HOMEGROWN

HOMEGROWN

ISIS in America

Alexander Meleagrou-Hitchens, Seamus Hughes

and Bennett Clifford

I.B.TAURIS

LONDON • NEW YORK • OXFORD • NEW DELHI • SYDNEY

I.B. TAURIS
Bloomsbury Publishing Plc
50 Bedford Square, London, WC1B 3DP, UK
1385 Broadway, New York, NY 10018, USA

BLOOMSBURY, I.B. TAURIS and the I.B. Tauris logo are trademarks of Bloomsbury
Publishing Plc

First published in Great Britain 2021

Cover design by Adriana Brioso
Cover images © MrsWilkins/iStock, kool99/iStock, DedMityay/iStock,
Lorado/iStock, Jordan Graff/Unsplash

A catalogue record for this book is available from the British Library.
A catalog record for this book is available from the Library of Congress.

ISBN: HB: 978-1-7883-1485-5
         ePDF: 978-0-7556-0211-7
         eBook: 978-0-7556-0212-4

Typeset by RefineCatch Limited, Bungay, Suffolk
Printed and bound in Great Britain

To find out more about our authors and books visit www.bloomsbury.com
and sign up for our newsletters.

CONTENTS

Acknowledgments   vi

INTRODUCTION   1

Chapter 1
THE ISLAMIC STATE IN AMERICA   11

Chapter 2
THE TERRORISTS   31

Chapter 3
THE TRAVELERS   55

Chapter 4
THE E-ACTIVISTS   85

Chapter 5
THE IDEOLOGUES   111

Chapter 6
COUNTERING VIOLENT EXTREMISM IN AMERICA   149

CONCLUSION   169

Notes   175
Index   225

ACKNOWLEDGMENTS

This book is the culmination of years of research, made possible and enhanced by a smart team of colleagues who shared their time, expertise, and brilliance. This includes a cadre of extremism experts at George Washington University's Program on Extremism. The Program is led by Lorenzo Vidino, who gave us both the personal encouragement and the professional freedom to follow the research wherever it took us. We are grateful for the support and scholarship of Audrey Alexander, Jonathan Lewis, Andrew Mines, and Haroro Ingram who read, commented on, and corrected numerous drafts. Without their feedback, this would be a lesser endeavor. We are also appreciative of David Sterman and Daniel Byman, who provided key insights as the research progressed and acted as sage sounding boards. Finally, we thank the countless number of sources, from both government and the public, who trusted us to tell their stories in a serious and respectful manner.

Finally, while professional support is always needed, personal support cannot be ignored. We would be remiss if we did not thank those in our lives who, unlike us, do not spend their days reading and researching terrorism, but nonetheless support our concerning efforts to do so. Alexander would like to thank his family, in particular his wife Lee-Anne. Similarly, Seamus would like to thank his wife, Alison, his three children, and other loved ones who supported him throughout this research project. Bennett thanks Dawn Wullschleger, Dr. Jeanne Clifford, and Ralph Clifford for their constant support.

INTRODUCTION

Since 2014, the United States has faced the most sustained period of domestic jihadist activity in its history. Compared to previous waves of participation by Americans in jihadist terrorist groups, the scale of current American involvement is unprecedented. This is mainly due to the activities and outreach of one specific group, namely the Islamic State of Iraq and Syria (ISIS). The Federal Bureau of Investigation (FBI) is actively pursuing over 1,000 investigations related to the group in all fifty states.

While the majority of American ISIS supporters sought to leave their country and join what they came to believe was an Islamic utopia in the territories held by the group overseas, there have also been deadly ISIS-inspired attacks in California, Minnesota, Ohio, Florida, and several other states. Others, meanwhile, found their calling online, using various forms of online technology to recruit, spread propaganda, and even use cryptocurrencies to fundraise for the group. Similar to the methods they pursued to further the goals of ISIS, the backgrounds of America's ISIS supporters and activists vary widely, from an underage minor interested in traveling from South Carolina to the caliphate to a 32-year-old man coordinating Syrian extremist organizations' pledges of allegiance to ISIS from a New York pizza shop.

For some, this wave of jihadist activity came as a shock. During the previous decade, jihadist attacks and plots in the United States appeared to be on a steady decline, as were instances of Americans leaving the country to join jihadist groups overseas. In the eyes of many, America was witnessing what amounted to the beginning of the end for the global jihad movement. Over a decade of sustained military pressure in jihadist safe havens, coupled with the FBI's aggressive pursuit of jihadists at home, had taken its toll on al-Qaeda and, so the thinking went, the domestic threat level was only going to continue to decline.

Then, on the morning of December 2, 2015, the threat of the Islamic State became a reality for many Americans. After using her Facebook account to pledge allegiance to the group's now deceased leader Abu Bakr al-Baghdadi, Tashfeen Malik, along with her husband Syed Rizwan Farook, went on a shooting spree in San Bernardino, California, murdering 14 and injuring another 24 before they were killed in a shootout with the police. Neither Malik nor Farook had any direct connections with ISIS or any of its members. They were inspired to act after hearing a September 2014 speech by ISIS' former spokesperson Abu Muhammad al-Adnani, in which he urged ISIS supporters around the world to commit atrocities in the group's name. Soon after the killings, official and unofficial ISIS media outlets released statements praising the attacks. While not claiming credit for directing Malik and Farook's operation, one of its media arms, *Amaq*, praised ISIS supporters in America and hailed their willingness to sacrifice all they held dear for the advancement of the caliphate.

Unlike Europe, where most major attacks with a nexus to ISIS involved direct interactions between ISIS members in Syria and Iraq or returned foreign fighters, this type of decentralized, inspired attack characterized the nature of the ISIS threat in America. San Bernardino was soon followed by media coverage of dozens more plots, along with reports of hundreds of Americans leaving their homes to wage jihad in Iraq and Syria. Almost all of these activities were carried out on behalf of ISIS, the new spearhead of the global jihad movement. Americans were increasingly inspired to travel as the group took over a large swathe of territory spanning both nations and covering an area roughly the size of Great Britain. In doing so, the Islamic State used its newfound success as an insurgency to launch an international outreach campaign which, in the West, has dwarfed the efforts of its jihadist predecessors in terms of levels of activity and lethality.

The result of this outreach was twofold. Firstly, ISIS attracted unprecedented numbers of Western Muslims to travel to its territory to join its self-proclaimed state. Secondly, the group used its popularity to launch a terrorist campaign targeting Western nations involved in the international effort to fight the group in Iraq and Syria. Those who could not travel were encouraged to become jihadis in their home country and conduct indiscriminate mass-casualty attacks without first seeking advice or permission. As ISIS' spokesman Abu Muhammad al-Adnani stated in his 2014 speech, "Do not ask for anyone's advice and do not seek anyone's verdict. Kill the disbeliever whether he is civilian or military, for they have the same ruling. Both of them are disbelievers."[1] In some cases travelers trained to become terrorists and returned to their country with an even deadlier assignment: plan and execute large-scale and lethal attacks.

In the West, it is Europe that has taken the brunt of this effort, but attacks like San Bernardino are a reminder that Americans are not immune to the ISIS call. While a topic of much interest in the media, ISIS-related activity in the US rarely receives in-depth analytical treatment. This book attempts to provide a clearer understanding of how and why the group was able to gain a foothold in the country and how that presence has changed since the Islamic State lost its geographical caliphate.

Although few authors focus solely on ISIS, the studies which have analyzed the jihadist movement in America can be broadly divided into two categories. Some have taken a qualitative, historical approach, explaining why jihad in America became "homegrown" after the September 11, 2001, attacks and how the threat has evolved since.[2] Other studies have relied more on statistics, explaining the nature of the threat through analyzing metrics such as demographics, attack type, frequency, and regional activity.[3]

This book combines qualitative and quantitative approaches to provide a comprehensive picture of the contours and dynamics of ISIS in America. Drawing on an array of exclusive primary sources, including interviews with American ISIS members and the agents tasked with thwarting them, this book will reveal how and why the Islamic State is able to successfully radicalize and recruit a new generation of jihadists in America. In doing so, it offers a number of new and unique insights and arguments about this multifaceted and constantly evolving phenomenon. Above all, we argue that, unlike in other Western nations, the Islamic State presence in America is surprisingly self-contained. While ISIS activity in many other Western nations is the result of long-standing and deep-rooted international networks based on connections to jihadist battlefields in Iraq, Syria, and beyond, in America (barring some notable exceptions), it has had little direct input and influence from external actors beyond the propaganda the group is able to spread via the internet. Thus, the story of ISIS in America offers a useful case study for furthering our understanding of jihad in the West, demonstrating the resiliency and adaptability of a movement that has faced, and to some extent overcome, seemingly overwhelming odds.

Before going any further, it is important to briefly discuss our decision to focus specifically on ISIS in America, rather than the wider homegrown jihadist mobilization which has taken place in the country since 9/11. There is no doubt that there is a significant ideological and operational overlap between al-Qaeda and ISIS in America. It can be argued that dividing these two is an arbitrary exercise. Indeed, in some cases Americans who have acted on behalf of the latter also claimed inspiration from al-Qaeda.[4] However, this division is nonetheless justified. Firstly, this is because the Islamic State is unique in that it was able to transform an insurgency into a large-scale proto-state with a variety of messages—from ultra-violence to utopian-society-building—that appealed to Americans. Secondly, and most importantly, while they share a similar ideology and recruitment strategy, there is no doubt that ISIS has been much more successful than al-Qaeda at attracting Americans and inspiring them to act. As such, this phenomenon is worthy of study in its own right.

There are a number of reasons why ISIS has been more effective than al-Qaeda at recruiting Americans. In practical terms, by controlling territory and largely prioritizing travel to the Islamic State over domestic terrorism, involvement with ISIS appeared to be a much more realistic, attainable, and fruitful prospect. Between 2014 and 2016, it was relatively easy to travel and join ISIS, certainly more so than it was to join any al-Qaeda-linked groups. Europeans and Americans could catch flights to Turkey, make their way to towns bordering Syria and arrange with Islamic State facilitators to be smuggled across the porous border to begin their training with ISIS. The group and its supporters even published instruction manuals with details of how to join them without getting caught.

As well as attracting unprecedented numbers of foreign fighters, however, ISIS also outperformed al-Qaeda in its ability to inspire Americans to commit domestic terrorist attacks in its name. In many ways, it has al-Qaeda to thank for this; its predecessor had spent years developing and promoting an "individual jihad" strategy which, by the time ISIS emerged, had begun to mature. ISIS took advantage of the groundwork laid by Western al-Qaeda strategists like Anwar al-Awlaki and Samir Khan, who, while members of al-Qaeda in the Arabian Peninsula (AQAP) in Yemen, developed new ways to attack their enemies in America. As early as 2010 they used their English-language magazine, *Inspire*, to call for "Open Source Jihad," which they defined as "a resource manual for those who loathe the tyrants." It encouraged de-centralized, small-scale attacks by lone actors, and provided crucial information including bomb-making techniques, counter-surveillance measures, and guerrilla tactics.[5] Awlaki and Khan claimed that this would be "America's worst nightmare" because it "allows Muslims to train at home instead of risking dangerous travel abroad."[6] For Westerners, jihad was "now at hands reach."

The lone-actor strategy which was introduced by al-Qaeda during the end of the 2010s has been adopted and refined by ISIS as a central component of the group's presence in the US. This has been made possible partly due to the now widespread availability of encrypted communications technologies that allow the group to securely communicate with and instruct its supporters from afar. This approach ensures that ISIS maintains a steady level of threat in a country where more complex plots involving the ISIS hierarchy are difficult to plan and execute. Unlike Europe, it has only been able to maintain a meaningful physical presence in America through those it has inspired to commit attacks in its name. This kept ISIS in the headlines, and on the minds of America's jihadists.

Although the strategic framework to strike America was therefore already in place, and al-Qaeda had some success in attracting foreign fighters, it struggled to get many Westerners on board. Its competitor, however, has been able to deploy a number of unique and inspiring messages, and this helps to partially explain its relative success. Particularly during the early stages of the Syrian conflict, the nature of its fight against Syrian President Bashar al-Assad had the appearance of a just cause. ISIS was able to portray itself as the only group which could effectively protect the Syrian Sunni population from the atrocities of Assad's Alawite-dominated regime. Indeed, many of the first Americans to travel and join ISIS were driven by moral outrage at the well-publicized actions of the Assad regime, and wanted to contribute to the protection of their fellow Sunni Muslims.

Additionally, in re-establishing the caliphate, ISIS was also seen as having succeeded where al-Qaeda failed. A distant pipe dream in the pronouncements of most of the al-Qaeda leadership, this utopian super-state that realized the vision of God on earth and protected the worldwide Muslim population (or *ummah*) became a central component of the ISIS mission. The mere existence of the caliphate was a powerful inducement to act, and living proof that the goals of the global jihad movement were attainable and worth fighting and dying for. It is, however, a mission with a wider appeal than just violence. The creation of the caliphate is a social program that goes beyond fighting and killing, providing social services and building the infrastructure of a fully functioning state. Thus, as well as fighting, some Americans were drawn to the promises of a utopia, hoping to be involved in the wider state-building project and offering themselves and their offspring to serve as teachers, doctors, and parents who could rear the next generation in this perfect Islamic society.

Not only is the Islamic State able to confidently claim that it was the first global jihadist group to re-establish the caliphate, but it did so in a region of great Islamic historical importance. When, in 2017, ISIS gained control of significant portions of Syria, it celebrated the significance of its presence in al-Sham, the ancient term for a region in modern-day Syria. Sham, and more specifically the town of Dabiq, is identified in the Quran as the site of the final battle between good and evil (or between Muslims and their enemies). This, it is believed, precedes the coming of the anti-Christ, who will help rid the world of evil and then bring about the apocalypse. Thus, not only were Muslims offered the opportunity to take part in the state-building project, but ISIS was able to present its mission as one which offers the final chance for Muslims to do their part for Islam before the apocalypse. The train was leaving the station, as it were, thus lending a sense of urgency to the ISIS mission, which al-Qaeda's never had.

Finally, any analysis of the success of ISIS compared to al-Qaeda cannot discount its effective exploitation of online communications, in particular social media. When al-Qaeda had begun to ramp up its Western outreach in 2010, mostly via Awlaki and *Inspire*, social media had yet to become a staple part of Western life. By the time ISIS began taking over from al-Qaeda, the amount of regularly active users on platforms like Twitter and Facebook had increased by hundreds of millions. Not only did the timing of ISIS' rise coincide with the exponential growth of the use of social media, but technology companies had barely begun to comprehend the extent to which their platforms were being exploited by jihadists, let alone implement policies to counter this. Between 2014 and 2016 specifically, Twitter was an open playing field for ISIS. It helped to create online networks of ISIS sympathizers, facilitated secure and direct contact between Americans and ISIS members in Syria and Iraq, and made access to propaganda easier than ever before. Westerners traveling to join the group were shockingly open about their intentions and actions on the platform, using Twitter to connect with ISIS facilitators and even share information about their journeys.

Indeed, more so than in any other Western nation, modern communications technology has been crucial to the spread and survival of the ISIS movement in America. Lacking in the sort of large, deep-rooted, and long-standing jihadist recruitment and mobilization networks found in many European nations, the US has proven to be a more difficult arena for jihadist groups to operate and establish themselves in. As a result, the US has faced a relatively small threat from ISIS, and the group relies heavily upon social media to maintain its presence and appeal among Americans. While it is important to avoid the simplistic explanation of "online radicalization," which erroneously suggests that people join ISIS purely due to their online involvement, it is impossible to ignore that the internet is more important to ISIS in America than in any other Western country.

This book represents the culmination of over four years of research into the presence of ISIS in America and the activities of its supporters that we conducted as colleagues at the Program on Extremism at George Washington University. As a center devoted to understanding this phenomenon, we gathered various types of data to build the clearest possible understanding of how this far-flung group managed to successfully implant itself into the United States. Of all the sources of information we drew upon, that which we relied upon most heavily was thousands of pages of court documents from ISIS-related terrorism trials. These were collected through a variety of means, including filing motions for the release of records in federal courts across the country and traveling to numerous courthouses to retrieve records only available in person. The documents include full court transcripts, trial exhibits, and the testimonies of those charged with an offense and the people who investigated them. In some cases, the authors also personally attended these trials and gathered information that was not made available on the public record. Additionally, more than three dozen Freedom of Information Act (FOIA) requests were filed. Alongside the information provided by the US courts, we also conducted interviews with US prosecutors, defense attorneys, federal agents directly involved in investigating and apprehending ISIS supporters in America, national security officials, and other officials tasked with implementing programs aimed at preventing Americans from adopting the beliefs and tactics of ISIS.

While interview access to American ISIS members remains difficult, our analysis was further strengthened by interviews with two former American ISIS members who have returned to the United States, one of whom was convicted for joining ISIS in Syria, and another who has thus far avoided prosecution. While not a large or representative sample, this is nonetheless the largest number of such interviews conducted for any publicly available study on ISIS in America to date. In addition to these primary sources, we also studied hundreds of pro-ISIS social media accounts and drew upon two extensive databases compiled at the Program on Extremism over three years. The first is a repository of 1,782 English-language Twitter accounts containing over 845,646 total tweets, which was designed and populated by our colleague Audrey Alexander. This database is fully searchable and is based on raw data using Twitter's Application Programming Interface. For more than a year, the database harvested tweets every 30 minutes posted by accounts that were still active. The second database focuses on Telegram, an encrypted social media platform which has now overtaken Twitter as the online platform of choice for ISIS members and supporters. The database holds a collection of more than 700 channels and chatrooms, including closed groups with limited membership. The Telegram channels range from general propaganda materials to detailed and specific instructions on bomb-making. To analyze the second database, the authors used a text and content scraper and various data analysis platforms to isolate key messages and themes within the sample. Taken together, these unique sets of data, from court documents to interviews and social media, have allowed us to produce the most detailed account of ISIS in America that is currently available to the public.

Similar to any other region where ISIS has found support, the group's activity in America can be broadly divided into four categories: terrorist attacks and plots, foreign fighter recruitment, online engagement and activism, and promoting the group's message through ideologues. Before delving into these different forms of ISIS activity in the United States, the first chapter provides a short history of ISIS and its establishment in Iraq and Syria, before using our unique ISIS terrorism cases database to review the landscape of the Islamic State's presence in the United States. Using statistics, facts, and figures based on original research, the authors will demonstrate how ISIS emerged in America and how its presence has grown, evolved, and survived despite the efforts to counter it. Since March 2014, for example, when the establishment of the caliphate was announced by ISIS, 204 people have been charged with terrorism-related activities in connection with the group. A near majority were accused of attempting to travel or successfully traveling abroad to Syria or Iraq, while 31 percent were accused of being involved in plots to carry out attacks on US soil. In addition, we will show how this review of the cases points to mobilization of individuals, not a widespread community-level problem. Despite concerns about secure borders and Muslim migration to the United States, the vast majority are US citizens or legal permanent residents, making this a truly "homegrown" phenomenon.

The book then shifts focus to the domestic terrorist threat posed by ISIS. Here, we delve into a detailed analysis of the more complex ISIS-related terrorist plots in America. By using a range of data described above, the chapter sheds new light on ISIS activities within the United States, detailing both successful (in terms of lethality) and not-so-successful plots. In doing so, we will provide insight into how plotters were radicalized and recruited by ISIS members and sympathizers, and the process by which they planned their attacks. Additionally, we explore and reveal the details of riveting FBI investigations which ultimately prevented massacres from taking place.

As the analysis and statistical breakdowns in Chapter 1 will demonstrate, all 13 ISIS-related successful attacks and plots in the United States were "ISIS-inspired." This term refers to attacks that are carried out in the name of ISIS but were not the result of any direct involvement from the group or its networks. These individuals did not receive training from ISIS, nor were they members of any international jihadist network. In this way, America is the exception to the rule of ISIS mobilization in the West. In Europe, for example, research shows that, despite common perceptions to the contrary, only a small percentage of plotters can be truly classified as lone actors in that they had no connections of any kind to ISIS.[7] In the majority of cases, attack plots included the involvement of an ISIS network of recruiters based abroad. The United States is the only Western country targeted by the group in which the opposite is true. The vast majority of attacks and plots in the country were undertaken by individuals or small groups unconnected to formal networks.

Moving on to the most popular form of ISIS mobilization among Americans, Chapter 3 reviews the stories of those who traveled or attempted to travel to the Islamic State. It is based on an exhaustive review of both legal cases and instances where the authors have uncovered previously unknown names of American travelers to Syria or Iraq. Additionally, the research is augmented by the authors' interviews of Americans who returned to the United States after joining the Islamic

State. The use of the term "travelers" (as opposed to the more popular "foreign fighters") to describe these cases reflects a conscious decision on our part to account for the many reasons why Americans joined ISIS in Syria and Iraq. While the majority went with the intention to fight, some sought to take up other responsibilities so as to be able to contribute to the group's wider state-building project.

American ISIS members' use of the internet, and in particular social media, is now a typical feature of modern terrorist organizations. Not only does ISIS utilize social media to disseminate propaganda and communicate its aims to Americans, but it has also been used to recruit new members, and even facilitate multiple terrorist plots. Chapter 4 therefore assesses how the group's use of modern communications technology has evolved and contributed to ISIS' diverse presence in America. By also identifying the latest and future trends of ISIS' use of modern communications technology, we hope to provide the reader with an in-depth and nuanced understanding of how ISIS has been able to increase its presence in America and survive despite its territorial losses in Syria and Iraq.

Behind much of the ISIS propaganda aimed at Westerners lie a number of influential Western ideologues who are crucial to tailoring the group's message so that it resonates with Americans. In the penultimate chapter, we identify some of the most important such figures who are either still operating within the United States, such as Ahmad Musa Jibril, or whose impact has outlived them, such as Anwar al-Awlaki, who was killed by a drone strike in 2011. Other preachers whose output and activism will be analyzed include Abdullah Faisal, a Jamaican-born cleric who is facing extradition to the United States on charges of soliciting acts of terrorism, and Suleiman Anwar Bengharsa, a Libyan-American sheikh currently living in Maryland who has been linked to five ISIS-related criminal cases in America. Drawing from some of their key lectures, court documents, and interviews with federal agents, the authors will detail precisely how these individuals have contributed to the establishment and growth of ISIS in America.

A combination of tough law enforcement approaches, intelligence work, and counter-radicalization programs are needed to help prevent jihadist radicalization in the United States. In Chapter 6, the book concludes by discussing the opportunities and challenges facing law enforcement and Muslim American community partners in pursuit of that goal. One of these is the question of how to devise and implement soft-power policies aimed at both preventing citizens from joining terror groups and deradicalizing returning foreign fighters. While often categorized together under the umbrella of Countering Violent Extremism (CVE), these are two very different concepts that require their own unique approaches. The analysis explains the history, evolution, and the current state of CVE in America, looking in particular at where and how it has been implemented and the key successes and failures the government has experienced thus far. The chapter is unique in that it is written largely from the perspective of one of the authors, Seamus Hughes, who, during his time at the National Counterterrorism Center (NCTC), helped to run the US Government's first CVE efforts. Among his roles was heading government engagement with Muslim American community leaders across the country and drafting and implementing the Obama Administration's policies on these issues.

As a whole, the following chapters provide one of the first comprehensive assessments of the ISIS presence in America. Drawing on a unique range of primary sources, it will help make sense of this phenomenon and contribute to a more extensive understanding of how international terrorist groups survive and grow in even the most hostile environments. As the group undergoes significant changes related to its almost total loss of territory in Syria and Iraq and the death of its leader Abu Bakr al-Baghdadi, it remains to be seen how, if at all, this impacts its desire and ability to continue targeting the United States. What is clear, however, is that the group has already demonstrated its ability to adapt and evolve while always keeping America firmly in its sights.

Chapter 1

THE ISLAMIC STATE IN AMERICA

In March 2014, three months before ISIS' declaration that it had re-established the caliphate, the FBI arrested two North Carolina men for conspiring to travel to Syria to join jihadist groups. In the months prior to their arrests, Avin Marsalis Brown and Akba "Jihad" Jordan extensively prepared for their journey by implementing a military training regimen and ordering brand-new passports.[1] During their initial months of planning, Brown and Jordan knew that they wanted to support jihadist groups overseas, but could not decide between Syria or Yemen as a final destination. In early 2014, however, Jordan caught word that a group in Syria, which called itself the Islamic State of Iraq and Syria, was on the verge of announcing the return of the caliphate. From that point onwards, Brown and Jordan's choice—to join ISIS—was clear.

In the grand scheme of federal terrorism cases, Brown's and Jordan's were generally unremarkable, save for one fact: they marked the first instances of individuals charged with ISIS-related activity in the United States. In the five years following the arrests of Brown and Jordan, federal and state authorities charged 204 individuals for activities on behalf of the organization. This period represents the largest wave of jihadism-related arrests in a five-year period in American history. At any given time between 2014 and 2019, the FBI ran approximately 1,000 active ISIS-related investigations in all 50 states.[2]

An examination of the 204 cases of Americans charged with ISIS-related activity sheds light on many aspects of the ISIS mobilization in the United States. The most important revelation is the sheer diversity of individuals who were drawn to the organization for various reasons. Among the 204 are individuals as young as 15 and old as 60, from 29 different states, involved in a variety of activities and charges of offenses on behalf of the group. They represent innumerable socioeconomic, ethnic, geographic, and educational backgrounds. Drawing comprehensive conclusions about an "average American ISIS supporter" is therefore close to impossible. While there are important, general trends— supporters tend to be young men, and either US citizens or permanent residents— it remains tremendously difficult to build a profile of ISIS' American adherents based on the legal cases.

The data used in this chapter comes from the Program on Extremism's unique database of over 20,000 pages of documents from ISIS-related terrorism cases in the United States. All documents are continuously updated and are made available to the public online.[3] Data garnered from legal cases often yields more information about American ISIS supporters than many other sources, such as social media, media reporting, and incomplete investigation records. Legal documents, unlike other sources, are open to the public, verifiable, and contain a wealth of information that can be connected to a particular case. As individuals are charged, prosecuted, and sentenced, law enforcement, prosecutors, and defense teams publish data about the subjects of the cases through legal filings at every step of the trial process. Using the Public Access to Court Electronic Records (PACER) system, as well as making formal requests for document release, filing injunctions to release sealed documents, and personally attending trials, researchers can garner a massive amount of information from federal and state terrorism cases.

Given the diversity of Americans charged with ISIS-related activity, one of the major questions facing policymakers, researchers, and local communities is how so many Americans from different backgrounds were persuaded by ISIS' message and ideology. Unlike in several other Western countries, ISIS lacked large-scale personal recruitment networks and infrastructure in the United States, making these questions especially pertinent. Throughout this chapter and the following chapters, profiled cases of American ISIS supporters will point to the overarching factors that allowed ISIS' narrative to diffuse within various communities in the United States despite the lack of traditional recruitment infrastructure. Small-scale, closed, and decentralized recruitment networks, the use of digital communications technologies, and the prominence of English-speaking jihadist ideologues all helped the Islamic State bridge the gap and reach thousands of Americans.

This opening chapter has three sections. The first traces the history of jihadism-related cases in the United States, and how ISIS positioned itself to take advantage of the popularity of the conflict in Syria as a *casus belli* for American jihadist supporters in the early 2010s. It then examines how legal cases for ISIS-related charges have changed over time from 2014 until the present day. The second section provides an in-depth look at the data, examining several demographics (e.g., age, gender, state of origin, and citizenship status) and behavioral (e.g., activities conducted on behalf of ISIS) variables within the sample of 204 American ISIS-related cases. The final section examines the outcomes of the legal cases, using data on prosecution and sentencing to assess how the American legal system typically responded to cases of American ISIS supporters. Each section will include statistical analyses from the Program on Extremism's database used in conjunction with individual cases of note.

Historical Development

According to a database compiled by the New America Foundation, the United States has charged 440 people with jihadist terrorism-related offenses since September 11, 2001.[4] From that number, over half were charged between 2014 and

2019.[5] More arrests and indictments against jihadists in the United States were handed down during this five-year period than at any other time in the country's history. Of those charged during the period, 204 were involved with Islamic State-related activity.[6]

The shift that occurred in legal cases of American jihadists before and after 2014 was not only reflected in their sheer number, but also in their qualitative difference. Notably, events in the early 2010s almost completely consolidated American support for jihadist groups into focusing on one battlespace—the Levant—and on one specific group—the Islamic State.

Before 2014, federal terrorism cases generally involved American jihadists with affiliations to multiple jihadist groups, spread out across the globe.[7] The most influential was al-Qaeda, which operated an affiliate network with various branches in the Middle East, North Africa, East Africa, Central Asia, and Southeast Asia. A perusal of the jihadism-related terrorism cases prior to 2014 generally shows that Americans charged with supporting jihadist groups were primarily interested in four main areas of operation: the Afghanistan–Pakistan border area, Iraq, Yemen, and Somalia.[8] Afghanistan, Pakistan, and Iraq had historical credibility for jihadists as the sites of major resistance efforts by *mujahideen* against non-Muslim armies. After the US interventions in Afghanistan and Iraq following 9/11, affiliating with groups in those regions had special relevance for American jihadists, as their support would benefit groups directly fighting the US military.[9] Yemen's major draw was a team of American jihadist propagandists based in the country who produced English-speaking content for al-Qaeda in the Arabian Peninsula (AQAP). The two most influential figures were the New Mexico-born ideologue Anwar al-Awlaki and his co-author Samir Khan, originally from North Carolina.[10] Many of the Americans attracted to jihadist groups in Somalia, in particular al-Shabaab, were first- or second-generation Somali-Americans. Ethiopia's military intervention in the Somali Civil War in 2006 sparked calls by al-Shabaab for foreign fighters to take up arms on behalf of the group.[11]

While many of the groups Americans supported in the pre-2014 period were affiliates of one organization (al-Qaeda), they differed in capabilities, objectives, and strategic priorities for foreign supporters. For instance, al-Shabaab had some capacity to take incoming foreign fighters. During the period between 2007 and 2014, at least 30 Americans successfully joined the group in Somalia, some of whom became de facto spokespeople for it.[12] The Americans who joined were primarily interested in traveling to join the group and fight in Somalia, not in conducting attacks in the United States. In contrast, AQAP had fewer American foreign fighters. The Americans with a nexus to AQAP tended to be less interested in travel and were more interested in using AQAP material and expertise to plan large-scale attacks in the United States.[13]

Legal cases of Americans involved with jihadist groups began to taper off in 2011, but they were quickly replaced by Americans interested in a new jihadist cause—Syria. After the Bashar al-Assad regime initiated brutal crackdowns on anti-government protestors in 2011, a widespread insurgency began in Syria. The revolution involved non-state armed groups of varying ideological factions, including violent Islamists.[14] Around the same time, jihadist groups gained new legs across the border in Iraq after a 2011 near-complete withdrawal of US military forces from the region. With a close eye to the events next door in Syria, Iraq-based jihadist groups saw the potential to expand. One outfit, the Islamic State of Iraq (ISI), sent advisors into Syria to explore the idea of starting a franchise in the war-torn country.[15] After ISI affiliates proved themselves as effective fighting forces against Assad, the revolution underwent two splits. First, violent Islamists connected to ISI split from their non-Islamist counterparts. Then, between 2013 and 2014, ISI fighters in Syria still loyal to the group's central leadership in Iraq separated from those who wanted to start a completely independent outlet.[16] The latter, led by Abu Muhammad al-Julani, formed the al-Qaeda affiliate Jabhat al-Nusra. Meanwhile, the former group, still loyal to ISI and its leader, Abu Bakr al-Baghdadi, now controlled territory on both sides of the Syria–Iraq border. A name change was in order, and the group became the Islamic State of Iraq and Syria (ISIS).[17]

Thousands of miles away, Americans interested in jihadist groups often had difficulty navigating the galaxy of jihadist outfits that set up shop in Syria during the early days of the conflict. A common feature of jihadist cases between 2011 and 2014 is Americans engaging in debates with others about the particularities of specific groups. Questions about groups' allegiances, alliances, tactics, methods, and adherence to core jihadist principles were standard. Regardless of what group American jihadists sided with during the early days of the Syrian conflict, the emerging consensus was that Syria was the only important battlefield for the jihadist movement. The cause—assisting oppressed Sunni Muslims in rebellion against an Alawite regime, backed by Shi'a Muslim Iran and primordial jihadist adversary Russia—was as close to a just war in the jihadist tradition as possible.[18] Major hardline Sunni Muslim clerics and leaders, even if they refrained from backing specific factions, argued that all Sunni Muslims had a moral obligation to assist their brothers and sisters in Syria by any means possible.[19] By this time, a steady trickle of foreign fighters was entering Syria via the Turkish border and embedding themselves in jihadist groups, sharing their perspectives, and inciting others using social media.[20]

These factors appear to be the primary motivators for the "first generation" of ISIS supporters in America, represented in many of the early cases in the dataset. Their support for ISIS derived from a perceived sense of duty to aid the group in Syria, which they viewed as actively defending local Sunni Muslims and doing so on a strong foundation of Islamic law (or, at least, the jihadist interpretation thereof).[21] The earliest cases of ISIS supporters in the United States demonstrate how quickly the group's popularity set in, and how one of the hundreds of contemporary jihadist groups operating in the Levant could reach a significant audience in the United States. By the spring of 2014, ISIS had established its credibility in American jihadist circles, in even the most unlikely of locations—including a nondescript pizza shop in Rochester, New York.

Mufid Elfgeeh, aged 32 and described by the FBI as "one of the first ISIS recruiters ever apprehended" in the United States, coordinated pledges of allegiance to ISIS from his Rochester pizzeria, Mojoe's Famous Pizza and Chicken.[22] Elfgeeh had a long track record of espousing jihadist extremism and was previously expelled from three Rochester-area mosques for making pro-al-Qaeda statements.[23] During the initial stages of the FBI investigation against Elfgeeh, he expressed support for several jihadist groups in Yemen, Somalia, and Syria on social media. However, his efforts quickly consolidated on ISIS. As early as September 2013, Elfgeeh operated several Twitter accounts that he used to promote ISIS and its activities in Syria, praising decisions by the group to block food aid into areas operated by the US-backed Free Syrian Army and highlighting media produced by ISIS foreign fighters.[24] In conversations with FBI cooperating witnesses in early 2014, Elfgeeh argued that ISIS was the only group that had been endorsed by al-Qaeda's former leader Osama bin Laden, and shared several videos produced by ISIS foreign fighters encouraging others to travel to join the group.[25] Elfgeeh directed the men to send money to ISIS fighters and travel to Syria specifically to join the group and connected them to facilitators that could ferry them across the Turkish–Syrian border.[26]

The FBI arrested Elfgeeh on May 31, 2014.[27] Two weeks before Elfgeeh's arrest, the State Department amended its foreign terrorist organization designation list to include ISIS as a separate entity.[28] One month after Elfgeeh's arrest, ISIS' activities, scope of operations, and perceived legitimacy amongst jihadists would take a turn that would permanently affect the dynamics of the global jihadist movement. In late June 2014, ISIS' senior religious leaders issued a statement claiming that the group had re-established the caliphate. From a pulpit in Mosul, Iraq's historic Great Mosque of al-Nuri, ISIS leader Abu Bakr al-Baghdadi made his first appearance as the newly declared caliph on July 4, 2014.[29]

The declaration of the caliphate was a watershed moment for ISIS support in the United States. The number of ISIS-related legal cases skyrocketed. In 2014, 17 people were charged with ISIS-related activity in the United States; ten of those charges came after al-Baghdadi's July 2014 address. By 2015, a banner year for ISIS-related cases in the United States, the number of cases ballooned to 65; 2015 remains the year with the highest number of arrests of jihadists in United States history. During the period where ISIS maintained its self-proclaimed caliphate and held significant territory in Syria and Iraq, the motivations and recruitment processes for American ISIS supporters also changed. Rather than supporters expressing a general interest in joining jihadist groups in Syria to defend Muslims, after the declaration of the caliphate, American jihadists tended to be directly attracted to ISIS as an organization.

The first "pull factor" drawing Americans to ISIS after it declared itself a caliphate was ideological in nature. Within the confines of the Islamic tradition of governance, the existence of a caliphate led by a divinely guided caliph entails several mandatory responsibilities for Muslims around the world. First, the obligation for Muslims to follow the caliph is a mandatory, individual duty (*fard al-'ayn*). It is incumbent upon every Muslim to obey their orders and rulings.[30] Muslims living in areas that the caliph does not control are obliged to perform migration (*hijra*) to live in the caliphate. The rule of the caliph rests on a foundation of divine authority; negating the authority of the caliph is rejecting the authority of God.[31] Of course, only an infinitesimally tiny minority of Muslims worldwide viewed ISIS' claims to have re-established the caliphate as legitimate, and even a majority of ardent jihadists rejected the claim.[32] But for American ISIS supporters, many of whom lacked the scholarly prerequisites to contest these claims, existed largely in "echo chambers" of like-minded ISIS adherents, or were attracted to other elements of ISIS' activities, the ideological pull of ISIS' caliphate declaration helped set the group apart from others. Moreover, ISIS' media teams issued propaganda and imagery depicting life in Syria and Iraq under ISIS as a utopian society, fulfilling the prophetic method.[33]

The religious arguments of ISIS were important, but far from the only factor driving Americans to support the group. ISIS' significant foreign recruitment, incitement, and information operations capabilities, driven largely by online social media, also helped ISIS' message reach an American audience and encouraged them to aid the group. The common assumption is that ISIS' online efforts were directed towards "online radicalization," which is a misnomer when it comes to most American cases. Radicalization processes usually derive from several reinforcing factors, the majority of which occur away from computer and mobile phone screens and involve human interactions.[34] Instead of online radicalization, the more apt term to describe ISIS' use of the online space is "online mobilization." ISIS and its American supporters used digital communications technologies to facilitate operations, logistics, and communications, to keep already-radicalized individuals within the online echo chamber of propaganda, and to push them towards action. ISIS was unlike many of its jihadist contemporaries in that it invested resources into specialized infrastructure and personnel designed to recruit English-speaking Westerners, including Americans, through the use of social media.

Finally, ISIS extensively used "propaganda of the deed" to recruit.[35] There is no denying that for a certain sub-section of American ISIS supporters, ISIS' hyper-violent acts were extremely attractive. ISIS' grotesque depictions of violence in its propaganda—including but not limited to the beheadings of journalists, aid workers, and religious officials, the mass murders of prisoners of war and religious minorities, and enforcing capital punishments against violators of religious offenses—drew significant interest from its American ISIS supporters, who often shared these videos and discussed them with other likeminded contacts. Some seemed to have bizarre fascinations with extreme violence, and ISIS was simply the outlet for their urges. Others saw the violence as legitimate retributions for war crimes committed by the Assad regime and other militaries in Syria and Iraq. Even more viewed the enforcement of capital punishments (such as the burning of the Jordanian pilot Muath al-Kasasbeh, or the executions of gay men) as evidence that ISIS was committed to enforcing justice prescribed by its interpretation of Islamic law. ISIS' use of violence may not have been the main factor behind why so many Americans chose to support the group. However, American ISIS supporters who claim not to have known about its violent streak are often offering half-baked, post hoc justifications for their actions.

These three pull factors, in various forms, are prevalent throughout the stories and radicalization pathways of Americans charged with ISIS-related activities. Each had a distinct impact on how Americans chose to participate in the movement. Those easily persuaded by the religious and ideological aspects of ISIS, especially the prophesied return of the caliphate, tended to view travel to ISIS-held territory as necessary to uphold their obligations. The Americans who were ensconced in ISIS' online ecosystem often tried to find ways to become "e-activists" for the group by spreading online propaganda, communicating with other supporters, and even attempting hacking. The ISIS supporters most attracted to violence attempted to beget violence themselves—through planning and executing attacks on behalf of the group. Each of these groups are covered in depth during the following chapters of this book.

The period between 2015 and 2017, where 143 Americans in total were charged with supporting the Islamic State, is considered the heyday of Islamic State-related legal cases in the United States. However, the number of publicly known cases began to decline after the record year in 2015, reaching its nadir (14 cases) in 2018. Law enforcement officials are quick to point out that, despite the seeming downfall in activity, FBI operational tempo remained high, with over 1,000 active investigations at any given time.[36] They explain that the publicly available numbers may not include an unspecified number of additional American ISIS supporters who faced sealed charges, indictments at the state level, or non-terrorism-related charges.[37]

Several changes in the global ISIS landscape in 2015 and 2016 were the likely drivers of the decline. First and foremost, ISIS began to experience significant setbacks in its ability to take in foreign fighters. Due to the efforts of Combined Joint Task Force–Operation Inherent Resolve (CJTF–OIR), a US-led global military coalition to defeat ISIS, it began hemorrhaging territory and losing personnel to targeted strikes. Among the first strategic areas ISIS lost in 2015 and 2016 were checkpoints along the Syrian–Turkish border, which previously allowed the group to process incoming jihadist travelers.[38] In tandem, airstrikes killed key English-speaking ISIS ideologues and travel facilitators, who were responsible for connecting with Americans via social media and directly encouraging them to travel.[39] Meanwhile, in the United States, federal and state law enforcement were able to disrupt several ISIS-inspired attack plots and prevent jihadist travel, hampering the efforts of US-based ISIS supporters to assist the group.

The period between 2017 and 2019 continued to deal significant setbacks to the Islamic State. In July 2017, three years after they initially overtook the city, ISIS forces were driven out of Mosul by US and Iraqi forces.[40] Months later, in October 2017, ISIS lost its Syrian de facto capital, Raqqa.[41] In combination with the Syrian Democratic Forces (SDF), CJTF–OIR pushed back ISIS forces into a sliver of land alongside the banks of the Euphrates River in southeastern Syria. By spring 2019, remaining ISIS fighters held one small Syrian village, Baghuz Fawqani, near the border with Iraq. The SDF prevailed against the ISIS fighters in Baghuz Fawqani after a short siege in March 2019, eliminating the last vestige of ISIS-held territory in Syria and Iraq.[42] The losses of cities, territory, and mid-level personnel deprived

ISIS leadership of safe havens, sources of revenue, and a base for producing propaganda and directing external operations. Many of ISIS' Syrian and Iraqi supporters went underground, retreating into cities to form "sleeper cells." A bulk of its foreign members were either killed, detained, or left the Levant. After ISIS' fall at Baghuz Fawqani, ISIS' senior leaders were cut off from their support base, and CJTF–OIR closed in quickly. In late October 2019, dual United States Special Operations Forces raids in northwest Syria led to the deaths of ISIS' first "caliph," Abu Bakr al-Baghdadi, as well as its spokesman, Abu Hassan al-Muhajir.[43]

In the midst of its strategic losses, ISIS' directives to foreign supporters changed. It began encouraging supporters to conduct attacks at home rather than attempting to travel to Syria and Iraq. As the next section of this chapter explains, American ISIS supporters also turned their efforts towards conducting attacks in the United States in response to the shifting directives. This effect demonstrates the unreliability of the number of ISIS-related arrests in any given year as a predictor of the overall threat of ISIS supporters to the United States. In fact, as the number of arrests tapered off from its peak in 2015, the proportion of cases in which supporters were planning attacks on US soil increased.

Nonetheless, the collapse of ISIS-held territory in Syria and Iraq, the deaths of its leaders, and increased success on the part of American law enforcement in investigating and prosecuting American ISIS supporters does not entail an end to the movement in the United States. The number of ISIS-related cases in the United States increased almost twofold from 2018 to 2019. ISIS supporters continue to explore the idea of traveling to ISIS-held territory outside Syria and Iraq, are finding new ways to support the organization, and, in some cases, have adopted new tactics to avoid detection by law enforcement. Thus, the staggering number of FBI investigations of ISIS supporters is unlikely to decrease in the coming years, even after key strategic losses for the organization in Syria and Iraq. The ideology and narratives that the group propagates maintain their relevance for a wide cross-section of Americans from various backgrounds. The stunning diversity of American ISIS supporters, exemplified in the 204 cases from 2014 to 2019, will therefore continue to shape the movement.

About the Cases

The 204 cases of individuals charged in the United States with ISIS-related activity between 2014 and 2019 include individuals from all walks of American life. As a whole, this demographic spans socioeconomic, ethnic, political, geographic, and educational divides. In examining their radicalization pathways, there are very few similarities between how individual Americans came to support the Islamic State. Certain ISIS narratives, ideologies, and pull factors seemed to have varying resonance, and their success was largely dependent on the individual's background. However, in recruiting foreigners to join its cause, one Islamic State metanarrative—the idea that it could forge bonds between Muslims of different backgrounds all over the world—appears to have some relevance for American ISIS supporters.[44]

This idea of the Islamic State as a jihadist *internationale* can also help explain why supporters within a country, in this case the United States, could arrive at a mutual cause despite widely varying backgrounds.

There is no single profile of an American Islamic State supporter. Variance within the sample is massive, and the factors that explain most of the population have little analytic value. As an examination of the demographic and behavioral data shows, however, there are some notable trends that help shed some light on ISIS recruitment in the United States. First, the general demographic most heavily represented in the cases is young males—the average age of the sample is 28, and almost nine out of ten supporters were men. However, the sample also includes individuals as young as 15 and as old as 60, and the proportion of cases involving minors has steadily increased. Meanwhile, the cases of ISIS-supporting American women, who compose a substantial minority of the sample, cannot be ignored.

ISIS recruitment in the United States is a homegrown phenomenon. The vast majority of cases involved US citizens or permanent residents. In some Western countries, recruitment heavily affected first- and second-generation immigrants, sometimes without citizenship status in their country of residence. In contrast, American ISIS supporters spent most of their lives in the United States, were part of the fabric of American society, and radicalized in the United States. Cases of ISIS support are also generally dispersed throughout the United States, involving individuals in 29 states and the District of Columbia.

For American ISIS supporters, traveling to join the Islamic State overseas took precedence over planning domestic attacks as an objective. However, the two activities appear to be inversely correlated. As terrorist travel became more difficult due to a range of factors, more American ISIS supporters became involved in attack plotting. The change in *modus operandi* from travel to attacks occurred as a result of individual ISIS supporters conducting cost/benefit analyses prior to mobilization. But additionally, the decision to plot an attack in some cases came as a result of law enforcement or other actors preventing supporters from traveling, in what is known as the "frustrated foreign fighter" phenomenon.[45]

Age

Islamic State recruitment in the United States primarily affected young people. The average age of an individual charged with Islamic State-related offenses was approximately 28 at the time of their arrest. However, age data from the sample is right-skewed: 118 cases, a majority of the sample, involved individuals younger than the mean of 28. The five-year age group most heavily represented in the sample are individuals between the ages of 20 and 25.

The prevalence of American ISIS supporters under the age of 30 reflects not only the increased susceptibility of younger people to violent extremist propaganda, but also familiarity with the digital toolbox that ISIS operatives used to reach its worldwide supporters. Without a doubt, the primary audience for ISIS in propaganda focusing on Western supporters was military-age men.[46] Social proximity also plays a role. Across age groups, American ISIS supporters tended to radicalize in close social groups, especially amongst friend and family networks. If one or two young people within a close-knit social group developed an interest in ISIS, it became easier to convince others in the group, many of whom were similar in age, to become involved.

With regard to age, outliers exist at both ends of the spectrum. More often, they tend to be younger rather than older people, with a few exceptions. The oldest person charged with ISIS-related activity in the United States was 60-year-old Abdul-Majeed Marouf Ahmed Alani, a former American Airlines mechanic who was arrested after allegedly attempting to sabotage an airplane.[47] Investigators reportedly found ISIS propaganda on his cellphone, and he once boasted to a friend that his family members in Iraq were senior ISIS members.[48] To date, eight people over the age of 50 have been charged with ISIS-related offenses. Among the notable figures in this subgroup are 52-year-old Gregory Hubbard and 50-year-old Darren Arness Jackson, two members of a cell of Florida residents who planned to travel to Syria to join ISIS;[49] 55-year-old Marie Castelli, who posted threats against US military servicepeople in a pro-ISIS Facebook group from her home in rural Kentucky;[50] and 53-year-old Abdullah Faisal, a notorious pro-ISIS imam and recruiter who is profiled in Chapter 5 of this book.[51]

On the other end of the spectrum, 45 people under the age of 21 have been charged with ISIS-related activity, including five under the age of 18. The proportion of cases involving individuals within this age bracket grew steadily since 2014. The question of how to address minors involved with terrorist activity has become a major concern for law enforcement authorities in the wake of these cases. The database of legal cases used for this book only includes minors who are charged as adults. Therefore, the number of minors involved in ISIS-related activity in the United States between 2014 and 2019 was much higher than the number reflected in the data. Due to a range of constraints, the Department of Justice (DOJ) traditionally avoids prosecuting minors for terrorism charges.

To date, the youngest person in the United States to be charged as an adult for ISIS-related activity is Santos Colon, a New Jersey resident who was only 15 years old when he was arrested in August 2015. Colon pleaded guilty in 2017 to an ISIS-inspired plot to kill Pope Francis during a visit to Philadelphia and is still awaiting sentencing.[52] In a similar case in the same year, a 16-year-old in South Carolina planned a jihadist attack against a local military facility. Zakariya Abdin pleaded guilty to a state-level gun charge and spent two years in a juvenile detention facility before being paroled in 2017.[53] Less than one year after his parole, Abdin, now legally an adult, attempted to travel to Syria to join ISIS. Due to his criminal record and his adult status, federal prosecutors charged Abdin with material support to terrorism. After pleading guilty, he was sentenced to 20 years in prison.[54]

Overall, DOJ prosecutions of minors on terrorism charges are few and far between. However, as the result of a recent decision by the Supreme Court of the United States, federal law enforcement's options for dealing with ISIS supporters under the age of 18 are even more restricted. In its 2018 ruling in *Sessions v. Dimaya*, the Supreme Court found that in order to charge juveniles with federal crimes transcending international boundaries—including the federal material support to terrorism statute—the juvenile has to have committed a "crime of violence."[55] As a result of this decision, the DOJ now faces two options in handling terrorism cases involving minors. The first, similar to the option used during the first case against Zakariya Abdin, is to allow state prosecutors to take terrorism cases involving minors. The second is to forego prosecution altogether and monitor under-18 jihadists until they reach legal age.[56] To ensure that they do not commit violent acts or attempt to travel overseas, law enforcement can schedule mentorship and counseling opportunities for young ISIS supporters while putting "tripwires" in place to allow legal intervention if they cross the threshold of criminal behavior.[57]

Gender

Of the 204 charged with Islamic State-related activity in the United States, 184 (90 percent) were male. The over-representation of men within this sample might lead to several assumptions about gender roles within the American pro-Islamic State movement, many of which would be erroneous. Before examining these assumptions, it is worth mentioning that data about the role of women in jihadist groups based on arrests and prosecution has a known tendency to undercount the number of women that are involved in the jihadist movement.[58] This occurs for several reasons. First, the jihadist movement is highly conservative regarding the participation of women in many public activities. While women have played key roles in jihadist groups like ISIS, many contribute in ways that are more likely to be concealed from the public eye and, therefore, less likely to reach the level of a chargeable offense.[59] Second, evidence shows that the United States criminal justice system demonstrates considerable leniency towards women extremists. Data compiled by the University of Maryland's National Consortium for the Study of Terrorism and Responses to Terrorism (START) show that American women extremists were, on average, less likely to be arrested and indicted for extremist-related offenses than their male counterparts, even when they participated in similar activities.[60]

Because of their statistical underrepresentation, drawing notions about American women participating in ISIS based on arrest data may not lead to analytically sound assessments. In our other, similar samples—especially the sample of American women who successfully traveled overseas to join jihadist groups—the percentage of women is considerably higher than 10 percent. Of course, there is no known sample of American participation in ISIS in which there is anything close to gender parity. However, the lack of representation of women within the sample of American jihadists charged with supporting ISIS does not entail that women were restricted to specific roles. Even within this small sample, women were involved in every major category of ISIS-related activity in the United States, from planning and perpetrating attacks to travel, financing, internet activism, and online operations. Most did so entirely of their own volition, and despite sensationalized and simplified accounts of their cases, often radicalized without the influence of a male co-conspirator. Overall, the evidence supports claims that "women have no fewer motives than men for engaging in jihad."[61]

Several cases within the sample show that American ISIS-supporting women were able to chart their own roles, sometimes outside the traditionally determined spectrum of women's participation in jihadist groups. In April 2015, the FBI arrested Noelle Velentzas and Asia Siddiqui for planning a bombing attack in New York City on behalf of ISIS.[62] The two Queens, New York women were active figures in the jihadist movement since the mid-2000s, when Siddiqui became in contact with American AQAP operative Samir Khan and incarcerated American al-Qaeda supporters.[63] In 2013, the pair began consulting a range of sources to plan a bomb attack, using instructions from AQAP's *Inspire* magazine, *The Anarchist's Cookbook*, and college-level chemistry books. In 2014, Velentzas and Siddiqui declared fealty to ISIS. They were on the verge of constructing a working improvised explosive device in early 2015 when they were arrested by the FBI's Joint Terrorism Task Force.[64] In August 2019, the pair pleaded guilty to distributing information pertaining to the making and use of weapons of mass destruction, to be used in federal crimes of violence.[65]

Cases like Siddiqui and Velentzas demonstrate how American women supporters of ISIS deviate from the traditional roles prescribed for them by the group, in this case by directly participating in planning attacks. Evaluating ISIS' stance on women's participation in combat operations is difficult. In theory, the group has been ambiguous in its ideological treatises and propaganda about whether women are allowed to engage in military activities or attacks. In certain periods, they attempted to issue moratoriums on women participating in combat, but in times of urgent need of combatants, such as during the 2017 sieges of Mosul and Raqqa, they lifted the ban.[66] However, in practice, ISIS and its predecessors have long histories of utilizing women in combat. During the mid-2000s, al-Qaeda in Iraq (AQI) and its Jordanian leader, Abu Musab al-Zarqawi, frequently employed women as suicide bombers.[67] After several evolutions, AQI was one of the groups that eventually formed the organizational core of ISIS.[68] Away from the battlefields in Syria and Iraq, American women jihadists may have more agency to interpret their roles within their organization. Referring to Siddiqui, Velentzas, and Tashfeen Malik, the woman who perpetrated the 2015 San Bernardino shooting, Audrey Alexander argues that "although their efforts might reflect changing attitudes about formerly gendered, now-permissible activities, violence by female jihadists in America could also be a symptom of the movement's increasing reliance on lone-actors, self-starters, and small, disconnected groups."[69]

Women participating in other activities on behalf of ISIS, from successfully joining the group in Syria and committing attacks in the United States to financing, online activism, recruiting, and cyber operations, are profiled throughout the various chapters of this book. In part, these accounts show that the roles and profiles of both men and women ISIS supporters are far from monolithic, and help challenge common misconceptions about the role of Western women within jihadist groups. While young men will likely continue to be the primary audience for ISIS and groups like it, to discount women's participation would not only leave out a substantial percentage of the data, but with it several pressing policy issues and national security threats.

Citizenship and State of Origin

The overwhelming majority of Americans charged for ISIS-related activity were United States citizens (154 cases) or permanent residents (19 cases). Most ISIS supporters were deeply rooted in the United States by either citizenship, long-term residence, or ties, and underwent the critical stages of their radicalization within the United States. To more closely encapsulate the nature of this threat, the FBI, National Counterterrorism Center (NCTC), and Department of Homeland Security (DHS) refer to these cases as "homegrown violent extremists" (HVE). The US Government joint definition of an HVE is

> a person of any citizenship who lives or operates primarily in the United States or its territories, and who advocates, engages in, or is preparing to engage in or support terrorist activities in furtherance of a foreign terrorist organization's objectives, but who is acting independently of foreign terrorist direction.[70]

In FBI, NCTC, and DHS publications, HVEs are considered one component of the threat from international terrorism, alongside members of foreign terrorist organizations who are located overseas and state sponsors of terrorism.[71] According to senior FBI officials, HVEs now take up the bulk of the international-terrorism-related investigations in the United States. In 2018, FBI Director Christopher Wray testified that the "primary terrorist threat to the homeland today, without question, is homegrown violent extremists."[72] Undoubtedly, ISIS and its recruitment efforts in the Islamic State helped create the meteoric rise in HVE cases in relation to other international terrorism efforts during the past five years. It also forced US counterterrorism authorities to account for domestic drivers of radicalization. No longer could terrorism be viewed solely as an external threat to the United States.

The characteristics of the HVE threat distinguish the United States from several other Western countries that have been affected by ISIS recruitment. Several European countries—including the United Kingdom, France, Belgium, and Denmark—experienced community-level radicalization involving dozens of individuals from a particular neighborhood or social network joining ISIS.[73] In these countries, ISIS had physical recruitment networks on the ground, through key ideologues and jihadist activist groups. Their targets were Muslim communities within these countries that, in comparison with the United States, were poorly integrated and isolated from mainstream society.[74] In the United States, ISIS recruitment dynamics largely involve individuals who were part and parcel of the fabric of American life. Radicalization was largely confined to groups of two, three, or four individuals who grew estranged from their own communities, and the process did not occur on a community-wide level.[75]

Further evidence for this distinction between Western European and American radicalization patterns can be shown in the geographic dispersion of ISIS supporters in the United States. In other Western countries, ISIS support was often concentrated in particular communities and areas within specific countries. Infamous examples include the Brussels neighborhood of Molenbeek in Belgium and the small Mediterranean town of Lunel in France, from which several dozen ISIS fighters each hailed.[76] No "hotspot" on this level exists in the United States, with minor exceptions. The FBI operates ISIS-related investigations in all 50 states, and supporters have been charged in 29 states (and the District of Columbia). Four of the five states with the highest frequency of cases are among the most populous states in the country (New York, Virginia, Florida, and Illinois). The prevalence of ISIS cases in these states appears to mainly be the result of their large populations rather than any specific phenomenon within the state. One outlier— Minnesota—does have a unique history behind the significant number of ISIS cases in the state, discussed at length in the second chapter of this book. Excluding the Minnesota example, ISIS cases tend to be distributed across states in proportion to their total population.

Travel and Attacks

On average, American ISIS supporters were more interested in traveling to join the group overseas than they were in planning attacks within the United States. Of Americans charged with ISIS-related activity, 39 percent were alleged to have attempted terrorist travel, versus 31 percent who planned terrorist attacks on US soil. At first glance, this result is surprising. Many consider ISIS' attempts to direct and inspire terrorist attacks against the United States to be the main objective of its outreach to Americans. However, for many radicalized Americans, ISIS' supposed re-establishment of the caliphate created a mandate of migration, requiring every supporter to travel overseas and come to the aid of the Islamic State.

However, if the data is broken down year by year, an interesting trend emerges. In 2014, 76 percent of Americans charged with ISIS-related activity planned to travel overseas to join the group. The proportion steadily declined in the following years: in 2015, 43 percent of the cases involved jihadist travel efforts, in 2016 36 percent, and in 2017 29 percent. The decline in Americans interested in travel over the period from 2014 to 2019 generally correlates with ongoing developments in the situation in Syria and Iraq. From 2015 to 2017, ISIS lost most of its physical and human infrastructure for recruiting and intaking foreign fighters. In 2018 there was a slight increase in the proportion of Americans attempting jihadist travel to 36 percent, although there were only 14 people publicly charged with ISIS-related activity that year. In 2019, eight of the 30 (27 percent) charged with ISIS-related activity traveled or attempted to travel to join ISIS. In total, the proportion of indicted ISIS supporters interested in jihadist travel peaked in 2014, steadily declined, and then plateaued from 2016 onward.

In comparison, the number of ISIS supporters interested in planning domestic attacks steadily increased. In 2014, only 12 percent of the cases involved domestic attack plotters. By the next year, although still smaller in comparison to the number of attempted travelers, the percentage shot up to 35 percent. Numbers remained constant in 2016 (33 percent) and 2017 (34 percent), but in 2018, nearly half (45 percent) of the ISIS cases in the United States involved an individual who plotted a domestic attack. The steady rise in the number of American ISIS supporters interested in attacks in the homeland matches the timeline of the group's increasing encouragement of these types of attacks, as well as the infeasibility of jihadist travel. In 2019, the percentage of attack planners dropped again to 27 percent.

Thus, travel and jihadist attack planning for American ISIS supporters appear to be inversely correlated. Because of its ideological significance, *hijra* was generally the preferred option for most ISIS supporters. However, when travel to Syria and Iraq became impractical, supporters chose violence at home. During one of many calls for Western supporters to engage in violent attacks in their home countries, ISIS' former spokesperson Abu Muhammad al-Adnani instructed supporters during a 2016 speech that "if the tyrants have shut the gates of *hijra* in your face, then open the gates of jihad in their face."[77] Following this call, and taking into account the unlikelihood of successful travel to Syria or Iraq, many American ISIS supporters began building the option of conducting attacks into their cost/benefit analyses. Thomas Hegghammer refers to this dilemma as a classic problem plaguing foreign jihadists: "should I stay or should I go?"[78]

In some American cases, ISIS operatives instructed individuals who were interested in jihadist travel to stay home instead. In 2015, Emanuel Lutchman, a 25-year-old Rochester, New York resident, used a messaging application to reach out to ISIS external operations facilitator Junaid Hussain, expressing interest in *hijra*.[79] Hussain told Lutchman to avoid travel. At the time, the borders between Turkey and Syria were closed, and Lutchman did not have anyone to vouch for him or his jihadist bona fides. Therefore, Hussain told Lutchman that his best option to help ISIS was to conduct an attack in the United States, and walked him through the process of designing a plot.[80] Lutchman was arrested on December 30, 2015, before he was able to carry out his planned attack on a New Year's Eve celebration the next day.[81]

In other cases, American ISIS supporters who made unsuccessful travel attempts turned towards attack planning after their efforts were thwarted. Houston, Texas resident Kaan Sercan Damlarkaya made two separate attempts to join ISIS in Syria in 2014 and 2015, both times as a minor.[82] According to Damlarkaya, his first attempt failed because he "didn't have a contact" in the group; the second failed because an individual with knowledge of the plot alerted his mother, who then tipped off the FBI.[83] After the second attempt, Damlarkaya told an FBI undercover employee that if he "[could not] make *hijra* to any *wilayat* [province of the Islamic State]...[he would] attack the *kuffar* here."[84] He was arrested in 2017 after attempting to build homemade explosives and firearms in furtherance of a jihadist attack plot. Damlarkaya's case highlights a trend that Daniel Byman refers to as the "frustrated foreign fighter" problem, wherein "policies that aim to block the flow of foreigners frustrate some of these would-be jihadists." In turn, would-be foreign fighters turn their efforts towards committing attacks.[85]

Investigation, Prosecution, and Sentencing

With 1,000 open investigations of ISIS-inspired homegrown violent extremists at any time, the FBI must determine which cases require immediate disruptions through arrest, and which cases must be prioritized or deprioritized. In full-field counterterrorism investigations against ISIS supporters, the FBI increasingly relies on three areas—partnerships, intelligence, and innovation—to reduce threats.[86] Partnerships with local communities, as well as state and local law enforcement, have been vital to the FBI's investigations of ISIS supporters. Intelligence gathering in these cases usually involves the strategic usage of FBI undercover employees and confidential human sources. Counterterrorism innovation relies on law enforcement's adoption of technology to conduct investigations on social media. A vast majority of today's ISIS-related investigations now involve the use of some evidence from online platforms.

It is safe to say that many of the 204 ISIS-related homegrown violent extremism cases would not have been on the FBI's radar without tips from concerned friends, family, and local community members. Senior federal law enforcement officials describe local partners, including state and local law enforcement, community organizations, local religious leaders, and human services providers, as the first line of defense in counterterrorism efforts.[87] In today's counterterrorism, federal law enforcement's relationships (or lack thereof) with local communities can be the difference between effective interventions and cases slipping through the cracks. The final chapter of this book examines many of the efforts that the FBI, DOJ, NCTC, and DHS have taken towards strengthening the lines of contact between local communities and federal counterterrorism authorities.

The FBI also continues to leverage the investigative approach of using undercover FBI agents (UCEs) and confidential human sources (CHS). Fifty-eight percent of ISIS cases in the United States involve either an undercover FBI agent or a cooperating source, who often contact or are contacted by terrorist suspects who unwittingly believe them to be co-conspirators in attack plots or attempts to travel overseas. Despite the frequency of their use in investigations, sting operations involving UCEs or CHS are controversial. The FBI argues that using undercover operatives or CHS are critical to human intelligence gathering and that, without them, law enforcement would be unable to identify active terrorist threats.[88] Critics claim that FBI operatives entrap terrorist suspects by pushing them to undertake criminal activities when it is unclear that they would have done so on their own volition.[89] Condemnations of this approach aside, significant changes to the way the FBI uses undercover agents are unlikely. This strategy has become a key component of counterterrorism investigations, and to date, there are no court rulings that found the FBI legally entrapped terrorist suspects.

Finally, the FBI's access to evidence from social media is a critical aspect of the investigative process for most ISIS-related suspects. Generally speaking, FBI agents gather intelligence from social media in one of two ways. First, FBI undercover employees pose as ISIS supporters online, connecting and engaging in conversations with targets. If the company that owns a social media platform is based in the US, the FBI has additional options to recover evidence relevant to terrorism investigations, even if it has been deleted or removed. As part of a search warrant, the FBI can subpoena US companies to provide information related to the targeted accounts of terrorist suspects.[90] In one form or another, evidence from social media is increasingly referenced in investigations of ISIS supporters in the United States. Two factors—the use of messaging technology with end-to-end encryption and platforms owned by non-United States companies—complicate some of the FBI's investigative procedures.

When the investigative process is concluded, and there is enough evidence to make an arrest, the DOJ can indict and prosecute ISIS supporters. The statute used to prosecute most ISIS supporters is Title 18 of US Code, Section 2339B, more commonly known as the "material support statute." According to the material support statute,

> whoever knowingly provides material support or resources to a foreign terrorist organization, or attempts or conspires to do so, shall be fined under this title or imprisoned not more than 20 years, or both, and, if the death of any person results, shall be imprisoned for any term of years or for life.[91]

In order to charge an ISIS supporter with violations of the material support statute, there are two necessary preconditions. First, supporters need to either conspire to, attempt to, or successfully provide "material support or resources." The definition of "material support" is broad and is designed to give leeway to prosecutors. It can include tangible and intangible property, services, money or finances, lodging, training, advice or expertise, facilities, weapons, lethal substances, explosives, and, most importantly for ISIS-related cases, personnel.[92] Courts generally interpret traveling to join a terrorist group as providing one's self as personnel to a foreign terrorist organization, thus violating the material support statute.[93] The other requirement is for the material support to go to a "foreign terrorist organization." This is determined by the State Department's designated list of foreign terrorist organizations (FTO), which has included ISIS since May 2014 after it amended the designation of its predecessor, AQI.[94]

Sixty-nine percent of the ISIS-related prosecutions between 2014 and 2019 involved some alleged violation of the material support statute. Other common charges of offense included making false statements to the FBI, violations of firearms statutes, use or distribution of information related to weapons of mass destruction, murder, and attempted murder. In these cases, it is important to review what the material support statute and other federal terrorism statutes do not cover. Making pledges of allegiance to the Islamic State, publicly professing support for the group, or praising its activities are all protected speech under the First Amendment and are not viewed as providing material support unless accompanied by tangible forms of assistance.[95]

In some cases, the federal government defers to states in prosecuting ISIS suspects. Between 2014 and 2019, nine ISIS cases were prosecuted at the state level in Alabama, Arizona, Florida, Minnesota, New York, Pennsylvania, and

Texas. State prosecutions are especially likely under three conditions. As previously mentioned, cases involving minors are now considered to be the responsibility of state prosecutors. Additionally, in cases where an ISIS supporter successfully carries out an attack, resulting in casualties, states sometimes take up prosecution. In the United States, state-level murder statutes are more expansive than federal ones. In certain circumstances, charging a jihadist attacker with a state murder or attempted murder charge may result in a substantially longer prison sentence than charging them with material support or a federal terrorism offense.[96] Finally, in some instances, zealous state prosecutors investigate terrorism cases that are too weak for federal investigators.[97]

At the federal and state levels alike, prosecutors usually convict indicted ISIS supporters. Of the 204 individuals charged with ISIS-related offenses 127 pleaded guilty, and 22 additional suspects were found guilty at trial. In fact, prior to March 2018, when Noor Zahi Salman was acquitted of making false statements to the FBI related to her husband, the Pulse nightclub shooter Omar Mateen, DOJ had never lost an ISIS-related case at trial.[98] Federal prosecutors continue a perfect record in ISIS-related material support cases.

After prosecutors secure a guilty plea or conviction by a jury, judges use federal sentencing guidelines, supplemented by arguments from the defense and prosecution, to determine how long convicted terrorists will spend in prison. The average prison sentence for a convicted ISIS supporter is 13.7 years, with a standard deviation of approximately ten years above or below the average. This number is slightly less than the mandatory minimum 15-year sentence for violations of the material support statute. Differences in the charges of offense used to prosecute ISIS supporters, their activities on behalf of ISIS, cooperation with authorities, and other factors (including age, gender, personal background, and mental health) all can have an effect on the prison sentence they receive. The result is a patchwork of prison sentences, from as short as a few months in prison to life sentences.

Convicted ISIS supporters are currently incarcerated throughout the federal prison system.[99] The Federal Bureau of Prisons (BOP), which operates and oversees the administration of prison facilities, places inmates under various levels of security conditions based on their charge of offense and the risk they pose to the institution.[100] The most dangerous ISIS-related prisoners go to the administrative security facility (ADMAX) at the United States Penitentiary in Florence, Colorado, where they are locked down in individual cells 23 hours of the day.[101] The rest are dispersed throughout high-, medium-, and low-security facilities in state and federal prison systems. There are ongoing concerns that convicted ISIS supporters behind bars could radicalize others. Citing limited instances in which ISIS-related radicalization in prisons occurred, the Bureau of Prisons views these as "low base-rate, high impact" incidents.[102]

From many perspectives, the US strategy of investigating, prosecuting, and sentencing ISIS supporters can be viewed as an overwhelming success. This is especially the case in comparison to many other Western countries, which, prior to the current ISIS mobilization, lacked the legal infrastructure to process ISIS supporters. With larger populations of ISIS supporters, fewer laws like the material support statute, and generally shorter sentences for convicted terrorists, many European countries found that trying ISIS supporters amounted to a "revolving door."[103] Arresting an ISIS sympathizer by no means guaranteed their conviction. Even when convictions were secured, the average EU-wide sentence for terrorism offenses is approximately five years in prison, meaning that convicted terrorists would quickly be back on the streets.[104] Sometimes, their stays in prison allowed them to connect with other incarcerated jihadists, leading to the development of networks that were responsible for some of Europe's most deadly terrorist attacks during the past five years.[105]

The situation is drastically different in the United States. When the FBI arrests an ISIS supporter, the DOJ can reasonably assume that a guilty plea or conviction, followed by sentences of more than a decade in tightly controlled federal prisons, are not far behind. However, this is not true for every case, and counterterrorism authorities in the US are increasingly forced to respond to releases of convicted jihadists from prison systems. Already, upwards of 20 Americans convicted for ISIS-related activities have been released from federal custody after serving time. The majority involve cases where convicted ISIS supporters were sentenced to less than five years in prison for charges other than material support. By 2023, at least 80 individuals incarcerated for jihadist activities since September 11, 2001, will have been released from BOP custody.[106]

Following their release, the office responsible for managing formerly incarcerated ISIS supporters is US Probations and Pretrial Services, part of the Administrative Office of the US Courts. Probations and Pretrial Services is currently developing its resources and strategies for handling cases of released violent extremists.[107] One of the main gaps in US policy towards released terrorist offenders is a lack of data about recidivism rates among the released extremist population. Some early studies in the US context suggest that the risk of terrorist recidivism is generally lower than the overall federal recidivism rate, but the coming release of dozens of terrorist offenders could potentially change the verdict.[108]

Processing ISIS supporters from the investigation phase through arrests, indictments, prosecution, sentencing, and prison time was a well-worn path in the US legal system's response to the uptick in jihadist activity in America between 2014 and 2019. As Chapter 6 of this book explains, however, during this period, US counterterrorism authorities became increasingly convinced that relying on arrests and prosecution alone was counterproductive. Through programs under the header of "countering violent extremism" (CVE), they attempted to install non-prosecutorial options as a potential alternative to arresting and trying every case of ISIS support in the United States. With the exception of a few notable examples, however, traditional investigation, prosecution, and sentencing are still the overwhelming choices for the FBI and DOJ and remain in use for a majority of terrorism-related cases.

Chapter 2

THE TERRORISTS

ISIS did not limit its brutalities to its controlled territories in Syria and Iraq. ISIS supporters perpetrated a litany of violent attacks around the world. In North America and Western Europe alone, ISIS is responsible for directing, assisting, and inspiring over 50 terrorist attacks in which more than 400 people lost their lives.[1] Compared to previous waves of jihadist mobilization in the West, the frequency of attacks is unprecedented.[2]

The methods and tactics employed by the perpetrators are, in some ways, a direct result of ISIS' strategy towards attacks in the West. The organization generally eschews extensive linkages between its core and its base of Western supporters, encouraging its followers to take matters into their own hands with ISIS' blessing, but not necessarily its support. "If you can kill a disbelieving American or European," exhorted the group's former spokesperson Abu Muhammad al-Adnani in a September 2014 speech,

> then rely upon Allah and kill him in any manner or way however it may be . . . If you are not able to find an IED or a bullet, then single out the disbelieving American, Frenchman, or any of their allies. Smash his head with a rock, or slaughter him with a knife, or run him over with your car, or throw him down from a high place, or choke him, or poison him.[3]

Heeding al-Adnani's call, supporters of ISIS throughout the world have employed dozens of methods in carrying out attacks, from firearms and explosives to vehicular assaults and stabbings.

Despite the new variety of methods, and the increasingly diverse backgrounds of the perpetrators, some common themes in ISIS-related attacks in the West emerge. Compared to the terrorist plots of the al-Qaeda generation, fewer of the ISIS-related attacks in Western Europe and North America required extensive logistical planning, financial resources, or trained attackers.[4] Notably, the lack of these factors appears to have decreased average plot lethality as compared to attacks by al-Qaeda.[5] Yet, concurrently, the total number of attacks perpetrated by ISIS supporters have substantially increased. Law enforcement agencies worldwide, who built a wide array of tools to detect and interdict attack planning based on financial transfers, identifying networks, and apprehending would-be perpetrators during the planning stage of their attacks, now have fewer avenues to detect when an attack may be on the verge of occurring.[6] Would-be jihadist perpetrators obtain everything that they need to pull off a plot via completely legal means, and do not cross a criminal threshold or raise any red flags until they are conducting the attack.[7]

Jihadist Attacks in the United States: 2014 to 2019

Between al-Adnani's speech in September 2014, which directly followed ISIS' claim that it had re-established the caliphate in June 2014, and the end of 2019, there were 23 jihadist attacks in the United States. The attacks resulted in a total of 88 deaths and 222 injuries.[8] An analysis of these attacks highlights the diversity of motivations, methods, perpetrators, and targets of jihadist plots in America.

Evidence collected from primary source records and court documents shows that approximately two-thirds (16) of the 25 attackers who perpetrated these attacks had been at least partially inspired by ISIS. The remaining nine individuals had no known nexus to ISIS. Four of this number (16 percent) claimed allegiance to or inspiration from al-Qaeda or another jihadist group only. ISIS officially claimed responsibility for seven of these attacks in its propaganda material:[9]

- Curtis Culwell Center attack, Garland, Texas: May 3, 2015[10]
- San Bernardino shooting, San Bernardino, California: December 2, 2015[11]
- Pulse nightclub shooting, Orlando, Florida: June 12, 2016[12]
- St. Cloud Mall stabbing, St. Cloud, Minnesota: September 7, 2016[13]
- Ohio State University stabbings, Columbus, Ohio: November 28, 2016[14]
- Lower Manhattan truck-ramming attack, New York, New York: October 31, 2017[15]
- Port Authority bombing, New York, New York: December 8, 2017[16]

The attackers utilized a range of different methods to carry out their attacks. Ten carried out their attacks using firearms, and nine used bladed weapons (knives and axes). Only two successfully perpetrated an attack involving an improvised explosive device, and, in one case each, jihadists conducted an attack involving arson and truck-ramming. The most effective method was to use firearms. Of the 88 deaths during the 23 jihadist attacks after June 2014, 78 came as a result of attacks using guns.

The 25 perpetrators of these attacks ranged in age from 17 to 49 years old, with an average age of 27 years old. The average attacker is not much younger than terrorist attackers of years past, and mirrors the average ages of jihadist travelers and other supporters in the United States. Only one attacker was under the age of 18. Corey Johnson, a 17-year-old Florida native, killed one and injured two in a knife attack during a sleepover at a friend's house in March 2018 after the young ISIS supporter believed that his friends were insulting the group and his religion.[17]

Still, two-thirds of the perpetrators were 24 years or older. The oldest attacker, Michigan resident Amor Ftouhi, was 49 years old when he injured two in a stabbing at Flint Airport in June 2017.[18] Twenty-three of the perpetrators were male, and two—San Bernardino shooter Tashfeen Malik and Minnesota arsonist Tnuza Jamal Hassan—were female (8 percent).

The location of attacks is dispersed throughout the US, spanning 14 different states. California, Colorado, Florida, Michigan, Minnesota, North Carolina, New York, New Jersey, Ohio, Oklahoma, Pennsylvania, Tennessee, Texas, and Virginia all experienced at least one jihadist attack in the observed period. Three states experienced more than two attacks: New York (4), Florida (4), and Minnesota (3).

Twelve perpetrators were killed in the commission of their attack, while 13 were arrested and charged in the US court system following their attack. While these 23 attacks were successful, during the same time period from 2014 to 2019 the FBI disrupted at least 58 ISIS supporters who were planning to conduct attacks in the United States. This chapter examines both successful and failed attack plots. Highlighting the differences and similarities between the two is a critical enterprise, as it can help reveal key insights into not only how terrorists develop their plan of attack and learn from others, but can also gauge the effectiveness of law enforcement's response.[19]

Lone Actors, Group Plots, and "Virtual Entrepreneurs"

The principal difference in the age of ISIS for jihadist attack plots in the West was the growing emphasis on lone actors, individuals inspired by a jihadist group's ideology who conducted attacks alone.[20] These make up the overwhelming majority of the jihadist attacks in the United States from 2014 to 2019 (21 out of 23, or 91 percent). The exceptions are the San Bernardino shooting from December 2015 and the Curtis Culwell Center Attack from May 2015, both of which involved pairs of attackers.

But an important distinction must be made: while lone-actor plots were the norm, this does not mean that America's jihadist attackers went through every step of their radicalization and mobilization processes by themselves. The term "lone wolf" is frequently used to refer to jihadist attackers in the West, but it has limited application here.[21] Many lone attackers drew support from a wider network of ISIS supporters, and a few received guidance from specific operatives in ISIS' external operations teams who provided them information and support for conducting an attack in the United States from bases in Syria and Iraq. We refer to these attack planners as ISIS' "virtual entrepreneurs," and they left an indelible mark on jihadist plots in the United States.[22] In reality, these virtual entrepreneurs served several roles beyond attack planning—from acting as "travel guides" for ISIS supporters who were considering *hijra* to key propaganda disseminators online—but their roles in guiding attackers were arguably their most significant.[23]

Since 2014, at least 20 US-based ISIS supporters were in contact with ISIS English-speaking virtual entrepreneurs located in Syria.[24] The most infamous team of virtual entrepreneurs conducted their operations from a small internet café in Raqqa. Led by the British former black-hat hacker Junaid Hussain, this group of online operators eventually became referred to by the US Department of Justice as "The Legion."[25] Hussain, alongside a crew of ISIS operatives that he hand-picked from his hometown of Birmingham, including Reyaad Khan and Raphael Hostey, had a simple *modus operandi*. Using a host of online messaging platforms and social media accounts, they reached out to ISIS supporters in English-speaking countries, including the US, encouraging and directing the supporters to commit attacks on the group's behalf.[26] Their efforts were so notorious that most of the Legion—including Hussain himself, who was at one time the third person on the US' list of high-value ISIS targets—were directly targeted in coalition airstrikes.[27] In addition to the Legion, another prominent English-speaking virtual entrepreneur was Abu Sa'ad Sudani, also known as Abu Isa al-Amriki.[28] Based in al-Bab, Syria, Sudani operated independently from many of the others, sometimes with the assistance of his Australian wife, Shadi Jabar Khalil Mohammad, and his British friend Omar Hussain (Abu Sa'eed al-Britani).[29]

The influence of virtual entrepreneurs is stamped throughout the map of ISIS attackers and attack planners in the United States. In December 2014, Justin Nojan Sullivan, a 19-year-old resident of the small town of Morganton, North Carolina, killed and robbed his 74-year-old neighbor, John Bailey Clark Jr.[30] Sullivan, in need of cash, stole his father's hunting rifle and waited until his parents left their home for a weekend getaway before committing a home invasion and murder. After shooting and killing Clark at point-blank range with a .22 caliber Marlin rifle, Sullivan stole hundreds of dollars from Clark's house.[31] On first glance, the murder-robbery seemed to be more related to a standard criminal motivation rather than an ideological one. However, evidence from the investigation revealed that Sullivan was accessing, viewing, and downloading ISIS propaganda in the months leading up to the murder. In the following months, Sullivan would engage in correspondence with Junaid Hussain. Sullivan told Hussain that he was planning to use the proceeds of the Clark murder to purchase an assault rifle, which he said he would use to "[carry] out the first operation of the Islamic State in North America."[32] Hussain instructed Sullivan to record video footage of the attack and send it to him.[33]

All four of the attack plots examined in this chapter have some nexus to an ISIS virtual entrepreneur. While the details and facts of each attack plot are markedly different, they also have similarities that can be traced back to the guiding hand of the virtual entrepreneurs involved in the plot. However, despite the frequency of their involvement, the involvement of ISIS virtual entrepreneurs in ISIS supporters' attack plots in the United States does not appear to have had any bearing on whether the plots were successful or not.[34] Law enforcement adapted to their strategies, and used the evidence of a connection between an ISIS supporter in the United States and a Syria-based virtual entrepreneur as a basis to investigate and interdict the supporter. Additionally, the deadliest ISIS-related attacks in the United States between 2014 and 2019 did not involve a virtual entrepreneur.

By far the most lethal ISIS-inspired attack occurred at 2:00 AM on June 12, 2016, when 29-year-old Omar Mateen stormed the Pulse nightclub in Orlando, Florida and began shooting, alternating between an assault rifle and a handgun.[35] Twenty-two minutes into the rampage, he called 911 and pledged allegiance to ISIS' leader Abu Bakr al-Baghdadi. Later, he told a police negotiator who arrived at the scene that he conducted the attack because of "the airstrike that killed Abu Wahid [*sic*]," referring erroneously to Shaker Wahib al-Fahdawi al-Dulaimi, also known as Abu Wahib, an ISIS field commander who was killed in a drone strike a month before Mateen's attack.[36] After a standoff, police shot and killed Mateen. In total, Mateen fired over 100 rounds of ammunition, killing 49 and wounding 53.[37] The Pulse nightclub shooting remains the second-deadliest mass shooting by a lone actor in United States history, eclipsed later by a 2017 shooting in Las Vegas.[38] ISIS' Amaq News Agency claimed that Mateen was "an Islamic State fighter" and carried out the attack on behalf of the group, despite few tangible links between them.[39]

Mateen's attack is an outlier in multiple regards. Only two other jihadist attacks in the post-2014 period, both claimed by ISIS, resulted in more than five deaths. On December 2, 2015, husband–wife team Tashfeen Malik and Syed Farook opened fire on a departmental event at the Inland Regional Center in San Bernadino, California. The assault, which ended in a police chase and both attackers' deaths, resulted in 14 deaths and 24 injuries.[40] Nearly two years later, on October 31, 2017 in New York City, Sayfullo Saipov drove a pickup truck onto a bike path in Lower Manhattan, killing eight and wounding twelve.[41] Following the vehicular assault, Saipov brandished a paintball gun and charged a New York Police Department officer, who shot him in the stomach and arrested him. Amaq News Agency claimed both attacks on behalf of ISIS.[42]

These three attacks, however, are exceptions to the norm. Thirteen of the 23 jihadist attacks in the United States between 2014 and 2019 resulted in no deaths, except for the attackers. Another important corollary is that in the same timeframe, federal, state, and local law enforcement in the United States successfully prevented at least 58 individuals who were planning to commit attacks on behalf of ISIS from following through, arresting and charging them before they carried out their plots. From the broadest view possible, the United States government has been effective in decreasing the risk of casualties from ISIS- and other jihadist-related attacks in the country since 2014.

That notwithstanding, responding to the threat entails significant challenges for law enforcement. While the FBI has a broad mandate to investigate would-be jihadist operatives in the United States who may be planning an attack, determining when to escalate the intervention to prosecution and successfully bring charges is increasingly difficult. The majority of modern jihadist perpetrators use means that may be completely legal in their jurisdictions, such as purchasing firearms and knives or renting vehicles, to carry out their attacks.[43] If they do not cross a criminal threshold, either by engaging in a financial transaction with a designated terrorist or terrorist organization, purchasing or distributing information necessary to make an explosive device or other weapon of mass destruction, or committing other forms of material support, law enforcement may not be able to arrest and charge would-be attackers in time.

This can result in one of two scenarios, both of which have led to criticism of US counterterrorism investigations. In one scenario, law enforcement may not be able to detect when an ISIS supporter is planning an attack. In November 2015, 18-year-old University of California Merced student Faisal Mohammad went on a stabbing spree on the university's campus, resulting in four injuries.[44] The FBI denied that Mohammad was subject to an investigation prior to the stabbings, but in a post-hoc review found ISIS propaganda and a manifesto on his computer.[45]

In other cases, the FBI launches an investigation against an individual, but they commit an attack before the investigation results in an arrest or charges. Omar Mateen and Tashfeen Malik both had touchpoints with law enforcement prior to committing their deadly attacks. Mateen was subject to FBI investigation twice, once for making incendiary, pro-jihadist statements while employed as a security guard in 2013, and again when his friend Moner Abu-Salha committed a suicide bombing attack while fighting for Jabhat al-Nusra in Syria during the summer of 2014.[46] According to standard operating procedure, Tashfeen Malik was subject to "three extensive national security and criminal background screenings" as she applied for permanent residency in the United States in 2014.[47] The reviews, however, did not find any irregularities or red flags, and Malik's application was approved months before she committed her attack in San Bernardino.[48]

The FBI's counterterrorism mission draws scrutiny from the public and elected officials when either of these scenarios occur. FBI officials and special agents across the country assigned to the Joint Terrorism Task Force (JTTF) understand the consequences when the Bureau is either unable to fully investigate an attacker prior to their violent act, or when an investigation does not herald arrest and prosecution before a supporter of a terrorist group strikes. They view their responsibilities as a zero-fail mission. "If we screw up," one FBI special agent assigned to JTTF explained, "we're going in front of Congress. That's part of working counterterrorism. If you blow a narcotics operation and a heroin dealer sells another kilo, OK. But if we mess up a counterterrorism operation involving someone who is planning an attack, we're fucked."[49]

The following three cases detail the push–pull battle between ISIS attack planners in the United States and federal law enforcement, documenting the often thin line between a successful attack and a failed plot. The difference can often be attributed to well-run investigations, human error on behalf of the planners, and, in many cases, some degree of serendipity and luck. In the following examination of these cases, we present a perspective that is not available in most media narratives about the three attack plots by including details from exclusive interviews with the FBI special agents in charge of the investigations, personally attending the trials of individuals arrested, and reviewing several hundred pages of previously unpublished investigative files and court documents. Federal agents successfully prevented three of the four attacks described below, while the fourth raised new questions about how the FBI conducts counterterrorism investigations in the age of ISIS.

Mohamed Bailor Jalloh

On the day before July 4 in 2016, a team of federal agents arrested 27-year-old former Virginia National Guardsman Mohamed Bailor Jalloh outside of his house in Sterling, Virginia.[50] Scouring media reporting on this arrest, there is very little to suggest that this arrest was fundamentally different from any of the dozens of ISIS-inspired plots disrupted in the United States since 2014. On second look, Jalloh's case illustrates many of the difficulties for law enforcement in responding to the new face of jihadist attack planning in the United States, but also how the FBI can successfully interdict ISIS-inspired or directed attack plotters.

Unlike most of his counterparts, Mohamed Bailor Jalloh had distinct advantages which would conventionally comprise a greater chance of attack success. Most importantly, Jalloh had military training from his stint in the Army National Guard.[51] According to publicly available evidence, Omar Mateen did not communicate online or receive instructions from ISIS operatives prior to his attack.[52] Jalloh, in comparison, was in direct contact with a notorious ISIS attack planner. To date, no person who conducted a lethal ISIS-inspired or directed attack in the United States traveled overseas to join a jihadist group. Jalloh met ISIS facilitators in one country and made it most of the way to ISIS-held territory before backing out.

For the FBI employees from the Washington Field Office tasked to Jalloh's investigation and apprehension, discovering that these factors were in play brought an understandable level of urgency to the case. In a wide-reaching interview, FBI Special Agents assigned to the Jalloh case told us about the investigative process, the split-second decisions they were forced to take, and why this case, out of the multitude of ISIS-related cases in their area of responsibility during the past five years, was the one that "kept them up at night."[53]

The person who would be identified later as Mohamed Bailor Jalloh first popped up on the FBI's radar as the result of ongoing conversations between a confidential human source for the FBI and a mysterious Syria-based ISIS attack planner, known only by his jihadist noms de guerre (*kunyas*) Abu Sa'ad Sudani and Abu Isa al-Amriki, and a variety of online handles.[54] After his death in an April 2016 airstrike, the Department of Defense described Sudani as an "influential ISIL recruiter" who was "involved in planning attacks against the United States, Canada and the United Kingdom."[55] In addition to Jalloh, Abu Sa'ad Sudani was in contact with at least two other people in the United States who were interested in committing attacks on behalf of ISIS.[56] One month before his death, Sudani put the FBI's human source, whom he believed to be an ISIS supporter, in touch with another supporter he knew, and told them to meet in person to plan an attack in the United States.[57]

At the time of this introduction, the FBI had little knowledge of who the mutual contact was, besides the evidence that they were in Sterling, Virginia and had contact with Abu Sa'ad Sudani, a known ISIS attack planner.[58] This basis alone moved the case up the list of the JTTF's priorities. "We needed to get a disruption as fast as possible that would also hold up in court," the FBI agent working on the case explained. "It's a push–pull. We have to be aggressive, but prosecutors have to prove it in court, and you have to consider sentencing. If we pick him up for something immediately, that may result in a lesser charge that will put him in jail for five years, but we will have to deal with him again very shortly."[59] In the first of a series of judgment calls, the FBI decided to let the in-person meeting between the source and the mutual contact transpire.

The call paid off. On April 9, 2016, the FBI confidential human source met with the mutual contact, who revealed a host of information about his life, intentions, and experiences.[60] The contact claimed to be a lifelong Muslim, born in Sierra Leone, who decided to quit the Army National Guard after watching videos of the Salafi-jihadist preacher Anwar al-Awlaki. More concerningly, the man claimed to have recently returned from West Africa, where he was in contact with what he described as "*khilafa* [Islamic State] brothers" in Nigeria.[61]

Additionally, he indicated interest in conducting an attack on a military target in the United States, praising Mohammad Youssef Abdulazeez, the shooter in a 2015 attack on military installations in Chattanooga, Tennessee, and Nidal Malik Hasan, the Fort Hood shooter.[62] The man told the source that he thought about conducting an attack all the time, and that he had experience with firearms from his time in the military.[63] Through visual surveillance and a car records check, the FBI identified the man as Mohamed Bailor Jalloh, and commenced a full-field investigation, with a crew of FBI agents rotating between 24/7 and 18/7 surveillance shifts.[64]

Indicative of new phenomena in ISIS-inspired attack planning, FBI agents were initially concerned, given Jalloh's background and experience and his stated interest, that he was at risk of conducting an attack at any time without warning.[65] An FBI records check after the first meeting also revealed that Jalloh had purchased a firearm. Again, agents were faced with a conundrum after the April 9 meeting: they knew Jalloh had the means, motive, and opportunity to conduct a terrorist attack, but did not have a sufficient level of evidence to arrest him or charge him with a crime. The agents let the investigation continue, with the risk that Jalloh would decide to commit an attack in the meantime. "We don't want to induce or push the conversation; entrapment is on the back of our mind at all times," the agent argued. "If he's breaking the law, he needs to do so with a clear heart and a clear mind."[66]

Investigators dug into Jalloh's claims about foreign travel and his time in the military as a window for establishing his radicalization and his ties to Sudani. Using Customs and Border Patrol records, they confirmed that Jalloh left the United States on June 11, 2015 and traveled to Sierra Leone alongside his father.[67] Later, Jalloh claimed that his father took him back to their home country directly after he quit the Army National Guard, when he noticed a substantial change in his son's behavior and wanted to "sort him out."[68] This effort appears to have backfired: during his trip to West Africa, Jalloh met his first contacts in the Islamic State.

In our interview, FBI Special Agents working on Jalloh's case attested that part of the evidence that would later be used to bring material support charges against Jalloh came from an interview with an ISIS facilitator who was arrested in Nigeria in February 2016.[69] The special agents got a tip that the facilitator knew American

ISIS supporters who were attempting to travel to Libya via Nigeria.[70] After receiving the information during the April 9 meeting between the confidential source and Jalloh that he claimed to have met "*khilafa* brothers" in Nigeria, the FBI sent a team for an interview. "The guy had a photographic memory," an FBI agent claimed.[71] Investigators found that Jalloh contacted the Nigerian facilitator via social media after his arrival in West Africa, traveled to northern Nigeria to meet him, and paid for a spot on a convoy of trucks headed to ISIS' province in Libya. At the last minute, however, Jalloh backed out before reaching Libya: he handed all of his money to the fixer and traveled back to Sierra Leone.[72]

While the FBI learned more about his travels, they worked with local police and Joint Terrorism Task Force officers from the US Army to gain more insight into Jalloh and his motivations.[73] Even after this review, they still felt that the information that they had was not sufficient to bring a material support for terrorism charge that would stick in court. Their only choice was to continue surveillance and hope to detect "out of pattern" behaviors which could indicate that Jalloh was about to commit a crime. As the FBI special agent put it: "There's out of pattern behavior like, 'he went to The Cheesecake Factory instead of Legal Seafoods,' and then there's out of pattern behavior like, 'he's talking to ISIS guys and just went to a gun store.'"[74]

Agents found a saving grace: Jalloh worked extensive shifts as an unarmed security guard and was an excellent employee. They could rely on the fact that Jalloh would be at work from early in the morning until late at night, limiting the window of time he could use to commit an attack.[75] In one out-of-pattern incident during the investigation, Jalloh drove to Dulles International Airport. Fearing that he was on his way to travel back to ISIS-controlled territory, FBI agents jumped into action, but pulled back when they realized that he was there to pick up family members who arrived on a flight from Sierra Leone.[76]

Jalloh's behavior, however, eventually took a quick turn towards committing chargeable criminal offenses. In a second in-person meeting between Jalloh and the confidential human source on May 1, 2016, Jalloh inquired about a potential attack during the Islamic holy month of Ramadan, which he felt would give him the maximum spiritual reward.[77] Among the targets that Jalloh suggested was the person responsible for organizing the "First Annual Muhammad Art Exhibit and Contest", a *cause célèbre* of many ISIS-inspired American attack planners.[78] He also asked the source about making monetary donations to ISIS fighters, and told him that he had a family member in North Carolina that could easily obtain assault weapons for an attack.[79] "Sometimes you just have to take action," Jalloh explained, "You can't be thinking too much . . . you have to pick a action [*sic*] and take it cause time is not on your side, since *Khilafah* was announced, what, June, 2014?"[80]

The May 1 meeting forced the Joint Terrorism Task Force to escalate their involvement in the case. To assuage Jalloh's desire to make a "charitable" donation to ISIS fighters, the source gave Jalloh a link to a money transfer service account operated by an FBI employee posing as a senior ISIS financier.[81] Jalloh sent $500 to this account, and in mid-June 2016, he contacted his family members in North Carolina to set up the purchase of an untraceable assault rifle.[82] Jalloh, who already owned a handgun, wanted the new weapon because he felt an attack with an assault rifle would be more lethal, and also believed that authorities would not be able to trace the weapon back to him.[83]

On July 1, 2017, an FBI surveillance team clocked Mohamed Bailor Jalloh entering a gun store in Virginia, taking an assault rifle off the wall and handling it while talking to employees.[84] He eventually left the store without purchasing the firearm, but the Joint Terrorism Task Force went into high alert. The next morning, before the store formally opened, agents from the Washington Field Office entered and interviewed staff about what had transpired. Those who interacted with Jalloh told agents that he did not have all the proper paperwork to purchase the gun and would be returning the next day with everything in hand.[85] "Please tell me this guy isn't some kind of terrorist," another employee allegedly asked FBI agents while reviewing store surveillance videos of Jalloh handling the rifle the day after. After a lack of response from the agents, he simply muttered, ". . . oh shit."[86]

As anticipated, Jalloh returned on July 2 to purchase the firearm. The store's employees kept their cool and sold Jalloh a Stag Arms AR-15 that had been rendered inoperable.[87] During the entirety of the July 4 weekend, the Washington Field Office agents, in conjunction with the Department of Justice, were already filing all the warrants, affidavits, and other paperwork necessary to apprehend and arrest Jalloh.[88] The case capped off a run of high-profile material support cases in the Washington Field Office's area of responsibility. FBI Special Agents said that due to how much time the Joint Terrorism Task Force spent on these cases, the field office decided to arrange a "spouse's appreciation picnic" for the July 4 weekend. "But then the Jalloh case picked up a week before, and everyone was so crushed. The last thing we needed was for people's spouses to come in to the office, so we canceled the picnic and decided to make it 'spend time with your family day.'"[89] That plan didn't come to fruition either: "When we heard Jalloh went to the gun store, we had to cancel that too."[90]

In the early morning hours of July 3, as Mohamed Bailor Jalloh was leaving his house on a cul-de-sac in Sterling to drive to work, a fleet of Chevrolet Suburbans swarmed in and closed off the street. An FBI SWAT team emerged from the blockade, and Jalloh quickly surrendered without incident.[91] FBI Special Agents executed search warrants on Jalloh's house and car where they discovered the magnitude of what Jalloh was planning to do with his newly acquired assault rifle. "When we got a search warrant for his Google search history, we found searches for 'Omar Mateen,' 'which kinds of rounds should I use for maximum damage,' and '4th of July Veterans Parade.'"[92] Had Jalloh successfully carried out this attack on the well-attended veterans parade on the Fourth of July in Washington, D.C., it may have been one of the deadliest terrorist attacks on American soil since September 11, 2001.

"I didn't sleep a lot during the three months of the Jalloh investigation," one seasoned FBI agent told us. "There's a lot of times where we're busy and don't sleep a lot, but this time I couldn't get to sleep because I was worried about what could happen. This case kept me up at night."[93] Mohamed Bailor Jalloh was eventually charged with attempting to provide material support to ISIS. In October 2016, he pleaded guilty; in February 2017 a judge sentenced him to 11 years in federal prison—slightly under the average sentence for most people charged with material support.[94] "My only hope," the FBI agent who investigated Jalloh told us, "is that Mohamed can make it through his prison sentence and come out as a functioning member of society. If that happens, nobody will be happier than me."[95]

During the investigation of Mohamed Bailor Jalloh, the FBI took a number of strategic risks to ensure that a successful, legal, and ethical criminal case could be built against an avowed ISIS supporter who was intent on committing a deadly attack. In several of the other cases involving individuals who successfully committed an attack, many of whom had less resources, skills, and connections than Jalloh, there were touchpoints with the FBI or full investigations where taking similar steps did not result in an arrest in time. This is less due to the FBI's ability to investigate terrorism cases, and more due to the very thin line between successful and unsuccessful attacks and ISIS' strategic and deliberate encouragement of unplanned terrorism, or, as one of the special agents put it: "at any point in time, a plotter can decide that it is 'that point in time' for an attack."[96]

Ultimately, how the FBI Special Agents handled the Jalloh case should be instructive to investigating and apprehending ISIS-inspired or directed attack planners. Through measured risk-taking and a strong commitment to the core investigative guidelines that shape the FBI's work in any investigation, they prevented what could have been an incredibly serious and lethal attack from taking place. Thus, in this rare case when an American ISIS attack planner had relevant military experience, had traveled overseas, and was in contact with virtual entrepreneurs, the attack plot was thwarted.

The Curtis Culwell Center Attackers

Jalloh's case helps illustrate the role of ISIS' virtual entrepreneurs guiding would-be attackers in the United States during the plotting stages of their attacks, but it was one instance in a long line of efforts by virtual entrepreneurs to strike the United States. A rude awakening to the impact of ISIS virtual entrepreneurs, their online networks, and their ability to strike the US came on May 3, 2015. It started in the afternoon, when a Twitter account with the handle @ataawakul went on an online posting spree. "Follow @_AbuHu55ain," the first tweet implored, directing the account's followers to a Twitter account run by Junaid Hussain.[97] An hour later, the account's tweets began to augur violence. "The knives have been sharpened, soon we will come to your streets with death and slaughter! #QaribanQariba," one tweet claimed, using a hashtag campaign utilized by ISIS with one of its catchphrases in Arabic: "soon, very soon."[98] Soon after, the account posted a final declaration. "The bro with me and myself have bay'ah [allegiance] to Amirul Mu'mineen [the leader of the believers]. May accept us as mujahideen [holy warriors]. Make dua [prayer]. #texasattack."[99]

Minutes later, at 6:50 PM, two gunmen attempted to enter the Curtis Culwell Center in Garland, Texas.[100] The target, time, and date of the attack were by no means random selections. The attack transpired as the Curtis Culwell Center hosted the "First Annual Muhammad Art Exhibit and Contest," wherein the event's organizers offered a $10,000 prize for the best drawing of the Prophet Muhammad.[101]

An off-duty guard quickly responded, shooting and killing both attackers.[102] The two men were later identified as 31-year-old Elton Simpson and 34-year-old Nadir Soofi, residents of Phoenix, Arizona.[103] In Phoenix, the pair were roommates in an apartment owned by a third man, Abdul Malik Abdul Kareem, who was later sentenced to 30 years in federal prison for supplying Simpson and Soofi with the firearms that they used in the attack.[104] Authorities would later track down Abdul Khabir Wahid, another friend of the pair in Arizona. In 2019, Wahid was found guilty of withholding information about the attack during an interview with the FBI.[105]

Like Tashfeen Malik and Omar Mateen, Simpson was not an unknown figure to the FBI at the time of the attack. In 2006, the Bureau launched an investigation into him, eventually collecting dozens of conversations between Simpson and a confidential human source. In these conversations, Simpson discussed traveling to Somalia to join the jihadist group al-Shabaab.[106] In 2011, a judge sentenced Simpson to probation for lying to the FBI about his travel plans.[107]

After the end of his probation in 2014, Simpson jumped on the emerging wave of jihadist extremism and began to make statements on his social media accounts praising the newly declared caliphate of the Islamic State.[108] Simpson's online interactions reached another man with deep connections to the American jihadisphere: the Minneapolitan jihadist e-celebrity Mohamed Abdullahi Hassan, more commonly known as Mujahid Miski.[109] Miski left the Twin Cities in 2008 for Somalia, where he joined al-Shabaab alongside at least 23 other Minnesotans who left Minneapolis and St. Paul between 2007 and 2013.[110] When the tide shifted in Syria towards the Islamic State, Miski became a notable online cheerleader for the group, and reportedly assisted several people in traveling to jihadist-controlled territory.[111]

According to publicly available records, Simpson first reached out to Miski in late 2014. Among other subjects, Simpson asked Miski to interpret dreams for him—including one where he claimed to have witnessed a vision of Anwar al-Awlaki.[112] But over time, their interactions via Twitter grew more operational. Weeks before the attack, Simpson's @atawaakul account tweeted: "When will they ever learn? They are planning on selecting the best picture drawn of Rasulullah (saws) [the Prophet of Allah, peace be upon him] in Texas."[113] Miski retweeted Simpson's post, with an incitement of his own: "The brothers from the Charlie Hebdo attack did their part. It's time for brothers in the #US to do their part."[114]

Miski, who built his success through his Twitter feed and preferred public interactions, spoke with Simpson exclusively on Twitter. In comparison, Junaid Hussain, a Syria-based attack planner with a large target on his head, mostly communicated with Simpson using messaging platforms with end-to-end encryption to avoid detection. "Afwan [Excuse me] for the disturbance," Simpson wrote to Hussain on Twitter. "Isnt surespot more secure than kik?" he asked, comparing two popular end-to-end encrypted messaging platforms.[115] "Yes akhi [brother] it is, I have surespot too," Hussain replied, and subsequently, the two promised to add each other on Surespot.[116] Due to this shift to encrypted communications, to this day, the details of Simpson's interactions with Hussain are not publicly available. In 2015, then-FBI Director James Comey testified before Congress that the Bureau was unable to access 109 encrypted messages between one of the Garland gunmen—presumably Elton Simpson—and an "overseas terrorist"—reportedly, Junaid Hussain.[117]

Unlike Simpson, Nadir Soofi's links to virtual planners or other extremist groups have not been as extensively documented. Soofi, born in Dallas to a Pakistani father and American mother, moved back to Pakistan after his parents' divorce at a young age.[118] Eventually, he moved in with his mother in Utah, working at a series of fast-food restaurants and racking up dozens of minor misdemeanor offenses—ranging from possession of alcohol to possession of drug paraphernalia.[119] According to his family, from 2011 onward Soofi became "obsessed" with the work of Anwar al-Awlaki following his death in Yemen, talking frequently about Islam and the role of US military presence in the Middle East.[120] Yet, they also claim that Simpson "brainwashed" Soofi after he moved in with him in Phoenix in 2014.[121] Soofi left behind a nine-year-old son.[122]

The third roommate in the Phoenix house involved in the Culwell Center attack, Abdul Malik Abdul Kareem, became the second person to be convicted by a jury of providing material support to ISIS. In 2017, a judge sentenced him to 30 years in federal prison.[123] As early as 2012, the FBI investigated Kareem after police found extremist material on his computer during an unrelated search. Kareem, according to court documents, researched travel to join ISIS as early as 2014, and during this period, he also encouraged Simpson and Soofi to move in with him.[124] Federal prosecutors argued that prior to the Garland attack, Kareem was interested in a much more extensive plot involving the use of explosive devices; the target was the 2015 Super Bowl, held in Phoenix, Arizona.[125]

But ongoing mystery, speculation, and even conspiracy theories surround another person linked to the attack on the Culwell Center. As the attack was about to transpire, a third man was driving in a car behind Simpson and Soofi, taking pictures and recording video footage of the attackers. When he saw Simpson and Sufi pull out their assault rifles, the third man U-turned and fled the scene. Garland police pursued the vehicle, and quickly surrounded the driver, forcing him out of the car at gunpoint and arresting him.[126] Later, while in custody, the third man shocked the arresting officers by revealing his credentials: he was an FBI undercover employee from a district thousands of miles away, who drove to the Culwell Center on a tip that "something was about to happen."[127]

The presence of an FBI undercover employee at the Culwell Center during the attack sparked a wave of speculation. Why did an FBI agent so auspiciously show up at the right (or, from another point of view, the wrong) place at the exact time of a jihadist attack? What knowledge did the FBI have about the attack? And more pressingly, why did the undercover employee cut and run while the attack happened, rather than staying and attempting to apprehend Simpson and Soofi?

If the FBI knew an attack would take place, why did they seemingly do nothing to stop it?

In October 2017, Bruce Joiner, the security guard wounded in the Culwell Center attack, sued the FBI and its Director, James Comey, for damages. In court filings, Joiner claimed that the FBI "even sent an agent to accompany the terrorists as they carried out the attack."[128] Also in 2017, two US Senators, Chuck Grassley (R-IA) and Ron Johnson (R-WI) sent inquiries to the FBI, asking the Bureau to explain its response and involvement in the attack on Garland, Texas.[129] The FBI, in an email statement to CBS, simply claimed that "There was no advance knowledge of a plot to attack the cartoon drawing contest in Garland, Texas."[130] Yet, in other filings, FBI agents attest that, at the very least, they received information about a potential incident—although not necessarily a terrorist attack—at the Curtis Culwell Center on May 3, 2015. Indeed, on the day of the attack, the FBI sent a bulletin to Garland, Texas police with a mugshot of Elton Simpson, informing the local authorities that he had previously been convicted of terrorism offenses and was "interested" in the event.[131] It did not, however, contain any insight that an attack would occur.

A great deal of the FBI's prior knowledge about the Culwell Center plot, why an undercover agent drove thousands of miles to witness the attack, and why the agent turned back as he saw the attack happen, is laid out in two court cases in an entirely separate jurisdiction. In June 2015, authorities in the Northern District of Ohio arrested Robert McCollum, also known as Amir Said Abdul Rahman al-Ghazi, for attempting to provide material support to ISIS, illegal firearms possession, and selling drugs.[132] This unlikely slate of activities helped al-Ghazi, who described himself as a "cyber jihadi," participate in, finance, and coordinate a group of individuals across the United States who were interested in conducting attacks on behalf of ISIS.[133] During an interview, FBI agents asked al-Ghazi if he knew anyone involved with the Garland, Texas attack. He replied: "Oh yeah, I'm sorry, yes, OK. Garland, Texas. Fuck. I didn't know about Garland before it happened but a brother contacted me. The one brother from [a social media application] . . . his name was Abu Harb."[134]

Corroborating al-Ghazi's reports about the Abu Harb account were a series of interactions between this same account, owned by a North Carolina man named Erick Jamal Hendricks, and an FBI undercover employee posing as an ISIS supporter. Hendricks, whom al-Ghazi described as the ringleader of a group that was attempting to form an ISIS attack cell in the United States, was described by federal prosecutors as "paranoid" about his online activities in furtherance of this plot.[135] He utilized at least four different applications with varying levels of encryption for communications, frequently rotated between accounts and account names, spoke cryptically, and inserted spaces between words in online communication to avoid detection.[136] Before the FBI undercover agent could even speak to Hendricks, he had to clear several religious tests and counter-surveillance measures.[137]

After passing these tests and engaging in a lengthy discussion about the merits and operation of an ISIS attack cell in the United States, on April 23, 2015,

Hendricks told the FBI employee that he wanted him to get in contact with "a good brother." "I vouch for this brother ..." Hendricks said; "don't ask him about details though."[138] The only detail Hendricks provided was the contact's username, "juba1911." The undercover agent and "Juba" exchanged messages later that day, with Juba voluntarily describing dozens of details about his life. Claiming to be a Muslim who converted 11 years ago, the account's owner also told the undercover that he had a criminal history: "I've been arrested b4 akh [brother] ... that's all I will say ... arrested not for some worldly affair ... Had a spy on me for 4yrs."[139] The undercover asked Juba if he did time in prison. "Not much ... 1 charge dropped, 1 stayed, 3yrs probation."[140]

The undercover knew why Hendricks put him in contact with Juba, but per Hendricks' request, did not ask any details about attack planning. Instead, Juba initiated the conversation about a potential attack. Days after Elton Simpson posted his first tweet about the cartoon contest in Garland, Texas, Juba messaged the undercover: "Did u see the link I posted? About Texas? Prob not."[141] He then sent a link to the article about the First Annual Muhammad Art Exhibit and Contest. "U know what happened in Paris ... I think ... yes or no?" Juba asked the undercover, referencing the January 2015 attack on the headquarters of the newspaper *Charlie Hebdo*, which infamously included a drawing of the Prophet Muhammad on its cover. "So that goes without saying ... No need to be direct."[142]

Two days before the attack on the Culwell Center, the undercover asked Hendricks about "Juba" and the drawing contest in Garland. "The AZ [Arizona] brother? You can link with him brother," Hendricks replied, "it's your call."[143] The next day, Hendricks told the undercover, "I wish someone could go to tx and harass them ... see what you and bro [Juba] can do."[144] Hendricks also directed the undercover to Juba's Twitter account, @atawaakul.[145] By this point, the FBI had already put the dots together: "Juba" was Elton Simpson, and something—a protest, incident, or even an attack potentially involving Simpson—was going to occur at the Curtis Culwell Center in Garland, Texas on May 3, 2015.

The undercover, based in the FBI Field Office in Cleveland, Ohio, decided to take Hendricks' advice and travel to Garland to investigate. There is no publicly available evidence that either the agent or the FBI knew that the attack would take place. The undercover likely traveled to the scene to investigate Hendricks, not Simpson or Soofi, and didn't know that the latter was even involved. The agent pulled into a parking lot across the street from the event early in the afternoon and began to send Hendricks messages about the event. Hendricks pestered the agent about event security: "How is security" "How big is gathering?" "How many ppl" "How many police/agents" "How big is building" "Is it wood" "Do you see feds there" "Do you see snipers" and "How many media?"[146] Minutes before the attack commenced, the undercover messaged Hendricks, telling him that he was driving closer to the event to get a better look.[147]

The next day, Hendricks, upon hearing about the aftermath of the Garland attack, posted a short manifesto on the file-sharing site justpaste.it about the events that occurred. Promising future attacks on the event's organizers, Hendricks addressed warnings to "the disbelievers who shot our brothers from Arizona, a new Muslim of 2 years and another of 11 years," indicating he believed the FBI undercover, and not Soofi (a lifelong Muslim), was killed during the attack.[148] After using a mutually agreed-upon code, the undercover eventually messaged Hendricks and informed him that he was alive. But at this point, Hendricks was even more paranoid. Two weeks after the Garland attack, Hendricks cut off communication with the undercover. The FBI arrested Erick Jamal Hendricks in August 2016.[149] In March 2018, almost three years after the Garland attack, a jury found him guilty of conspiring to provide material support to ISIS, and he was sentenced to 15 years in federal prison.[150]

Usaamah Rahim, Daoud Wright, Nicholas Rovinski and Zulfi Hoxha

Hendricks, Simpson, and Soofi were not the only Americans who were planning to conduct an attack on the organizers of the event at the Curtis Culwell Center on May 3, 2015. Mohamed Bailor Jalloh, relaying messages from Abu Sa'ad Sudani, talked about attacking the organizers of the event nearly one year after the attack on Garland. Only minutes after the attack happened, over 1,500 miles away, a group of men in Boston made a pact to behead one of the leaders of the group that organized the art contest. The first person that they attempted to contact for guidance was Junaid Hussain.

The group was composed of three men: an unemployed, morbidly obese video-game fanatic named David "Daoud" Wright, his uncle Usaamah Rahim, and their friend Nicholas Rovinski, a young Rhode Islander with cerebral palsy.[151] Wright, despite being glued to his computer for most of the hours of the day, was nonetheless the ringleader of this unlikely trio.[152] He was the first of the three to declare his support for ISIS, and, before the beheading plot, had assisted another American who successfully traveled overseas to join the group. That American, Zulfi Hoxha, was later assessed by the Department of Justice to be "a senior ISIS commander."[153]

Hoxha, a pizza-shop employee from Margate City, New Jersey, met Wright online. Their record of interaction dates back to 2010, and both men were involved on the online video-gaming platform Steam and the forum site Paltalk.[154] Prosecutors claim that by November 2014, Wright and Hoxha both had adopted support for ISIS, and were actively engaged in a plot to travel overseas to support the group.[155] Using Skype and Paltalk, the pair traded ISIS propaganda material, and discussed the benefits of supporting the caliphate.[156]

By the spring of 2015, Hoxha was committed to traveling. Wright enlisted the help of his uncle, Usaamah Rahim, who sold his laptop to raise funds for Hoxha's plane ticket.[157] For logistical support, Rahim and Wright found a contact through Twitter that could help Hoxha cross the Turkish–Syrian border after he arrived in Turkey. This contact turned out to be Junaid Hussain.[158] On April 6, 2015, Hoxha left New Jersey for Istanbul. Shortly thereafter, Rahim and Wright communicated with Hussain, who told the pair that Hoxha had safely crossed the border and was "in training" at an ISIS camp in Syria.[159] Hoxha's last reported message was to

Rahim, sent on Kik on April 10, 2015: "Hurry up and talk to me because [ISIS] will take my phone for and be training for about three months." He also told Rahim and Wright to delete his contact information from Skype.[160]

With Hoxha out of the country, Wright and Rahim began to look towards ways that they could support ISIS while remaining in the United States. They brought in Nicholas Rovinski, another ISIS supporter whom Wright met in December 2014 on Facebook.[161] The trio began operational planning in February 2015, when Wright forwarded an ISIS manual called "How to Survive in the West" to the other members of the cell.[162] One of the chapters in this manual provides instructions for Western supporters on how to form "sleeper cells," which Wright was especially interested in.[163]

The turning point for the Boston group came after the attack on the Curtis Culwell Center. Directly afterwards, Junaid Hussain tweeted: "2 of our brothers just opened fire at the Prophet Mohammad ... art exhibition in texas!" later instructing supporters to "Kill Those That Insult the Prophet #GarlandShooting."[164] Wright decided that the organizers of the event would be his "sleeper cell's" first beheading target, and, using Hussain's information, compiled a dossier on the assassination target with personal information and instructed the trio on the best methods and tactics for the operation. He also told Rahim to purchase combat knives, in case the police prematurely disrupted the plot. The goal was to behead one of the organizers during an event on July 4, 2015.[165]

The hitch in Wright's plot came two days before the planned attack. Usaamah Rahim, knives in hand, called Wright and told him that he could not wait for July 4 to act. He saw some local police officers while he was shopping in a convenience store and now wanted to attack "the boys in blue" immediately.[166] Wright sanctioned this plan, and told Rahim to conduct a factory reset on his computer and phone to clear any evidence. Rahim managed to clear his computer—preventing the FBI from accessing "even a single line of text" from his laptop—but did not clear his phone.[167] As Rahim was cornered by police in a Roslindale, Massachusetts parking lot on June 2, 2015, he lunged at an officer with one of the combat knives he bought on Wright's advice. The officers opened fire, killing Rahim.[168] Police arrested Wright and Rovinski shortly thereafter. Both are now serving extensive federal prison sentences.[169]

The failed plot in Boston also had massive implications for the broader effort to hunt down ISIS' virtual entrepreneurs. Federal authorities caught another lucky break in tracking down Junaid Hussain as a result of the interdicted Boston plot. Hussain usually communicated via encrypted messaging applications, for which law enforcement faces additional barriers in obtaining search warrants and access to communications. The FBI knew that Hussain was in communication with Elton Simpson but could not obtain the content of the messages.[170] Hendricks' messages to undercover agents on encrypted platforms were fair game, but the rest of his communications—including any evidence that he convened with overseas virtual entrepreneurs—were inaccessible.[171] However, when Boston police killed Usaamah Rahim, authorities obtained a search warrant for his phone, which was on Rahim's person at the crime scene. Because Rahim forgot to clear the data on his phone as

David Wright instructed him before the attack, investigators were able to access all of Rahim's Kik and Surespot messages with Junaid Hussain—and garnered evidence about what the virtual entrepreneur was planning in the United States, new account information, and even some locational evidence.[172]

Two months later, on August 24, 2015, as Hussain left a Raqqa internet café used as the de facto base of operations for the Legion, a US drone armed with a Hellfire missile struck the area, killing Hussain instantly.[173] At the time, Hussain was the third-highest priority target in Syria and Iraq on an internal Pentagon "kill list," behind only his countryman Mohammed Emwazi (a.k.a. "Jihadi John") and the caliph himself, Abu Bakr al-Baghdadi.[174] Theories regarding how US and UK authorities were able to track down Hussain abound; some suggest that he was sent a compromised hyperlink by an undercover law enforcement agent; others suggest that Western intelligence agencies found a backdoor into one of Hussain's preferred encrypted messaging platforms.[175] Many versions of the story, however, suggest that the FBI drew a significant deal of its evidence on Hussain's activities and location from the people he interacted with in the United States.

Meanwhile, David Wright and Usaamah Rahim's friend Zulfi Hoxha quickly rose through the ranks of ISIS. In an October 2015 release, a masked militant with a New Jersey-inflected accent gruesomely executed a Kurdish soldier while addressing a message to then-President Obama.[176] Two years later, in May 2017, the ISIS regional media office in Ninawah province, Iraq released "We Will Surely Guide Them To Our Ways," a 45-minute video montage depicting Western fighters serving numerous roles in the group. An American with a New Jersey accent, identified as "Abu Hamza al-Amriki," shows off the spoils of military technology captured by the group in one of its raids and directs his countrymen to conduct attacks in the United States.[177] "Are you incapable of stabbing a *kafir* [non-Muslim] with a knife, throwing him off of a building, or running him over with a car," Abu Hamza asks, "liberate yourself from hellfire by killing a *kafir*."[178] In 2018, multiple law enforcement sources confirmed that the American who appeared in both videos was indeed Zulfi Hoxha, the only member of Wright and Rahim's cell still alive and out of prison.[179] There were heated debates within the US Government about whether Hoxha's activities rose to a level that would justify his inclusion in a targeted military airstrike list. Ultimately, the decision was made that it did not, resting largely on the fact that Hoxha was an American, and thus subject to a higher bar for a kinetic strike than ISIS members of other citizenships.[180] At the time of writing, Hoxha's whereabouts are unknown.

Mohamed Elshinawy

After Junaid Hussain was killed in the summer of 2015, the Islamic State's external operations wing tapped Siful Haque Sujan, a late-20s Bangladeshi based in Cardiff, Wales, as his replacement.[181] While Hussain's approach to external operations was based on his computer savvy and bona fides as a black-hat hacker, Sujan's approach mirrored his experience in the white-collar tech business world. Prior to joining

ISIS in Syria in 2014, Sujan was director of the IBACS Group, a computer equipment distributor established in 2005 by Sujan and his brother, Ataul Haque.[182] The business mainly sold computer equipment to restaurants, had offices in Bangladesh, the UK, and Spain, and switched between several names and incorporations.[183]

After Sujan's arrival in Syria, he continued to operate the company, putting nearly a decade of technology distribution experience to nefarious aims. He set up an independent distribution center in Şanlıurfa, Turkey, 20 miles from the Syrian border.[184] Sujan, with the cooperation of his business' offices in Dhaka, Seville, and Cardiff, utilized his expertise with computers and years of experience running an online ordering firm to ensure the equipment reached its intended destination.[185]

As he took up his new role as "Director of the Islamic State's computer operations" after Hussain's death in 2015, his priorities were clear: revolutionize the virtual entrepreneur model, while ensuring that his staff were not subject to the same fate as Junaid Hussain.[186] Using Ibacstel Electronics Limited, a subsidiary of the IBACS Group, Sujan put in orders for $18,000 worth of infrared cameras, antennae, and other monitoring equipment through his company, shipping the components from Spain through Turkey into Syria.[187] Sujan's orders and shipments for "bug-sweeping" tech reflected his primary concern: coalition airstrikes. "We would win the war if not for the drones, the drones are killing us," he reportedly lamented.[188]

Even before Hussain's death, Sujan experimented with new ways to reach out to individuals in the West who were interested in planning attacks. On June 28, 2015, a 30-year-old newspaper deliveryman named Mohamed Elshinawy drove to a convenience store on the outskirts of Baltimore, Maryland, to pick up a Western Union remittance from his childhood friend in Egypt.[189] He picked up the money order, $1,000 in total, and deposited $800 of it in his bank account. This was the last of several transfers Elshinawy received from the same source, totaling $8,447.23.[190] The FBI, concerned about the source of the transfers, the irregularity of Elshinawy's financial behavior, and the amount, brought Elshinawy in for an interview.[191]

FBI agents informed Elshinawy that they had tracked the payments for months, and caught him receiving money from a known foreign terrorist—his friend Tamer Elkhodary, an Egyptian man who, following his release from Egyptian prison for participation in the Muslim Brotherhood, fled to Syria and joined the Islamic State.[192] Elshinawy was not fazed by the accusations and offered an unconventional explanation. With an air of self-assurance, he claimed that he had just successfully scammed the Islamic State, and suggested that the FBI should be thanking, not questioning him.[193] He admitted that he had reached out to his childhood friend in ISIS and received money from him, but claimed it was all a ruse to raise money for home furnishings.[194] The interviewing agents were incredulous but did not yet have enough evidence to determine why Elshinawy had received this money order from an ISIS member.[195]

Before questioning Elshinawy again, the FBI went to work, mapping out the backers and entities behind the transfer of money from Egypt to Maryland. The trail was long and winding, but eventually revealed perhaps the most complex Islamic State-directed terrorist financing plot in the United States to date. Working backwards, investigators found that Elkhodary was an intermediary for five separate payments wired through PayPal from three separate shell companies, one in Bangladesh, one in Turkey, and a third in Cardiff, Wales.[196] As a front, Elshinawy posted advertisements for several laser printers on Ebay.[197] A Cardiff-based IBACS Group executive, Abdul Samad, made payments to Elshinawy for the printers using an account registered to Ibacstel Electronics Limited, a front for the group in Cardiff.[198] The printers did not exist and were never transferred or delivered to the UK. This activity was coordinated from Syria by the IBACS Group's director, Siful Haque Sujan.[199]

Sujan and his colleagues made the purpose of the financial transfers clear to Elshinawy. Sujan, IBACS Group directors, and Elshinawy used encrypted applications such as Surespot and Telegram to communicate.[200] They ordered Elshinawy to purchase computer equipment, a virtual private network, and a data self-destruct feature in case of apprehension.[201] According to the US Attorney's Office, the virtual entrepreneurs and the Maryland man talked "every day, for several months."[202] Sujan initially gave Elshinawy three choices: a suicide bombing, a planned terrorist attack, or travel to Syria. Elshinawy chose the attack.[203]

Notably, as an example of which attack targets could be beneficial for the Islamic State, Sujan and his cohort directed Elshinawy to seek out attacks on the organizers of the "Draw the Prophet Muhammad" contest.[204] But Sujan eventually decided he wanted to include a mass-casualty attack in his legacy. The virtual entrepreneurs instructed Elshinawy to create a Dropbox account where he received "16–17 videos with step by step instructions … on how to make a peroxide bomb."[205] While no publicly available evidence suggests that Elshinawy successfully constructed a working explosive device, he made several Google queries for the addresses of federal buildings in the Baltimore area after his handlers in Syria asked him to give progress reports on target selection.[206]

While Sujan and Elshinawy's plot followed many of Junaid Hussain's previous objectives, the methods used had Sujan's personal signature on them. Most importantly, it was the first known instance where Islamic State officials financed a plot in the United States. Sujan's international network of shell companies under the IBACS Group played an extensive role in this new dynamic. But, like his predecessor Junaid Hussain's reliance on encrypted messaging platforms, Siful Haque Sujan's business network eventually led to his downfall.

In December 2015, a judge granted the FBI a search warrant of Mohamed Elshinawy's house in Maryland, including his personal computer.[207] During this time, Elshinawy was under 24/7 FBI surveillance, and agents working on the case conducted upwards of 20 search warrants and 300 grand jury subpoenas to build their case.[208] They discovered the full extent of Elshinawy's interactions with Sujan and the IBACS Group and filed charges in federal court.

In conjunction with the FBI investigation, British, Spanish, and Bangladeshi law enforcement closed in on the IBACS Group's activities on three different continents. In a joint operation, Bangladeshi police shuttered Wahmi Technologies,

IBACS' Dhaka-based outfit, while Spanish authorities simultaneously closed a virtual office in Seville administered by Sujan's brother Ataul Haque and his wife, Ana Maria Gonzalez.[209] Abdul Samad, the Cardiff administrator of the IBACS Group who was responsible for transfers to Elshinawy, was arrested in the UK on December 10, 2015.[210]

Months after the sweep, IBACS Group attempted to revive itself. In February 2016, Haque and Gonzalez created a new subsidiary, ISYNCTEL Technologies, Inc. Again, Spanish authorities moved on the pair, arresting them for terrorism financing.[211] According to a 2016 indictment, "ISYNCTEL recreated the business model of its founder, Siful Sujan Haque, and maintained the same members, providers, and commercial clients."[212] The charges came after Haque and Gonzalez made a transfer to Wahmi Technologies Inc., which had also apparently re-emerged in Bangladesh after its forced closure by police for terrorism financing in the December 2015 operation.[213]

On the same day as Abdul Samad's arrest in the UK, Combined Joint Task Force–Operation Inherent Resolve (CJTF–OIR) launched a targeted drone strike on Raqqa, Syria. Despite his best efforts to protect himself and his contemporaries from airstrikes, the December 10, 2015 strike killed Siful Haque Sujan.[214] "Now that he's dead," CJTF–OIR spokesperson Colonel Steve Warren explained, "ISIL has lost a key link between networks."[215] A day after Siful Haque Sujan's death, the FBI arrested Mohamed Elshinawy.[216] After he pleaded guilty to several counts of material support for ISIS, a judge sentenced him to 20 years in prison in March 2018.[217]

Sujan's tenure as computer operations director for ISIS was not as lengthy as his predecessor's, nor did it result in the same tempo of operations in the United States. Part of this is undoubtedly due to how much time and energy the wing spent protecting itself from drone strikes: with self-protection as a priority, the Legion could not afford to draw more attention to itself by reaching out to American operatives.[218] But the Elshinawy plot nonetheless reveals interesting insights into how the Islamic State may continue to direct attacks, even in lieu of losing its most infamous virtual entrepreneurs and the majority of its territory in Syria and Iraq.

First, in the US context, it is worth considering the utility of the virtual entrepreneur model from ISIS' perspective. Most attacks planned by "the Legion" and other anglophone planners in the US were unsuccessful. John Mueller notes that the attacks planned by virtual entrepreneurs in the United States resulted in very few casualties, and individuals like Junaid Hussain, Abu Sa'ad al Sudani, and Siful Sujan made basic operational security mistakes that potentially led to the apprehensions of their collaborators and their deaths.[219] Self-started attacks without remote virtual assistance—such as the Pulse nightclub shooting and the San Bernardino attacks—resulted in far more casualties than any plot involving a virtual entrepreneur.

Nonetheless, virtual entrepreneurs left their mark on the American jihadist scene in a number of ways. It is no coincidence that several would-be jihadist attackers—including many of those mentioned in this section—converged on a particular set of targets after communications with several attack planners. They encouraged supporters to take advantage of advancements in technology and cybersecurity, creating roadblocks to law enforcement officers who attempt to apprehend them. In the case of Mohamed Elshinawy, they used an extensive, complex, and transnational financing network involving several shell companies, intermediaries, and fronts to disguise attack plot financing. None of these developments, despite the empirically low casualty rates from virtual entrepreneur-inspired plots, give law enforcement agencies any respite in their efforts to interdict potential terrorist attacks.

The Future of Jihadist Attacks in the United States

The threat of ISIS-inspired jihadist attacks in the United States has certainly changed since the group's declaration of the caliphate in 2014, but it has not subsided. Factors extrinsic to the group's success or failure in Syria and Iraq, or specific personnel, remain significant concerns. The "flash to bang" ratio, or the period between an individual's radicalization and their decision to commit an attack, grows shorter and shorter.[220] In the United States, would-be attackers can legally attain what is necessary for an attack without crossing a criminal threshold. Easy access to firearms in several jurisdictions makes this picture more complicated: all but three of the lethal attacks in the past four years used firearms, and over 85 percent of the deaths in jihadist attacks during the same timeframe came in these attacks.[221] But even without access to firearms, jihadists find other ways to commit deadly attacks, from stabbings and beheadings to explosives attacks and vehicular assaults.

The group's loss of territory in Syria and Iraq has not stopped ISIS-inspired attackers from taking matters into their own hands. Those suggesting that the territorial demise will diminish its Western supporters' desire to strike in their native countries should remember that much of the impetus for the group's initial switch to attack planning came largely as a result of territorial loss. As ISIS relinquished control of the Turkish–Syrian border towns that it used to process foreign fighters, its media outlets began instructing supporters to stay in place. At present, the group's media outlets promote a narrative of *qisas*, or retribution: the United States and its coalition are destroying the caliphate, so it is mandatory for followers to strike them down in retaliation.[222] This narrative will continue, and may even strengthen, as the organization loses the last vestiges of the territory it once controlled in Syria and Iraq.

Meanwhile, the United States will remain a priority target for the group's supporters, and even those outside of Syria and Iraq may attempt to assist would-be attackers using the innovative methods developed by virtual entrepreneurs. As the Elshinawy plot demonstrates, establishing front companies in Western countries and subsidiaries around the world for terrorism financing is an avenue available to supporters of the Islamic State even outside of its central territory. In some ways, the virtual entrepreneur model itself may be more successful outside of ISIS-held territory: arguably, its biggest downfall was drone strikes, and that option is unavailable for the United States and its coalition partners outside particular geographic areas. ISIS-affiliated attack planners can set up shop in areas where police enforcement is weak, the state's legal capacity to apprehend terrorist organizations is limited, or where the state has fewer incentives to counter ISIS operatives.

An additional layer to the threat of jihadist attacks in the US is the innovations in online security encouraged by virtual entrepreneurs. The "going dark" problem, as authorities refer to it, masks the activities of ISIS-inspired plotters and restricts the ability of law enforcement to monitor ongoing threats.[223] By using platforms operated by companies that are outside of US jurisdiction, ISIS online activists have fewer capacities to detect threats and notify US authorities, and may adopt an ethos of preserving privacy at all costs, would-be attackers have and will continue to avoid law enforcement. Beyond messaging and communication, ISIS affiliates use platforms with file-sharing capabilities to disseminate the instructions for attacks once distributed by the virtual entrepreneurs—preserving their innovations and influence long after their deaths.

As documented in the investigations of the aforementioned ISIS attack planners, much of the United States' response to jihadist attacks hinges on the efforts of US law enforcement, in particular the FBI and the Joint Terrorism Task Force. The special agents assigned to these cases are frequently forced to make split-second decisions during investigations, with potentially successful and lethal terrorist attacks on US soil hanging in the balance. Through a combination of elbow grease, old-school investigative tactics, and newer developments involving the use of technology, agents successfully disrupted a multitude of ISIS-inspired and directed terrorist plots in the United States during the past four years.

Simultaneously, however, the FBI's tactics in counterterrorism investigations have elicited a significant degree of criticism from civil liberties groups. The use of confidential human sources and undercover employees are a lightning rod of controversy, with critics claiming that they are used to entrap unwitting individuals who would not have successfully carried out an attack without the intervention of the FBI. The legitimacy of this criticism is outside the scope of the chapter. But pushback on these grounds, and the general imperative for the FBI to gather evidence without endangering civil liberties and maintaining a working relationship with the communities in which they operate, add additional concerns during any investigation.

According to testimony from FBI Director Christopher Wray during an October 2019 hearing before the House Committee on Homeland Security, "the underlying drivers for domestic violent extremism ... remain constant" and "domestic violent extremists collectively pose a steady threat of violence and economic harm to the United States."[224] The rise in domestic terrorism attacks in the United States in the past several years, paired with the persistent and evolving nature of the threat, creates a varied and diverse threat landscape for local and federal law enforcement agencies. Recent data from the FBI suggests there are approximately 5,000 terrorism cases under investigation, with more than 3,000 cases tied to groups designated as foreign terrorist organizations, 1,000 cases related to homegrown violent extremists, and another 1,000 focused on domestic terrorism.[225]

This milieu lends itself to the dynamic of reciprocal radicalization, where two competing, antagonistic forms of extremism (such as jihadi and far-right extremism) use the other's narrative to promote their own group.[226] The recent resurgence in far-right attacks may help feed fuel to the fire of ISIS support in the United States. In 2019, the FBI arrested Mark Steven Domingo, a 26-year-old former US Army private, for plotting a terror attack in the suburbs of Los Angeles. According to the criminal complaint, Domingo was a recent convert to Islam who purchased "several hundred nails to be used as shrapnel inside an explosive device,"[227] ensuring that he had "specifically bought three-inch nails because they would be long enough to penetrate the human body and puncture internal organs."[228] Domingo was reportedly "enraged" after watching the video of the 2019 mass shooting at a mosque in Christchurch, New Zealand, and discussed with an FBI Confidential Human Source his desire to "kill in retaliation,"[229] as well as expressing his desire to target individuals walking to their local synagogue.[230]

While Domingo was arrested a month later in the process of preparing a terror attack against a different target, this case exemplifies the complex and evolving nature of terrorism within the United States. With the death of Abu Bakr al-Baghdadi and subsequent leadership succession within the Islamic State, it remains to be seen how the internal priorities and messaging themes, both by the core remnant of the Islamic State and by its disparate affiliates, will change and develop. During the rise and fall of the Islamic State as a territorial force, the messaging and propaganda used by the group has had an appreciable impact on ISIS sympathizers and supporters worldwide. As the group lost control of land in the caliphate, its messages, both official and unofficial, encouraged supporters who could not safely travel to commit attacks domestically. In addition, as ISIS continues to lose territory, trends may emerge to suggest that individuals are choosing simply to commit a lone-actor attack in the homeland instead of attempting risky travel to a far-flung ISIS affiliates in the West Africa or South Asia.

Therefore, as ISIS, other jihadist groups, and their respective supporters adapt and evolve to the geopolitical situation they face, the methods they use to plan attacks in the United States may change. What will likely not change is their commitment to attacking the United States, or the push–pull dynamic between would-be terrorists and law enforcement that can determine success or failure. The next few years may be a critical period of ISIS affiliates charting a new course for the organization's external operations in the wake of the loss of its territory. As the lessons of the past five years suggest, how US law enforcement adapts will be crucial.

Chapter 3

THE TRAVELERS

Early reports about the nature of the Islamic State threat to the West centered mainly around the foreigners—termed by the group as *muhajireen*—that flocked to the battlefields of Syria and Iraq to assist the group. By late 2015, officials already estimated that more than 5,000 citizens from Europe had traveled to Syria and Iraq to participate in jihadist groups.[1] The initial concern was that battle-hardened fighters from these countries, trained by ISIS and connected to its global network of recruits and supporters, could return to their home countries and commit attacks.[2]

These fears were realized during the twin attacks in Paris and Brussels, in late 2015 and early 2016, respectively. In tandem, these assaults killed over 150 people; they remain among the deadliest jihadist attacks in Western Europe.[3] Investigators uncovered a cell of jihadists based in Brussels who were responsible for planning and executing both attacks.[4] More perturbingly, some group members were returning jihadist travelers from Syria and Iraq who had been directed to carry out the attacks by members of ISIS' intelligence wing, the *Emni*.[5]

The attacks in Paris and Brussels sounded the alarm for many countries and prompted them to develop effective responses to the specter of returning jihadists. Policymakers on both sides of the Atlantic had already raised constant fears about the threat from ISIS returnees. In 2014, then-FBI Director James Comey testified before Congress in a hearing on the terrorist threat to the United States:

> Foreign fighters traveling to Syria or Iraq could, for example, gain battlefield experience and increased exposure to violent extremist elements that may lead to further radicalization to violence; they may use these skills and exposure to radical ideology to return to their countries of origin, including the United States, to conduct attacks on the homeland.[6]

Since that time, the rate of jihadist travel to the Syrian and Iraqi battlefields has largely abated due to a decline in ISIS-held territory, increased border-protection measures, and enhanced penalties for terrorist travel.[7] As ISIS lost territory and strongholds in Syria and Iraq, security services in Europe and the United States interdicted would-be travelers from reaching their final destinations in the caliphate. But once again, the anticipated droves of ISIS fighters returning to their home countries has not yet been realized.

The scope and nature of the threat in America differs greatly from the situation facing European countries. First, estimates suggest fewer Americans traveled to Syria and Iraq to join jihadist groups. Compared to over 1,900 from France, 900 from Germany, and 850 from the UK, the FBI estimates that only 300 Americans attempted to travel or actually traveled to the Levant.[8]

Additionally, many of the same factors that inhibited American ISIS sympathizers from traveling to Syria and Iraq also have prevented successful travelers from returning home. Current estimates suggest that around a dozen travelers have returned to the US. In contrast, more than 400 British jihadists in Syria and Iraq are reported to have returned to the UK.[9] Compounding these factors, while approximately three-quarters of American returning travelers were arrested and prosecuted, only a minority of the UK returnees have faced any criminal charges.[10]

Second, while ISIS-inspired or directed attacks in Europe since 2014 were carried out by a mix of returning travelers (e.g., Paris, Brussels, and Manchester) and homegrown extremists (Nice, Berlin), none of the 23 jihadist attacks that occurred in the United States during the same period were carried out by a returning traveler. One returnee in the US was planning an attack at the time of his return—and was directed to do so by the then-al-Qaeda affiliate Jabhat al-Nusra. He was arrested during the early planning stages of his attack.[11]

Nevertheless, the United States remains rightfully concerned about American jihadist travelers, who pose threats in different ways than those in Europe. They serve as key nodes in jihadist recruitment networks that target Americans and can inspire, direct, or augment the success of domestic jihadist plots even if the traveler is not directly involved. Many of these lessons stem from the US experience with previous waves of jihadist recruitment to conflict zones including 1980s Afghanistan, 1990s Bosnia and Chechnya, and Iraq, Pakistan, Yemen, and Somalia during the 2000s. A pre-Syrian War study places the number of Americans who participated in these conflicts at over 1,000.[12] Many of the travelers who joined jihadist groups in these areas and lived to tell the tale recruited Americans, directed US-based jihadist cells or plots, and were critical to forming transnational jihadist networks.[13] This phenomenon, colloquially referred to as the "wandering *mujahideen*" problem, helped set the stage for major jihadist plots in the US and the West, including the 1993 World Trade Center bombing and the September 11, 2001 attacks.[14] After 9/11, former American jihadist travelers were also notably involved in several failed attack plots, including attempted bombings on the New York City subway system in 2009 and in Times Square in 2010.[15]

Thus, while American jihadist travel to Syria and Iraq has largely ceased and early evidence does not suggest a massive influx of returnees, it is dangerous for policymakers to ignore American jihadist travelers. As the dust settles on the former territories of ISIS' self-proclaimed caliphate, the United States struggles to identify the key figures, demographics, and trends that can be drawn from the study of individuals from the US who traveled to the Levant.

To collate our database of Americans who traveled to Syria and Iraq to join ISIS, the authors obtained thousands of legal records from district and appellate courts. We filed more than three dozen Freedom of Information Act (FOIA) requests for additional information. Finally, we also filed motions seeking release of sealed records in federal courts across the country. We drew from the Program on Extremism's extensive database of jihadist social media accounts, and conducted interviews with US and foreign prosecutors, national security officials, defense attorneys, the American travelers, and their families.

We found 62 US residents who traveled to join ISIS overseas since 2011 with full legal names and basic identifying information. An analysis of these travelers finds a range of ages, ethnic backgrounds, states and cities of origin, and socioeconomic statuses. While establishing a single profile is impossible, some trends are notable. The average age of these individuals is 27, and 79 percent are men. The majority were US citizens or permanent residents prior to their departure. They come from 20 different states; the states with the highest per capita rate of ISIS travel are Minnesota, Virginia, and Ohio. While approximately 30 percent died overseas while fighting with the group, a substantial number are still at large. The remainder either are in US custody (16 percent), in the custody of a foreign country (8 percent), or returned to the US without facing charges (6.5 percent)

Syria and Iraq were by far the most popular destinations for ISIS recruits after 2011. Several individuals chose other battlefields, mainly on the African continent and the Arabian Peninsula. For instance, Mohamed Rafik Naji, a US permanent resident and Yemeni citizen, traveled to Yemen in 2015 to join the regional ISIS affiliate. He eventually returned to New York, where he was arrested and pleaded guilty to providing material support to ISIS.[16] Around the same time, in June of 2015, the aforementioned Mohamed Jalloh joined a local ISIS-affiliated smuggling ring in the northern provinces of Nigeria. From there, he attempted to travel to Libya to join ISIS' emerging province.[17]

Even a perfunctory glance at the statistics shows that it is difficult to succinctly classify travelers by their motivations, as this is personal and hard to quantify. A better methodology is to classify American ISIS travelers by their life experiences, connections to networks to which they belong, and their eventual roles in jihadist groups. This allows for more distinct categories of analysis. To this end, we refer to American ISIS travelers in three groups: pioneers, networked travelers, and loners.

Pioneers

Pioneers represent the upper limits of what Americans in ISIS are usually able to achieve. The popular picture of an American ISIS recruit is a young, bumbling, but bloodthirsty idiot who, due to a combination of quixotism and bloodlust, is lured into traveling overseas to join ISIS.[18] While these descriptors are apt in describing several American travelers, it undersells the experiences of ISIS pioneers, who are generally experienced, have previously participated in jihadist or militant movements, and have a greater sense of their roles and responsibilities.

Pioneers have experience with critical skills needed by ISIS and are able to attain positions within a group's leadership. These skills include military training, bomb-making, engineering, mechanics, computer expertise, and even the production of ideological material and propaganda. As a result of the wide slate of skills desired by ISIS, the profiles of American ISIS pioneers vary.

This category contains a motley crew of Americans from starkly different backgrounds, all of whom managed to become leaders in ISIS. John Georgelas, a convert from Greek Orthodoxy, used fluency in the Arabic language and training in Islamic law, combined with over a decade of participation in online jihadi e-forums, to become a senior propagandist for the Islamic State.[19] Abdullah Ramo Pazara's experience fighting for the Bosnian Serb Army partially enabled him to become a tank commander in ISIS nearly 20 years later.[20] But perhaps no story exemplifies this category more so than Ahmad Abousamra, the Bostonian who was the brains behind the ISIS official online magazines, *Dabiq* and *Rumiyah*.

Abousamra, born in France to Syrian parents, moved to a suburban area south of Boston at an early age.[21] His father, Dr. Abdulbadi Abousamra, was an endocrinologist at Massachusetts General Hospital and a prominent community organizer and activist linked to the Muslim Brotherhood.[22] After graduating from a Catholic high school in 1999, Ahmad Abousamra attended Northeastern and the University of Massachusetts-Boston. He graduated with a degree in computer science.[23]

After 9/11, Abousamra and a close group of friends began looking for ways to assist jihadists overseas. The friends used a combination of Salafi-jihadist web forums and in-person connections to find information about journeying to Pakistan to join an al-Qaeda training camp.[24] Abousamra reached out to Hassan Masood, the son of Imam Hafiz Muhammad Masood, the imam of the Sharon Mosque.[25] Masood, a Pakistani national, was well acquainted with the landscape of al-Qaeda networks in Pakistan: his uncle Hafiz Muhammad Saeed was a co-founder of the al-Qaeda-affiliated jihadist group *Lashkar-e-Taiba* (LeT).[26]

In 2002, Abousamra made his first attempt to join an overseas jihadist group. He traveled to Pakistan intending to join an LeT training camp.[27] This attempt was unsuccessful; camp administrators would not admit Abousamra because he was not Pakistani and lacked military experience.[28] Abousamra continued to attempt to find people who could vouch for him (a process called *tazkiyah*) to enter a training camp, eventually meeting a facilitator named Abdulmajid. However, Abdulmajid convinced Abousamra to return to the US, where he claimed he would be more useful to the jihadist cause.[29]

Abousamra agreed and returned to the US. After his return, Abousamra and his friends Tarek Mehanna and Daniel Maldonado discussed committing attacks in the Boston area. They reportedly considered malls, a local US Air Force base, and also a political assassination.[30] When they were unable to attain weapons necessary for these plots, they turned towards traveling overseas. In 2003, when the US began its military engagement in Iraq, a new ideologically significant destination emerged. The group began to plan a trip to Iraq to join al-Qaeda.[31]

Unlike Abousamra's travel to Pakistan, however, the men had no local contacts that could facilitate their travel to Iraq. Eventually Abousamra connected with a returned LeT fighter named Jason Pippin. Pippin, who had spent time in a madrassa in Yemen during the 1990s, met with Abousamra in Sacramento, California in October 2003.[32] He instructed Abousamra to travel to Yemen, participate in an AQAP-administered training camp, and then transfer to the Iraqi battlefield.[33]

Several months later, Abousamra, Mehanna, and an unnamed co-conspirator traveled to the United Arab Emirates en route to Yemen.[34] The third co-conspirator returned to the US after arriving in the UAE; he received word from home that his father was sick.[35] Mehanna and Abousamra traveled onward to Yemen, but once again, they failed to find a suitable training camp. The two split paths: Mehanna returned to the US, where he continued to assist al-Qaeda affiliates by translating propaganda material into English, and Abousamra ventured into Iraq.[36]

For Abousamra, his third attempt to join a jihadist group was not a charm. After only a few weeks in Iraq, having failed to enter a training camp, he crossed the border into his father's native country, Syria, and eventually returned to the US in February of 2004, where he regrouped with Mehanna and assisted him in efforts to translate al-Qaeda propaganda into English.[37] In 2006, Abousamra and Mehanna were once again hatching a plot to travel to an LeT training camp in Pakistan. Their plans were disrupted, however, when the FBI arrested their associate, Daniel Maldonado.[38]

While Mehanna and Abousamra were re-investigating the Pakistan option, Maldonado left the country with his family and another American, Omar Hammami (who later became well-known under his *kunya*—Abu Mansur al-Amriki).[39] After a brief stint in Cairo, Egypt, Maldonado arrived in the newly opened jihadist destination of Somalia, where al-Shabaab began to operate training camps that would take foreign fighters.[40] Maldonado spent only a few weeks in the al-Shabaab camp before he, and his entire family, contracted malaria. They traveled to neighboring Kenya to receive medical treatment but were arrested by Kenyan forces in January 2007 and extradited to face trial in the US.[41]

The Maldonado investigation may have burned Mehanna and Abousamra. Prior to his arrest, Maldonado called Mehanna from Somalia to tell him of his whereabouts and his participation in an al-Shabaab camp.[42] In December 2006, FBI Joint Terrorism Task Force agents interviewed Mehanna and Abousamra. Mehanna lied to the FBI about Maldonado's call and his whereabouts, and was eventually arrested, tried, convicted, and sentenced to seventeen and a half years in prison.[43] Abousamra, anticipating apprehension, left the US weeks after his JTTF interview.[44] Citing "operational reasons," the FBI claimed that Abousamra was not on a watchlist prior to his departure from the US.[45]

In December 2013, the FBI listed Ahmad Abousamra as a "Most Wanted Terrorist," offering a $50,000 reward for information leading to his arrest.[46] The notice claimed that he was living in Aleppo, Syria, with his wife and daughter. Inferentially, due to his extensive history of association with jihadist groups, his current location in 2013, and the ongoing conflict in Syria after 2011, it was assumed that, at this time, Abousamra was a participant in the Syrian conflict.[47] However, exact information about which organization he affiliated with was unavailable. Nearly a year after the Most Wanted listing, a senior US law enforcement official told CNN that Abousamra had finally found a group he could join: ISIS. Abousamra was now a critical figure behind the production and dissemination of online pro-ISIS propaganda.[48]

After nearly a decade of unsuccessfully trying to join a jihadist group, Ahmad Abousamra, and the unique skills he developed, fit perfectly into ISIS' strategic vision. Abousamra's path to ISIS is detailed in the eighth issue of the ISIS official English-language magazine *Rumiyah*, a publication that Abousamra helped develop.[49] "Among the Believers are Men" eulogizes Abousamra, explaining how he became involved in ISIS' media infrastructure.[50]

The article claims that in the "early days" of the Syrian resistance in the town of Aleppo, Abousamra was wounded while fighting for an unnamed jihadist faction.[51] While he was too badly wounded to continue participating in the battle, he stumbled across soldiers affiliated with the Islamic State in Iraq (ISI), one of ISIS' predecessors. He recognized the soldiers of ISI as the scions of al-Qaeda in Iraq, the group he swore *bayaa* (allegiance) to during his sojourn in Iraq nearly a decade prior.[52] The wounded Abousamra was not allowed to participate in combat, but he quickly found a role "preaching *aqidah* [creed]" to the ISI soldiers. When ISI split, and its soldiers either pledged allegiance to Jabhat al-Nusra or ISIS, Abousamra joined the latter.[53]

However, Abousamra quickly outlived his usefulness as a wounded preacher. His ISIS commanders were planning to send him on a suicide bombing mission when he stumbled across one of the chiefs of ISIS' media division, Wa'il al-Fayad (Abu Muhammad al-Furqan).[54] Al-Fayad reportedly recognized Abousamra's talent for propaganda and gave him a job in the media division, at first "ghostwriting" *fatwas* (religious rulings) for al-Fayad under the pen name Abu Maysarah ash-Shami.[55] One of Abousamra's tracts written under this pen name, *Yahud al-Jihad: Qaidat al-Zawahiri* (Jews of Jihad: Zawahiri's al-Qaeda) gained prominence as one of the key texts distinguishing the approach of ISIS from that of al-Qaeda and its leadership.[56] The phrase "Jews of Jihad" also became a common pejorative for ISIS supporters to refer to al-Qaeda's leadership. Following the success of this text, and others, Abousamra was given a role as co-editor in chief of ISIS' new officially-released online magazine, *Dabiq*.[57]

Following the first release of *Dabiq* by ISIS' al-Hayat Media Center, al-Fayad and Abousamra produced 15 issues of the flagship magazine, all of which were translated into multiple languages. After the release of the 15th issue in July 2016, the two began work on a new magazine, *Rumiyah* [Rome]. Eventually, the first issue was released on September 5, 2016. It eulogized the recently killed ISIS spokesperson, Abu Muhammad al-Adnani.[58] Some sources claim that Wa'il al-Fayad was slated to become al-Adnani's replacement, leaving Abousamra as his likely successor as director of the media division. However, two days after the inaugural release of *Rumiyah*, al-Fayad was killed in a Pentagon airstrike.[59]

Abousamra had a chance to become the highest-ranking American in ISIS' brief history, but after the death of his mentor, he decided to leave for the battlefield. *Rumiyah* later reported that he was "greatly saddened" by the death of his mentor, and rather than taking his place, he immediately requested a transfer to *ribat* (the front lines).[60] In January 2017, Ahmad Abousamra was reportedly killed during a battle in al-Thawrah, Syria. The US Government has yet to confirm his death, claiming that ISIS has previously issued false death reports to obfuscate the current whereabouts of their leaders.[61]

The eighth issue of *Rumiyah,* released in April 2017, contains a eulogy for Abousamra, a poem written by him, and some details which are not typically included in the group's profiles of its leaders.[62] First, and most notably, halfway through the eulogy it identifies Abousamra by his real name. Its biography of Abousamra includes information about his life in the US that generally matches the accounts contained in media reporting and trial documents, noting that Abousamra:

> completed his studies in Computer Science at the University of Massachusetts in Boston, graduating as an engineer and programmer, before resolving to go forth in the cause of Allah with some of his friends. So they left as muhajirin [travelers] to Allah, not coordinating their journey with anyone. They roamed between Yemen, Pakistan, and Iraq, hoping to meet someone who would bring them to the mujahideen. But once they became weary of finding the way, and as they feared inciting the suspicions of intelligence agencies, they returned to America, asking Allah to guide them towards their goal.[63]

It also documented a previously unknown ISIS plot to kill a US citizen tied to Abousamra. The eulogy claims that in 2016, he "took part in planning to kill the American apostate Hamza Yusuf during his last trip to Turkey."[64] Indeed, Yusuf, an Islamic scholar and the co-founder of Zaytuna College, did make a trip to Turkey in the summer of 2016. However, the eulogy does not go into further detail about this plot.[65]

By the time of his death in 2017, Abousamra had attempted to participate in jihadist organizations in Pakistan, Yemen, Iraq, and Syria over the course of 15 years. Abousamra, a computer scientist by training, spoke Arabic and English fluently and was a skilled propagandist with a deep understanding of jihadist ideology. At the time he joined, ISIS was in the process of revolutionizing its branding through stark points of departure from the current debates in Salafi-jihadism and propaganda that could appeal to Westerners (and especially English-speaking Westerners) through a comprehensive use of digital communications technology. Assisting in these efforts may not have constituted an automatic entry ticket into the leadership ranks of LeT, AQAP, or AQI, but they sufficed for ISIS.

Although they represent a comparatively smaller percentage of the Americans who traveled to Syria and Iraq to join jihadist groups, pioneers have outsized influences as they combine experience and connections to drive recruitment to other battlefields. A review of previous mobilizations of American travelers reveals that the central nodes of recruitment networks responsible for recruiting Americans to the conflicts in Afghanistan, Bosnia, Chechnya, and Somalia were often jihadist pioneers.

A second category—the networked travelers—help dispel the notion about their lack of connections to like-minded individuals. The data does not substantiate the idea, prevalent in many media reports about American ISIS supporters more broadly, that the majority "self-radicalized" or were "lone actors" or "lone wolves." On the contrary, many found that they had a better chance of carrying out activities on behalf of the group whether it was, in some small number of cases, planning attacks or more likely traveling overseas, if they built connections to others.

Networked Travelers

Out of the 62 American ISIS travelers covered in this book, 87 percent had connections to another ISIS traveler, attack planner, or supporter charged with ISIS-related activity in the United States. Their relationships generally fit into one of three subcategories: friends, families, and clusters. Examples of friendship-based traveler groups include Sixto Ramiro Garcia and Asher Abid Khan, two young Texans who embarked on a journey to join ISIS in Syria in 2014.[66] In some cases, family members traveled to join the group. For instance, Arman and Omar Ali, two brothers from Texas, reached Syria in 2014 and fought for ISIS together.[67]

Less common in the American context are clusters—large, networked groups comprising several family-based and friendship-based connections. Usually, clusters center around particular communities and hotspots. Overseas, particularly in European towns and cities, clusters of jihadist supporters resulted in extensive foreign fighter networks, wherein 10 to 20 individuals from one neighborhood traveled in close succession to one another to the battlefields of Syria and Iraq.[68]

These clusters, and the factors behind them, rarely occur in the United States. Although networked connections are just as important in shaping foreign fighter travel, they generally stay confined to small family and friendship groups and rarely branch out into larger clusters. Relatedly, terrorist travel from the US usually occurs in groups of twos, threes, and fours, and almost never in larger numbers.

However, there is one exception to this trend. Between 2013 and 2017, about seven people from Minneapolis and St. Paul, Minnesota traveled to Syria and Iraq, with at least ten more attempting to travel.[69] The state of Minnesota had the highest rates of foreign fighter travel per capita to Syria and Iraq, prompting then-acting US Attorney for the District of Minnesota, Andrew Luger, to admit that "we have a terror recruiting problem in Minnesota."[70]

The numbers of ISIS travelers from Minnesota are an American anomaly but resemble the dynamics in Europe where tens of travelers, all connected to a specific community, journeyed to Syria and Iraq. In examining the Minnesota case, three important factors emerge: the close family/friendship ties between the travelers and connections to the Somali-American community in the Twin Cities, the experience of previous mobilizations of jihadist travelers, in this case to the 2000s conflict in Somalia, and finally, the use of criminal conduct to finance terrorist activities.

These factors are apparent in the indictment against Abdullahi Ahmed Abdullahi, a resident of Edmonton, Alberta, Canada and former resident of Minneapolis and San Diego. The indictment charged Abdullahi and 14 others with a conspiracy to kill, kidnap and maim across four countries: America, Canada, Turkey and Syria.[71] The conspiracy was born in the fall of 2013 with Abdullahi and his three cousins, Hersi Karie, Hamsa Karie, and Mahad Hersi. According to the FBI, "Abdullahi conspired ... to provide personnel and money to individuals engaged in terrorist activities in Syria, including the killing, kidnapping and maiming of persons."[72]

In November 2013, Abdullahi sent an email to the Karie brothers, Mahad Hersi, and two associates in the United States: a cousin in Minnesota named Hanad Abdullahi Mohallim and a family friend in San Diego, Douglas McCain.[73] Abdullahi told the five men that it was time to raise money for their brothers in Syria, and finance Mohallim and McCain's travel to join them. In a request that echoed a ruling by Anwar al-Awlaki, Abdullahi encouraged them to "steal and commit fraud against the *kuffar* (non-believers)," noting that Islamic law sanctioned these activities as long as the proceeds were used to finance jihad.[74]

Abdullahi taught by example and participated in an armed robbery of a jewelry store in Edmonton. He pawned the proceeds and wired over $3,000; $450 went to Douglas McCain in San Diego, who then re-routed $350 to Gaziantep, Turkey at the orders of the Karie brothers.[75] In late February and early March of 2014, Abdullahi sent two payments of $900 and $1,700 to McCain and his brother Marchello to help finance McCain and Mohallim's travel to Syria.[76]

Despite not being Somali, the McCains had ties to the Somali community from the time they lived in Minneapolis and attended Robbinsdale Cooper High School.[77] Douglas McCain, nicknamed "Duale" by his Somali colleagues, previously lived with Troy Kastigar, a Minnesotan who traveled to join al-Shabaab in Somalia in 2008.[78] At the time of his departure to Syria, McCain was working in a Somali restaurant in San Diego.[79] Both McCains had extensive criminal records: Douglas was a career petty criminal and Marchello picked up weapons charges while still in Minnesota.[80]

On March 9, 2014, Douglas McCain and Hanad Mohallim traveled from the Twin Cities and San Diego, respectively, to Istanbul, Turkey, with the intent of traveling onward to Syria.[81] Their plane tickets were paid for using a credit card belonging to Marchello McCain's girlfriend, and the balance was paid off using the proceeds of Abdullahi's armed robbery in Canada.[82] After arriving in Syria, the five men linked up with another Minnesotan in ISIS, Abdifatah Ahmed.[83] Meanwhile, Abdullahi remained in the fold. His social media and emails to co-conspirators provided daily updates and running details about his friends' experience in Syria and Iraq fighting for ISIS. Their responses were "disguised" by using basketball and American football terminology to describe military actions.[84]

Each of the first five American ISIS fighters died within their first year in Syria. Douglas McCain was killed in August of 2014 fighting against the Free Syrian

Army. He became the first American citizen the US Government acknowledged to have died fighting for ISIS.[85] Abdifatah Ahmed was killed at about the same time.[86] Hanad Mohallim, the Karie brothers, and Mahad Hersi were all killed four months later during the 2014 siege of Kobani by Kurdish forces.[87]

Although their tenures as ISIS jihadists were short-lived, they paved the way for several other young acolytes from the Twin Cities. Some members of the cluster had direct personal connections to this initial group of Americans, while others built on contacts they made while the five were still alive.

Hanad Mohallim told Abdullahi Yusuf, his best friend from back in Minnesota, about life in the caliphate. Yusuf, in a series of text messages and calls to Mohallim in Syria, expressed his interest in joining him in the fight.[88] In addition, Mohallim and Yusuf had a group of friends who all attended the Dar al-Farooq Youth and Family Center, the local Muslim community center in Minneapolis, where they used to hang out and play basketball.[89] One of Mohallim and Yusuf's friends from the center was Guled Omar, described as the "ringleader" of the second wave of Minnesota travelers. Omar was already on the FBI's radar and they were not surprised to hear of his attempt to join ISIS. FBI agents stopped Omar at the airport in 2012 while he was traveling to Nairobi, Kenya.[90] The agents believed he intended to travel into Somalia, where his brother, Ahmed Ali Omar, had already become a member of al-Shabaab.[91]

Through Omar, Yusuf connected with Abdi Nur, a young man who was also interested in the Islamic State. Yusuf and Nur both began planning to depart for Syria together, going on shopping trips at the local mall to buy clothing and gear and purchasing plane tickets. On April 24 and 28, 2014, Nur and Yusuf made fateful trips to the Minneapolis Passport Agency to obtain US passports for their journey.[92] Nur went on the first day, listing his travel destination as Australia. His application for a passport was approved. Four days later, Yusuf submitted his application, with a stated travel destination of Turkey. Yusuf, however, gave an inconsistent account of his travel purpose, was visibly nervous, and could not sustain eye contact with the agent. This behavior unnerved the agent conducting the interview, who promptly notified their supervisor, who then alerted the FBI.[93]

However, Yusuf's application was eventually approved. He used the new passport to open a checking account, which he subsequently used to purchase his ticket to Istanbul. Nur, around the same time, purchased a plane ticket to Istanbul for the day after Yusuf's scheduled departure.[94] On May 28, 2014, Nur drove Yusuf to the train station, where he traveled onward to Minneapolis–St. Paul International Airport. However, Yusuf could not board his flight. FBI agents were there to meet Yusuf at the airport and arrested him.[95] Undeterred, Abdi Nur traveled to the airport the next day and boarded his flight to Istanbul. Days later, Nur communicated with members of his family in Minnesota. He told them that he had "gone to join the brothers" and that "everybody dies but I want the best death … take care of hooyo [mother] for me inshallah."[96]

After Nur's successful arrival in Syria to join the ranks of the Islamic State, he reached out to other jihadist travelers from the Twin Cities for advice. In August 2014, he contacted Mohamed Abdullahi Hassan, now more commonly known as

"Mujahid Miski," on Facebook.[97] Hassan was involved in a previous mobilization of young men from Minnesota to the battlefields of Somalia, to join the jihadist group al-Shabaab. At the time of his conversation with Nur, Hassan had spent over five years in Somalia, and was beginning to reach out to other American jihadists. As previously mentioned, he would be involved in the planning processes of several ISIS-inspired attacks in the US, including the 2015 attack on the Curtis Culwell Center in Garland, Texas.

In one of their online conversations, Hassan asked Nur how many "brothers from mpls [Minneapolis]" traveled to the battlefields in Syria. Nur replied that, besides him, three had successfully entered Syria and "others" were planning to travel.[98] Hassan gave Nur some sage advice, from one Minnesotan traveler to another. After asking Nur if he knew "Duale" (Douglas McCain), Hassan informed him:

> try to all connect and make one of you guys *mas'uul* [a Somali term referring to a guardian, or someone that is responsible for others' affairs] . . . being connected in jihad make you stronger and you can all help each other by fulfilling the duties that allah swt put over you . . . like us in Somalia the brothers from mpls are well-connected so try to do the same . . . It is something we have learned after 6 years in Jihad.[99]

By the end of 2015, at least ten people who knew Nur personally had tried to join ISIS by traveling to Syria and Iraq. Only two succeeded. The first successful traveler was Yusuf Jama. Jama was amongst the group of friends who met outside the Dar al-Farooq Center, and an acquaintance of the group's ringleader, Guled Omar.[100] He went on a "dry run," a one-day, round-trip flight between Minneapolis and Chicago in early June 2014 to make sure he was not on the no-fly list.[101] One week later, he traveled from Minnesota to Istanbul, and onward to Syria. On June 25, 2014, using a Turkish SIM card, he called a family member in the US. Investigators later found that Abdi Nur used the same SIM card to call his family around the same time.[102]

The second successful traveler, Mohamed Amiin Ali Roble, was Abdi Nur's nephew.[103] In August 2014, weeks after Nur's conversation with Mujahid Miski, Roble applied for an expedited US passport.[104] Using money from a personal injury settlement that became available to him on his 18th birthday, Roble purchased plane tickets for him and his mother (Nur's sister) from Minneapolis to Shanghai, China. In December 2014, he bought another plane ticket from Shanghai to Istanbul, and absconded into Syria.[105] His friends in Minnesota identified him fighting for ISIS in a series of early 2015 pictures distributed through social media.[106]

However, eight members of this group (including Abdullahi Yusuf) who attempted to travel were not nearly as lucky as Mohallim, Nur, Jama, and Roble.[107] A multi-state FBI operation in April 2015 resulted in the arrests of Guled Omar, Zacharia Abdurahman, Abdirahman Daud, Adnan Farah, Mohamed Farah, and Hanad Musse in the Twin Cities and in San Diego, California.[108] Each of these men not only assisted the successful Minnesota travelers, but also made several failed attempts to reach Syria themselves. In the following six months, two more Minnesota men, Hamza Ahmed and Abidirizak Warsame, as well as Douglas McCain's brother Marchello, were arrested for their roles in the conspiracy.[109] Finally, in September 2017, Abdullahi Ahmed Abdullahi was arrested by Canadian authorities for armed robbery. After losing an appeal, he was extradited to the US to face charges of providing material support to a terrorist organization.[110]

The trials of the individuals charged with recruiting for ISIS in the Twin Cities uncovered several successful travelers, multiple attempted travelers, and a handful of others who provided financial support or services to ISIS. Seven members of the cluster pleaded guilty and three were convicted at trial.[111]

The cases also heralded innovative approaches to how the US Government responds to terrorist recruitment. Abdullahi Yusuf, one of the first attempted travelers, currently takes part in a program aimed towards rehabilitating jihadists. He was granted supervised, conditional release in November 2017.[112] The others are serving sentences ranging from two-and-a-half to 35 years in federal prison.[113] Guled Omar, Mohamed Farah, and Abdirahman Daud—the three men that received the harshest sentences—are currently appealing their convictions. In 2019, they appealed to the Supreme Court of the United States to review their case.[114] However, their appeal was denied.[115]

In Syria and Iraq, the "second wave" of Minnesotan travelers met the same fates as the Karie brothers, Abdifatah Ahmed, Douglas McCain, and Hanad Mohallim. Yusuf Jama was killed in battle in Syria in March 2015.[116] Abdi Nur is presumed dead, and the status of his nephew, Mohamed Roble, remains unclear.[117]

Two more Twin Cities residents who are seemingly unconnected to the cluster also reached Syria and Iraq. In August 2014, a young woman named Yusra Ismail borrowed a family member's passport claiming that she needed to use it to travel to a wedding in Africa, and later told her family that she had reached Syria.[118] Another Twin City teenager, Abdelhamid al-Madioum, left his family vacation to Morocco in July 2015 to work at an ISIS-controlled hospital in Mosul.[119]

The extent of ISIS recruitment in the Minnesota Twin Cities sparked a flurry of news reports, analyses, and Congressional inquiries. While the Minnesota case is an anomaly in regard to the recruitment of American ISIS travelers, what is equally obfuscated is the factors that motivated this outflow. The Twin Cities during this time period exhibited trends seen in other, non-US contexts, and these variables may have contributed to the extent of the traveler phenomenon there.

First, the nature of face-to-face interaction and deep personal connections shaped not only the dynamics within the Minnesota cluster, but also expanded the number of individuals involved in the cluster. Unlike its counterparts, which usually involve isolated groups of two or three members, the Minnesota cluster transcended several friendship and family groups and included at least 15 people directly. All participants in the cluster were at minimum two or three degrees of separation away from one another. Close family and friendship connections created a "snowball effect," ensnaring a significant number of people in the same social circles into the travel facilitation network. Also notable is the fact that this cluster involved individuals with connections to the same Somali-American community in the Twin Cities, but who lived in two different US states and one Canadian province.

Next, the previous mobilization of Minnesotans to jihadist groups in Somalia played a part in shaping the mobilization to Syria and Iraq. The 2007–2013 recruitment wave to Somalia entailed that the new generation of jihadist recruits had access to organized formations of jihadist travelers, with experience, knowledge, and skills that could be used in future recruitment. It is no coincidence that upon arrival in Syria, Abdi Nur reached out to Somalia-based Minneapolitan Mohamed Abdullahi Hassan for guidance. Several other co-defendants had family and friendship connections to al-Shabaab members. Drawing from this structure, and the charismatic personalities it produced, the Minnesota travelers formed tight-knit kinship and friendship groups to facilitate their travel.

Finally, several participants in the Minnesota cluster either had extensive criminal records (for instance, the McCain brothers) or used criminal means to facilitate their travel attempts. Efforts ranged from attempts to fraudulently acquire illegal passports, to the armed robbery in Edmonton the proceeds of which eventually reached ISIS members in Syria. The "crime–terror nexus," or linkages between jihadist and criminal underworlds, has been a prominent feature of ISIS travel facilitation networks in Europe, where estimates suggest that a majority of European ISIS foreign fighters and attackers had criminal records prior to their mobilization.[120] Additionally, several used criminal activities and connections to the criminal underworld to acquire the means necessary for their plots.

While most of the American contingent in ISIS used personal connections and contacts to reach Syria and Iraq, the cluster in Minnesota represents the most extensive and clear example. It is distinguished by factors—connections transcending several family and friendship groups, linkages to previous jihadist mobilizations, and the crime–terror nexus—which are extant in other wide-reaching facilitation networks on both sides of the Atlantic.

Loners

If a majority of American ISIS travelers made connections to like-minded supporters prior to their travel and used their contacts to reach their destination, where does this leave the remainder? While it may be the case that the final category of travelers—the so-called "loners"—have stories that may be less generalizable than their pioneer or networked equivalents, their insights reveal a great deal about the radicalization process. In our review of these cases, we found that for the loners, the role of binding ideologies and the use of digital communications technologies played especially pertinent roles in lieu of face-to-face connections with other supporters.

In May 2017, we interviewed "Mo," a young man from New York who traveled to Syria to join ISIS in June 2014.[121] During this interview, he discussed some of the factors that motivated him to travel, and provided an account of his journey and his experiences after joining the group. While his story helps to shed some light on why some young Western Muslims have been radicalized in the cause of ISIS, those hoping for a simple, or even clear explanation will be disappointed. The reasons people join extremist groups like ISIS are complex, multifaceted, and involve a range of unique personal and situational factors. There is rarely a so-called "tipping point" at which one simply becomes a traveler, or any sort of linear progression in the radicalization process. To add complexity to the picture, recruits themselves can rarely provide a full and comprehensive explanation for why they joined a specific group, and often choose to alter their stories to avoid their complicity.

When our interview started, we first asked Mo the obvious question: "Why did you join ISIS?" He declined to answer, directing us instead to another question: "You should ask me why did I go there [to Syria]."[122] At the time that Mo was deciding whether to travel to Syria, many argue that ISIS had not fully established its ideological bearings by declaring the caliphate, although it did exercise some proto-governance functions. Mo claimed that he had no strong affinity to ISIS at the time of his travel, and that he departed the US for Syria simply because he was interested in living in a *sharia*-compliant environment.[123]

In our first line of questioning, we explored the factors behind his radicalization that eventually led him from studying at a prestigious American university to the battlefields of Syria. From his perspective, the factors that he saw as most relevant included a screening of the 2004 Dutch film *Submission* in his university class at Columbia, the death of his sister and her unborn child, and a turn online to understand his identity as a Muslim living in a Western country. After this conversation we presented many of these ideas to Mo in a general, linear narrative about how he became involved in jihadism, as researchers and academics tend to do. Mo promptly rejected this as an attempt to "put me in this box and explain my decisions . . . it's not that simple."[124]

To that end, Mo is correct that radicalization cannot be explained using any single "moment" or root cause. The stories of how travelers reached their decision often involve a complex, multivariable explanation, involving a host of psychological, sociological, and personal factors. However, our interview with Mo also yielded one of the most in-depth, publicly available explanations about mobilization—in other words, the process that already-radicalized individuals undertake to reach a decision about which actions are appropriate, and how they facilitate their actions. In this case, Mo explained the choices he made once he was convinced that he could no longer live in the US as a Muslim, and the labyrinthine process of traveling to Syria and eventually joining the Islamic State.[125]

In this regard, Mo's claim that Syria was not his first destination of choice was fascinating. After committing to leaving the US for a *sharia*-compliant environment, his intent was to travel to the Kingdom of Saudi Arabia and enroll in the University of Medina. Unfortunately, Mo lacked the basic requirements, including knowledge of the Arabic language and Quranic verses, to matriculate.[126] As a result, Mo began to consider other options.

One of those options was traveling to the Levant to join a group that, at least in Mo's estimation, was an upstart new outfit that made the bold claim that it was re-establishing an Islamic state. In this time period between 2013 and 2014, this group, which now called itself the Islamic State in Iraq and Syria, released a host of propaganda depicting its held territory as the only true Islamic utopia where Muslims could thrive under the implementation of *sharia* law.[127] "There were all these videos showing the public works ISIS was taking part in; it looked like a good Islamic community to raise a family."[128] At the time that he was researching the group, the brutal videos which ISIS is now known for (including the beheadings of the American journalists James Foley and Steven Sotloff) had not yet been released. "The effort of ISIS as I saw it was Islamic government, and that's what I wanted."[129]

In a similar vein, Mo claims he was not aware that ISIS was a group that was "like al-Qaeda." According to Mo, he abhorred al-Qaeda because of his disdain for the tactic of suicide bombing, which he viewed as unjustifiable under Quranic law. "Al-Qaeda put me off, I was always against terrorism and especially suicide bombing."[130] Despite numerous reports of ISIS utilizing suicide bombings, Mo held fast to his glorified notion of the group's goals and activities: "As far as I could see at the time, ISIS was not the same as al-Qaeda, the effort of ISIS was Islamic government and that's what I wanted. It felt legit, and the clue was even in their name!"[131]

At best, Mo's idealized depiction of ISIS displays significant naïveté. At worst, he was fully cognizant of ISIS' violent nature. ISIS was not a "new player on the scene" as Mo thought; it was a well-established jihadist group with roots in al-Qaeda's franchise in Iraq, dating back to the early 2000s. Nevertheless, Mo concluded his search for a *sharia*-compliant environment to live in, and reached the decision to travel to Syria to join ISIS.

Mo started to follow influential members and supporters of the group on Twitter. At the time, he found Twitter particularly useful, as it allowed him to receive news about the group's activities "straight from the source."[132] As he followed and read about the experiences of fellow Americans and other English-speakers in Europe who joined ISIS, many of whom were presented as being "just like him," the prospect of journeying to Syria in pursuit of fighting for the caliphate seemed more realistic. Mo also learned about which routes were optimal: "I knew from following these guys that the border [between Syria and Turkey] was porous, and that Urfa [Şanlıurfa, a Turkish town near the Syrian border] was the place to go."[133]

However, authorities quickly caught wind of Mo's plans after he became more active online. FBI Joint Terrorism Task Force agents interviewed him in early June 2014 about his travel plans. "When they came to visit me, all of a sudden it became real. It wasn't just something on my computer anymore."[134] Mo consented to the interview, but when asked about ISIS, he claimed that he supported rebel groups in Syria, but did not have the means, knowledge, or wherewithal to travel. Nevertheless, the FBI visit added a sense of urgency to Mo's decision-making: "The train now felt like it was leaving the station, I had to either go soon after that or not at all." [135]

On June 12, 2014, one week after his FBI interview, Mo booked a flight from New York to Italy via Istanbul. To hide his path, he did not select Istanbul as his final destination as many unsuccessful travelers did. As an illustration of his commitment at the time, when he left the US he was recovering from an ankle injury and required crutches to walk. Yet this did not deter him from braving the rough, mountainous terrain of southern Turkey and Northern Syria to reach his destination.[136]

Mo immediately made his way to Şanlıurfa after arriving in Istanbul. Surprisingly, prior to his arrival, he had not made a direct connection with any ISIS members or border smugglers. His plan was more spur of the moment, based on reaching out to contacts he knew from Twitter once he arrived in Şanlıurfa or, if that failed, "even just go there and cross by myself."[137] His first choice for contacts was a famous pro-ISIS Twitter user who went by the handle @Shamiwitness—at the time, one of the group's leading online "fanboys." Authorities in India later discovered that the account belonged to a Bangalore man, Mehdi Biswas, who was eventually arrested in December 2014 in India.[138]

From Şanlıurfa, Mo reached out to @Shamiwitness on Twitter, who put him in contact with three local ISIS facilitators, including a British ISIS fighter named Abu Rahman al-Britani. Moving from Twitter to Kik, the encrypted messenger of choice for ISIS travelers at the time, he reached out to al-Britani. He gave Mo the number for a border smuggler, and gave Mo permission to use his name for *tazkiyah*.[139]

That night, the smuggler picked up Mo outside the hotel and took him to a safe house which held other prospective ISIS members from around the world. Among the more colorful recruits that Mo recalled was a Russian former neo-Nazi convert to Islam. After a few hours in the safe house, the recruits were taken across the border into Syria and dropped off—"he [the smuggler] pointed to Orion's Belt and told us to follow it until we came to a village."[140] Mo was still limping in his surgical boot from his injury as they trekked to reach the village, and to complicate matters, his group were arrested by Turkish border guards, beaten up, and briefly detained. However, they were quickly released, and the group eventually arrived at the village. Subsequently, they were picked up by ISIS members and transferred to another safe house in Suluk, a Syrian town about seven miles south of the border with Turkey.[141]

Mo stayed in the safe house in Suluk for two weeks with dozens of other travelers. He claims that during his stay, he began to realize the severity of his mistake. While ISIS propaganda portrayed its supporters as a "band of brothers," regardless of their origins, Mo realized that many "weren't the type of Muslims I grew up with."[142] Mo referred to them as lacking in *akhlaq*, which translates directly from Arabic to "disposition," and refers to the strong moral and virtuous character of a person.[143] The fraternal bonds and camaraderie among travelers, frequently highlighted as motivating factors for those who join jihadist groups, appeared to be a sham: "They prayed differently, they had a bad attitude towards sharing food, they weren't doing *wudu* (ritual ablution before prayer) properly, and the bathrooms were kept terribly."[144]

Mo claims that he had no intention of fighting when he arrived in ISIS-held territory. Instead, he hoped to start a new life within a *sharia*-compliant environment: "I wanted to maybe start a business and eventually raise a family."[145] Like Mo's hope for brotherhood with other recruits, this ideal was quickly shattered as well. At the Suluk safe house, an ISIS member carrying a suicide vest asked the new recruits to familiarize themselves with it. Mo began to see the group in a different light, and became concerned for his safety. After evening prayers, this member also gave a lecture to the group about suicide bombing and argued that, despite the lack of legal justifications for the practice in Islam, ISIS supported the tactic. Mo was shocked: "They know it is legally weak, but they still accepted it, and he told us that 'we gain benefit from it, so we do it.'"[146]

As time passed, Mo claimed to grow increasingly despondent about his new home. He had lost his glasses during the scuffle with Turkish border guards and was unable to see what his surroundings looked like until another recruit lent him a pair. "That was the first time I got a full view of where I was—just this desolate desert—I felt hopeless and thought 'how the hell do I get back home from here?!'"[147]

Some of the other English-speakers at the Suluk house were also having second thoughts about their decision, including a man he knew as Abu Salman al-Hindi. This was the *kunya* of Talmeezur Rahman, an Indian national raised in Kuwait who attended a university in Texas between 2012 and 2014.[148] Rahman, who studied computer science in college, hoped to offer his technical expertise to ISIS; like Mo, he claimed to have no intention of fighting.[149] Mo and Abu Salman bonded over their outlook and became friends: "Salman was one of the only guys there I could relate to."[150]

However, Mo claimed that other Americans in the Suluk house were more extreme in both their beliefs and also their commitment to fighting. The recruits were all allowed to use a single burner phone to contact their families in their native countries. After Mo spoke to his parents one day, a Somali-American from Minneapolis that he knew as "Omar" confronted him. "He asked me how strong my parents' Islam was, and if I had made *takfir* on [excommunicated] them."[151] An uncompromising hardcore jihadist ideologue committed wholeheartedly to jihad, Omar represented the other end of the spectrum of the Western ISIS recruits in Suluk. According to Mo, this category represented the majority: "Most of the Americans I met during my time in Syria were very ideological and ready for fighting."[152]

Notably, during Mo's time in Suluk, ISIS leader Abu Bakr al-Baghdadi announced the establishment of the caliphate at the al-Nuri mosque in Mosul in June 2014. Mo recalled the celebrations in the house but noticed that some of the members were calling themselves *irhabeen* (Arabic for "terrorists"). When jihadists themselves use this term, it connotes their endorsement of their group's violent tactics. Mo claims that this was further confirmation that he had grossly misunderstood the group he joined.

The most insightful information we drew from our interview with Mo was his explanation of how new recruits were processed and trained. After waiting in Suluk for two weeks, his group of recruits were taken to the Farooq camp. Mo described Camp Farooq as a "*sharia* camp" focused on ideological indoctrination.[153] At the time that Mo attended, Camp Farooq was under the control of the Emir of

Sharia and Teaching, whom Mo knew only by his first name, "Amari." While Mo could not place the camp's exact location, he knew it was south of Raqqa, in north-central Syria.[154]

Raqqa is approximately 50 miles away from Suluk, and during the time Mo was there, the road linking the two cities was under direct ISIS control or contained corridors through which the group could safely pass.[155] At Farooq, recruits were separated by their native language and put through various forms of ideological training, including classes on creed (*aqidah*), methodology of religion (*manhaj*), Quranic study, and some basic tactical training. In regard to the religious ideology promoted by the camp, Mo claimed that the instructors "were basically teaching us Wahhabi stuff," referring to a Saudi Arabian branch of conservative Islam with its roots in the eighteenth-century Arabian Peninsula.[156]

During his time in Camp Farooq, Mo continued to harbor doubts about ISIS, and again was subjected to questioning by more committed Americans. One day, an ISIS commander asked his group if they wanted to go and fight in Deir ez-Zor, a town to the southeast. Mo hesitated to volunteer: "I sort of half-raised my hand but then quickly put it back down."[157] Some of his fellow Americans noticed this fence-sitting, including "this one guy from Harlem [who] saw what I did and criticized me in front of everyone."[158]

Mo claimed that he eventually became so confused that he expressed doubts about his commitment to his teacher. "I told him I was experiencing *waswas*," an Arabic term used in Islam to refer to the evil whispers of *Shaytan* (the Devil) which sow doubt in one's mind. He immediately regretted making this complaint: "After expressing doubts about Deir ez-Zor, I was stupid to put attention on myself again."[159] Directly after this incident, a sheikh at the camp warned his students to "watch out for those who make doubt, they have question marks on their heads." This terrified Mo, who viewed the remark as a direct threat to his life.

After three weeks in Camp Farooq, Mo moved again to Camp Abdallah Azzam (known colloquially as Camp AA). At Camp AA, named after the "father of jihad" who fought with the *mujahideen* against the Soviet Union in Afghanistan, the focus was much more on military training. The facility where Camp AA was located was previously a Syrian army base. During tactical drills, recruits who were especially adept in fighting were transferred to what Mo said was called "commando training."[160] Understandably, Mo was neither mentally nor physically cut out for commando training. At both Camps Farooq and AA, ISIS administrative staff required Mo to fill out a Microsoft Access form with personal details, including age, experience, and what he felt he could offer ISIS.[161]

The electronic form for Camp AA also asked Mo to request a specific military role. His choices included being a regular soldier, a suicide bomber, or an *inghimasi*, which refers to someone who fights on the front lines while wearing a suicide vest. Mo, still intent on avoiding military service in ISIS altogether, tried to find another role as a "researcher": "I didn't want to fight, so I told them I went to a very good school, and my value to them was my mind."[162] Mo pitched a half-baked idea to ISIS commanders about constructing an electro-magnetic pulse (EMP) device, which he claimed could resolve a growing problem for ISIS: taking aircraft out of the skies before they could issue devastating air strikes. This, even in Mo's estimation, was an eleventh-hour effort to avoid fighting: "I didn't know shit about making an EMP, but I figured this could buy me some time."[163]

Astoundingly, Mo's concocted story worked. His commanders sent him to Manbij in northwestern Syria to work with an ISIS emir who was responsible for local transport logistics, designing bunkers, and digging underground tunnels. Interestingly, Mo claims that this office utilized former Hamas members with experience in tunnel-digging to carve underground routes for ISIS between Syria and Turkey.[164] Mo still had no proficiency in Arabic, and he was only of limited use to his new emir, who eventually tasked him with training other members in computer programs.[165]

When he arrived in Manbij, however, Mo had already committed to leaving ISIS-held territory and the group altogether. He had been devising an escape route since his stay at Camp AA. In Manbij, he had access to an internet café, where he researched the border crossings between Syria and Turkey that were still open. But even before picking a specific crossing, he would first need a legitimate excuse to get out of Manbij. Exploiting the traditional sensitivities of his commander, he claimed that he had met a girl online and needed to travel outside Manbij to seek her father's hand in marriage.[166]

The commander gave Mo permission, and he departed via minibus to the town of Raqqa, transferring to a taxi to the border crossing point at Tel Abyad. He planned to cross the border on foot but noticed ISIS guards at the checkpoint. Without a contingency plan, Mo had to turn back and returned via taxi to Manbij.[167] By a stroke of luck, his driver on this route understood the situation that Mo was in and told him that he could help him cross into Turkey in a few days. At that time, many of the local taxi drivers in the area developed lucrative side businesses by trafficking individuals who were attempting to leave Syria across the northern border.[168]

In the meantime, he had to explain to his emir why he was returning without a new wife. His story was that she refused his proposal, but "they didn't believe me and got suspicious." He grew paranoid, claiming that his commander treated him differently, and "people got cold towards me very quickly."[169] Exacerbating these fears, ISIS adopted an aggressive policy towards dealing with its Western members who were perceived to have questionable loyalties, and the secret police were actively hunting spies and defectors. Mo had also noticed that many of the English-speaking members he knew were being sent to the front lines and dying in battle.[170]

Mo was forced to take extraordinary risks to secure his extraction from Syria; he knew the danger was overwhelming if he stayed. Against ISIS' rules for members, he bought a SIM card which allowed him to send emails.[171] On October 31, 2014, just five months after he embarked on his journey, he sent a message to the FBI. He hoped they would be able to verify his identity from his interview with JTTF agents while he was still in the US and send American government personnel to pick him up once he crossed the border. "Please help," he wrote, claiming that "my window is closing," and "I'm fed up with this evil." Rather fancifully, he also asked for "complete exoneration" and to "have everything back to normal with me and my family."[172]

FBI officials eventually responded, although their answer was not particularly reassuring to Mo. He was informed that the US had no consular presence in Syria and could not help him until he reached Turkish territory. Mo's only hope was the cab driver he met on the way back from Tel Abyad, but he would still have to find a way of escaping Manbij. Fortunately for Mo, fighting around the area had been particularly intense, and ISIS guards had left their posts at the gates of the camp to participate in battle. "I just walked out of the front gate and got a ride into town," Mo claimed; after leaving the camp, he went to Raqqa and met the smuggler.[173]

The taxi driver took Mo from Raqqa to a border crossing where a young boy guided him on foot across the border. On November 4, 2014, four days after he had contacted the FBI, Mo announced himself at a US consulate in southern Turkey.[174] Officials took him into custody, and during a series of interviews, Mo recounted his experiences over the last five months with ISIS. He also willingly provided all the intelligence he could offer, including smuggling routes, locations of the ISIS camps he had visited, and the names of the Western members of the group whom he encountered during his travels.[175]

During a break from his meetings at the consulate, Mo went outside to smoke a cigarette—a criminal act punishable by 20 lashes in ISIS-held territory—and was joined by a US Marine working consulate security.[176] Mo considers this one of the most surreal experiences of his five-month journey: "Just 24 hours earlier I was with a bunch of ISIS guys, and now here I am standing and smoking with a Marine."[177]

Mo was charged with providing material support to a foreign terrorist organization and receiving military training from a foreign terrorist organization.[178] After returning to the US in custody, he pleaded guilty to both charges in late November 2014. Today, he actively cooperates with federal authorities.[179] In August 2018, a federal judge sentenced Mo to time served—a sharp downward departure from the normal 15-to-20-year sentence for material support. But the decision was made due to Mo's cooperation with the government and participation in an innovative program in the Eastern District of New York, where he provided interventions for radicalized youth who were considering joining jihadist groups. More information on these programs is contained in Chapter 6 of this book.

Most aspects of Mo's story, including his claims that he never participated in military activity during his stint as an ISIS member, have been corroborated by US authorities.[180] Unsurprisingly, numerous Americans and other Westerners who traveled to Syria or Iraq before returning home or being captured on the battlefield by Western forces or their allies made similar claims, offering the constant refrain of "I was just a cook" or "I was just a mechanic."[181] Of course, these claims are suspect, and many are attempts to avoid harsh penalties that are connected to terrorism offenses. Nonetheless, even when the false claims are sorted out, Mo's experience highlights that some Westerners who are legally treated as "foreign fighters" may never have seen any actual combat.

Mo's expressed desire to "live under Islam" reiterates that the utopian and religious appeal of ISIS' message must not be ignored. While some members can accurately be estimated as violent psychopaths out for a cheap thrill, some Westerners are committed to ISIS' religio-political ideal and view it as the most effective vehicle for the Islamist vision. Many fit both categories, as well. For Mo, he appears to have rejected the zealous idealism that drove him towards Syria: "All the shit I've been through, I don't care anymore. America is my home."[182]

Undoubtedly, his view of the US is also shaped by how he has been treated by federal authorities since his surrender. Prosecutors have given him significant leeway and assistance in return for cooperation, which some may believe is too lenient for a returning ISIS member. Irrespective of the legitimacy of his treatment, his experiences following his return have countered his initial notions that the US Government is responsible for a "war against Muslims". Mo's experience can be essential in the future in convincing radicalized Americans who are considering foreign terrorist travel to disembark from their paths. Few can speak to the same experience as Mo can, having seen first-hand the inner workings, bureaucracy, and violent brutality of a major terrorist organization. His message to those considering joining ISIS is simple: "Don't be impulsive; think and sit still before you do something stupid."[183]

Mo's story, alongside those of the young men from Minnesota and Ahmad Abousamra, clearly shows the diversity in travelers' profiles, and the reasons that they chose to leave the US to join ISIS. Some, like Mo, traveled primarily to fulfill perceived religious obligations. As another American ISIS recruit described it during his trial:

> I wanted to go to the Islamic State, the caliphate, and see for myself how it is, how are people living there, and one day tell my kids, I have been there. You know, it's not all like it seems . . . I just wanted to, you know, just share with them like history, like places, places I have been . . .[184]

For these travelers, the extensive base of ISIS propaganda displayed a prophesied land that was administered and governed solely by the law of God and promised rewards in the hereafter if they participated in its broader project. Some of these same recruits were undergoing identity crises, leading them to question whether they could legitimately live and exist as a Muslim in a predominantly non-Muslim society. Defying the odds, a select few were able to overcome their lack of in-person connections to like-minded individuals and reach Syria and Iraq with the assistance of online contacts and, in some cases, a healthy dose of luck.

Personal and social factors compounded ideological matters, particularly for the networked travelers and pioneers. Many travelers were swept up by the febrile atmosphere created within a group of peers, all of whom sought the excitement and adventure of fighting together to protect fellow Muslims. Turning to "strength in numbers," networked travelers improved their chances of travel success by expanding their network of contacts, learning from each other's mistakes, and ensnaring a wider social circle of individuals in their plots.

An even smaller sub-section of pioneers, including travelers like Ahmad Abousamra, had extensive experience in the jihadist movement and were able to garner the skills and contacts that they developed to assist them in their journey. Once they arrived in Syria, their record of distinctions set them apart from other American travelers and allowed them to reach positions in ISIS that many of their compatriots could only dream of.

The manifold experiences of jihadist pioneers, networked travelers, and loners in Syria and Iraq caution against ascribing a single motivating factor to the problem of jihadist travelers. Commonly cited factors, such as the role of ideology, personal grievances, and personal networks undoubtedly play a significant role. However, there are less tangible, often serendipitous, causes which scholars and analysts often ignore. If history is any guide, a future large-scale jihadist mobilization is likely. As the current wave of jihadist travel slows to a halt, understanding the key figures and trends in what drove so many Westerners, including Americans, to the battlefields in Syria and Iraq is of paramount importance.

These three categories are heuristics for evaluating not only jihadist travel to join the Islamic State, but jihadist groups in general. With regard to American outflow to ISIS-held territory, two additional designations transcend the pioneer, networked, and loner categories. First, while the travel of women to an overseas jihadist group has historical precedent, it is unparalleled in scope to the wave of American women who traveled to Syria and Iraq to participate in the caliphate-building process. The second issue, concerning American jihadist travelers overseas who were returned to the United States by the US Government, came back on their own volition, intend to return, or are stranded overseas in non-state-actor-administered camps or third countries, is now the defining policy issue facing US officials within the field of jihadist travelers.

Women Travelers

Recent estimates place the number of women from around the world who traveled to Syria and Iraq to join the Islamic State at more than 6,700. This represents approximately 13 percent of the total count of foreign ISIS affiliates. From this number, at least 15 women are American, representing 19 percent of the total number of known American jihadist travelers who joined ISIS.[185]

Like men, the American women in ISIS joined the group for varying reasons, served in a wide array of capacities, and pose different threats to the US. Yet, as a result of their gender, accounts of these women in popular sources are fraught with analytical error. They frequently simplify the radicalization process for women ISIS recruits, conflate their roles within the organization after they travel, and discount the critical impact played by women in jihadist groups. This has a distinct effect on US counterterrorism, particularly when it comes to the prosecution of ISIS-affiliated American women in the criminal justice system.[186]

Much of this error is predicated on the fact that jihadist organizations, including ISIS, are extremely socially conservative and relegate women to roles outside the public space, including a general (but not absolute) prohibition on women's participation in military activity. While this is correct, many of the assumptions that are drawn from this assessment are overly reductive. The first critical error is the oft-repeated claim that the core, driving motivations of most (or all) women jihadist travelers is to either go along with their husbands or, if unmarried, to find a husband.

Within popular sources, the common referent for foreign ISIS women is "jihadi bride," a term that quickly fell out of favor with almost all serious scholars and analysts of terrorism. Both the term and the assumption behind it fail to account for the varying radicalization pathways of women travelers, which several studies find are as complex and multivariate as male ISIS fighters.[187] Moreover, it erases the agency of women ISIS travelers, many of whom traveled on their own accord. Meredith Loken and Anna Zelenz write that Western women jihadists are "not running after men for excitement or reward." Like most jihadist travelers, "they are committed actors making decisions they view as fundamental to their faith."[188] In fact, although well-known examples of Western male ISIS travelers who went to ISIS to find a wife are legion, references to "jihadi husbands" are generally absent from popular sources—highlighting the bizarre dichotomy with which popular sources often treat the role of gender in jihadist travel.

Undoubtedly, some American women were influenced by male relatives into traveling to Syria and Iraq. When we interviewed Tania Joya, the British-born Texas resident and former jihadist who traveled with her family to Syria in 2013, she discussed how her abusive and controlling husband concealed their final destination from her on the way to the country from Egypt.[189] Only a month after arriving in Syria and five months pregnant with their fourth child, Tania became ill and demanded her return to the United States.[190] She split from her husband, took the children and was smuggled back into Turkey before journeying back to Texas. Her husband, John Georgelas, became a high-ranking figure in ISIS' media department.[191] However, despite her husband coercing her into travel to Syria, Tania nonetheless rejects the "jihadi bride" label: "I talked to a professor who referred to me as the 'first lady of ISIS' ... well at least that's better than 'jihadi bride'; I wasn't a bride, I was a divorced woman with four kids."[192]

Even for women who do travel to ISIS-held territory with their spouse or in search of a spouse, this does not entail that it was the only factor behind their travel or that they were not as ideologically committed. Within the corpus of American women in ISIS, the story of Ariel Bradley exemplifies this point. In 2014, Bradley's story made headlines after she was one of the first known American women to join the Islamic State.[193] On first glance, the story of the young Tennesseean and convert to Islam from Pentecostalism appeared to confirm many of the media's assumptions about why American women joined ISIS. She traveled alongside her husband, a Swedish ISIS supporter whom she met online, to join the caliphate in Syria in 2014.[194] Yet, a closer look at her extensive social media presence confirms that she both independently adopted a staunch Salafi-jihadist outlook years prior to meeting her would-be husband, and directly and openly supported jihadist violence, including infamously praising the 2015 attack in Chattanooga.[195]

Relatedly, the second analytical pitfall is related to the roles of women within ISIS. American women, and their foreign peers, found ways to serve a variety of functions within the Islamic State.[196] The narrative of "jihadi brides" not only assumes that women of ISIS serve only in the function of homemaker or housewife, but discounts the variety of roles that women played. Erin Saltman and Melanie Smith found that despite the "primary role of Western women under ISIS-controlled territory is to be the wife of the jihadist husband they are betrothed to and to become a mother to the next generation of jihadism," women made active efforts to serve in a wide range of capacities within ISIS' state-building process, including but not limited to propagandists, online recruiters, educators, medical staff, and ISIS' religious police (*hisba*).[197]

Within the context of American travelers to the Islamic State, Zakia Nasrin's story exemplifies the array of roles that women affiliates found within the group. Leaked ISIS personnel files revealed that Nasrin, a 24-year-old Ohioan, officially joined ISIS in July 2014 with her brother Raisel Raihan and her husband Jaffrey Khan.[198] She was the valedictorian of her high school outside of Columbus, Ohio, and once aspired to be a doctor.[199] Within the context of the Islamic State, she was able to achieve her goal. According to her father-in-law, when Nasrin and her husband contacted him in September 2014, he received information that Nasrin was working as a doctor in a hospital controlled by ISIS in the city of Raqqa.[200]

Finally, as women in ISIS were largely relegated to non-combat support roles or out of the public space altogether, a final mistaken assumption is to devalue the impact of women participants in ISIS. It is far from the only jihadist group to utilize women in strategic positions; for both ISIS and its competitors, women can, according to Nelly Lahoud, "advance jihad in the domestic sphere and also in the public sphere through raising money for jihadis and preaching the merit of jihad to others in mosques, print, and online publications," alongside other roles.[201] Even within private life, women were predominantly responsible for educating their children, training what ISIS hoped would be the next generation of jihadist combatants for the caliphate.[202] Although their roles were different, in many ways foreign ISIS-affiliated women were as important to the organization's strategic vision as their male counterparts.

The result of these analytical mishaps is frequently seen in justice systems around the world, including the United States, when legal systems determine whether and how to prosecute women travelers and other ISIS-supporting women. Several studies point to a wide disparity in sentencing outcomes of women travelers.[203] In many instances, defense attorneys and judges play up gendered biases about women jihadist travelers, sometimes resulting in lighter sentences or, in some cases, non-prosecution.[204] The gap in treatment of men and women travelers can potentially lead to women who are as ideologically committed to the ISIS project slipping through the cracks of the criminal justice system, and potentially posing a threat of recidivism or attacks. It is paramount, therefore, for analysts, policymakers, and the public to cast off erroneous assumptions about the role of American women within the Islamic State and jihadist groups more broadly.

Returning Travelers

The situation for foreign jihadist travelers following the operations that took the Islamic State's last territorial holding is constantly in flux. Throughout the waning days of the Islamic State's exertion of territorial control, foreign jihadists remaining in the Levant had several options: attempt to return to their countries of origin or travel to another ISIS territorial holding, surrender to ISIS' regional adversaries or switch affiliations, or, as ISIS propaganda instructed them to, hold out to the bitter end and risk death or capture. By 2017, the third option was the most feasible: many states issued harsh penalties for participating in the conflict, surrender or attempting to play turncoat likely resulted in summary execution, and traveling onwards to another ISIS *wilayat* was logistically difficult. Not surprisingly, the final years of the recent iteration of the caliphate saw the deaths or detention of a substantial percentage of jihadist travelers.[205]

Arguably, the largest issue related to foreign jihadist travelers to Syria and Iraq currently facing governments around the world is the cadre of ISIS affiliates presently detained in the region by non-state actors. Following ISIS' last stand in Baghuz, the Syrian Democratic Forces (SDF), a Kurdish-led coalition of local militias that currently acts as de facto administrator of much of northeast Syria, holds tens of thousands of men, women, and children suspected of ISIS affiliation in a series of refugee camps.[206] The most infamous is the al-Hol camp, a processing center in the Hasakah governorate of Syria that currently holds more than 60,000— over 50,000 of which arrived after 2018.[207]

The situation within al-Hol and other camps housing ISIS affiliates in eastern Syria is grim. The systems are stretched far beyond their capacities for resources, staff, and security. Camps like al-Hol, designed to temporarily shelter approximately 10,000 refugees, are now at over six times their limit.[208] As no permanent solution to house ISIS affiliates is in place, the SDF-administered camps are now indefinitely detaining them. Access to food, water, health services, and consular assistance is minimal. Meanwhile, security problems abound: al-Hol reportedly has a detainee-to-staff ratio of 175 to 1, and foreign ISIS affiliates (mainly women) who remain steadfastly committed to the Islamic State frequently cause disturbances, threaten staff and guards, and enforce ISIS' draconian interpretations of Islamic law on other detainees.[209] After visiting the camp in April 2019, British journalist Quentin Sommerville described the SDF camps as "an overflowing vessel of anger and unanswered questions."[210] In October, State Department Special Envoy on Syria Ambassador James Jeffrey confirmed that more than 100 ISIS fighters escaped prisons in the days following the withdrawal of US troops.[211]

For years, Western governments showed very little initiative to repatriate their citizens from detention in Syria and Iraq. Select governments even stripped citizenship from their foreign jihadist travelers to avoid responsibility, effectively making detained ISIS affiliates stateless people.[212] This situation, however, has not been true with regards to United States policy. To date, the Program on Extremism's databases count 19 American jihadists—14 men and five women— who are known have returned to the US from Syria and Iraq. Fifteen of them faced federal charges for their participation in a jihadist group; the majority of these travelers were repatriated by the US Government. In addition, the US brought back at least a dozen children, either forcibly taken by their parents to the caliphate or born in ISIS-held territory to US citizen parents, from Syria and Iraq.

With issues pertinent to foreign fighter returnees at the top of the agenda for countering the ISIS threat in many Western countries, the situation with American returned travelers deviates from the picture painted by US law enforcement and intelligence officials during the early days of recruitment. First, contrary to grim expectations about their potential intentions to return, no American traveler affiliated with ISIS so far has successfully conducted an attack on US soil after returning. In fact, no ISIS-affiliated returnee was even known to have planned an attack at the time of their apprehension.[213]

In many ways, this dynamic is a result of American officials interdicting travelers before they could return home. Active cooperation with Iraqi justice officials and non-state forces responsible for detention in Syria helped the DOJ and FBI successfully repatriate travelers to the US directly from jails and prisons in the Levant.[214] Repatriating travelers while successfully maintaining evidence that is admissible in court is a tricky procedure, fraught with a minefield of legal issues. In cases where a detained ISIS fighter is thought to be an American, the FBI typically sends one team of special agents to liaise with foreign officials and prison guards and conduct a preliminary, voluntary, and informal interview with the detainee.[215] If the intelligence suggests that the detainee is a US citizen who may be implicated in a federal offense, the FBI then sends a second team, which is responsible for conducting a formal, Mirandized interview with the suspect.[216] Through this process and active extradition agreements, the FBI and DOJ are able to legally and formally repatriate American ISIS affiliates.[217]

This process can take a considerable amount of time, and today, American ISIS affiliates remain in detention in Syria, Iraq, Turkey, and several other countries, in limbo until the DOJ can finalize their repatriation.[218] In two notable cases, the US Government declined altogether to repatriate American ISIS affiliates from Syria and Iraq. It should be noted, however, that despite the massive amount of press attention they received, these cases constitute exceptions to the norm of US policy vis-à-vis American jihadist travelers. Hoda Muthana, a young woman from Alabama who traveled to Syria to join ISIS in November 2014, later surrendered to the SDF in 2019 with her young son in tow, and requested repatriation to the United States.[219] In January 2016, the Obama Administration issued a decision to revoke Muthana's passport.[220] In 2019, Muthana challenged this ruling in federal court, but a judge found that Muthana's US citizenship was invalid due to her Yemeni father's diplomatic status at the time of her birth.[221] Abdulrahman Ahmad al-Sheikh, a dual US–Saudi national from Louisiana, was also prevented from returning to the US after he was detained in Syria by the US military in 2017.[222] As part of a negotiated settlement in his legal case against the Department of Defense, the military transferred al-Sheikh out of custody into Bahrain in 2018.[223]

These exceptions aside, US policy can be considered unusually proactive in its response to repatriation, a process that has been difficult to justify in most Western countries. The major differences between the US and Europe on this issue are threefold. First, as previously mentioned, there were far more Western European citizens in ISIS than Americans; where the US was able to apply a case-by-case approach to its limited number of returnees, European officials lacked freedom of movement. The US legal system, which includes statutes that criminalize jihadist travel and established backchannels to Syrian and Iraqi authorities, found itself far more suited to legally processing incoming returnees than many of their European counterparts. In many Western European countries, repatriating an ISIS fighter into a legal system in which charging them with crimes or attaining convictions was difficult and putting them behind bars for a significant period of time even more so was an unnecessary gamble.[224] Finally, and most importantly, the European history with returnees committing horrific attacks—like the Paris and Brussels attacks—created an insurmountable political disincentive for most European politicians.[225] Foreign fighter repatriations in the US are quiet and rarely make headlines; failures to repatriate generate wall-to-wall media coverage. This situation is precisely the opposite in most European countries.

This is not to suggest, however, that the US did not face any issues with its system of processing jihadist returnees through the legal system. On average, the 13 American returnees who were charged in federal court received less time in prison than those who attempted to travel, but were arrested before they could reach Syria or Iraq. On first glance, this differential appears to be illogical. There are few crimes for which an attempted violation carries a more severe prison sentence than an actual violation. In the case of American travelers, this result is due to two factors: charging and cooperation. Successful travelers were more likely to slip under the radar of federal officials prior to their travel, and once they arrived in Syria and Iraq, it is difficult to gather evidence about their activities. As a result, charging successful travelers with material support violations is substantially more difficult—in turn, prosecutors often charged returnees with violations of other statutes that carry shorter prison sentences. Like "Mo," a substantial number of returnees also cooperated with law enforcement, providing invaluable intelligence on ISIS' activities in Syria and Iraq. With a few exceptions, the majority entered guilty pleas. Having intelligence to trade for a shorter prison sentence benefited successful travelers. In contrast, the failed traveler, who was arrested at a US airport, never stepped foot in the caliphate, and may have never met an actual ISIS member in real life, had far less to offer.

Between 2014 and 2019, the US managed to avoid many of its worst-case scenarios regarding the return of Americans in ISIS. The evidence suggests that alongside built-in resiliency and other policy responses, bringing back Americans to face justice in US criminal courts was a relatively successful strategy. While many of the factors that led to the success of US policy are difficult to replicate elsewhere, the US has also been at the forefront of encouraging other nations to return their citizens from Syria and Iraq.[226] For the US and its international partners, the threat in the future will continue to be determined by "known unknowns"—the greatest risk is from cases where ISIS fighters are able to slip under the watchful eye of US and Western European intelligence and law enforcement agencies.

More likely than not, the United States will face another wave of jihadist travel in the future. As the ISIS mobilization was shaped by its predecessors in Somalia, Yemen, Afghanistan, Iraq, and elsewhere during the mid-to-late 2000s, the ISIS mobilization will likely inspire a future generation of American jihadist travelers.[227] Foreign fighter waves are cyclical. While the US and its partners learned invaluable lessons about how to counter foreign fighter travel during the ISIS foreign-fighter wave, and developed mechanisms for detecting and interdicting travelers, the jihadist movement is also learning from mistakes. It remains to be seen whether ISIS and other groups will be able to overcome advances in biometrics, intelligence sharing, legal developments, and best practices developed during the ISIS mobilization.

Several scenarios could lead to another wave of foreign fighters. First, ISIS could regain a foothold in Syria and Iraq, re-opening the "gates of *hijra*" to interested Americans by controlling the international borders into their territory. Given the tenuous situation in Syria and Iraq today, counting ISIS out of the long-term picture in the Levant may be a costly mistake. In the past, the group and its predecessors cycled through historical periods of rise and fall, strategically capitalizing on failure and reinvigorating itself for future campaigns.[228] While it is unclear what a future ISIS reincarnation following its 2019 defeat may entail, a revanchist organization may attempt to restore its credibility by regaining access to its steady flow of foreign fighters. If this occurs, the number of American jihadists considering travel to Syria and Iraq may jump up again.

Before ISIS' territorial collapse in Syria, it established a network of affiliates in several traditional jihadist hotspots around the world. As part of the establishment of these *wilayat* (provinces), ISIS called on its Western supporters to join jihadist groups outside Iraq and Syria. So far, 11 Americans in the past five years are known to have heeded that call, attempting or succeeding in joining the Islamic State's patchwork of affiliated provinces around the globe.[229] Most flock to the areas that were previously popular destinations for American jihadists— Somalia, Yemen, Afghanistan, and Iraq. Recent evidence shows that American ISIS supporters are increasingly considering these destinations. In the first month of 2019, the FBI arrested three Michigan men for conspiring to travel to Somalia to join ISIS-affiliated groups.[230] In July 2019, Ahmed Mahad Mohamed and Abdi Yemani Hussein were arrested in Arizona during the planning stages of an effort to travel to Egypt to join ISIS' fledgling province in the Sinai Peninsula.[231]

Alternatively, one of ISIS' competitors in the jihadist movement could re-seize the mantle of foreign fighter recruitment, and use techniques popularized during the ISIS mobilization to target Americans. Other jihadist groups are beginning to position themselves as tangible alternatives to ISIS in recruiting Americans. In July 2019, a Bronx man named Delowar Mohammed Hossain was arrested for attempting to travel to Afghanistan to join the Taliban; several months earlier, two men from Texas and New York were charged with attempting to provide material support to the Pakistani jihadist group Lashkar-e-Taiba.[232] ISIS' jihadi competitors may be uniquely positioned to take advantage of ISIS' recent misfortunes, and if they are interested in foreign support, can return to the radar of recruitment of Americans.

Chapter 4

THE E-ACTIVISTS

More than ever before, digital communications technologies serve as a potent tool for contemporary terrorist organizations. The Islamic State serves as one of the best examples of how such groups opportunistically leverage various digital tools to disseminate propaganda, communicate aims, and mobilize recruits.[1] Despite ongoing efforts in both governmental and nongovernmental spheres to mitigate the ISIS online presence, the group has managed to continue making use of numerous emerging communications technologies to help maintain its presence around the world. From social media accounts and messaging applications to SIM cards and cryptocurrencies, ISIS supporters in the United States exploit a range of digital communications technologies to aid and abet the group on a global stage.

Of all the regions in which the Islamic State is active, it is in America where the group relies most on communications technology to maintain its presence. For reasons already outlined in Chapter 1, ISIS is unable to draw upon extensive real-world networks of members and supporters in the way it has done in Europe. As a result, the group has made innovative use of emerging communications technology as a way to redress this balance. While it is not able to replace the size and effectiveness of real-world networks, there is evidence which suggests that the internet provides a very viable alternative.

Through digital means, the group was able to chart out a path for its American supporters beyond conducting terrorist attacks or terrorist travel. ISIS' doctrine viewed its propaganda arm as strategically important, on the same par as its fighting capabilities.[2] To maintain the steady stream of propaganda targeting Western audiences, translate existing media into Western languages, and keep a foothold on the social media channels necessary to disseminate the media, ISIS relied on "e-activists": supporters who conducted most of their activities for the group in the digital space.

This chapter on American ISIS e-activists begins with a brief overview of research on the use of communications technology by extremist groups with a focus on how it is used and the impact it can have on terrorist groups' ability to recruit and mobilize supporters. The following section analyzes the constant back-and-forth game between ISIS e-activists and the social media platforms they occupy, which will help to provide a fuller understanding of how specific platforms offer unique advantages (and disadvantages) to American ISIS supporters. The final section will use case studies to illustrate the various ways in which the online communications have been used by American ISIS supporters, namely travel to ISIS territory, propaganda dissemination, hacktivism, and fundraising.

The data used for this chapter combines the Program on Extremism's database of American legal cases with its extensive database of social media data from the accounts, channels, and groups of English-speaking ISIS supporters.[3] While focusing on the ebb and flow of activity on several social media platforms, the project assesses a range of tools to help illuminate the functions, goals, and ideologies of ISIS, their English-speaking supporters, and the wider jihadist movement. Since 2015, the Program on Extremism has collected over 800,000 tweets from more than 1,500 English-speaking, pro-ISIS accounts, and over 100,000 pages of data from more than 700 pro-ISIS channels and groups on the instant messaging platform Telegram.[4] The following section explains the strategic utility of both these platforms for ISIS supporters and their role in ISIS information operations targeting Americans. By combining data from major legal cases with this unique corpus of social media information, our analysis of how ISIS used digital communications technologies situates American ISIS e-activists within their broader online networks.

How Extremists Communicate Online

During the early years of the internet, American right-wing groups were among the first to make extensive use of this technology to disseminate propaganda and virtually connect like-minded extremists. The American white nationalist Louis Beam was a visionary in this regard and is credited with pushing the right-wing extremist movement in America "from the age of the Xerox to the age of the computer."[5] However, it is a former Ku Klux Klan member named Donald Black who set a new precedent after creating Stormfront in 1995, which at the time was the first website of its kind and to this day remains one of the internet's largest and most influential neo-Nazi and white supremacist online platforms.[6]

Soon, jihadist leadership figures and their respective groups also created officially sanctioned websites as a way to communicate their goals and collective grievances through a cheap and largely unregulated platform with global reach.[7] These websites were used mostly to disseminate both ideological and tactical documents while also providing opportunities for group sympathizers to forge contacts, safe in the knowledge that there would likely be no law enforcement oversight. Over time, the websites also served as databases for the storage and archiving of the output produced by extremists.[8] Among the first such sites was *al-neda.com*, which was set up in 2001 and overseen by the al-Qaeda leadership while being hosted by a server in Malaysia.[9] Other senior al-Qaeda strategists and ideologues also set up their own sites around this time, using them as clearing houses for their latest publications.[10]

These centrally controlled top-down websites began to experience a significant decline in the years after 9/11. This was due to a combination of the sites being blocked or taken down, growing concerns over government surveillance among users, and a general shift to other platforms, including social media.[11] This, however, did little to stop jihadists from moving on to the next innovation in online communications: forums and chatrooms. By the mid-2000s, password-protected forums and online chatrooms had all but replaced websites as the main platforms from which to spread jihadist propaganda and create online networks.[12] As the platforms evolved, jihadist propaganda began to be produced in a variety of languages, making it accessible to a wider audience.[13] Online forums and chatrooms provided new opportunities for members and supporters of extremist movements to interact with each other, creating what has been referred to as the "jihadisphere."[14]

According to Aaron Zelin's 2013 analysis of jihadist forums, whereas previous jihadist online activism was limited to top-down official Al-Qaeda websites, these new forums "shattered the elitist nature of *jihadi* communications."[15] This began to create a space for more bottom-up, grassroots involvement in the jihad movement's online activities. The communication between group and supporter was no longer a one-way street, and jihadist internet users around the world were able to feel more connected to the group and able to contribute more actively to its online messaging goals.

Due to the online anonymity that these platforms offered, they proved especially useful for extremist propagators who wanted to avoid both the attention of the security services and possible repercussions in their social or professional lives. It provided those who were averse to engaging in high-risk activism and criminality in the real world the chance to experiment with extreme ideas in the safety of an anonymous online world.[16] This allowed extremists more freedom than ever before to discuss and ask questions about what were often seen as taboo subjects, while also granting a veneer of authority and legitimacy to users who wished to pose as experts and ideologues.[17] Online anonymity can contribute to what the psychologist and expert on online behavior John Suler has called the "online disinhibition" effect. This phenomenon allows internet users to avoid responsibility for their virtual pronouncements while also testing out new ideas. As they test these ideas out, extremists may find an audience which sympathizes with and supports them, thus giving a false sense of the existence of a critical mass in the real world. In its most toxic form, online disinhibition can engender an increase in hostility, polarization, and even violence.[18]

Similar to the static websites, in 2010 public scrutiny around these forums began to increase, leading to their infiltration by counterterrorism agencies and large-scale shutdowns of the most popular among them. Users became increasingly weary of the true identities of fellow forum members, and forum administrators conducted mass culls of users they believed were behaving suspiciously. Many forums imploded as a result of growing paranoia and, somewhat counterintuitively, online jihadists began looking at more open and publicly available forms of communication.

Instead of driving online jihadist networks further underground, the squeezing of the forums sent them out into the open during a time when social media networking sites began emerging. This use of social media made online jihadist activism far more accessible to the general public. It also meant that the traditional relationship between mainstream media and violent actors was reversed—with the former now relying more on the latter's social media output for information gathering, and terrorist groups no longer requiring the mainstream media to disseminate information.[19]

Jihadist groups quickly recognized the potential of online social networking sites, and these platforms maximized the accessibility of their content and linked sympathetic users with group members. The full utility of social media to the jihad movement was realized during the early stages of the Syrian conflict. Twitter in particular became crucial to the recruitment of jihadists in Europe who left their homes to join ISIS and other jihadist groups fighting the Syrian regime.

The opportunities created by these technologies and the interconnectivity between these platforms optimized networking among like-minded extremists. For groups like ISIS, an active command of the digital landscape was instrumental in establishing global recognition. ISIS and its media department embraced the ubiquity and growing popularity of these new technologies, which offered them access to a range of new audiences, strategically shifting away from hierarchical websites and forums.[20] With expansive networks of communications, ISIS managed to combine the efforts of both official members of the group who were using the platform with those of highly motivated sympathizers and fellow travelers to advance its propaganda efforts.[21] This further increased the pool of talent the group could draw upon, while incurring almost no risk or financial cost. Ultimately, by coordinating distribution of pro-ISIS materials, and weaving together influential messages and mediums, ISIS built what one of the leading experts in ISIS online activity, Nico Prucha, refers to as a "multiplatform zeitgeist" that allowed the group to inject its ideas into conversations across many digital networks.[22]

In addition to ISIS' technical finesse, the organization's production of media in multiple languages, including English, made the group all the more accessible to supporters around the world.[23] This overarching method helped facilitate a global movement, posing a threat that defied borders, to push and pull actors both inside and outside of ISIS-controlled territory to rally for the cause. Likely inspired by a range of factors, sympathizers in America enthusiastically heeded ISIS' calls to action.

ISIS online propaganda has also been able to appeal to a range of interested parties. Although formal propaganda by the group gained notoriety for its displays of extreme violence, materials produced by ISIS and its sympathizers traditionally cover a range of themes. Surprisingly, given the nature of most media coverage on ISIS propaganda, studies have repeatedly found that depictions of executions and other harsh punishments make up a relatively small percentage of the group's overall output.[24] In *Communication Breakdown*, a study by the Combating Terrorism Center at West Point, scholars specifically analyzed ISIS' strategic output between January 2015 and August 2016.[25] The study parses such materials into six thematic categories: military, governance, commercial, religious, lifestyles, and other topics.[26] ISIS' apparatus of communications emphasized its efforts in multiple arenas, reaching far beyond fear-inducing propaganda videos. Moreover, official English-language ISIS magazines like *Dabiq*, and later *Rumiyah*, employed a wide range of narratives in order to ensure that it could reach out to and find resonance with the interests and concerns of a broad range of potential supporters and recruits.[27] In this way, ISIS' top-down communications efforts made the group's activities accessible, and empowered supporters around the world.

While ISIS and its more formal organizational associates created and spread strategic propaganda products, the movement's increasingly extensive web of online sympathizers responded to ISIS' calls to action, and also created their own content.[28] In the digital sphere especially, supporters advanced the aims of the group by disseminating existing media, workshopping their own materials, and engaging in discourse with other supporters in both public and private channels.[29] With communications technologies fusing the top-down components with the bottom-up mobilization, the entirety of the network became more than the sum of its parts.

Among the first studies to demonstrate how influential ISIS supporters were using social media to encourage Westerners to join the group came from King's College London, in which researchers drew from a database of Twitter accounts used by English-speaking ISIS members and supporters to show how the platform was being used to establish webs through which they could connect with one another and with "disseminators." These Western-based leadership figures used Twitter to present themselves as legitimate Islamic scholars and formulate convincing extremist narratives justifying support for ISIS and encouraging foreign fighter travel. They were able to build up a large base of followers as a result, providing them with real-time updates from ISIS contacts in far-away battles, and soon became major sources of conflict information for foreign fighters.[30] Ali Fisher and Nico Prucha found in a 2013 study that Twitter was serving as a gateway to other less publicly accessible extremist material hosted on relatively unknown file-sharing sites. This made it one of the main hubs for access to propaganda hosted on a range of other platforms.[31]

Studies such as this contributed to an increased awareness among social media companies of the extent of extremist exploitation of their platforms. In response, they began to both review their terms of service and more strictly enforce them. Over the last few years, this has led to the large-scale removal of ISIS-related accounts and the implementation of various initiatives aimed at countering extremist use of social media, which will be discussed in more depth in Chapter 6. While these efforts were certainly successful in significantly reducing extremist activity on open platforms, there were also some unintended consequences. These efforts happened to coincide with the proliferation and increased accessibility of encryption technologies and the so-called "dark web." As is so often the case, these new opportunities did not go amiss for entrepreneurial extremists.

From Twitter to Telegram

By 2017, as researchers, government authorities, and major technology companies became increasingly aware of the presence of ISIS on open social media platforms, the group's members and supporters began seeking out other avenues for online activism. Not only were many being arrested after being identified, but they also found that their accounts were being shut down at an increasingly rapid pace. This growing scrutiny inadvertently played a role in pushing them on to less transparent, more secure online mediums. These included the anonymous internet browser Tor and the encrypted email service ProtonMail, along with a range of apps that offered end-to-end encryption such as Telegram, Surespot, Kik, and WhatsApp.[32]

Telegram, an application which allows for fully encrypted chats between users, is particularly significant in the context of the ISIS presence in America; it has not only become the most important encrypted communications platform for the group, but since 2015 has also been used to recruit and guide jihadist plotters throughout the West.[33] In their study of ISIS-related terrorism in Europe, Petter Nesser and his co-authors discovered that out of 38 ISIS plots and attacks in Europe between 2014 and October 2016, 19 were found to have involved "online instruction from members of ISIS's networks."[34] Although various digital communications remain relevant, they explain that "the ways in which attackers are instructed via encrypted social media are unprecedented."

In the face of territorial losses on the ground in Iraq and Syria, and compounded by increasing regulation by technology providers, it is clear that ISIS and its supporters are not immune to pressures in the physical or digital arenas. Indeed, this can also be measured to some extent. Research has already found that online communications and activity are fundamentally linked to real-world events, and that the success of the ISIS media arm is dependent on how things shape up for the group on the battlefield.[35]

Twitter's content moderation and regulation policies, in combination with a strategic shift by supporters to closed forums, facilitated an exodus of English-speaking online ISIS supporters to Telegram.[36] Unlike Twitter, Telegram offers users four different communication options: end-to-end encrypted chats and voice calls, groups of up to 100,000 members, and channels, wherein one user broadcasts messages to an unlimited number of followers.[37] It also offers a broadened range of media file-sharing options. The company behind Telegram, founded by the Russian technology entrepreneurs Pavel and Nikolai Durov, uses a distributed data infrastructure to house data in multiple facilities worldwide, and has pledged to share "zero bytes of user data" with governments.[38] These features, as well as Telegram's commitment to online privacy and security, are understandably attractive for ISIS supporters looking to exploit digital communications services. Substantiating this observation is the finding that operational security guides were a common form of instructional material posted on pro-ISIS Telegram channels, along with tactical information about attack planning.[39]

Indeed, the sharing of files in and of itself, something which Telegram helps to facilitate, tends to receive far less attention than it should given how important a dissemination tool this is for ISIS propagandists. While Telegram is used to host files, it is also a useful platform on which to provide links to external file-sharing sites where ISIS supporters can access the group's latest media release. These releases, in particular the videos, can be up to 1.5GB, meaning that they can only be shared on sites that specialize in transferring such large files. The top five most popular external file-sharing sites among ISIS supporters in our Telegram dataset are archive.org, YouTube, Justpaste.it, Top4top.net, and Google Drive.[40]

Two of these may come as something of a surprise. Given Google's efforts to respond to extremist use of their platforms, they would surely be disappointed to see YouTube and Google Drive on this list. However, while the big tech companies are often the focus of discussions about extremist use of the internet, file-sharing companies have yet to face similar scrutiny. This is likely to do with the rather unglamorous nature of the platforms, which have no social media component and can be very dry and technical. Archive.org, also known as The Internet Archive, is undoubtedly one of the most important file-sharing services for ISIS propagandists and, unlike other similar platforms, is a nonprofit entity. Its mission is to "provide Universal Access to All Knowledge," and it works to achieve this by "building a digital library of Internet sites and other cultural artifacts in digital form."[41] Of course, the site plays host to countless documents, video and audio related to a wide array of topics, and extremist material makes up only a fraction of the millions of files found on it. This makes it harder to' control the content; even if they were looking for extremist material to remove they may struggle to come across it. Relatedly, the staffing sizes of file-sharing websites like The Internet Archive pale in comparison to the tech giants and, even if they wanted to address extremist use of their platform, they simply do not have the personnel or budgets required to continuously monitor and remove extremist content.

The existence of a large and ever-expanding market of file-sharing websites means that, even if the major companies do succeed in cleansing their platforms of ISIS materials, it is likely these will remain accessible online for some time yet. While access may become slightly more complicated, those who truly want to view it will always find a way. Much will instead depend on the legislation that Western states enact in coming years, which may seek to further criminalize the accessing, downloading, and viewing of such materials, an issue which we discuss in more depth in the concluding chapter of this book.

It is beyond any doubt, then, that the wide and expanding range of digital communications technologies, and the myriad options they afford, create virtual spaces for extremists to share their views, promote ISIS, disseminate information and create social networks. Conventionally, some platforms are conducive to extremist activity whereas other tools are more regulated and inhospitable to ISIS supporters. Before it began to rigorously enforce its terms of service, Twitter was once the ideal platform for American ISIS supporters seeking to quickly inject themselves into networks of like-minded people, some of whom could assist them in traveling to the Islamic State or attack planning back home.[42] Encrypted services like Telegram, meanwhile, allowed the most committed extremists to take their conversations to unregulated platforms where they could discuss sensitive details about travel or attack plans. Extremist users of these platforms have, however, relied heavily on the facilities offered by numerous file-sharing and archiving sites, which continue to offer largely unregulated platforms to share huge volumes of materials. In order to better understand how some of these dynamics play out, the remainder of this chapter will focus on specific cases of American ISIS supporters, and the various ways they have deployed the communications technologies at their disposal.

American ISIS E-Activists

The influence of digital communications technologies permeated almost every aspect of ISIS sympathizers' operations in the United States. Throughout every sub-category of American ISIS supporter profiled in this book, individual ISIS "e-activists" made innovative uses of social media, file-sharing, and encrypted instant messaging to promote ISIS' cause. While many used various technologies towards various ends, there is utility in breaking down some of the common trends. Following the other chapters of this book, this section identifies how the three other areas of support (travel, attacks, and propaganda) were impacted by the advent of new digital communications technologies, and also assesses their impact on a fourth area of support: terrorism financing.

Technology and Travel

Given their lack of access to the on-the-ground networks that helped Europeans make the journey to the Islamic State, new communications technologies also have proven to be a critical logistical tool for Americans seeking to join the group. Although digital communications technologies are an integral part of most people's efforts to travel to ISIS-controlled territory, individuals make different considerations to achieve operational security along the way. The case of Mohamad Jamal Khweis, a bus driver from Northern Virginia who traveled to Syria to join ISIS in late 2015, is one of the best examples of how technological expertise and discipline can often be enough to plan a successful journey to ISIS.[43]

On February 3, 2017, just days after taking part in the military operation that removed ISIS from Mosul in Iraq, Colonel Arkan of the Kurdish allied forces fighting the group began searching through a pile of papers in one of the ISIS office buildings found in the city. As he sifted through the documents, one piece of information caught his eye. It was a paper containing details of an ISIS recruit named Abu Omar al-Amriki. The colonel, who had years of experience in fighting alongside American forces, was regularly on the lookout for information that would be useful to American intelligence. Any ISIS member with a *kunya* that ended in al-Amriki ("the American") was to be taken very seriously. On the spreadsheet detailing the recruit's personal information, he also found his real name: Mohamad Jamal Amin Khweis. Under the category of "current mission" was written *muqatil*, Arabic for "fighter."[44]

Nearly a year before this find, which would serve as a critical piece of evidence in Khweis' trial, Peshmerga forces in Northern Iraq arrested a young American who, it was later revealed, was Khweis.[45] He had fled ISIS some days earlier and handed himself in to Kurdish forces. After spending over two months in Kurdish custody and being interrogated by the FBI, he was extradited to the US to face charges of fighting for a designated foreign terrorist organization.[46] He reportedly told no one of his plans before he left, was largely influenced by his online activities, and was not involved in any known physical jihadist networks in the US. Khweis made this trip at a time when the online activities of Western ISIS supporters were beginning to receive increased levels of scrutiny. As a result, he took extraordinary measures to mask his communications and movements. This makes the case a particularly useful one to unpack as it reveals how Americans were able to use technology, including the latest encryption and location-masking apps, to join ISIS.[47] Through his use of a suite of online tools, Khweis was able to plot his route into ISIS territory apparently without any outside assistance until he reached the Turkish border with Syria.

Less clear, however, are Khweis' motivations for joining ISIS. Unlike other cases analyzed in this book, there is little evidence that Khweis experienced any semblance of a religious awakening. During his trial, he claimed that he was not devout, rarely prayed, and had even been drinking alcohol while making his way to ISIS territory.[48] Some insight, however, can be gained through an analysis of a series of interviews Khweis gave to the FBI while still in Kurdish custody in Erbil, Iraq.

During these discussions, Khweis explained both why and how he joined ISIS in Syria, including an admission that he had agreed to become a suicide bomber for the group. He recounted how, while still in America, he was an avid consumer of the group's propaganda, including the video depicting the burning alive of Jordanian pilot Muath al-Kasasbeh.[49] He also viewed numerous sermons from well-known English-language jihadist preachers, including Abdullah Faisal, Anwar al-Awlaki, and Ahmad Musa Jibril.[50] According to one of the agents who conducted these early interviews, Khweis' inspiration to join ISIS was driven by his desire to be part of the establishment of the caliphate. This was despite being aware of ISIS involvement in overseas terrorism, including the November 2015 Paris attacks, which took place just a month before Khweis left to join the group.

While the evidence strongly suggests that Khweis was sympathetic to ISIS, and he was found in possession of phones containing numerous pieces of the group's propaganda, he also later claimed during his trial that he believed aspects of ISIS' ideology went against Islam. These perspectives represented a significant part of his defense, in which he argued that he disagreed with ISIS' use of violence, had joined the group out of curiosity and was forced to agree to become a suicide bomber out of fear for his life rather than due to his deep commitment to the organization.[51] Further contributing to the lack of clarity surrounding Khweis' motivations was his evasiveness during discussions with the FBI. The agents noted in the trial that he changed his story on a number of occasions. For example, on the subject of his agreeing to be a suicide bomber, he first claimed he did so to prove his commitment to the group and only later made the claim that he agreed out of fear. He also initially claimed to the FBI that he had "given" himself to the group.[52] It "controlled" him and he would have acted on orders he received from superiors whether or not he agreed with them.[53] Later on during his trial, however, Khweis testified that he traveled to ISIS territory to satisfy his curiosity about a group he had been researching for many months. During cross-examination, he claimed that:

> I wanted to go to the Islamic State, the caliphate, and see for myself how it is, how are people living there, and one day tell my kids, I have been there. You know, it's not all like it seems . . . I just wanted to, you know, just share with them like history, like places, places I have been.[54]

Considering that Khweis had mounted a vigorous defense after his "not guilty" plea, it is difficult to determine why he joined ISIS. His assertions denying his support for the group during the trial must be seen in this context, while also not being dismissed out of hand. Among the claims that were not disputed by the prosecution was that he was not profoundly ideological and had no links to a wider jihadist network. However, there is irrefutable evidence that he was in possession of a wide array of ISIS propaganda, had traveled to ISIS territory in the full knowledge of its role as an international terror group that was targeting the US, and had willingly gone through the official ISIS intake process for all new recruits. Like many similar stories of ISIS recruitment, there may never be a fully comprehensive account of what drove Khweis to join.

The details of Khweis' journey, however, are much clearer. After approximately a year of planning, one of the first steps he took once he decided to make the trip was to sell his car to help both pay off his credit card debts and finance his travel.[55] While it may seem a strange priority, these credit card payments were likely a diversion to distract investigators from his plans, by suggesting that he intended to return to America and continue his life. According to the FBI, this is a common tactic among both successful and unsuccessful ISIS travelers.[56] He also created the first of several new email addresses that he would use during his journey. Within minutes of setting this account up, he used it to book his flights from the US to Turkey.[57]

On December 16, 2015, Khweis, equipped with five cellular phones and a laptop, took the Iceland-based budget transatlantic airline WOW Air from Baltimore–Washington International Airport, via Iceland to London Gatwick.[58] While at the airport in London, he attempted to contact a well-known British extremist and member of the al-Muhajiroun network named Abu Bara'a, but he did not receive a response.[59] From Gatwick, he flew to Amsterdam, where he spent two days staying in the city's red-light district. His final flight was from Amsterdam to Istanbul.[60]

While still in America, Khweis also purchased a separate ticket for a flight from Istanbul to Greece which, like Mo's ticket to Italy, he never intended to use.[61] Instead, he hoped it would mask his final destination from any suspicious border or law enforcement agencies. This also explains the circuitous route he took through Europe on his way to Turkey, which helped him avoid any undue attention from authorities. While in Turkey, he booked a flight back to Washington, D.C. which he never boarded. This step was yet another effort to conceal his intentions and give the impression that he planned to return home after an innocent trip.[62]

Upon his arrival in Istanbul on December 20, Khweis took a bus to Gaziantep.[63] While in the border town, Khweis created another email address with the name "Zach K."[64] He used this to set up two Facebook accounts, and a Twitter profile using the handle @fearislove1, which he intended to leverage to contact ISIS members who could facilitate his travel into Syria.[65] One of his two Facebook accounts was set up using a non-existent email address, again a standard tactic for ISIS travelers attempting to mask their identity.

Khweis' new email address was also used to set up an Apple ID which he used to download a variety of secure messaging applications he hoped would help him speak with ISIS members and mask his location and online activity. Between the time of his arrival in Turkey and his crossing of the border into Syria, he downloaded a host of apps that were based on encrypted communication and masking online activity including Kik, Surespot, Telegram, VPN Master, VPN Defender, VPN InTouch, and a Tor browser called VPN Browser.[66] Following his passage into ISIS-controlled territory, he continued expanding his digital toolbox. Among the apps he downloaded in Syria were secure/encrypted calling applications, including Vodafone Secure Call, VIVA Secured Call, Cryptotel, and Secure Video Calls Free.[67] He also used an app called Snaptube to download ISIS videos from YouTube, including videos of executions and mass graves.[68]

After four days of trying to contact ISIS members using his new Twitter account, he had gained little traction and decided to create a second account with a name that was more explicit in its support for the group: the username "Greenbird" with the handle @iAGreenBirdiA.[69] As Khweis would later admit to FBI interrogators and in court, the names were an open advertisement to online ISIS recruiters of his sympathy for the group and his desire to die fighting for it. The "iA" is an acronym for the Arabic term *inshallah*, meaning "God willing," while "GreenBird" refers to the belief that people who die fighting for ISIS are martyred and turn into green birds for their ascent to heaven. One of the agents who interrogated Khweis testified in court that he "acknowledged that [ISIS] and other violent terrorist groups use this to reference martyrdom, violent jihad, suicide bombing."[70]

Using his new Twitter account, he reached out to at least three different Twitter users whom he had identified as actively assisting people who wanted to travel to Syria and join ISIS. The first responded to his request for help by telling him "I am a sister," suggesting that she was only able to interact with and help other women.[71]

An account named "Mad Mullah" (@martenyiii) eventually helped Khweis.[72] The account's biographical information stated that the user was based in Syria and offered advice on *hijra* and other matters related to ISIS. Subsequent investigations by the authors have found that this account was involved in helping at least one other person travel to join the group.[73] This account also interacted on Twitter with Shawn Parson (Abu Khalid al-Amriki), a Trinidadian national who fought for ISIS and appeared in one of the group's recruitment videos targeted at other Trinidadians.[74]

On December 25, Khweis sent a direct message to Mad Mullah: "Salaam akhi [brother] do u have Telegram?"[75] He was then asked to move their conversation to the encrypted messaging application. On this app, Khweis was told to download a second similar encrypted messaging application to which they moved and proceeded to have a detailed conversation about arranging Khweis' safe passage into Syria.[76] This three-tiered communication approach—from Twitter, to Telegram and finally to a third encrypted messenger application—demonstrates the length to which ISIS members were going to hide their tracks online, making it very difficult for authorities to track their activities in real time.

This example mirrors the tradecraft of ISIS travelers attempting to avoid detection online as they plan their route to the caliphate and reach out to ISIS recruiters and facilitators. This approach appears to have worked in Khweis' case. Based on the information currently available, Khweis' interest in ISIS and his trip to join the group was completely unknown to authorities until his arrest by Kurdish forces in March 2016. Khweis' journey was only uncovered after his arrest, when he informed the FBI of his online activity and usernames. Despite volunteering this information, authorities do not appear to have been able to access the encrypted discussions Khweis had on Telegram and other similar applications.

Khweis was staying in his hotel room in Gaziantep when he contacted Mad Mullah. Later that day, he received a call telling him to meet with ISIS smugglers outside the hotel. Khweis left Gaziantep in a taxi, continued on foot across the border, and then traveled into ISIS-held territory in an SUV.[77] He was joined by other new recruits, including, according to his own account, three men from Paris who claimed to have been inspired by the recent attacks in the city.[78] During the journey they were instructed to put their phones on airplane mode and, if possible, remove the batteries to avoid possible detection.[79] Similar to Mo's account, they too were stopped by Turkish police near the border but were released after negotiations between the police and the taxi driver.[80] After their release, Khweis successfully reached an ISIS training camp in Syria.

Technology, Attacks, and Cyber Operations

In the second chapter of this book, we examined the role that new communications technologies played in planning and executing physical terrorist attacks in the United States. To a limited extent, American ISIS supporters also attempted to use technology to conduct offensive cyber operations. However, their capabilities remain rudimentary at best.[81] While in one case, ISIS-affiliated hackers successfully breached a company's website to retrieve personally identifiable information of US military servicepeople, most ISIS hacktivists used techniques that relied on open-source information, such as identifying accounts on social media that had fallen out of use, accessing them and turning them into ISIS dissemination platforms.[82]

The efforts of the Junaid Hussain-led ISIS Hacking Division were the basis for most American e-activists' endeavors in cyber operations. In August 2015, weeks before his eventual death, Junaid Hussain posted a link to a document on his Twitter account. The document contained personally identifiable information for over 1,300 members of the US military, along with a message:

Target United States Government And Military – The Head of The Crusader Coalition

Hack US Military And Government Emails, Passwords, Names, Phone Numbers and Location Information Leaked

Peace Be Upon The One Who Follows True Guidance O Crusaders, as you continue your agression towards the Islamic State and your bombing campaign against the muslims, know that we are in your emails and computer systems, watching and recording your every move, we have your names and addresses, we are in your emails and social media accounts, we are extracting confidential data and passing on your personal information to the soldiers of the khilafah, who soon with the permission of Allah will strike at your necks in your own lands! "So wait; we too are waiting" – Islamic State Hacking Division.[83]

This message was followed by the personal details of more than 1,300 individuals from the US military, including full names, email addresses, email passwords, cities of residence and phone numbers. This, it would later be revealed, was the work of Ardit Ferizi, a citizen of Kosovo living in Malaysia, who passed illegally obtained information about US Government personnel to virtual entrepreneur Junaid Hussain in 2015.[84]

As early as April 2015, Ferizi supported ISIS by acting as an administrator for Penvid.com, a platform housing extremist videos and content like *Dabiq*, one of ISIS' official English-language magazines.[85] After the website was removed for its links to terrorism, and promotion of violence and criminal activity, Ferizi defended ISIS, the website, and his beliefs against critics on Twitter.[86] On April 26, 2015, Ferizi provided members of ISIS, including a British ISIS fighter named Hamayun Tariq, with "what appeared to be" personally identifiable information "belonging to people living in the United States and abroad."[87]

Later that year, in June 2015, Ferizi obtained high-level access to a server hosting the website of a company in Illinois without authorization, accessing information on "tens of thousands" of the company's customers.[88] After parsing out employees with designated US Government and US military email addresses, ending in ".gov" and ".mil," Ferizi amassed personal information belonging to approximately 1,300 people.[89] Ferizi shared the data with Junaid Hussain.[90] While Hussain had since become infamous for being an ISIS virtual entrepreneur, he first gained notoriety in 2011 for hacking Former British Prime Minister Tony Blair's address book, and posting it online for the hacking group "TeaMp0isoN."[91] In fact, court filings reveal that Ferizi was "associated with Hussain" when Hussain assumed the alias "TriCk," and worked with "TeaMp0isoN."[92]

From June to August, Ferizi continued to access the company's server without authorization and maintained communications with Hussain.[93] In August 2015, acting as a member of the Islamic State Hacking Division, Hussain shared communications on Twitter that contained the information Ferizi had shared with him.[94] About two months later, Malaysian authorities arrested Ferizi on a US provisional arrest warrant; US officials charged Ferizi with providing material support to ISIS and "computer hacking related to the theft and distribution of US military and federal employee personal information."[95] In September 2016, then Assistant Attorney General for National Security John Carlin commented on Ferizi's case, explaining that it "represents the first time we have seen the very real and dangerous national security cyber threat that results from the combination of terrorism and hacking."[96] Ferizi received a 20-year prison sentence for his actions.[97]

After Ferizi's arrest and Hussain's death, a smattering of unofficial ISIS hacking affiliates emerged, with varying and sometimes tenuous ties to the central organization. Largely recruiting their members from hacktivist circles, a new type of American e-activist became attracted to the ISIS cause. These unofficial groups largely followed the techniques, tactics, and procedures of Junaid Hussain's Islamic State Hacking Division. Through low-level intrusions, they engaged in two tactics: unauthorized dissemination of personally identifying information (also called doxing) and taking down or altering websites and social media accounts (defacement).[98] Lora Shiao, NCTC Acting Director for Intelligence, commented in 2017 that ISIS had "minimal hacking skills" but were nonetheless "able to deface websites" and "put out 'hit lists' of personally identifiable information on westerners, but this is primarily for intimidation. It's not a key strength for them."[99]

Hussain's death led to the end of the Islamic State Hacking Division, and the formal effort quickly devolved into a number of individual hacking collectives. In April 2016, several informal pro-ISIS collectives merged into one organization, which they referred to as the United Cyber Caliphate (UCC).[100] The UCC and its sub-groups' efforts followed Ferizi and Hussain's *modus operandi*: publish kill lists of Americans based on information collected during rudimentary intrusions and open-source intelligence.[101] In July 2017, an American member of the Kalachnikv E-Security Team, one of the groups under the UCC's banner, contacted the FBI and requested an interview. What the hacktivist told the FBI peeled back the curtain on many of the operations of ISIS' unofficial hacking teams, their capabilities, and their reach into the United States.

The hacktivist, a 20-year-old Georgia woman named Kim Anh Vo, went by "F@ng," "SyxxZMC," "Zozo," "Miss.Bones," "Sage Pi," "Kitty Lee," and other names online.[102] Between 2016 and 2017, Vo provided services to the UCC after her hacking group merged into the conglomerate. Vo's responsibilities included recruiting other Western hackers and hacktivists to join ISIS' cause, working with a larger team to translate UCC media releases into English, and reporting successful defacements of websites by the UCC's hackers.[103] Vo told the FBI that most of the senior leadership for her team was based in Iraq, and in conversations with other team members, she claimed that her group's leadership were "individuals that been with former Junaid Hussain. In hacking before he was announced shaheed [martyr]."[104] After one senior leader "disappeared," Vo claims that she was nominated to head her team, but eventually declined the nomination.[105] Overall,

Vo believed becoming a leader of the team would lead to unnecessary attention from law enforcement, as evidenced by the executions, arrests, and deaths of its personnel in several countries. After hearing that one UCC leader was scheduled to be executed in an unnamed country, Vo asked an FBI undercover agent to issue this message in response:

> In the name of Allah, who is the most gracious and merciful. A very important reminder for all of our beloved brothers and sisters. Do not be sad and plunge yourselves into sorrow. [Unnamed Co-Conspirator], Junaid Hussein, [Unnamed Co-Conspirator], and [Unnamed Co-Conspirator] have won victory over the enemies who drill in the path of the righteousness. The brothers have fought among the tyrant leaders of the world with their courageousness; one that allows himself to face all obstacles and danger in front. The Islamic state cyber division has not lost. Drone us as much you can infidels! By the next morning you will find another kind of us ready to wage war of Jihad! This isn't something new to us. We pledge to Abu Bakr Al-Baghdadi the Islamic state will expand in regions across the seven seas. O' you infidels do not think this is the end. There will be blood today, tomorrow and until your last breath.[106]

As part of her responsibilities for the UCC, Vo was also tasked with recruiting new Western members for the group's activities, as most of the leadership could not communicate in English. In December 2016, she began recruiting two unnamed co-conspirators: a 14-year-old minor living in Norway and a Dutch man.[107] Using Telegram to communicate, the three coordinated the release of a new "kill list," including information on over 8,000 residents of New York City that was illegally obtained by the UCC through hacking a website.[108] They also published a video on YouTube threatening a New York-area non-profit dedicated to countering ISIS' use of social media.[109] After Norwegian and Dutch law enforcement arrest her co-conspirators in March and June of 2017, respectively, Vo volunteered for an interview with the FBI. She was charged in March 2019 with conspiring to provide material support to ISIS.[110]

Beyond "kill lists" and defacing websites, ISIS e-activists viewed defacements of social media as especially important in light of several social media companies' efforts to remove ISIS supporters from their platforms. Rather than create new accounts, American e-activists led campaigns to hack into and take over existing ones. In June 2018 Waheba Issa Dais, a Wisconsin woman, was charged with attempting to provide material support to ISIS. Dais aided the group by promoting its agenda, "facilitating recruitment ... and maintaining a virtual library of instructions on how to make bombs, poison, and suicide vests" to assist attack planning.[111] She used many social media platforms, including Facebook and Twitter, to disseminate pro-ISIS propaganda and incite violence among her followers.[112] As a means of facilitating her support of ISIS, Dais hacked into several old accounts on Facebook, and made them her own.[113]

After taking over each private Facebook account, Dais tailored it by "changing the profile picture, friends list, and display name." Dais utilized a specific profile picture throughout all of her hijacked accounts; a professionally shot photo "of a young girl wearing a blue dress."[114] On a tactical level, she used this method to bypass Facebook's efforts to disrupt the flow of information Dais was sharing when the company shut down each profile.[115] According to "open source searches and information provided by Facebook," Dais, and those communicating with her, "used hacked Facebook accounts as a way to avoid law enforcement detection of their communications."[116] She exchanged private messages with a number of people, including an undercover employee of the FBI, in an attempt to provide them with information on how to better support ISIS.[117]

Through private messaging, Dais used her hacked Facebook accounts to encourage interested followers to visit a separate social media channel, likely on Telegram, where they could find videos and guides on creating poison, and on bomb-making.[118] She advised one follower to learn how to make ricin, a naturally occurring poison, and provided him with the necessary means to do so.[119] While easy to manufacture, ricin can be "lethal to the touch," making it an attractive mode of operation for Dais to recommend.[120] Dais was arrested on June 13, 2018 and pleaded guilty in April 2019. She faces up to 20 years in prison.[121]

Technology and Propaganda

American ISIS sympathizers, based both in the US and in ISIS territory, often use technology to assist in disseminating the group's propaganda and furthering its strategic aims in the West. They do this through a variety of means. In rare cases, some American ISIS supporters use their technological skills to find new ways to ensure the wide accessibility and dissemination of ISIS propaganda. More commonly, however, they use social media and digital communications technologies to attract fellow Americans by disseminating propaganda, praising acts of ISIS-inspired violence in the West, and making calls to action. This type of bottom-up grassroots propaganda production and dissemination has become a main feature of ISIS activism in America and has helped to maintain its presence and ensure the output remains accessible and relevant to the lives of its American audience.

In some instances, ISIS sympathizers choose to stay in the US, seeing themselves as ideally placed to contribute to the group's recruitment efforts by publicly vocalizing their support and calling for targeted attacks online over broad-based social media platforms. In February 2016, authorities arrested Safya Yassin, a Missouri resident, for transmitting threats online to murder federal government employees.[122] Although Yassin maintained different Facebook, Google+, and Twitter accounts, the offense leading to her arrest occurred on Twitter, when Yassin shared personal information about two FBI agents with the caption, "Wanted to Kill."[123]

Yassin had initially come to the attention of the FBI in January 2015 as a result of a complaint made to the agency's Public Access Line (known as PAL) by a member of the public. They claimed to have known her for several years after striking up an online friendship via Facebook, during the course of which Yassin convinced them to convert to Islam. In the first years of their conversations, she expressed moderate, mainstream Islamic views; however, since the rise of ISIS, the friend told the FBI that Yassin had begun to take much more extreme and uncompromising positions. She had also, according to her friend, become convinced that ISIS was "going to save the world" and that it was her mission to further its goals in America.[124]

Subsequent investigations by the FBI uncovered multiple social media accounts linked to Yassin that were engaged in, as one of her Facebook accounts described it, "disseminating information" related to ISIS.[125] They also found that she was making little to no effort to hide her true identity, using her real name or close variations of it in her various usernames and email addresses linked to her accounts. She also included pictures of herself on her Facebook page, which the FBI used to formally identify her by matching them to her driver's license records. In private messages found on Yassin's phone when seized by police following her arrest, it was also revealed that she was using Telegram to discuss with a fellow ISIS contact how easy it was for the group's supporters to purchase firearms while lamenting the failure of American Muslims, in particular men, to take fuller advantage of this. It is worth reproducing parts of this conversation in full in order to better understand how Yassin saw her role in spreading propaganda online, along with inciting and helping to plan attacks:

Safya Yassin "They're [guns] pretty much everywhere in USA. I can go to flea market tomorrow and buy one. LOL."

Contact "I can't believe that."

SY "No background checks."

C "You're in a Muslim haven. That is what Muslims wish for. Not Murtadeen [apostates], G[uns] everywhere."

SY "And all these men here and very little attacked."

C "Kuffar everywhere, perfect mix."

SY "I met Muslim men everywhere and hardly any attacks."

C "Unfortunately, yeah."

SY "It makes me so sick. Like get off Twitter and do something. My posts are directed at men and Jihad a lot."

C "I know. So sad."

SY "Trying to incite."

C "Number one enemy."

SY "Yes."

C "NG everywhere. Come on. So, many bars."

SY   "LOL. That's how I feel. It's ridiculous."

C   "So many gay parades, so many Jews."

SY   "I have thought of many things and places. LOL."

C   "So many police and vets."

SY   "I have toured many too."

C   "Hee, hee, hee."

SY   "I know every synagogue where I live and most cities. LOL."

As discussed in the previous chapter, research on female Western ISIS members has demonstrated that, on the whole, they perform auxiliary roles in support of jihad.[126] Yassin's comments here and elsewhere certainly suggest this was the case for her. Through using technology to spread ISIS propaganda from her home in Missouri, Yassin was primarily concerned with encouraging and supporting the violent acts of men and identifying possible tactics and targets for attack. In her public Twitter posts, she also often focused on calling upon Muslim men in America to fulfill their duty of jihad, with messages such as "a sincere request from our Muslimah [female Muslim women]: The Ummah Needs men of action not hashtags."[127]

One of the first public calls to violence she made was in May 2015. During this time, an anti-Muslim protest march under the banner of "Freedom of Speech" was being planned in response to the ISIS-inspired attack in Garland, Texas earlier that month. The organizers planned to protest outside of the Islamic Community Center in Phoenix, Arizona, which was reportedly attended by the plotters.[128] On the day of the rally, Yassin used one of her Twitter accounts, @Mu5limah_o01, to draw attention to the rally among her ISIS-supporting followers, writing, "they are only getting bolder because no one was killed at their last event, but if it goes the other way ... they have courage now, but if a backpack was left at the scene w/ nothing in it, you would have a stampede. . ."[129] This post, while avoiding any direct threats, was an early, experimental, and subversive injection of violence into the discussions about how American Muslims might respond to anti-Muslim activism in their country. Yassin was likely testing to see the responses of her followers and using these to gauge how to more explicitly call for violence in future posts. This post prompted the FBI to interview Yassin about her online activity in support of ISIS in June 2015. While she complied and answered all of their questions, she denied any support for ISIS when shown examples of her posts, including ones depicting children with ISIS flags. She also denied any intent to travel to join ISIS or incite violence in America.[130]

This brush with the authorities, however, did little to dampen Yassin's enthusiastic online support of ISIS activities and propaganda. Her regular explicit support for ISIS led to regular suspensions of her social media accounts for breaching terms of service but this too did little to dissuade her. In response, she continued to set up new accounts, particularly on Twitter; shortly before her arrest, the FBI identified approximately 97 Twitter accounts that were "likely" linked to Yassin.[131] Despite using so many accounts, Yassin appeared to almost always use a variation of the word "Muslimah" (female Muslim) for her Twitter username. This made it relatively easy for the FBI to track her new accounts, along with her use of similar profile pictures (a small green "Twitter" bird icon) and a banner picture of a road sign with "Dabiq" written across it.[132] She also often poked fun at the platform for failing to silence her, while suggesting that Twitter's efforts to shut down pro-ISIS accounts were further proof of an anti-Muslim bias in the West: "Twitter suspends thousands of Muslim accounts in 48 hours. Then … everyone comes right back within 2 minutes."[133]

Yassin was being regularly kicked off of Twitter for a reason: her posts were becoming increasingly extreme and violent. In July, just a month after the visit from the FBI, she tweeted in support of what at the time appeared to be an ISIS-inspired shooting in Chattanooga, Tennessee, in which an American citizen named Mohammad Youssef Abdulazeez killed four US Marines and a Navy sailor.[134] Alongside a picture of two of the victims she suggested that the attack was a legitimate act of revenge because of US military actions in Muslim-majority countries: "both participated in slaughtering Muslim babies."[135] Shortly after this, she also posted encouragements for her followers to murder non-believers by beheading them, stating that "Americans aren't even smart enough to know where to cut on a neck" and posting a picture of a torso and neck with a dotted line over the throat accompanied by the words "cut here."

Then, in August, Yassin finally crossed the line between protected speech and criminal solicitation for murder. When the Islamic State Hacking Division released their 2015 "kill list" compiled by Ardit Ferizi and Junaid Hussain, Yassin shared it enthusiastically, writing "ISIS leak HACKERS GUIDE to hundreds of military personnel."[136] She also made a specific effort to create her own content using the data, creating a Twitter post with images of eight of the individuals identified in the documents, each accompanied by their names and personal details.[137] A few days later, the same group of ISIS hackers released another set of documents containing the personal details of 150 US Air Force personnel, and Yassin was again quick to disseminate the information, along with a call from the hacking group to use it in order to conduct targeted killings in America on behalf of ISIS: "This information was seized from American sites belonging to the American crusader army by a hacker of the Islamic state, may God grant it strength and support through victory. Rejoice, O supporters of the Caliphate State, with the dissemination of the information to be delivered to one wolves. God said: 'And slay them wherever you may come upon them.'"[138]

Yassin was also in direct contact with Twitter accounts linked to this team of ISIS hackers, and as well as communicating openly with them, shared tweets they produced which identified two specific FBI agents by name, city, and personal phone number and called for their killing by ISIS supporters based in America. While none acted on the information provided by the two hacks promoted by Yassin, a number of the individuals identified in the documents received direct death threats, including one Air Force Major who was called on his personal line and threatened with the beheading of members of his family.[139] This was the final straw for Yassin, and she was arrested soon after. She is now serving a nine-year prison sentence for soliciting violence in the name of ISIS.

For other American ISIS supporters, failed attempts at traveling to join the group led them to seek out other ways to help further its mission online. In Virginia, Haris Qamar attempted to travel to Syria but ultimately chose to support the group in the US through online propaganda dissemination after his parents took his passport, preventing him from going abroad.[140] Reports suggest that Qamar drew the attention of law enforcement due to a series of pro-ISIS Twitter accounts operating under various iterations of the username "newerajihadi."[141] Between May 2015 and April 2016, the FBI identified over 60 Twitter accounts that were operated by Qamar, and by July 2016, Qamar allegedly told a confidential witness that "he'd gone through almost 100 accounts."[142]

In addition to sharing graphic material and promoting ISIS' worldviews, Qamar was an avid consumer of violent propaganda videos, including infamous ones like "Flames of War."[143] After watching a video where ISIS encourages lone wolf attacks in Washington, D.C., Qamar offered to help an undercover FBI witness, whom he believed was a fellow ISIS sympathizer, take pictures for a supposed propaganda product.[144] According to court filings, Qamar believed that "taking photographs and providing them to the Islamic State was different from being a 'fanboy' online, and constituted active support for ISIL."[145] By snapping photos and recording video footage at various landmarks in D.C. and Arlington, Virginia, including the Pentagon, Qamar believed he was going beyond being simply a "keyboard warrior" and was actively assisting the group.[146] He also offered the confidential witness tactical recommendations for how to deliver the files to ISIS operatives in a secure fashion.[147] Authorities arrested Qamar in July 2016, and charged him with attempting to provide material support to the group.[148] Thus, while Qamar did not overtly plan to conduct an attack in the US, his case represents a category of American ISIS supporter who believe they could advance the organization's aims by using digital communications technologies to aid the production and dissemination of propaganda.

In November 2019, a 20-year-old Illinois resident and computer science university student became the first known American to be charged with attempting to provide material support and resources to the Islamic State in the form of computer programs. These were explicitly designed to aid in the dissemination of ISIS propaganda to Western audiences through digital communications technologies. Thomas Osadzinski's activity is among the more unique examples of the type of innovative approaches taken by American ISIS supporters to further the spread of the group's propaganda in the US.

Over the course of its investigation, the FBI found that Osadzinski was using his specialist IT skills to code and disseminate an online tool designed to efficiently preserve, archive, and spread ISIS propaganda across various social media platforms, in particular Telegram. In doing so, he hoped to subvert efforts by technology companies to rid their platforms of extremist materials while also automating the process of sorting and accessing ISIS output. He was also aware of likely FBI surveillance and as a result made no plans to attempt to travel to ISIS-held territory, instead deciding to put his IT skills to use at home.

Speaking in early March 2019 to an undercover FBI employee in Arabic via Telegram, whom Osadzinski believed was a member of an official ISIS media organization based in Syria, he offered to help by translating their material into English for an American audience.[149] He also claimed to have been working for a another well-known ISIS media outlet, al-Hayat, translating propaganda into English and even providing the voiceover for at least one video, the popular production from 2014 mentioned above entitled "Flames of War: The Fighting Has Just Begun." In the video, his voice urges Muslims in the West to "return the flames of war into the countries of the aggressors just as the planes of the crusaders burned the homes of Muslim residents in Iraq and Sham the Muslim in their lands will retaliate with an equivalent strike."[150] Offering his services to what he thought was his new ISIS contact, he wrote, "if you need any help I will help too ... sometimes I am busy with school, but jihad is always more important than relaxing and games."[151] In his view, he was performing "jihad of the media" on behalf of ISIS as opposed to "jihad of the sword," which he said he was not ready for due to his plans to have a wife and children who "will be slaves of Allah."[152]

It was in late March, however, when Osadzinski unwittingly unveiled to the FBI his plans to create software that was to streamline how ISIS supporters could access and disseminate ISIS propaganda on Telegram. After taking several classes in university on basic coding and computer science, Osadzinski attempted to construct two products for ISIS. The first was a Linux-based computer operating system specifically for "the ansar [ISIS supporters] to use" while "preventing exploitation by crusader intelligence agencies."[153] The second was a Python script that would allow quick and efficient downloading of material within Telegram channels and groups to help supporters build their own archives of ISIS propaganda, immune from takedown efforts.[154] Osadzinski allegedly referred to these dual efforts as "Operation: Heralds of the Internet," and built an operational manual for both programs.[155]

According to the charging documents, Osadzinki viewed his "operation" as paramount to the jihadist movement, even describing the efforts as "the highest form of jihad ... no more than ten brothers know how to do this kind of [media] jihad."[156] At the time of development, Telegram was beginning to embark on a more expansive campaign to delete accounts and channels promoting terrorist content on its platform.[157] Osadzinski saw the preservation of content in the face of these takedowns and protecting e-activists from criminal prosecution as the major goals of his activities. "Before i was muslim," Osadzinski texted an undercover FBI employee, "I wanted to find dawla [ISIS] videos but never could. Its very good for dawah [recruitment]. The news lies about dawla videos and never shows it full."[158]

Osadzinski allegedly took several steps to obscure his activities. He believed that using The Onion Router (Tor), an anonymous browser, would prevent law enforcement from detecting him.[159] He developed his script for downloading content from Telegram in a way that would sidestep its process for detecting bots and malicious users. Telegram auto-bans channels that post more than 500 messages in one minute; to avoid bans, Osadzinki programmed his Python tool to automatically create a new channel to post in after every 500 messages.[160] He attempted to encrypt all the files that he posted online and recommended the use of the program "BleachBit," a secure means of deleting content from a computer permanently and without leaving a data trail.[161] He kept the passwords for all of his devices on a single piece of paper, on him at all times, and said that he would swallow the paper if apprehended.[162] Despite employing extensive online operational security measures, Osadzinki's offline operational security was suspect. He printed out a large ISIS propaganda poster on a physical printer at his school, and hung it in his dorm room.[163] He also unwittingly told several FBI undercover employees and confidential human sources about every aspect of his operation, resulting in his arrest on November 18, 2019.[164]

Technology and Financing

While some ISIS supporters sought to use their technical skills to hack sensitive information in order to assist the group in America, others researched ways to raise funds to finance activities such as traveling to join ISIS or planning attacks at home. In July 2014, an article entitled "Bitcoin wa Sadaqat al-jihad" was posted on an American pro-ISIS blog called "Al-Khilafa Aridat", and a link was posted shortly after on Twitter by a user under the handle @AmreekiWitness, who had around 4,000 followers at the time.[165] Translated as "Bitcoin and providing charitable giving for violent jihad," the article presented the funding of jihad as linked to one of the five pillars of Islamic worship, namely *zakat*, or alms-giving. The author was Ali Amin, a Virginia-based teen who also helped his schoolmate, Reza Niknejad, join ISIS and promoted pro-ISIS tactical advice online. In writing the article, Amin hoped he could help assist his fellow American ISIS supporters use cryptocurrency to fund the group's interests. He begins the article by lamenting the state of the current "kufr" financial system, which is corrupt and has led to "intense poverty in the United States." Unlike the Islamic financial model, which in his view prevents usury and helps the conditions of the Muslim *ummah*, the Western system and its currencies "feed directly into taxes that go to funding their oppressive, murder[ous], military forces," while also effectively eliminating the ability to provide alms for jihad. Wealthy Muslims who support jihad, he argued, are able to use their resources to channel money to jihadists, but the majority of Muslims needed alternatives to ordinary currencies.

Amin saw the solution in the expanding market of cryptocurrencies, especially Bitcoin. Its decentralized system and "Dark Wallet" feature meant that financial transactions were "untrackable by kafir governments," and he even went as far as to suggest that it would provide the basis for a new form of Islamically compliant online marketplace for the Islamic State in which Islamic judges, or *qadis*, could be introduced in order to preside over contracts and transactions to ensure they met the standards of *sharia* law. Most importantly, however, it allowed for Muslims in the West to both avoid paying taxes to their government by hiding their money and "secretly fund the mujahideen with no legal danger upon them."[166] Thus, Bitcoin provided an opportunity to "revive the lost *sunnah* [tradition] of donating to the mujahideen," that the Western financial system had prevented for so long.

Amin was arrested in February 2015, before he was able to pursue the use of Bitcoin himself. However, he was not the only American to recognize the utility of Bitcoin. In December 2017 authorities indicted Zoobia Shahnaz, a woman from New York, for bank fraud and money laundering in support of ISIS. Digital tools, in particular financial technologies, were a critical component of her efforts. Shahnaz engaged in a scheme to defraud several financial institutions, amassing $85,000 in illicit funds.[167] She used a series of credit cards, some of which were fraudulent, to purchase around $62,703 in Bitcoin and other cryptocurrencies, then siphoned most of the funds into one bank account under her name.[168] From there, Shahnaz eventually made several wire transfers to various individuals and front companies in Pakistan, China, and Turkey, employing methods to evade detection and circumvent financial transaction reporting requirements.[169] Evidence suggests that "these transactions were motivated to benefit ISIS."[170]

Prior to and in the midst of her laundering scheme, Shahnaz also sought to join the group in Syria; her web history contained searches about travel to ISIS-controlled territory, including maps of cities along the Turkey–Syria border, jihadi social media accounts, and information about moving around Turkey with money.[171] Authorities intercepted Shahnaz in July 2017 at John F. Kennedy international airport when she tried to board a plane to Islamabad, Pakistan with a layover in Istanbul, Turkey.[172] Upon investigation, federal authorities recognized a concerted effort by Shahnaz to delete information and communications off of several electronic devices prior to her travel, yet another attempt to avoid detection using technology.[173]

All of these cases demonstrate the dynamic interplay between digital communication technologies and ISIS sympathizers in America. Put simply, an ever-evolving list of tools affords countless opportunities to sympathetic actors, offering various degrees of participation including terrorist recruitment, facilitation, and tactical planning. Concurrently, ISIS adherents' exploitation of, and reliance on various digital communications technologies intimately connects with the roles they seek to fulfill in the movement.

We have seen how, in some cases, American ISIS supporters made use of communications technology, in particular a range of lightly regulated social media platforms that for many years did little to mitigate ISIS activity, to create and disseminate propaganda tailored for and targeted at Americans. This category represents the majority of cases of Americans who made use of technology—their work required a deep devotion to the ISIS cause and a skill for propaganda but needed little technical expertise.

For those who successfully joined ISIS in Syria or Iraq, technology and the ability to effectively exploit it proved to be pivotal. Not only did it allow Mohamad Khweis to gather intelligence on the most effective routes to the group's strongholds, but it also masked his movements and communications to such an extent that, as far as the available evidence shows, the authorities were wholly unaware of his presence in Syria until his subsequent surrender to the Kurds in Northern Iraq.

Rarer, but equally innovative, were the efforts of the hackers who attempted to demonstrate the apparent weaknesses and vulnerabilities of American government data security and encourage the killing of those working in counterterrorism. This was not simply a call for murder, but also an attempt to undermine what appeared to be an unassailable hegemonic foe, hoping to inspire others with the belief that ISIS could, in fact, prevail. Similar technical experience and imagination was demonstrated by the online fundraisers, who in cryptocurrencies identified a way to circumvent the powerful anti-terror-financing infrastructure in America. Turning the concept of almsgiving in Islam into a terror-financing imperative is nothing new—many jihadists have argued that jihad is a worthy charitable cause—but Americans like Ali Amin were among the first in the county to suggest a digital version.

Despite the breadth of cases analyzed here, it is worth keeping in mind that it likely does not represent the entirety of ISIS supporters' virtual activity in America and abroad. Court filings and other open-source materials are incredibly useful in highlighting sympathizers' use of technology, but the scope is still limited to publicly identified individuals. In this context alone, the collection of cases shows that ISIS adherents differed in their technical abilities and awareness of operational security practices. While authorities may continue to investigate some tech-savvy individuals, as the Khweis case demonstrates, it is possible that other people conducted operations without drawing attention from law enforcement.

One of the ways for non-indigenous terrorist groups such as ISIS to sustain themselves in inhospitable environments like the United States is through deft and innovative use of the ever-increasing range of communications technologies available to them. As we have seen, this technology has allowed for everything from travel planning for those seeking to leave, to attack planning and propaganda creation and dissemination for ISIS supporters who remain in the United States. In this way, the timing could hardly have been better—ISIS emerged just at the time when social media use was becoming widespread but had yet to be subject to any serious scrutiny. At the same time, services offering various forms of encrypted communication and online activity masking began to proliferate, offering the online security all users had come to expect. Americans that found themselves far from the battlefield with little chance of successfully joining ISIS could not have asked for much more opportunity to remain involved, while those who did travel were able to draw upon an unprecedented amount of useful, and often free, technology.

Does the Internet Create Terrorists?

Despite all of this, a burning question among analysts remains: How much can the internet alone truly influence an individual's behavior and decision to take part in ISIS-inspired activities (or any form of terrorism for that matter)? As yet, we lack the empirical data to answer this in a satisfactory way. However, researchers continue to contribute to a fuller understanding of this issue.

In the "real world," the importance of friendship and kinship networks and face-to-face interaction in the radicalization process has long been accepted.[174] Some authors now ask, or even go so far as to argue, that online social networks can have the same or a similar effect.[175] Jerome Bjelopera and Mark Randol take this argument further, claiming that the level of interactivity between jihadists and their audience encourages the consumers "to more easily see themselves as part of broader jihadist movements and not just casual readers or online spectators."[176]

Matthew Costello, Pedro Manrique, and Daniel Koehler, amongst others, argue that extremist use of social media helps to create an impression among online followers that a critical mass has built up within the movement.[177] This effect then motivates individuals to become further involved in the movement and take part in more extreme actions.[178] This trend, often referred to as the "filter bubble effect," also mirrors the group dynamics that have been observed in the physical world, where groupthink can take hold and opinions become increasingly extreme as members of the group become more insular and exclusively reliant on one another for social interaction.[179] While more work needs to be done on proving the assertion that online networks can have the same impact as physical ones, it remains an interesting and fruitful avenue for future research. It may also be the case that the dividing of the virtual world from the physical one may no longer be a valid distinction. As younger generations create personas and forge relationships online in greater numbers, future research may have to find ways to treat both of these worlds as one and the same.

Ultimately, social media platforms emerged as a key tool for extremist groups because they provide a level of accessibility that allows users to selectively implant themselves in communities and milieus of like-minded individuals. The process of isolation has been described as entering into "echo chambers" or "cyberbalkanization."[180] Many studies argue that such echo chambers allow for the unchallenged support and amplification of the most extreme views in a community. This also leads to fewer dissenting voices, and helps users embrace extreme ideas: "As a result," according to Peter Neumann, "people acquire a skewed sense of reality so that extremist attitudes and violence are no longer taboos but—rather—are seen as positive and desirable."[181] Zeynep Tufekci and others argue that open platforms like Twitter and Facebook are particularly conducive to the creation of echo chambers because they help users curate content using complex algorithms.[182] In doing so, social media companies inadvertently expose their extremist users to content that reinforces their interest and beliefs, failing to integrate dissenting voices and alternative opinions.

With a clearer understanding of the dynamic network of digital communications leveraged by ISIS and its sympathizers in America, it is increasingly evident that counter-extremism strategies targeting virtual facets of the movement are insufficient. Put simply, a synergistic fusion between top-down strategic messaging and bottom-up grassroots mobilization comprises ISIS' apparatus of communications.[183] As a result, the organization benefits from a wide range of official and unofficial media products that proffer the worldviews of the group. While the issue of the Islamic State's online efforts draws attention from a range of stakeholders, amassing considerable resources, contemporary measures to combat violent extremism in the digital sphere lack flexibility and struggle to account for the various ways extremists exploit technology. As articulated at the outset of this chapter, political strategies adopted by Western states depend on the compliance and efficiency of major social media providers in removing extremist content. Regrettably, this emphasis on leading technology providers, like Twitter and Facebook, sidelines other enduring aspects of the digital threat matrix, such as web archives, encrypted messengers, file-sharing services, protected email platforms, mobile security applications, and VPNs.[184]

Another fundamental weakness in the method of regulation encouraged by policymakers, and employed by major tech companies, is the overarching dependence on the practice of account takedowns and content removal. Even if the leading social media providers could remove all of ISIS' propaganda on their sites, it would not necessarily prevent the rise of other extremist groups or keep ISIS and its sympathizers from migrating to other platforms.[185] Moreover, the expeditious removal of materials that violate a company's terms of service regarding the promotion of terrorism is not always a feasible aim, especially for smaller companies that do not have the resources to police their channels of communication.

To more effectively confront ISIS in the digital sphere, it is crucial for policymakers, practitioners, technology providers, and scholars to be cognizant of the evolving apparatus of communications and stay up to date on the mediums and methods of communication that matter to groups like ISIS and their supporters. In the face of pressure in both the physical and digital arena, ISIS sympathizers in America are adaptable and resilient in their exploitation of tools. As opposed to one monolithic form of online engagement, supporters in the US alone leverage a range of digital communications technologies to fulfill their personal aspirations within the organization. Those tasked with preventing and disrupting the proliferation of violent extremists in the digital sphere can make considerations for these observations in policy design and implementation. In addition to holistic responses that address the entirety of extremist networks online, not just the most obvious tools, more attention should be devoted to exploring how interventions might integrate synergistic online and offline components. By understanding the interplay between ISIS sympathizers and the tools they use to engage with the group, and calibrating measures to embrace the same dexterity, improved responses to ISIS exploitation of digital communications technologies can set a more productive precedent for how to confront violent extremists in the virtual arena.

Chapter 5

THE IDEOLOGUES

While American jihadist travelers, terrorists, and e-activists struggle on the front lines to promote the Islamic State, there is a final category which helps to bind all of these together, ensuring the maintenance of a common purpose, identity, and ideology: the ideologues. English-speaking ISIS ideologues issue the opinions and decisions that shape and justify the worldview of American ISIS members and supporters. Few in number but powerful in influence, American jihadist preachers, propagandists, and partisans are therefore a central component within the milieu.

Understanding these ideologues' outlooks, backgrounds, and arguments is therefore essential to examining cases of ISIS support in the United States. However, their contribution is not simply a matter of translating the ideology into English so that Americans can access it. Collectively, they have helped package and reframe ISIS and wider jihadist ideology so that it resonates with the beliefs, experiences, and fears of American and Western audiences. In a country where ISIS has almost no physical presence, ideologues offer a service that ensures the group's presence, survival, and ability to remain connected to supporters.

Previous studies of jihadism in the West often highlight the importance of charismatic leaders who hold authority and legitimacy in the eyes of their followers. In his influential study on jihadist radicalization in the West, Quintan Wiktorowicz provides multiple overlapping causes of this phenomenon. Among them is what he refers to as the importance of the "credibility and sacred authority" of leadership figures, who use these qualities to persuade individuals to join and take part in jihadist activism.[1] Thus, it is not only the packaging of the message that matters, but the reputation of the messenger themselves. Others, such as Tomas Precht, have noted the role of leadership figures as one of a number of possible "trigger factors" which help move individuals along the process of radicalization, often from holding a grievance or experiencing an identity crisis to adopting extreme ideas and solutions to their perceived problems.[2] Similar to Wiktorowicz, Precht argues that ideologues "are especially likely to influence young persons' belief systems by speaking from a position of authority on religious issues."[3] Haroro Ingram, in his research on what he refers to as the "charismatic leadership phenomenon", describes them as "architects of identity" who are able to construct both in-groups and out-groups in order to "shape their followers' cognitive perceptions and mobilize them towards collective action."[4] At their most effective, these ideologues are able to create meaning for American ISIS supporters by identifying new grievances or exploiting pre-existing ones, constructing a new collective identity, and creating frames through which they comprehend the world around them.

Due to their open support for jihadist violence or the organizations that carry it out, these ideologues exist on the extreme fringes—both within the vast landscape of worldwide Islamic scholarship and within American Muslim politics and society. They are figures of exceptional interest to law enforcement and intelligence agencies in the US and around the world, and their activity is constantly monitored. In many countries, the hate-filled and violence-inciting rhetoric contained in these ideologues' speeches and rulings would be standalone grounds for prosecution. In the US, however, several conditions allow jihadist ideologues to reach a broad audience while avoiding arrest. These factors help the Islamic State and other jihadist groups retain key nodes for reaching potential supporters in the United States despite lacking an expansive physical network.

The first and arguably most important factor is the First Amendment right to free speech, an essential freedom enshrined in the US Constitution that can also provide a wide berth for hate preachers and extremists. Jihadist ideologues in the US are renowned for their longevity; most of the prominent American figures who declared their support for ISIS are longtime contributors to the jihadist movement who continue promulgating their outlandish views despite scrutiny, ostracization, and legal difficulties. Meanwhile, many other countries whose laws lack the scope of free-speech protections in the US were able to disrupt prominent jihadist ideologues through arrests. The United Kingdom, for instance, jailed the outspoken pro-ISIS cleric Anjem Choudary and many of his followers in the al-Muhajiroun movement for inviting support for a proscribed organization.[5] Even after Choudary was released from prison in 2018, the UK courts imposed a gag order, preventing him from continuing to proselytize.[6]

For those who espouse jihadist ideology, the line between freedom of speech and incitement to violence is often paper-thin. The most successful jihadist ideologues in the US have a clear-eyed understanding of precisely where this distinction exists, and how to avoid falling on the wrong side of it.[7] Their speeches and pronouncements reflect an understanding of their constitutional rights and what types of speech are covered by the First Amendment. Starting from this understanding, jihadist ideologues constantly test the upper bounds of these rights by endorsing violence, vitriolic hatred and sectarianism, conspiracy theories, and the aims, objectives, and actions of terrorist groups, all without directly inciting their followers to commit specific violent acts. In this manner, they can have a pronounced influence on the decisions of others to commit violent acts or materially support terrorism while they cannot be held legally responsible for the acts their followers commit.

This places US law enforcement in an especially difficult position regarding ideologues. In most cases, traditional prosecutorial options (such as the material support statute) are statutorily inapplicable to cases involving jihadist preachers.

Instead, law enforcement defaults to "Al Capone tactics," attempting to disrupt their activities through smaller charges. In the period following 9/11, the FBI arrested jihadist imams for a smattering of offenses, ranging from tax fraud to immigration violations.[8] On several occasions, the DOJ built non-terrorism criminal cases against ideologues who were then deported, incarcerated, or placed on probation.[9] Whether these disruptions were successful or unsuccessful is a matter of debate. What is clear, however, is that they were temporary. Ideologues often continued promoting jihadist causes after their release from prison or expulsion from the US.

Secondly, many American jihadist ideologues overcome their dearth of traditional bona fides and real-life followers by projecting influence using digital communications tools. As discussed in the previous chapter, the internet had a far-reaching impact on American jihadists across categories, and many of America's jihadist clerics were early adopters of internet communications tools. The internet allowed these figures to transcend their local communities and masquerade as widely accepted religious authorities to audiences that often could not distinguish between legitimate and illegitimate religious sources. From behind a computer screen, ideologues had the potential to connect with other English-speaking jihadists living in small pockets throughout the world, and vice versa. Travelers, terrorists, and activists with jihadist sympathies could reach self-reported "scholars" that shared their opinions.

Research on the growth of support for ISIS in the West has found that ideologues acting as charismatic leaders have benefited particularly from the access they are granted to large audiences by social media. In her research on the influence of "charismatic preachers," Angela Gendron also finds that not only are they "highly influential in accelerating and guiding" the multifaceted process of radicalization, but that they have effectively harnessed the internet. She argues that many of these figures now rely primarily on the internet to not only spread their message but to create a "charismatic bond" with their followers.[10] This is particularly relevant to the focus of this chapter, which looks at American ideologues who act as leadership figures online, often without much real-world interaction with their followers.

This two-way accessibility is a critical feature of how Islamic scholars become "credible" in the modern era. Jarret Brachman and Alix Levine write that the initial English-speaking entrants to the jihadist e-verse

> rocketed to stardom . . . because they were viewed—at least by Western, English-speaking hardliners—as more accessible facsimiles of legendary Arabic-language sheikhs. These "lite" versions resembled the previous incarnation closely enough, even though they may have lacked the same level of intellectual horsepower or religious legitimacy. The "lite" sheikhs were more effective in speaking to Western hard-liners precisely because their message required less baseline knowledge to understand.[11]

American ideologues are essential interlocutors of jihadist ideology, presenting concepts from the stories of the Prophet Muhammad and his contemporaries, medieval Islamic law, and sermons from the eighteenth and nineteenth centuries in a vernacular that is comprehensible and digestible to followers across the English-speaking world.[12] Successful American jihadist preachers are accessible in two forms: both in linguistic accessibility and in virtual connectivity. Not only can they relay the message and methodology of jihadist groups to an audience in their native language but they are also one click away from their adherents.

Finally, the work and ideas of successful American jihadist ideologues survive their arrests, deaths, and the frequently shifting dynamics within the global jihadist movement. Multiple generations of American jihadists, regardless of space, place, or affiliation, find relatable insight from their writings and lectures. This effect is related to the other traits of successful American jihadist ideologues—because they are incredibly difficult to disrupt, and manage to maintain virtual personas, the shelf-life of their ideas is virtually unlimited. As a result, despite the small number of American jihadist preachers, their influence appears and re-appears in widely different cases of Americans supporting jihadist groups across decades.

Before examining some of the individual figures that took center stage in ISIS recruitment in the United States as ideologues, it is first useful to provide a brief explanation of the schools of thought within Islam that influence their thinking and its historical development in the United States. Next, we explore the ongoing impact of the infamous American al-Qaeda affiliate and ideologue Anwar al-Awlaki, who despite his death years before the rise of ISIS and support for al-Qaeda (one of ISIS' competitors) had an outsized influence on the ideas of the group and its American recruits. Finally, the chapter examines three other English-speaking ISIS ideologues—Ahmad Musa Jibril, Suleiman Anwar Bengharsa, and Abdullah Faisal—who have all played notable roles in the radicalization and mobilization of American ISIS supporters from 2014 until the present.

Salafism and Salafi-Jihadism

Commentators on the Islamic State are in constant disagreement about the role of religious ideology within the group and whether it is a factor in the radicalization of its Western supporters. Put simply, one interpretation is that religious ideology is a critical component of supporters' decisions to commit violent acts; the other argues that unrelated political or socioeconomic factors drive radicalization, and religion is irrelevant.[13] This chapter, which focuses on a small subset of American ideologues with backgrounds in Islamic scholarship and law, will not settle this debate. Regardless, as a result of their backgrounds and training, ideological issues within Islam are critically important to understand American ideologues' endorsement of the Islamic State.

A common denominator between American jihadist ideologues in this chapter is that from the standpoint of ideological affiliations, they all can be classified as adherents of Salafi-jihadism. This classification is a subset of Salafism, a broader strain of thought within Islam. Salafism is characterized by more disputes between its followers than areas of consensus, but its core principles include a revival of the practices, legal thought, and sources of jurisprudence from the foundational period of Islam, in combination with a strict interpretation of monotheism (*tawhid*).[14] The word "Salafism" is derived from *al-salaf al-salih*, the Islamic referent for the first three generations of Muslims.[15]

Salafism is a revivalist movement that attempts to restore the beliefs and practices of Islam to their form during the time of *al-salaf al-salih*.[16] This is the first and central precept of the Salafi movement. Thus, despite the diversity of Islamic thought and legal reasoning developed over the centuries, Salafis limit the acceptable sources of jurisprudence to what they consider primary source texts. These are the Quran, the sayings and deeds of the Prophet Muhammad (*hadith*), and the consensus of the Prophet's companions (*sahaba*). Any practice that does not have a basis in these sources is considered a deviant innovation (*bida*). Moreover, the Salafi interpretation of *tawhid* argues that God is a single, united, indivisible entity, and that the attribution of God-like attributes to human figures is a form of idol worship (*shirk*).[17]

While it stresses adherence to early Islamic practice, several more recent figures have drastically influenced the development of Salafism in the modern context. Modern Salafis draw heavily from the work of the fourteenth-century Damascene jurist Taqi ad-Din Ahmad ibn Taymiyya and the eighteenth-century theologian Muhammad ibn Abd al-Wahhab, whose religious ideals influenced the foundation of the Kingdom of Saudi Arabia.[18] More recently, events including the decolonization of the Middle East and South Asia, geopolitical conflicts in the Arab world and beyond, and the growth of the Muslim population in the West have all contributed to disputes within the Salafi movement.[19]

Oftentimes, "Salafism" is used interchangeably with other terms used to reference currents in political Islam, such as "Islamism" or "Wahhabism." There are subtle but distinct differences between these terms. "Islamism" refers to any movement that believes that Islamic law should be the blueprint for the construction of an Islamic state. While there are overlaps, not all Islamists are Salafis and not all Salafis are Islamists. Wahhabism, referring to Muhammad ibn Abd al-Wahhab, is the state religion of the Kingdom of Saudi Arabia. While some consider it a branch of Salafism (and many of its basic precepts are the same), Wahhabism is technically part of the Hanbali school of Islamic jurisprudence. Salafism rejects all of the four main schools of Islamic jurisprudence due to the belief that they cause divisions among Muslims and that Muslims should not require interlocutors, with their own agendas and interests, to explain their religion to them.[20]

Arguably, intra-Salafi disputes center around their methodology and theory of political change. All Salafis likely agree that the way Islam is practiced in most places today must be transformed in order to align it with the practices of the original Muslims. Yet, a plethora of arguments exist within the Salafi movements about the best method (*manhaj*) to accomplish this goal.[21] Within Western academic literature, Salafis are often classified by how willing they are to engage in modern politics. While it does not comprise a complete classification system, distinctions between groups of Salafis on this question can help explain the emergence of violent Salafi extremism.

Wiktorowicz made a significant contribution to our understanding of Salafism by providing an analysis which separates Salafism into three branches: *Salafi purists* (or quietists), who eschew political engagement or active contestation of the state, *Salafi politicos* (or activists), who openly participate in non-violent political action, and *Salafi jihadis,* who view violence and the use of force as the most effective and legitimate version of political action.[22] The first group's ideology is characterized by several scholars who are part of the religious establishment in Saudi Arabia, and stresses personal introspection and educational outreach as key to restoration of true Islamic practice.[23] The second group, associated with the *sahwa* protest movement in 1980s Saudi Arabia, represents a combination of Salafi thought with the methods and practices of Islamist groups (in particular, the Muslim Brotherhood).[24] They view engagement with the political system through forming political movements or parties as a necessary pre-condition to the re-establishment of Islamic states.[25] Salafi-jihadists, the final group, endorse the use of violent force to establish Islamic states.[26]

Over the last few decades, all three Salafi sub-groups made some inroads in the United States. Oftentimes, key ideological figures within the movement would switch from one strain to the other based on personal developments, tensions in the movement, or geopolitical events. The first Salafis in the US were quietists, mainly followers of African-American converts to Islam who studied the religion in Saudi Arabia during the 1980s and 1990s.[27] The Salafi politico movement, sustained by immigrants from the Middle East and South Asia, blossomed during the early to mid-1990s but faced severe difficulties in the post-9/11 period.[28] Since 9/11, the two branches are forced to share the stage in the US with their most extreme relative—Salafi-jihadism.

Salafi-Jihadism

In his 2016 book *Salafi-Jihadism: The History of an Idea,* Shiraz Maher argues that five concepts shape Salafi-jihadist ideology: *tawhid* (which has already been discussed), jihad, *al wala wal bara*, *hakimiyyah*, and *takfir*.[29] Salafi-jihadists believe in jihad as a holy, civilizational war fought on behalf of the *ummah* (global Muslim community) in which all Muslims are obliged to participate.[30] They also argue that fighting jihad is in itself an act of worship. *Al wala wal bara* (loyalty and disavowal) is the principle that Muslims should only practice, believe, and worship what is endemic to Islam, while rejecting and even developing hatred for other faiths and their beliefs.[31] According to Joas Wagemakers, it seeks to simplistically divide "the world into two separate spheres of which one is good and one is evil."[32] *Tawhid* is central to this concept as it is based on protecting and promoting practices and beliefs that preserve the oneness of God as the sole deity to be worshipped while rejecting anything that threatens monotheism.

For all Salafis, *al wala wal bara* is a concept that helps to protect their beliefs and identity from non-Muslim beliefs and practices. As such, it is a useful tool for creating, and defining the parameters of, a collective identity. It helps define both the beliefs and practices that characterize the in-group who properly practice Islam and the qualities of the enemies of Islam against whom an Islamic identity must be constructed. Salafi-jihadists, most notably the influential Jordanian scholar Abu Muhammad al-Maqdisi, have also made the concept a key pillar of jihadist thought by applying it to politics, specifically the application of Islamic law. In his landmark work on the issue, *Millat Ibrahim*, al-Maqdisi argued that, by accepting man-made laws over sharia law, a Muslim was showing their loyalty to a power other than Allah. This was, in his view, an act of idol worship (*shirk*) and could lead to their excommunication from the faith. The main targets of his work were leaders of Muslim countries who applied man-made law—in his view they were presenting themselves as idols, or *tawaghit* (singular: *taghut*), who should no longer be considered Muslims and had to be fought and overthrown through jihad.

Hakimiyyah, based on the writings of the Egyptian thinker Sayyid Qutb and South-Asian writer and activist Abu Ala Maududi, is the basis of this militant version of *al wala wal bara*. It inspired al-Maqdisi's own work by providing the argument that if God is the sole deity to be worshipped then he is also the only legitimate source of governance; Salafi-jihadists operationalize *hakimiyyah* (which they also refer to as *tawhid al-hakimiyyah*) to argue for the destruction of governments that are not completely governed by Islamic law.[33] Finally, there is *takfir* or excommunication. Using *takfir* liberally, Salafi-jihadists argue that Muslims who violate *tawhid* through pursing deviant beliefs and practices have removed themselves from the faith—and are therefore legitimate targets for violence. This also includes governments in Muslim-majority nations that do not fully apply *sharia* law.[34]

Like the disputes within Salafism more broadly, different Salafi-jihadist ideologues also disagree on matters of praxis. Classical (or defensive) jihadists believe that declaration of jihad is only legitimate in situations where a non-Muslim state invades or occupies Muslim territory. Then, it is acceptable to attack the invading state's military targets, but it is unacceptable to target civilians.[35] In the defensive jihad model, it is strictly forbidden to target Muslims.[36] This model is strongly associated with the *mujahideen* who fought against the Soviet Union in Afghanistan during the 1980s, in particular the writings of Abdallah Azzam.[37]

Global (or offensive) jihadism also considers jihad against a non-Muslim state invading Muslim territory to be legitimate. But this is not the only condition for legitimate declarations of jihad. In the framework of global jihad, external non-Muslim powers that back others to invade Muslim territory (often referred to as "the far enemy"), even if they do not invade themselves, are also acceptable targets.[38] Moreover, it is permissible to attack the noncombatant civilians of invading countries, using whichever means—including suicide attacks—to increase casualties.[39] Global jihad is most closely associated with al-Qaeda and its founders, Osama bin Laden and Ayman al-Zawahiri. In general, this model disapproves of targeting Muslims wherever possible.[40]

Arguably, the Islamic State and its predecessors in Iraq fostered a third form of jihad—which can be referred to as "caliphate jihadism"[41]—related to but ultimately deviating from the al-Qaeda model of global jihad. The two major differences are its interpretation of *takfir* and the necessary preconditions for establishing an Islamic State. The ISIS brand of global jihad widely applies excommunication, arguing that all Shi'a Muslims, and Sunni Muslims who oppose the establishment of an Islamic State, are not Muslims and are legitimate targets for violence.[42] Second, unlike al-Qaeda, who view military defeat of all occupying forces as a prerequisite to the establishment of an Islamic state or the caliphate, the ISIS brand of global jihad reverses the obligations.[43]

American Salafi-Jihadists

Salafism is a long-standing current within American Muslim thought. However, the emergence of American Salafi-jihadist ideologues, and Salafi-jihadism in the US more broadly, has a much shorter history. By most accounts, the first introductions of the ideas behind the Salafi-jihadist subcurrent to American audiences came in the 1980s, when figures associated with the jihad against the Soviet Union in Afghanistan traveled to the US to garner support.[44] From this point onward, several Americans journeyed overseas to join jihadist groups— including in Afghanistan, Bosnia and, Chechnya—but very few of the ideologues promoting Salafi-jihadism at the time were Americans or located in the US.[45]

Two inflection points shaped the American clerics who are involved with the Salafi-jihadist movement. The first was September 11, 2001. Prior to 9/11, some of the earliest examples of American Salafi-jihadist ideologues were involved in the quietist or activist branches of Salafism in the US. However, the events of 9/11, and the subsequent involvement of the US in wars in Afghanistan and Iraq, influenced the range of actions and political responses they believed were acceptable.[46] For the first time, the US was directly involved in large-scale conflicts against jihadists within the traditional definitions of Muslim territory. The framing on both sides of the Global War on Terror as a civilizational conflict between Islam and the West also influenced many of these early ideologues towards the jihadist strain of Salafism. Jihad, in this case interpreted as use of violent force to defend the *ummah*, shifted from the theoretical realm to an immediate and mandatory duty.[47]

The second inflection point was ISIS' declaration of the re-establishment of the caliphate in 2014. Within the American Salafi-jihadist milieu, the symbolic moment convinced some ideologues that ISIS had finally achieved the long-standing dream of all Salafi currents: the re-establishment of a global state for Muslims operating solely under a strict interpretation of Islamic law, with a divinely guided religious leader at the helm.[48] Many American Salafi-jihadists who were previously ardent defenders of al-Qaeda soon shifted allegiances. In their opinions, speeches, and *khutba* (sermons), they quickly began supporting various aspects of ISIS, from goals and objectives to tactics and methods.

Anwar al-Awlaki

Born in Las Cruces, New Mexico to Yemeni parents in 1971, Anwar al-Awlaki remains the most effective and influential figure in Western jihadism. After a fifteen-year career as an ideologue, preacher, and external attack planner, in 2011 Awlaki was declared by the US Government to be "public enemy number one" following the death of Osama bin Laden.[49] Four months after bin Laden was killed during a raid in Abbottabad, Pakistan, Awlaki was killed by a US drone strike on his convoy passing through al-Jawf province in the north of Yemen.[50]

During his career, Awlaki personally influenced several individuals who would later go on to commit or attempt to commit terrorist attacks in the US. Three of his more notable protégés are Umar Farouk Abdulmutallab, Zachary Adam Chesser and Nidal Malik Hasan. Abdulmutallab was trained and directed by Awlaki to carry out a major terrorist bombing in the United States; on December 25, 2009, he attempted a suicide attack on Northwest Airlines Flight 253 from Amsterdam to Detroit by smuggling explosives in his underwear, but was apprehended by his fellow passengers before he could detonate the bomb.[51] Chesser, an online propagandist turned attempted foreign fighter, was arrested in 2010 while trying to board a plane in order to join al-Shabaab in Somalia. He was active on the jihadist website Revolution Muslim and famously threatened to kill the creators of the cartoon show *South Park* after an episode depicted the Prophet Muhammad.[52] Nidal Malik Hassan, the 2009 Fort Hood shooter, is one of America's deadliest jihadist lone attackers, who acted after being inspired by Awlaki's work and communicating directly with Awlaki via email.[53]

Awlaki's work remains critically important in the ISIS age. Based on US court documents and other open sources, between 2009 and 2016, of the 212 total cases of individuals charged in America for jihadist-related offenses, 66 (31 percent of cases) were in some way inspired by or linked to Awlaki. The New America Foundation has also found that between January 2007 and January 2015, Awlaki influenced, and in some cases was in direct contact with, 63 out of 259 individuals who were either convicted of terrorism-related offenses in US courts or died in the process of their attacks.[54] A 2016 study, based on the court filings for 101 Americans who have been indicted for ISIS-related offenses, found that Awlaki's name was cited as an influence in 24 cases. This was only one reference fewer than ISIS' first self-proclaimed caliph, Abu Bakr al-Baghdadi, and 13 more than Osama bin Laden.[55] Finally, in George Washington University's Program on Extremism database of more than a million ISIS English-language tweets, Awlaki was the second most popular preacher, bested only by Ahmad Musa Jibril.[56]

Through most metrics, it is clear that Awlaki remains an essential source for American ISIS supporters, and for American Salafi-jihadists more broadly. This remains the case despite Awlaki's affiliation with al-Qaeda, and the resultant dispute between ISIS and al-Qaeda that solidified after his death. Yet, Awlaki's influence is unsurprising; of the few individuals worldwide who preach Salafi-jihadist ideology in the English language, Awlaki is the figure who most comprehensively and conclusively presented the ideology in a Western (and

American) context. Awlaki's influence on the global Salafi-jihadist movement not only survived his death, but may have increased posthumously and continues to play a significant role in present-day jihadist activity in America.

The "Americanization" of Salafi-Jihadism

Awlaki's main contribution to the Salafi-jihadist movement was transforming the ideological subcurrent into an easily accessible format for Muslims in the West. Presenting the key elements of Salafi-jihadist ideology with motifs resonant for Western Muslims in an American vernacular, Awlaki ensured that his audience could digest the critical premises of Salafi-jihadism. Because of his efforts, Salafi-jihadism evolved from a set of arcane ideas about foreign conflicts and ancient Islamic history into a theory and praxis that are directly relevant to the everyday lives of Western Muslims.

Awlaki's early appeal as a preacher in America during the 1990s and early 2000s was rooted in his recorded lectures which translated stories from the Quran and *hadith* as well as prophetic biographies called *sirah*. From the outset, he recognized the value and effectiveness of presenting Islam using a storytelling approach, noting that "stories are a powerful method of teaching . . . they are memorable and filled with lessons."[57] While he began his career as a preacher in small mosques in Colorado and San Diego, Awlaki's recorded audio lectures were soon widely distributed as CDs. His style reinvigorated the study of Islam for a young Western audience seeking accessible and relatable expressions of their faith. In a new context, he retold stories from the Quran and *hadith* in Americanized, idiomatic English, often drawing parallels between the time of the Prophet Muhammad and current social issues and politics.[58] Awlaki's skill in transposing situations from the early history of Islam into a modern context made him immensely popular and easily accessible. As he began to turn towards promoting violence after the 9/11 attacks, he employed this skill as a highly effective mobilization tool, using examples of the original Muslims resorting to and justifying violence to legitimize modern jihadist activity.[59] Awlaki produced hundreds of hours of lectures about Islam and its relevance to Muslims living in the West, the vast majority of which contained no extremist content. These lectures formed a cornerstone of Islamic learning for an entire generation of Western Muslims.[60] Compared to other Salafi-jihadist ideologues, Awlaki was able to draw in a larger pool of followers due to his status; those who started out as fervent jihadists could only recruit active hardliners.

Alongside his accessible style, prior to his turn to more openly inciting violence Awlaki was a credentialed, mainstream Muslim scholar with some theological training and knowledge, and many American Muslims came to consider him an authority on the religion. Before moving to Yemen in 2004 and eventually joining al-Qaeda, he held several prominent positions, including as the imam of mosques in San Diego, California and Falls Church, Virginia, and chaplain at George Washington University.[61] Due to his apparent understanding of the hearts and minds of American Muslim youth, the Pentagon and Congressional staff associations both invited him to give lectures or lead prayer services.[62]

Awlaki's legacy is that his Western Muslim adherents now view the global jihadist movement—irrespective of which form it takes—as propagating the purest possible form and practice of Islam. His intent in designing his specific brand of Salafi-jihadist thought was for the ideas, goals, and objectives of the movement to survive the collapse of any organization, and the death of any leader.[63] Thus far, the evidence suggests that this was an effective strategy. Despite the death of Awlaki and other key leaders in al-Qaeda, Awlaki's contributions to the global jihadist movement live on in not only the numerous al-Qaeda affiliates worldwide, but also in the emergence of ISIS in the West.

The foundation of ISIS occurred several years after Awlaki's demise, although the organization's enduring relevance and ability to recruit Americans has been significantly augmented by Awlaki's work. A striking number of Americans who have either joined ISIS in Iraq and Syria, or acted on its behalf as lone-actor terrorists in the West, were introduced to jihadist thought and activism by Awlaki's work which they accessed online. Several individuals profiled throughout the previous chapters were directly influenced by the cleric. Abdi Nur, one of the main players in the network of young Minnesotans who joined ISIS in Syria, frequently posted material from Awlaki on his Facebook page; his social media handle "DustyFeet" refers to a verse in the Quran relayed by Awlaki in his treatise "44 Ways to Support the Jihad."[64] Elton Simpson, one of the attackers at the Curtis Culwell Center in 2015, had a picture of Awlaki as his avatar on social media profiles.[65]

More broadly, ISIS affiliates have attempted to re-appropriate Awlaki as an ISIS supporter. Using a counterfactual, ISIS supporters argue that if Awlaki had survived the 2011 drone strike until the present day, he would have eventually declared support for ISIS. After all, many of Awlaki's ideas and opinions were eventually adopted by ISIS.[66] This theory is underscored by the fact that, among the first English-language propaganda videos produced by the Islamic State's official al-Hayat Media Center, one featured a lecture Awlaki had given in 2008 praising the establishment of the precursor to ISIS, the Islamic State of Iraq (ISI).[67]

Open Source Jihad and the Islamic State Model

Awlaki was not only an ideologue, but was also integral to the transition from violent jihadism as an idea to violent jihadism as praxis in the West. Through his effective presentation of Islam as a revolutionary ideology, he convinced significant numbers of Western Muslims that violent action was the only acceptable response to the condition of the Muslim world. Three areas in which Anwar al-Awlaki's ideas have critical relevance for ISIS and its American supporters are in attack-planning strategies, the use of the internet for propaganda and instructional material dissemination, and in pursuing criminal methods within the framework of jihad. These concepts are represented throughout Awlaki's later work, particularly within the pages of *Inspire*. ISIS and its supporters borrowed heavily from Awlaki's contributions to these areas, and his writings are some of the key reasons why Awlaki is still heavily referenced by American ISIS supporters almost a decade after his death.

In the latter phases of his career, Awlaki helped to develop and codify jihadist lone-actor terrorism, or, as al-Qaeda termed it, "open source Jihad."[68] This encouraged individuals to carry out acts in support of the movement without a direct connection to any terrorist organization. Awlaki propagated his concept of "jihadist lone-actor terrorism" prior to officially joining any specific jihadist group or organization: because his theoretical work on jihad was not tied to a particular group, it could be used by a variety of organizations, and thus became the ideological, motivational, strategic, and tactical foundation of the "new wave" of jihadist movements worldwide.[69] When Awlaki formally associated with al-Qaeda in the Arabian Peninsula (AQAP), the group's official magazine *Inspire*, published by Awlaki's Saudi-American associate and expert propagandist Samir Khan, used work from Awlaki and others to call for small-scale attacks in the West carried out by Muslims who lived there and had no direct connections to any group.[70] This ensured that this idea in particular would survive Awlaki's death and allow other jihadist groups—in this case the Islamic State—to take advantage of the open-source jihad model.

Within the jihadist realm, Awlaki's conception of "open source jihad" represented a major shift from the al-Qaeda-directed attacks of the late 1990s and early 2000s, which relied on extensive planning, operational logistics, and bases of operation. By directing and legitimizing supporters of the jihadist movement in the US toward small-scale attacks, Awlaki set off a wave of American homegrown violent extremists who conducted or attempted to conduct attacks on US soil.[71] Many jihadist attackers still utilize the "Open Source Jihad" series from *Inspire* due to its easy-to-follow guides for a range of potential attack methods, from explosive device construction to vehicular attacks and train derailments.[72]

This is particularly true for the subset of American attack planners interested in building improvised explosive devices (IED). The article "Make a Bomb in the Kitchen of Your Mom," featured in a 2010 issue of *Inspire*, provides blueprints for rudimentary bombs that many jihadist attack planners have attempted to replicate during the past decade.[73] While the 2013 Boston Marathon bombers were among the article's most infamous readers, several ISIS-inspired attackers in the US also followed Awlaki's guidance in the following years.[74] Before Syed Farook conducted the 2015 shooting in San Bernardino, California, his path to radicalization was influenced by Awlaki's "The Hereafter" series.[75] Later, although Farook eventually abandoned the plot idea, he constructed several pipe bombs based directly on the recipe in "Make a Bomb in the Kitchen of Your Mom."[76] Several other ISIS-affiliated attack planners in recent years also followed this exact recipe.

Awlaki not only revolutionized how jihadist groups conceived of attack planning, but also propaganda distribution. He was one of the first jihadist ideologues with a massive online presence, and encouraged jihadist operatives worldwide to adopt digital communications tools on an industrial scale. Awlaki understood that the internet allowed jihadist ideologues, from wherever they resided, to achieve "maximum penetration" of the ideas of Salafi-jihadism around the world.[77] By the mid-2000s, his lectures and sermons were largely disseminated across the internet through new file-sharing websites, including on YouTube. Awlaki made himself a reachable commodity through his blog, *www.anwar-alawlaki.com*, as well as through Islamic e-forum sites and the video chat service Paltalk.[78] This adoption of communications technologies ensured Awlaki's accessibility and relevance for young Western Muslims, including Americans.

Around this time, Awlaki issued several works through the internet that would be critical to translating the ideals of Salafi-jihadism to English-speaking audiences. In 2005, after Awlaki left the US, he recorded "Constants on the Path of Jihad," his translation of a work of the same name by the Saudi Salafi-jihadist scholar Yusuf al-Uyayri.[79] The Department of Homeland Security assessed in 2008 that Awlaki's lecture "[commanded] US Muslims to conduct violent attacks in the Homeland and against US targets abroad ... the sermon also attempts to inoculate readers against popular counter-violence messages."[80] In 2008, he gave a video lecture on Paltalk in response to several questions he had received about the ongoing controversy related to depictions of the Prophet Muhammad in the Danish newspaper *Jyllands-Posten*.[81] In the lecture, entitled "The Dust Will Never Settle Down," Awlaki used an analogy from the life of the Prophet Muhammad regarding the proper treatment of those who mocked the Prophet—in this case, suggesting that execution was religiously justified.[82] This lecture and its ruling remain critically relevant for American ISIS supporters, several of whom referenced the sermon during plots to target individuals that commissioned the 2015 "Draw the Prophet Muhammad Day" in Texas.[83]

In March 2010, Awlaki published "44 Ways to Support Jihad" on his blog.[84] Shortly thereafter, Awlaki and Samir Khan released the first issue of AQAP's *Inspire* magazine.[85] The magazine represents the culmination of Awlaki's efforts to make global jihadism as accessible as possible to Westerners. While it was only made available online as a PDF file, the style of production mimicked the appearance of glossy Western magazines. It also provided Awlaki and other global jihadists a platform from which to provide reactions and analysis to current events, and helped to solidify, explain, and facilitate the tactical shift within al-Qaeda towards promoting the individual jihad model for terrorist operations in the West.[86]

The first issue also introduced what it refers to as the "Dust Will Never Settle Down Campaign," which drew inspiration from Awlaki's lecture of the same name about the Muhammad cartoons. A section of the magazine is devoted to discussing the necessity to respond to the defamation of the Prophet Muhammad with violence, culminating with an article on the subject by Awlaki himself.[87] This article also includes an infamous "hit-list" containing the names of people whom AQAP identified as the main instigators behind the campaign to insult Muhammad, including the author of *The Satanic Verses*, Salman Rushdie, and outspoken former Muslim Ayaan Hirsi Ali.[88]

Through *Inspire*, we can see yet another example of how Awlaki was able to harness the power of new media to achieve his goals. He used it as a platform to continue making Salafi-jihadism more accessible and relevant to his audience of Western Muslims. Moreover, Awlaki and his team within AQAP were able to reach out to a wider pool of Westerners for recruitment and offer explanations and justifications for attacks very shortly after they took place. This would ultimately set the foundation for how later groups, including the Islamic State, would attempt to release and disseminate English-language propaganda. *Dabiq* and *Rumiyah*, ISIS' flagship English online magazines, are directly modeled on *Inspire*, in both design and content.[89]

Another area in which Awlaki contributed to ISIS' outreach strategy to Americans was in his growing acceptance of criminal means to support jihadist objectives. In a 2011 volume of *Inspire*, Awlaki issued an opinion permitting "dispossessing the disbelievers' wealth" for the sake of jihad—in other words, legitimizing theft and robbery so long as the proceeds supported jihadist groups.[90] Many Americans, citing this decision by Awlaki, used this method to finance their attacks or travel plans on behalf of ISIS. The first wave of American ISIS travelers from Minnesota paid for their plane tickets to Turkey through the proceeds of a jewelry store robbery, which they justified by citing Awlaki's ruling that it was *halal* to steal from disbelievers to support jihad.[91]

ISIS' interpretation of Awlaki's ruling on criminal methods for the sake of jihad also extended into their recruitment strategies. In his 2011 ruling on the topic, Awlaki expounds the legitimacy of theft, robbery, and other criminal enterprises for building revenue, even arguing that they are preferred forms of employment for Muslims over holding jobs with "regular" salaries.[92] Per Awlaki, Muslims working in the non-criminal economy are forced to pay taxes from their salaries, which feeds wealth directly into the hands of governments that oppress Muslims.[93] ISIS used these rulings to argue in favor of recruiting Western Muslims with criminal pasts, as a critical component of what has come to be known as the "new crime–terror nexus."[94]

Throughout the Western world, the new crime–terror nexus revolutionized the way that ISIS recruited individuals to join the ranks. It opened up new ideological arguments for recruiters, including a redemption narrative that even career criminals could reinvent themselves and be absolved by participating in ISIS.[95] The tactic solidified ISIS' presence in several arenas for recruitment, especially by building recruitment networks within prisons and probations systems in the West.[96] Finally, new recruits with criminal backgrounds brought key skills to ISIS. Jihadists with criminal pasts had access to networks that could source firearms, finances, and other key resources, and had long-standing practice in staying underground and avoiding law enforcement.[97] Awlaki's then-groundbreaking rulings on the permissibility of criminal means and methods in jihadist groups were vital to opening the door for each of these developments.

ISIS is notable for its production of propaganda material in several languages encouraging Westerners to either travel to ISIS-controlled territory or conduct attacks in their homelands, and the bulk of this material (especially the latter category) draws directly from Awlaki's work. Without a doubt, ISIS messaging would not be nearly as potent if not for Awlaki, who helped to lay the groundwork for the global jihad movement in the years preceding the ascent of ISIS. For many young Western Muslims who are now exposed to ISIS propaganda, the messages being relayed to them are built on established memes articulated and popularized by Awlaki during the previous decade. As a result, Anwar al-Awlaki's name and writings are ubiquitous in cases in the current wave of ISIS recruitment in the US, and will likely continue in future waves of Salafi-jihadist recruitment of Americans.

Ahmad Musa Jibril

While Anwar al-Awlaki remains the poster cleric for the Salafi-jihadist movement in the United States, his contemporary Ahmad Musa Jibril also retains an outsized influence. Jibril, a Dearborn, Michigan resident, has been active in the Salafist movement in America since the 1990s.[98] His path towards the violent iteration of Salafism was different than Awlaki's and many others. Unlike Awlaki, who was a mainstream scholar in the Salafi activist tradition prior to adopting a jihadist outlook, the classically trained Jibril was outwardly supportive of violent jihadism since the early 1990s. Despite being one of the earliest American-born Muslim scholars to come out in favor of a violent interpretation of jihad and the groups that perpetrate it, Jibril has still avoided federal terrorism charges. Understanding the interactions between Jibril and law enforcement reveals critical insight about the way that American Salafi-jihadist clerics are able to narrowly avoid prosecution, and how the Department of Justice manages these cases.

Ahmad Musa Jibril was born in Dearborn, Michigan in 1972. His father, Musa Abdallah Jibril, enrolled at the Islamic University of Medina when Ahmad was a child; the younger Jibril would later return to Saudi Arabia to attain a degree in Islamic law from the same institution.[99] While studying Islamic jurisprudence, Jibril focused his studies on prominent Saudi Salafi activist clerics like Salman al-Awda and Safar al-Hawali, among others.[100] Their influence in shaping dissent against the Saudi state in the early 1990s—drawn mostly from the Kingdom's decision to house American troops during the Gulf War—played a significant role in Jibril's formative years as a scholar and ideologue.[101]

When Jibril returned to Dearborn in 1989 after studying in Medina, he began forging new relationships with Dearborn's Muslim community at a number of local universities and mosques. Jibril's initial lectures and sermons promoted political, activist Salafism rooted in the ideology of prominent Muslim Brotherhood members. He also drew on scholarship of the *sahwa*, a movement born from the fusion of Egyptian Muslim Brotherhood political refugees in Saudi Arabia in the 1960s and 70s and local Saudi Salafists.[102] Yet, unlike many of his Salafi activist contemporaries in the United States, Jibril openly supported global interpretations of violent jihad.[103] This interpretation not only put Jibril at odds with many of his ilk, but also precluded his participation in many of the nationwide Salafi-activist organizations that had taken root at the time.

These views are apparent as early as 1995, when Jibril sent a fax to *CNN* praising the 1995 Khobar Towers bombing, carried out by Salafi-jihadists in Saudi Arabia. The attack, which was later tied to al-Qaeda, resulted in the deaths of 19 people, including US military personnel.[104] Jibril, using similar justifications as Osama bin Laden's 1996 communique declaring war on the United States, argued in the fax that:

> The first and main goal behind this first series of bombing [*sic*] is to kick the Jews, Christians and Infidels from the purified lands of the Arabian peninsula ... A third goal is basically a mere lesson for the Saudi regime who over the decades of their oppressing leadership never thought something this big and damaging was imaginable let alone possible, well now we can tell our government it's possible and where that came from there is much ... much ... more ...[105]

Despite his views, Jibril was able to attract followers at the local level in Michigan. His wider Islamic scholarship, which did not only focus on jihad, meant that he was still regarded as a legitimate voice and he was invited to several local universities and mosques in the early 2000s.[106] His extremism soon caused tensions, however. Jibril's highly visible support for violent global jihad led many to view him with suspicion. Even at that time, Jibril was a virulent sectarian, and a Detroit-area mosque permanently banned him from speaking due to his anti-Shi'a pronouncements.[107] These views developed in parallel with Abu Musab al-Zarqawi's controversial attacks on Shi'a holy sites and civilian targets in Iraq. In addition, officials at one Brownstown, Michigan mosque encouraged its members to completely avoid Jibril.[108] Despite the efforts to marginalize Jibril, he continued to attract a significant number of followers from the local community and later, around the world due to his innovative use of new media tools, the status boost he received from a brief prison sentence in the mid-2000s, and the newfound application of his rulings and viewpoints to the post-2014 jihad in Syria and Iraq.

Early Online Activism

As early as the late 1990s Jibril was one of the early pioneers to use the internet as a tool to spread Salafist ideology online. On his website, *alSalafyoon.com*, he regularly encouraged his readership to undertake violent jihad against non-Muslims.[109] In addition, he offered lengthy online tirades elucidating other underlying themes from Salafi thought, including anti-Shi'a sectarianism and declarations that modern, secular Muslims were committing apostasy. Well before 9/11, he regularly contributed articles to *alSalafyoon.com* espousing extremist beliefs.

The web archives of Jibril's now defunct website contain records from 1999 onwards and show the plethora of content and services offered by the site, including audio tapes, articles, discussion boards, *fatwas* on business and family issues, and a matrimonial service. In August 2001, just weeks before 9/11, he posted an article entitled "The Call to Jihad in the Quran", in which he praised violent jihad and urged Muslims to embrace its hardships. The post also scolds contemporary Muslims for ignoring their duties as they relate to *al wala wal bara*:

(Muslims) resemble the pre-Islamic ignorant nations, against whom they used to fight in the past. So they have turned on their heels back as apostates from Islam, they have imitated them in their civilization, in their social affairs, in their political affairs, in their character and in the pleasures of their lives.[110]

Another post, "Jihad in Allah's Cause", recounts various stories about jihad. Jibril argues that even paradise is no match for martyrdom: "Nobody who dies and finds good from Allah (in the Hereafter) would wish to come back to this world even if he were given the whole world and whatever is in it, except the martyr who, on seeing the superiority of martyrdom, would like to come back to the world and get killed (in Allah's Cause)."[111] In a post titled "Jihad and Expedition," readers are told that non-Muslims must accept Islam or pay a special tax (*jizya*) for non-Muslims: "If they accept neither option, fight them: If they refuse to accept Islam, demand from them the Jizyah. If they agree to pay, accept it from them and hold your hand. If they refuse to pay the tax, seek Allah's help and fight them."[112]

The website also featured a poem which contained praise for Osama bin Laden and Taliban leader Mullah Omar:

Yes, you're neither Sheikh Osama nor Mullah Umar / But, don't forget you're a Ummah of fighter Apostle / Why are you waiting go and thrust / In the lines of enemies and have them crushed / Hit them on the neck and send them to hell / If you're killed, you'll be received there well / . . . Give them a knife and a bulletful of gun / Ask them to battle with joy and fun / Fight, Fight & Fight, it must be our aim / What we learn from Quran and Elder's theme.[113]

Sectarian messages, a feature of all forms of Salafism, were also common on *alSalafyoon*. In one post, Shi'as are described as non-Muslims and "followers of the Devils."[114] Perhaps the most striking post of all was in relation to a major earthquake which took place in Turkey in 1999, resulting in the deaths of over 17,000 people. The disaster was, according to Jibril, the result of a divine punishment for Turkish secularism and the Israeli soldiers who were permitted to be stationed in the country by Turkish authorities at the time:

Many have differed in opinions and thoughts about it some sympathizers and some who felt Turkey deserved more, and we are of the second category, and one must ask why? . . . It is the Turkish government and along with the support of the Turkish population that declared war upon Allah in the past few years and especially in the past few months. It is the grand kids of the heroic men of the Ottoman empire who saved Islam for a long period of time who have come now to throw their fore fathers teaching behind their back and declare war on Allah openly and clearly without fear of anything or anyone.[115]

Whereas many in America's Salafist community sought to cover up their previous statements in support of violent jihad in the wake of 9/11, Jibril made no such efforts. Even after he launched a second website, *ahmadjibril.com*, he maintained his online activity through *alSalafyoon* through at least early 2013. Jibril's activity on *ahmadjibril.com* included referencing jihad as a means of attaining paradise, denouncing secular leaders as tyrants (*tawaghit*), promoting a strict legal code (*sharia*), and covering appropriate applications of excommunication (*takfir*) on Muslims. He also provided a schedule on this website of his classes and lectures at various local universities and mosques, in addition to at his family's home in Dearborn.[116]

Starting in 2003, Jibril also created a Yahoo! message board, "AhmadJibril-IslamClasses," for his students and other interested parties, serving as content moderator.[117] Some of the online forum's 485 members followed Jibril's father, Musa Jibril, who was also preaching in the Dearborn area at the time. As with his website domain *ahmadjibril.com*, Jibril posted information about his upcoming campus lectures, and members of the forum could post links to audio files they had recorded from these events. He received significant buy-in from local communities, with many spiritual leaders and imams on college campuses promoting Jibril's online presence and hosting him on campus.[118] That relationship took shape as the local scholar-turned-spiritual guide gained the trust of members of his community before attempting to isolate them gradually from the broader Dearborn area community. Jibril encouraged his followers to avoid associating with non-Muslim locals, enforced wearing the hijab for observant Muslim women, and espoused his disdain for American involvement in the Middle East.[119]

Known among his followers and friends in Dearborn as "AJ," Jibril was also the focal point of many local social gatherings and events. In a post from August 2003, he asked which of his followers would like to join him on a boating trip:

> we're going on a boat this morning (Wed. 8-13-2003) with Abdelrazzak (Adel's brother) as our captain there is room for one or two more brothers,,,,
> Call me asap if your interested in going . . .
> (IF more brother call than we can take priority is for those consistant in coming to our halakas) :)[120]

Soon after he writes about his experience of presiding over the wedding of two of his followers, joking that the brother of the groom "told him moments before I performed the *nikah* [marriage rites] if he wants to escape there is window behind him."[121] This is one of a number of weddings he mentions in the message board, and it is likely that he was offering various pastoral services for the community.

His tone often reflects the experiences of a close-knit circle of friends, of which Jibril was at the center as a spiritual leader and mentor. He provided his personal mobile phone number, and was regularly consulted by followers on a range of religious issues. During one particularly busy period, he wrote an apology for being more difficult to access than usual:

> *I know PLENTY of brothers and sisters are mad that i'm not good in responding to email and phone calls,,,
> PLEASE FORGIVE ME!!!!

It's not personal,,, inshallah during this week and after it i will be catching up on calls and emails,,,

I WILL BE ANSWERING MY PHONE inshallah everynight from 9:30pm to 2am for any questions, and concernns.

Please leave a message if i do no respond because I may be speaking to someone else,,,,[122]

Other postings from Jibril on the forum take the form of articles on issues of creed and politics, including one essay on the grandson of Muhammad ibn Abd al-Wahhab, in which Jibril refers to al-Wahhab as the "reviver of Islam." The article, from January 2004, is written as a critique of the Saudi establishment, and was inspired by the anti-regime activism of the *sahwa*. The purity of the vision of al-Wahhab was lost, according to him, under "the so-called al-Saud" regime which "became enslaved by British and Western foreign policies."[123] The final sentences of the article are among his most aggressive in the message board:

O Allah, You alone we worship and to You we pray and prostrate, for your sake we strive. We hope for your mercy and fear your punishment, for your punishment will certainly reach the disbelievers. O Allah, punish those who are preventing others from following and spreading your way.[124]

Shortly before his trial in 2004, when Jibril was the focus of a federal investigation, he posted an article about the imprisonment of Ibn Taymiyya during the early fourteenth century. While he does not explicitly refer to his own circumstances, this can be seen as an attempt to present himself, like Ibn Taymiyya, as a victim of powers intent on stopping him from spreading Islam in its purest form. "Legends" like Ibn Taymiyya," he wrote, "live on forever," while "savage ... informants [and] sellouts ... die out fast."[125] Jibril's final post on the message board was in November 2004, and soon after he was arrested and eventually imprisoned. The effects of Jibril's activism both online and in person had a lasting effect, and long after his arrest, his students and followers continued to be active online and express support for their spiritual leader.[126]

Imprisonment and Release

In 2004, a federal district court found Ahmad Musa Jibril and his father guilty of a laundry list of charges, including bank fraud, mail fraud, social security fraud, money laundering, possession of firearms and ammunition by a felon, and failure to pay income taxes.[127] According to a supplemental sentencing memorandum from the case, the father–son duo were found to have been "systematically destroying their rental properties for the insurance proeeeds, and bullying and threatening tenants in the process."[128] Jibril was sentenced to eight years in prison, and spent most of his time in the Federal Correctional Complex in Terre Haute, Indiana.[129] Though Jibril was not convicted on terrorism statutes, the government's prosecution argument made ample use of Jibril's activities on *alSalafyoon.com*, an incriminating photo album extracted during a sweep of Jibril's house, and multiple pro-Hamas images displayed openly in his house, to argue for an enhanced sentence.[130]

While Jibril was in prison, his Dearborn followers continued to maintain his website, allowing him to send articles from behind bars for them to post online. After Jibril engaged in what one counterterrorism official from the Federal Bureau of Prisons (BOP) described as "conduct detrimental to the security infrastructure" at other prisons—likely a reference to the continued communications with his followers in Dearborn—he was transferred to FCC Terre Haute,[131] one of the two BOP facilities to house a Communications Management Unit (CMU), a special prison unit first established around the time of Jibril's conviction to house inmates whose communications with the outside world could pose a special risk.[132] Inmates housed in the CMU can communicate freely with one another, but their ability to contact anyone outside the unit is severely restricted.[133] Sending Jibril to the unit substantially hampered his ability to radicalize and inspire extremists from behind bars. Rather than reforming Jibril's extremist views, however, prison appears to have only hardened his resolve. More importantly, it gave Jibril access to several other convicted jihadists and a platform within the prison.

At the time, a substantial percentage of the inmates housed in FCC Terre Haute's CMU were convicted terrorists.[134] Jibril became an influential figure among the Muslim prisoners, and was soon their unofficial spokesman, often taking their concerns and requests to the prison authorities. While the specific stories below could not be confirmed, the BOP official commented that Jibril did act as an informal religious leader within the CMU, pointing to his behavior as an instance of "offense paralleling," where offenders engage in the same conduct behind bars as they do outside of custody.[135] An article on Jibril's website, purportedly a letter from a prisoner who was held with him in the CMU, makes similar allegations. The prisoner praised Jibril's leadership qualities and backed the claim that he was influential among Muslim prisoners, even referring to him as their "emir":

> Prior to his arrival we had many internal problems. Muslims with each other, Muslims with non-Muslims and Muslims with staff. The problems among the Muslims themselves stem from the diversity of the brothers here; we have modernists, we have nationalists who fought with the PLO in the 80's, we have Salafis, we have *Ikhwan* [Muslim Brotherhood], we have very young brothers . . . As soon as this blessed Shaykh arrived we all saw in his apparent *taqwa* [piety] . . . vast amount of knowledge, charisma and personality; a man who would change our situation. The Muslims here for the first time since the CMU opened and I was among the first to come to this unit when it opened all agreed by consensus for the first time that he should be our Amir days after he arrived.[136]

According to the letter, the prisoner's respect for Jibril was seemingly due to both his training as an Islamic scholar in Saudi Arabia and his knowledge of the American justice system: "He is also a graduate of Law from Michigan so he knows how to deal with the staff and their intrusions upon our rights!! I'm not sure if it's respect or fear (I lean more to the latter) but he is running this unit by the blessing of Allah."[137] Similar to how he operated in Dearborn, he held daily sessions with prisoners and instructed them in a range of topics related to Islam and Islamic law.

Among the attendees of Jibril's lectures was a man who became a household name in the United States after serving a 20-year sentence for providing material support to the Taliban: John Walker Lindh.[138] Jibril allegedly harbored a deep fondness for Lindh, gaining his trust and admiration as he did a number of Terre Haute prisoners and Dearborn community members before them.[139] In one letter to his congregants in Dearborn, Jibril praised Abduwali Muse, a Somali pirate and the sole survivor of the gang of pirates who hijacked the *Maersk Alabama* off the coast of Somalia in April 2009.[140] Muse was also an inmate at Terre Haute, and Jibril wrote that he was allowed to visit him, even though Muse was being held in solitary confinement. Jibril also wrote that he spoke "on behalf of the Muslims" in the prison when he asked the authorities to place Muse in the general population, which he claims that "they gladly did."[141]

Jibril's imprisonment led his followers to lionize him, claiming that he was a prisoner of conscience, unjustly arrested by infidels. By the time Jibril was released from prison in 2012, a new conflict had begun in Syria that would create a massive new recruiting pool for American Salafi-jihadists, and many of the al-Qaeda generation of Salafi-jihadist ideologues (including Anwar al-Awlaki) were either dead or still in prison. The newly freed Jibril was an excellent candidate to fill the void created by Awlaki's death and became the iconic American preacher behind the mobilization of Salafi-jihadists to Syria and Iraq.

Ahmad Jibril and the Jihad in Syria

Jibril's status in the American Salafi-jihadist movement exploded after his release from Terre Haute. He is consistently referenced by English-language pro-Islamic State social media accounts, outpacing references to major jihadist leaders. In an analysis of over 845,646 tweets from 1,782 English-language pro-ISIS accounts in the Program on Extremism's database, Jibril was referenced more than Anwar al-Awlaki, ISIS' spokesperson Abu Muhammad al-Adnani, and even Osama bin Laden and Abu Bakr al-Baghdadi. Within the Program on Extremism's catalog of the English-language pro-ISIS Telegram ecosystem, Jibril is the most referenced ideologue or leader with over one thousand mentions.[142] The Dearborn native catapulted into his status through his consistent knack for using digital communications technologies to his advantage and figuring loopholes in the US law enforcement response.

Days after leaving prison, Jibril created an account on Facebook to further disseminate his teachings. In a 2014 study by the International Centre for the Study of Radicalisation (ICSR), Jibril's Facebook page was the most-liked account by Western foreign fighters who traveled to join the Islamic State.[143] He was purportedly the most influential ideologue for these fighters on Twitter, too, and many of his lectures recorded by his acolytes remain available on YouTube. While some of Jibril's more fiery expositions were watered down after his imprisonment, content available on Facebook, Twitter, and YouTube provides substantial evidence of his continued dedication to Salafi-jihadism. It mirrored Jibril's early adoption of web-based tools for spreading his message almost two decades prior.

Jibril constructed his infamous web persona despite strict monitoring by law enforcement. As part of the conditions of his release from Terre Haute, a federal judge restricted Jibril's travel to Eastern Michigan and ordered him to surrender his computer to federal officials if asked by probation.[144] To avoid returning to prison under this intense scrutiny, Jibril's post-prison lectures do not directly incite his followers to violence like his mid-1990s and early 2000s content. He also avoids directly supporting any specific jihadist group. However, he remains in the role of a "cheerleader" for armed Salafi-jihadist groups; supporting the theoretical use of armed force with an underlying current of extremely sectarian, religiously imbued, and emotive language.[145] In analyzing his online lectures, one can see how his followers connect the dots between these themes, and although Jibril does not directly encourage it, the only legitimate action based on Jibril's arguments would be to join a Salafi-jihadist group.[146]

One of his most well-known lectures, "The Only Path to Victory," calls on American Muslims to practice *al wala wal bara* in the extreme so as to preserve and protect the supremacy of Islam from Western influences, warning them that "our religion was sent to be supreme not equal and we must be different than other faiths … whoever imitates a group will be amongst them."[147] Continuing his criticism of Western Muslims who have taken on the values of their nations, he laments the "catastrophe" of them "downplaying the *sharia*" and supporting democracy over the law of God by "saying that the rule of the majority should rule."[148] He goes on to pronounce *takfir* on them, claiming that "those who follow other that what Allah legislated are *mushriqin* [idol worshippers]." In order for Muslims to be "victorious," they had to fulfill the "simple condition" of *tawhid al-hakimiyya* which "reforms … civilizes … [and] humanizes." This is a recurring theme in many of his other sermons. American Muslims, he believes, are putting their faith at great risk through committing acts of *shirk* and *kufr* (disbelief) by accepting and involving themselves in man-made systems of law.[149] For Jibril, there is "no ideology, no law, no system of governance that can be even compared to the laws given to us by Allah."[150]

In addition, Jibril is also celebrated by many in the Salafist community for his expressed beliefs on the Syrian civil war and support for jihadist groups fighting against the Assad regime. Jibril falls short of openly and explicitly encouraging Westerners to travel to the conflict theater, which helps to explain why his work remains widely accessible online. He stokes sectarian divisions by emphasizing Shi'a militia involvement in the rape, torture, and murder of Syrian Sunni Muslim women, condemns those in the West who stand by and watch, and argues that it is impossible for Western Muslims to fully practice the tenets of Islam while living in a secular, democratic society. Instead, he encourages them to travel to places where the *sharia* is being enforced so that they are able to fully practice their faith.[151]

In his most popular lecture on the topic, "Syria in our Hearts," Jibril laments the violence against Sunni Muslims in the country by both the Syrian Alawi soldiers and Shi'a militias, and criticizes his audience for not acting in their defense. Using what by now had become a preferred theme of his, Jibril highlighted crimes committed against the honor and dignity of Muslim women: "They entered a house full of females, they raped every single one of them . . . the Rafida [derogatory and sectarian term for a Shi'a Muslim] gang-raped your sisters in Syria . . . if our women, our honor, are being raped and you don't get mad then our faith is at stake." Muslims must act now as "their [Syrian Sunnis] honor is your honor, their blood is your blood, their soul is your soul" and yet "we eat while our brothers are hungry . . . we laugh while they cry."[152]

Despite these horrors, the United States, Jibril argues, does little to prevent the suffering. This is not due to any specific foreign policy, but because they "are perverted in their nature when it comes to Sunni Muslim blood, they are waiting for the maximum amount of deaths to pleasure and delight their hearts."[153] Discussing the role of the United States in a separate lecture, Jibril suggests to followers that they should make *hijra* (migrate from non-Muslim lands) as a result of the nation's secular laws. In his view, if they are not allowed to "believe in Allah and reject the *taghut* [secular leader]," then they must seek out where they can travel in order to live under Islamic law.[154]

Inflammatory rhetoric such as this is often deployed in Jibril's commentaries on Syria. It is designed to shock, shame, and enrage his audience, likely in the hope that this will spur them on to fight jihad to defend the honor of Muslims in Syria. His attacks on other Muslim sects, calls to make *hijra* to lands governed by Islamic law, and past support for jihad, leaves his audience to conclude that ISIS the only legitimate force operating in Syria. This line of argument, along with his American-accented English and obvious charisma and oratory skills, helps to explain why he is so popular among Western ISIS supporters.

Due to these factors, Jibril's works feature constantly in the radicalization process of jihadist attackers, plotters, and travelers in the West. Most infamously, Jibril is alleged to have inspired the perpetrators of the June 2017 London Bridge and Borough Market attacks.[155] Jibril also leaves a large footprint on the American ISIS scene. The FBI claimed that Mohamed Elshinawy and his co-conspirators, profiled earlier in this book, would constantly share Ahmad Musa Jibril's video lectures with one another, and court documents from that case refer to Jibril as "an ISIL supporter and Salafi shaykh from Michigan."[156] Khalil Abu-Rayyan, an ISIS sympathizer from Jibril's hometown of Dearborn, referred to Jibril's lectures during a conversation with an undercover FBI employee; he was arrested for making plans to "shoot up" a local church on behalf of ISIS.[157] Sebastian Gregerson, another Detroit-area ISIS sympathizer arrested for planning an attack in the US, was also a follower of Jibril's.[158]

Following these reports, and especially after Jibril was implicated in the 2017 London Bridge bombing, public pressure to shut down or disrupt his ability to gain a following through the internet substantially increased.[159] Jibril's terms of probation, including mandatory computer monitoring, expired in 2015.[160] While it is clear from recent cases that he remains on the FBI's radar, to date he has not been accused of committing any crimes following the end of his last prison sentence. In addition to law enforcement, efforts against Jibril's ability to recruit also fall in the lap of social media companies. To this day, Jibril and his followers maintain accounts on Facebook, Twitter, and YouTube, using the platforms to continually release and re-release Jibril's lectures. But even under the rubric of these companies' respective terms of service, very little of Jibril's content could be subject to takedown. Despite its proven value in radicalization and extensive extremist content, Jibril rarely directly incites violence or hatred and does not explicitly support known terrorist organizations or individuals. Even if the case could be made that Jibril's videos and lectures should be removed from the internet—like his contemporary Anwar al-Awlaki—his active group of supporters are likely to continue uploading and re-uploading content at a pace that companies cannot manage, on sites away from their reach, and in ways that avoid content detection algorithms.

Jibril retained relevance throughout multiple previous waves of jihadist mobilization, including the time he spent in federal prison. It is reasonable to expect that his ideas and arguments will maintain their persuasiveness for future generations of American Salafi-jihadists. Federal law enforcement and social media companies alike will attempt to continually pressure Jibril and others of his ilk, but he has consistently tailored his message to avoid prosecution and becoming *persona non grata* on social media. Of the ideologues profiled in this chapter, Jibril may be the most likely to take advantage of a future Salafi-jihadist mobilization: unlike Awlaki, he is an active ideologue who can tailor his own message to ongoing developments, and unlike Suleiman Anwar Bengharsa, he is a well-known entity within the American Salafi-jihadist movement. Even if Jibril adopts an under-the-radar approach, other jihadist ideologues in the US will without a doubt attempt to emulate his model.

Suleiman Anwar Bengharsa

Suleiman Anwar Bengharsa is a relatively obscure Salafi preacher who gained notoriety during recent years for a dubious honor: he is one of the only American imams who have publicly declared their support for the Islamic State. Not much is known about his life prior to 2016, when he received media attention after being linked to several cases of arrested ISIS supporters in the US.[161] A native of Libya raised in the United States, Bengharsa is a graduate of Al-Azhar University in Egypt, the oldest and most prestigious Islamic university in the world. In addition, he claims to have received a master's degree in Islamic Jurisprudence and Law from Sana'a University in Yemen, and a master's degree in comparative Islamic jurisprudence (comparative schools of thought) from the International Islamic University in Islamabad, Pakistan.[162] He served as chaplain for the Maryland Department of Corrections between 2006 and 2009, and later took the position of imam in two Maryland mosques between 2010 and 2014. Since the early 2000s,

Bengharsa has been the administrator of an Islamic online services center, the Islamic Jurisprudence Center (IJC).[163]

Prior to the ISIS mobilization, Bengharsa never established the same foothold in the American Salafi scene as Awlaki or Jibril. While he did give touring lectures at a number of mosques in North America, he never reached the online or offline following of his contemporary Salafi-jihadist ideologues. His YouTube channel, which remains active, has fewer than 200 subscribers, and his most-watched video has less than 1,000 views.[164] It is unclear how many individuals utilize the services offered by Bengharsa's IJC, or access his personal website, *www. suleimananwar.com.*

Bengharsa's outlook and ideology fits clearly within the Salafi-jihadist paradigm, and tenets of Salafi-jihadist thought have been present in his lectures dating back a decade. In 2010, he gave a lecture at a mosque in Toronto, Canada on the jurisprudence regarding interactions between Muslims and non-Muslims. Bengharsa claimed that the use of violence was a prerequisite to establishing Islamic governance, disagreeing with "Muslims among us these days who want to go around and say: 'Oh, Islam was never spread by the sword ...' That's a blatant lie ... the *sharia* was spread by the sword."[165] Furthermore, he argued that several places around the world had established Islamic governance—notably the Taliban-controlled areas within Afghanistan and areas controlled by al-Shabaab within Somalia—and that Western Muslims should travel to those areas. The recommendation becomes an individual obligation if any jihadist group establishes the caliphate. As Bengharsa argued: "When the Caliphate is established, you need to pack your bags and go."[166]

Bengharsa's rulings on the IJC site and his personal webpage also clarify his extreme interpretation of Salafi teachings. Similar to how Jibril used the online forums he created in the early 2000s to facilitate dissemination to and discussions with his followers, Bengharsa used his website to promote his status as a scholar of Islamic law, capable of ruling on a variety of topics relevant to the *sharia*, from consultation for businesses on compliance with the *sharia* in business practices, to settling legal disputes outside the traditional American court system, and guidance for married couples to avoid divorce.[167] While the IJC site has since been taken down, Bengharsa seems to have adopted Jibril's approach and switched to his own personal website, *suleimananwar.com.* But a common thread throughout many of these generally mundane topics is an extremely strict interpretation of the Salafi idea that Western culture and Islamic law are fundamentally incompatible, to the point that Muslims who acknowledge or practice any form of Western culture have removed themselves from Islam.

Like other Salafis living in the West, Bengharsa stresses the importance of living a *sharia*-compliant life and criticizes Western secular and liberal culture. He also espouses *al wala wal bara* as a mechanism to condemn inter-faith initiatives, claiming that they undermine the superiority of Islam above all other faiths.[168] The tell-tale sign of Bengharsa's Salafi-jihadist outlook, as opposed to similar positions expressed by all Salafis, is through his heavy emphasis on *takfir*. The Maryland imam used the IJC as a service to issue *fatwas* outlawing participation in democracy and other secular systems of governance, and declaring those Muslims who did willingly participate as *kuffar* (disbelievers).[169] He regularly deploys the term *taghut* (tyrant) in reference to the US and other secular countries to substantiate his descriptions of the treatment of Muslims under secular states around the world. The only acceptable alternative to the secular systems are states governed fully by Islamic law, underlying Bengharsa's adamant support for the restoration of the caliphate.[170]

Bengharsa virulently criticizes other Muslim scholars—even other Salafis— who disagree with his extreme interpretations in favor of jihad, the re-establishment of the caliphate, and *takfir*. Indeed, non-jihadist Salafis appear at times to be Bengharsa's primary target. He regularly calls out Salafi quietist scholars in America who do not pronounce their disavowal of the US Government, and posted a list to the IJC site of "puppet" scholars that named several Salafi quietist scholars as mouthpieces for the Saudi state, including the Grand Mufti of Saudi Arabia.[171] Bengharsa denounces Salafi quietists as blind puppets of the Saudi government, but he also brings political Islamic groups into his critical purview. Groups like Muslim Student Associations (MSAs) on college campuses are, to Bengharsa, prime examples of Muslim organizations that sacrifice key tenants of their beliefs in order to gain influence, citing their participation in democratic processes as a betrayal of their faith that makes them subject to *takfir*.[172]

Bengharsa's sweeping proclamations of *takfir* declare that, apart from a tiny minority of like-minded believers, all American Muslims are apostates. He ruled in 2017 that anyone who participates in any form of democracy cannot be Muslim.[173] In 2018, Bengharsa issued a ruling declaring that any Muslim who attends a mosque that preaches "Western/Modern Islam," identified by Bengharsa as anything that deviates from strict Salafi thought, participates in any inter- or intra-faith work, or cooperates with authorities, is a disbeliever.[174] Moreover, Bengharsa also considers Muslims who fail to stop associating with apostates to be apostates as well.[175]

Bengharsa's influence appears in at least three cases related to Islamic State recruitment in the United States, including one case in which Bengharsa is alleged to have provided direct support to an individual who was planning an attack in the United States. Yet, like Ahmad Musa Jibril, Bengharsa has never been charged for terrorism-related offenses. In documents related to Sebastian Gregerson, the ISIS supporter whom Bengharsa is believed to have assisted, the FBI assesses that Bengharsa is an "avid ISIL supporter and disseminator of ISIL propaganda."[176] This assessment draws on information about Bengharsa's activities garnered through the Gregerson case, as well as the others in which Bengharsa was directly or indirectly involved.

Gregerson appeared on the FBI's radar after an anonymous tip from a local Muslim community member in Michigan who expressed concerns about a congregant's increasingly supportive stance towards the Islamic State.[177] The anonymous source also detailed statements from Gregerson that indicated his desire to travel alongside his family to the Islamic State's territory in Iraq and Syria. Subsequent searches of his online activity turned up a steady pattern of consumption and dissemination of Islamic State propaganda on Facebook under the pseudonym Abdurrahman Bin Mikaayl.[178] On his Facebook page, Gregerson consumed and disseminated ISIS propaganda, including posts supporting the 2015 Paris attacks as a legitimate act of war against the enemies of Islam.[179] Later, search warrants uncovered several copies of ISIS' official English-language magazine *Dabiq* and 96 CDs containing a collection of lectures by Anwar al-Awlaki.[180] Gregerson communicated his support for ISIS terror attacks to an FBI undercover employee who befriended him, often referring to ISIS attackers as "brothers" fighting "jihad in the cause of Allah."[181]

The investigation also uncovered ties between Gregerson and Suleiman Anwar Bengharsa. While Gregerson still lived in Maryland, he introduced himself to Bengharsa after attending one of his lectures at a local mosque.[182] Although Gregerson moved to Michigan in 2014, he maintained contact with Bengharsa, and the two exchanged messages detailing their approval of ISIS-inspired and coordinated attacks in the West as they were occurring. Both men began actively sharing ISIS propaganda online. Bengharsa posted links to several ISIS propaganda videos, including one entitled "Capture and Slaughter of a Safavid Soldier" which depicted the execution of an Iraqi Army soldier.[183] On one occasion, commenting on a news article he posted describing ISIS' execution of a senior Iraqi army official, Bengharsa commented, "Allahu Akbar!! [God is great]."[184] By 2015, the FBI claimed that it had opened an investigation into Bengharsa to determine whether he was conspiring to provide material support to ISIS.[185]

Bengharsa and Gregerson's relationship evolved beyond simply messaging and sharing propaganda online. In June 2015 and June 2016, Bengharsa sent Gregerson two checks totaling $2,500.[186] While it is unclear whether Bengharsa intended for Gregerson to do so, he used the proceeds to purchase military equipment, including firearms, knives, ammunition, explosives materials, and a grenade launcher.[187] These purchases were not sufficient to arrest Gregerson, as he did not indicate to the FBI, Bengharsa, or anyone else that he was planning to use the weapons to support ISIS in any way. However, after Gregerson purchased grenades from an undercover FBI agent in July 2016, he violated the US statute criminalizing unregistered possession of explosives. He also was charged with an unrelated illegal firearms purchase in Virginia.[188] In May 2017, Gregerson pleaded guilty to these charges, and was sentenced to 45 months in prison.[189]

In a statement, Bengharsa denied giving Gregerson $2,500 to purchase firearms, claiming that he donated the money for charitable purposes.[190] But as part of their case, federal prosecutors claimed that Bengharsa had immense assets and had made other questionable financial transactions. From 2014 until 2015, they showed evidence that Bengharsa received a dozen wire transfers into his bank account, totaling over $900,000.[191] During the same period that he transferred money to Gregerson, he also wired money on three occasions to an unnamed individual in Yemen.[192] Based on their shared support for ISIS, the checks sent to Gregerson that he used to buy weapons, and the regular contact between the two, the FBI concluded that "there is reason to believe that Bengharsa and Gregerson [were] engaged in discussions and preparations for some violent act on behalf of ISIL."[193]

Gregerson's trial documents also connect Bengharsa with another ISIS-related case in Maryland. In July 2017, Yusuf Wehelie was convicted of being a felon in possession of a firearm and sentenced to 120 months in prison.[194] While sentencing guidelines for this offense range from 33 to 41 months, Wehelie received a higher sentence because the judge determined that he was a danger to the public after investigations revealed his professed support for ISIS.[195] While in contact with an undercover agent, he mentioned a desire to either travel to ISIS territory or plan an attack on a US military recruitment station. According to media reports, investigators also knew that Bengharsa was in contact with Wehelie and were exploring their communications as part of the Gregerson case.[196]

More recently, in December 2018, the FBI arrested a 21-year-old ISIS supporter named Damon Joseph for attempting to attack a synagogue in the Toledo, Ohio area. Joseph, a convert to Islam, communicated with several undercover employees about his plans to conduct a similar attack to the Tree of Life synagogue shooting carried out by a right-wing extremist in October 2018.[197] On Joseph's Facebook page, he frequently shared content from Salafi-jihadist ideologues alongside a barrage of anti-Semitic invective. As well as quotes from Anwar al-Awlaki and Ahmad Musa Jibril, Joseph shared a post referencing one of Bengharsa's *fatwas* on whether Muslims were obliged to live under the laws of the countries in which they lived.[198]

In the midst of these allegations, Bengharsa remains active and bullish on his viewpoints. In 2017, in response to the claim that he was responsible for radicalization of young Muslims, Bengharsa flipped the interpretation of the term "radicalization":

> "radicalization" is a term used to categorize people who disagree with the status quo (*taghut* system), and who are considered disloyal to it . . . when someone is de-radicalized, it simply means that he/she is once again loyal to the system of *taghut*. He is no longer a threat to the status quo (the way things are and should be).[199]

Bengharsa also has continued to expand his social media presence. In late 2018, he opened an online study program on his website for a course in the foundations of Islamic practice.[200] To accompany the course, Bengharsa opened a SoundCloud channel with audio recordings of his lectures.[201] Following the Program on Extremism's release of its 2018 study on Salafism in America, which profiled Bengharsa, he posted a link to the report, commenting that "one of the highest honors and excellent credentials a muslim can receive is that the enemies of Allah take him as their enemy."[202]

Despite maintaining an online persona, Bengharsa's rise to prominence in the American Salafi-jihadist scene would appear to stem less from his online presence and more from in-person connections. His interactions with the American ISIS scene were limited mainly to people he met in his own backyard, and he never enjoyed the nationwide or global appeal of Anwar al-Awlaki or Ahmad Musa Jibril. However, like the other ideologues profiled in this section, Bengharsa remains within his First Amendment rights despite being one of the few American imams to openly pronounce their support for the Islamic State. To this day, prosecutors have been unable to make a case against Bengharsa, especially without proof that the payments that he made to Sebastian Gregerson were directly intended to be used to facilitate a terrorist attack. In dealing with Bengharsa and others like him, these conundrums leave law enforcement with the difficult task of managing potential national security threats without infringing on fundamental rights provided in the Constitution.

Abdullah Faisal

While not American nor based in the United States, the influence of the firebrand Jamaican-born cleric Abdullah Faisal must be included in any account of English-speaking ideologues' influence on the ISIS-supporting scene in the United States. Faisal, born Trevor William Forrest in Jamaica in 1963, was an ardent supporter of the Salafi-jihadist movement dating back decades, from his time preaching in the United Kingdom in the late 1990s and early 2000s.[203] Due to his caustic lectures promoting al-Qaeda and its attacks, and inciting violence against Jews and Hindus, the UK jailed Faisal for inciting racial hatred from 2004 to 2007. He was deported to Jamaica following his prison sentence and set up a base of operations from his home in Kingston.[204] Despite his fringe extremist beliefs, Faisal underwent rigorous scholarly training for around seven years at one of the most respected Salafi institutions in the world, the Imam Muhammad ibn Saud University in Riyadh, Saudi Arabia. As a result, he is able to project an image as a legitimate Islamic scholar who closely follows the primary texts in all of his lectures.

Faisal's imprint on the American Salafi-jihadist scene includes acting as the de facto spiritual leader of Revolution Muslim, a New York-based cell of al-Qaeda supporters that were connected to several prominent American jihadist operatives.[205] He also used his own US-hosted web platform, entitled *Authentic Tauheed*, to share lectures, teachings, and other propaganda content promoting violent jihad.[206] Zachary Chesser and Younus Abdullah Mohammad (Jesse Morton), two major leaders of Revolution Muslim who had extensive correspondence with Faisal, were both arrested in 2010 and 2011 respectively for inciting murder and attempting to provide material support to a terrorist group.[207] The 2009 "underwear bomber," Umar Farouk Abdulmutallab, as well as the 2010 Times Square bomber Faisal Shehzad, both claimed that they were influenced by Faisal's teachings.[208]

Between 2014 and 2017, operating from his base in Jamaica, Faisal continued to play a role in the recruitment of Americans when the conflict in Syria began and ISIS came to the fore. Using the *Authentic Tauheed* platform, as well as several Twitter, Facebook, YouTube, and WhatsApp accounts, Faisal made declarations in favor of the legitimacy of ISIS' self-declared caliphate and argued that making *hijra* was mandatory for all Muslims.[209] Like Awlaki, he also used Paltalk to deliver live audio lectures, and it appears to have been his preferred platform. Using a chatroom also called "Authentic Tauheed," he would not only provide lectures, but also interacted with listeners using a live chat function. Among the audience were usually members of the *Authentic Tauheed* website admin team, who would transcribe his lectures in real time in the chatroom then later also post the text on the website. These individuals took on the role of his students, and his demeanor was one of a strict, perfectionist, and scolding teacher, often chiding them for misspelling Arabic terms in the transcript or otherwise not meeting his standards: "No, no, no, delete that!"; "Put those words in small letters!" He would also instruct them to find and post quotations from the Quran and *hadith* which he used to back up his every claim, again often scolding them for using the wrong citations or taking too long to post them in the chatroom.

Faisal used this platform for well over a decade to preach jihad to Western, English-speaking audiences. After the rise of ISIS, he used Paltalk from his base in Kingston to promote the group by trying to prove its Islamic authenticity while urging Westerners to either join it in Iraq and Syria or otherwise assist in any way they could. Indeed, of the ideologues discussed here, Faisal is arguably the most explicit in his endorsement of ISIS and in his instructions to Americans to join the group.

One of his first and most influential lectures on the topic, "The Importance of *Hijrah*," was given in July 2014, soon after the establishment of the Islamic State. In it, he gave ISIS' claim to be an authentic Islamic state, or *dawla*, his full endorsement and also urged Americans to leave their homes and join it. The focus of the two-hour-long talk was the duty of Western Muslims to make *hijra* now that there was a legitimate Islamic state for them to live under. Prior to the existence of the caliphate, he argued, many Muslims in the West used the excuse of its absence to remain in the West as law-abiding citizens.[210]

The world, according to Faisal and many other Salafi-jihadists, is split into three "abodes": *dar al-kufr*, in which there is no *sharia* law but the society is not "antagonistic" to Muslims; *dar al-harb*, in which "the infidels are locking up innocent Muslims and killing innocent Muslims abroad" while "their newspapers are used to insult the Prophet in the name of democracy"; and *dar al-Islam*, a "land in which *sharia* is implemented."[211] Living in the first category is considered by Faisal as *makruh*, or an offensive act in Islam but one which is not considered forbidden or a major sin. Living in *dar al-harb*, however, was *haram*, or strictly forbidden in almost any circumstance. Meanwhile, *dar al-Islam* was now a reality with the establishment of the Islamic state: "the *dawla* has been established in Iraq and Syria."[212]

America was now *dar al-harb* due to its wars in Muslim countries and domestic oppression of Muslims. Any Muslim in America who is able must therefore "try to the best of their ability to live in *dar al-Islam* before they die."[213] With the establishment of the Islamic State there should no longer be any reason for forsaking this duty, and yet excuses were still being used. These included the claim that no respected Islamic scholars had recognized al-Baghdadi as the new caliph or sworn *bayaa*, or allegiance to him. This proved, in his view, that some Muslims will always find a reason not to leave the comfort of their Western lives, where they fed themselves using government welfare money and enjoyed sinful romantic relationships with non-Muslims: "They worry about their bellies and their private parts ... they always come with a new excuse!" In addition, he argued that al-Baghdadi himself was a respected Islamic scholar due to his PhD in Islamic Studies. This was an issue that caused Faisal particular frustration; raising his voice he declared that "Abu Bakr al-Baghdadi himself has a PhD in Islam, you fool! Shut up, you hypocrite!" In a separate lecture from November 2016, he also instructed his followers that it was now "compulsory" to swear allegiance to al-Baghdadi because ISIS "fight jihad against God's enemies and implemented the Sharia."[214] Muslims also need not worry about the conditions of life in the caliphate, with Faisal claiming that he was in "direct contact with people living in the *dawla*" who reassured him that "the *dawla* provide for them food ... the *dawla* control oil wells that they took from the kuffar, they sell the oil and use the money to buy food for the people migrating there."[215]

Why, he asked, would a Muslim want to continue living with non-Muslims in the West? They were, after all, "human garbage" who would turn "your children into prostitutes and homosexuals."[216] It was not just for personal reasons that Muslims had to leave, however. Those who stayed continued to bolster the enemy, in part by working and paying taxes which were being used to "kill Muslims." They were helping the *kuffar* "morally, physically and financially." As a result, a believing Muslim could no longer legitimately reside in America and still be considered a believer. In effect, Faisal argued here that the choice not to join ISIS placed an American Muslim out of the fold of Islam. He puts this in crude and explicit terms to his listeners, using a popular Salafi source to argue that, for those Muslims "who prefer to live with the Jews and Christians ... you should chop off this person's head because he refused to live in the *dawla*."[217] It is worth noting here that Faisal, perhaps more so than any other Western jihadist ideologue, has for most of his career put emphasis on *takfir*, and is famous for excommunicating countless Muslims, including well-known jihadis who, in his view, were not correctly practicing Islam.

By joining ISIS, American Muslims were fulfilling what he argued was their religious duty to make *hijra*. They were choosing to "swell the ranks of the Muslims." Not only were they practicing *hijra* by joining ISIS but they were also proving their devotion to *al wala wal bara* by rejecting the non-believers and the *taghut* who were not implementing *sharia* law: "you cannot be a Muslim until you reject the *taghut*—when you make *hijrah* it proves you are a real Muslim and practice *al wala wal bara*."

Faisal meticulously backed up every claim he made with lengthy evidence from either the primary Islamic sources or respected Salafi scholars. Barely a sentence is uttered in his lectures without it being followed by long citations which he often impatiently demands the chatroom admins find and post while transcribing his lectures live. Responding to comments from followers in the chatroom that he was too abrupt with his demands that the citations be found and posted promptly, he argued that this was due to his strict Islamic training, which demanded close reliance on orthodox Islamic sources: "That is how I was educated—if you're going to open your mouth and speak about Islam bring Quran and *sunnah*. I was educated at Muhammad ibn Saud which is the most orthodox university in the world!" Opinions on Islam without such scholarly backing were worthless: "We don't want your opinion. You and your opinions can go to hell!"[218]

His lectures, imbued with authority by this carefully contrived image of scholarly legitimacy that he projected, attracted a variety of American ISIS supporters. The Authentic Tauheed Paltalk room was featured in a number of ISIS cases, including that of Masoud Khan, who was charged in June 2016 with lying to federal agents who interrogated him about his contact with Faisal, including providing the preacher with financial support. In documents related to the case, federal agents described how Paltalk was used by Faisal to incite terrorism and encourage support for ISIS and its leader. They also recount email and other online conversations from late 2012 to mid-2017 between Khan and Faisal that help shed further light on his relationship with and influence over American ISIS supporters. In total, there were over 1,100 messages exchanged between them.[219]

As in many such interactions with ISIS ideologues, the esteem in which Faisal is held by Khan is clear throughout their exchanges. Khan, who was also an avid follower of Anwar al-Awlaki, sees Faisal as not only a leading authority on Islam, but also a source of life advice, especially when it comes to how best to serve Islam.[220] In one of the first emails from Khan in which he discusses his desire to leave the West, fight jihad, and die as a martyr, his deference for the preacher is very apparent, despite never having met him in person:

> So shaikh I need some advice. I was born and grew up in the states . . . I want to get out of here make hijrah and jihad. What is considered a valid place in todays me [i.e., Middle East] to make hijrah to? Im thinking of Medinah, but can you still give me a list of countries that you would recommend. I dont want my children growing up in a kaffir state, where things are just getting more corrupt as days go by. Also I would like to make Jihad InshaAllah for His sake. How can one become a shahid these days? Where is a genuine place I can fight fisabilillah? Palestine maybe? I dont understand the Syria situation that much whos on whos side and or who if any are right or on the truth, let alone whats actually going on over there besides the media here and there. Also my parents want me to finish school and get a degree. They seem to have different expectations of life than I do. So now what should I or can I do? Thanks for your time shaikh.[221]

Masoud received a response from Faisal on the same day, advising that he heed the advice of his parents and "secure a degree before leaving for hijra." He even had a recommendation for which studies to pursue, telling Masoud that the caliphate "is in dire needs of all types of engineers at the moment."[222] Faisal was also often keen for his supporters to send him money, supposedly so that they could do their part in helping him spread "true Islam." Soon, he convinced Masoud to wire a total of $350 to him using Western Union and MoneyGram.

The two also communicated extensively via an unnamed encrypted messaging application, likely to be Telegram. Khan regularly sought out Faisal's advice on how to argue in favor of ISIS with close friends and family who criticized the group and its leader. This included Khan's own mother: "How do I respond to my mom who was using the argument of the recent daesh [ISIS] blasts in the city market that they are evil etc? Her excuse is all they do is kill other muslims."[223] Faisal's response was to send a video depicting the victims of chemical attacks in Syria conducted by Syrian Government forces, suggesting that ISIS was justified in its actions due to the atrocities being committed against Muslims.

In one of the more surreal episodes of their relationship, in April 2017 Faisal informed Khan that his wife would be traveling through Washington, D.C., near where Masoud lived, and wondered if he might be able to buy a car part he needed and give it to his wife. Masoud duly obliged, purchasing the item for $100 and providing it to Faisal's wife after a brief meeting in the D.C. area.[224] Soon after this, Masoud was approached by both the FBI's Washington Field Office and the United States Secret Service, members of which had become aware of his communications with the preacher. In this and subsequent voluntary interviews he denied both the extent of his communications with Faisal and sending funds to Jamaica.

In between each of the at least three voluntary meetings he had with federal agents, Masoud maintained contact with Faisal via the encrypted messenger, informing him of his encounters and asking for advice on how to proceed. Faisal urged him not to provide any information and to lie about their relationship.[225] Masoud, unaware of the intelligence that agents had already gathered, followed the advice. After being given several opportunities to provide the full story, Masoud was eventually charged with providing false statements and pleaded guilty soon after, receiving a 20-month prison sentence. This incident tells us more about Faisal than it does about Khan, whose intentions beyond supporting Faisal financially remain unclear. Faisal, however, was keen to engage in wide-ranging conversations with American ISIS supporters in order to better understand their true intentions and assist them in both developing an understanding of ISIS and its ideology and, if they so desired, traveling to join the group.

More so than others analyzed here, Faisal acted as a direct link to ISIS for Americans, helping to vouch for and put his followers in America in touch with ISIS members who could assist them in traveling to join the group. In his online talks he repeatedly claimed to be in direct touch with ISIS members, and in email conversations with both American ISIS supporters and undercover agents posing as such he provided names and contact details for a range of ISIS members who could be of assistance. He often told followers that they should not attempt direct contact with ISIS themselves due to the chances of being caught in a sting operation, claiming that he could offer them "safe" contacts. Ironically, among those he made his claim to was an undercover investigator online, warning that "I can link u with someone there [the caliphate] ... I don't want U to talk to anyone in dawla from where you are it's too risky ... I don't like talking about D[awla] online bcs the kuffaar will read our text."[226]

In at least one case, Faisal directly recruited an American to join the group. During 2014 and 2015, he was in contact with Keonna Thomas, a Philadelphia woman who attempted to travel overseas to join ISIS.[227] She was also an avid user of Paltalk, which she described in a Facebook conversation as a platform on which she felt "more comfortable to speak freely" because the authorities "don't monitor it."[228] In order to join the group in Syria, she would need to find a suitable marriage partner within ISIS, and she sought Faisal's help in suggesting an appropriate candidate. Not only did he find this for her, but he also conducted an online marriage ceremony and provided her with a marriage certificate that she hoped to use as verification when trying to join ISIS.[229] Thomas was one of a number of female ISIS supporters Faisal offered to help find an appropriate husband whom they could marry upon arrival in ISIS territory. On one occasion, he emailed an unnamed woman who had reached out to him, telling her he had the contact details for "a brother in the dawla who wants to interview u for marriage. Pls Whatsapp him."[230]

Faisal's role as an ideologue also manifested in several prominent domestic terrorism cases. When authorities searched an apartment shared by Elton Simpson, Nadir Soofi and Abdul Malik Abdul Kareem, the 2015 Garland, Texas attack plotters, they found CD recordings of Faisal's lectures.[231] Abdul Razaq Ali Artan, who in November 2016 carried out an attack at Ohio State University in the name of ISIS, was also influenced by Faisal, along with Anwar al-Awlaki.[232]

After an intensive sting operation by the NYPD, the New York state district attorney indicted Abdullah Faisal in August 2017 on state charges of conspiracy as a crime of terrorism and soliciting terrorism.[233] Soon after this, in December 2017, Faisal was also named by the US Treasury Department's Office of Foreign Assets Control (OFAC) as a "Specially Designated Global Terrorist."[234] According to OFAC Director John E. Smith, "Faisal has recruited for and provided support to ISIS and his actions have influenced terrorists who engaged in bomb plots and other horrific attacks on innocent civilians."[235] During the NYPD investigation, Faisal attempted to recruit and sent ISIS propaganda to at least one undercover officer. Jamaican authorities, pursuant to an extradition request, arrested Faisal shortly thereafter. Today, he remains in Jamaican custody awaiting extradition to the United States.[236]

The Future of American Jihadist Ideologues

Extremist ideologues are a persistent counterterrorism problem for United States law enforcement. On one hand, Salafi-jihadist ideologues who can translate the movement's complex ideas about religion, faith, practice, and politics into an American vernacular are critical elements of how groups like ISIS are able to recruit Americans. In each of the cases profiled above, ideologues served important functions: *legitimization* of ISIS' tactics and objectives through the selection, adaptation, and presentation of religious precepts; *incitement* of supporters to act on behalf of the group through whatever means necessary; and, in some cases, *recruitment* of supporters to formally join ISIS' cause. While not all American ISIS supporters had direct links to ideologues, the ideas they promote consistently appear in narratives about their radicalization process, as key pieces of evidence in their prosecution, and sometimes as abstract concepts that passed through multiple links in the chain of dissemination before they reached a supporter. Ideologues and ideology should not be viewed as the only factor in why Americans support the Islamic State, but it is nevertheless an important one.

As the profiles in this chapter demonstrate, several constraints hinder the response of the US to American jihadist ideologues. These likely entail that ideas promoted by Anwar al-Awlaki, Ahmad Musa Jibril, Suleiman Anwar Bengharsa, and others will survive long after the age of the Islamic State, and that the next generation of ideologues will draw from their example. The first and most important constraint is that the traditional arsenal of American counterterrorism responses—leadership decapitation through kinetic measures or prosecution—has been marginally effective at best against American jihadist ideologues. The long-standing maxim that ideas are impossible to kill is especially appropriate in this circumstance. As counterterrorism authorities found out in the years after the 2011 death of Anwar al-Awlaki in a drone strike, his ideas survived and gained new relevance during the ISIS age.

Arrests, trials, convictions, and prison time also do not appear to have been an effective response to ideologues. In the first place, it is very rare that the Department of Justice is able to build terrorism cases against ideologues, unless they move from legitimization and incitement into direct recruitment. It is imperative that First Amendment protections—even for religious extremist ideologues—be upheld, and that law enforcement does not cross the line into arresting ideologues for voicing opinions or support for Salafi-jihadist groups, no matter how reprehensible they are. To disrupt ideologues through prosecutorial means, US law enforcement is forced to build non-terrorism cases against ideologues, like Ahmad Musa Jibril's prosecution for fraud, money laundering, and firearms possession. This is a disruption, but ideologues quickly find themselves back on the street after serving shorter sentences. Oftentimes, like with Jibril or Abdullah Faisal, their time in prison lends to the perception amongst supporters that they are prisoners of conscience, and they can use their time behind bars both as a status boost and an effort to build new networks and connections.

Another constraint for law enforcement is that it is increasingly difficult to detect, identify, and monitor who the key American ideologues in the Salafi-jihadist movement are. The movement's predilection towards web forums, social media, and other communications technologies allows individuals to project themselves as ideological influencers, sometimes even when they lack traditional bona fides. Trends that exist in other facets of the Salafi-jihadist movement—such as the reduction of the "flash to bang" timeframe for radicalization and networked decentralization—also have distinct effects on the ease and quickness of building an ideologue persona in the movement.[237] Without a doubt, the "usual suspects," including historical (e.g. Ibn Taymiyyah, Muhammad ibn Abd al-Wahhab) and contemporary (Awlaki, Jibril, and Bengharsa) figures, will continue to play decisive roles in influencing the next generation of American Salafi-jihadists. However, keeping up with the American interlocutors that present their arguments to new generations will require a close eye towards new tools used by the movement.

A recent example of American jihadist ideologues using new digital tools to build influence is that of Said Azzam Mohamad Rahim, a Dallas, Texas man who was convicted in May 2019 of conspiring to provide material support to ISIS.[238] Rahim, a convenience store owner with an extensive criminal record and no apparent religious training, also operated a 10,000-member channel on the internet-based walkie-talkie app Zello where he acted as a quasi-religious authority.[239] On the channel, entitled "State of the Islamic Caliphate," Rahim answered various questions posed by followers across the world, providing religious sanction and justification for ISIS and encouraging others towards conducting specific attacks in the name of the organization.[240] Rahim's real-life credentials were shaky at best, but thousands of Salafi-jihadists across the world looked towards him for answers on religious matters. Among the ISIS supporters who asked Rahim for advice was Salman Abedi, one of the perpetrators of the 2017 Manchester Arena bombing. Responding to a question that Abedi asked via the Zello channel prior to the attack about its potential legitimacy, Rahim responded: "to the boy from Manchester I say, OK, kill them! Show no mercy to civilians."[241]

Outside of the traditional counterterrorism methods used by US law enforcement, the strategies that digital service providers have used to counter the influence of ideologues on their platform also have proven ineffective. In November 2017, YouTube made a landmark decision, taking down thousands of videos of Anwar al-Awlaki's lectures and imposing a full platform ban on any of his content.[242] Nevertheless, videos of Awlaki, including his most infamous lectures, are constantly uploaded and re-uploaded onto the platform by supporters who use several methods to sidestep the platform's detection protocol. Beyond YouTube, archives of Awlaki's lectures alongside other prominent jihadist ideologues are stored on platforms that are easily accessible to English-speaking supporters. Where traditional military or law enforcement responses intended to disrupt the influence of Salafi-jihadist ideologues have failed, internet-based takedown measures are even more difficult. Taking down a video or removing a website rarely signals the end of an ideologue's online presence. Ideologues and their supporters are especially persistent about spreading content through as many websites, social media platforms, and accounts as possible.

Less traditional methods may not have completely eliminated the influence of America's Salafi-jihadist ideologues, but they have in some cases created a fissure between the ideologues and potential followers by containing the ideas and preventing their virality. It is worth noting that many of these ideologues were denied critical platforms because of their extreme ideas—such as decisions by several Dearborn-area mosques to ban Jibril from preaching. In the digital space, preventing ideologues from reaching a broader audience through re-posting caps, "shadow banning" (deleting or banning accounts without informing the user that they have been banned), or redirects all help limit the virality of content produced by ideologues.[243] These solutions are far from perfect, but they address some of the gaps in using traditional disruptions against such figures, attempting to contain the impact of ideologues and ideology while recognizing that completely eliminating either is a fundamentally unattainable goal.

Nevertheless, ideologues are likely to be just as relevant for the American branch of the Salafi-jihadist movement in the future as they were in decades past and during the current wave of ISIS recruitment. Like others in "support" roles within the movement, such as attack planners, travel logisticians, or e-activists, they tie critical threads between the American Salafi-jihadist milieu and the global movement. Through religious legitimization of the movement's activities, inciting followers to take action, and sometimes recruiting them to join the group, the roles played by a handful of English-speaking Salafi-jihadist ideologues in the United States had an outsized effect on the development of the movement, even in a circumstance where ISIS had few physical networks of operatives on the ground. In future generations, a combination of the old guard of Salafi-jihadist "scholars" and new ideologues will continue to motivate the American Salafi-jihadist movement. If lessons from the cases of Anwar al-Awlaki, Ahmad Musa Jibril, Suleiman Anwar Bengharsa, and Abdullah Faisal are any indication, disrupting the cross-generational potential of Salafi-jihadist ideas, ideologues, and ideology is a herculean task for counterterrorism authorities.

Chapter 6

COUNTERING VIOLENT EXTREMISM IN AMERICA

In March 2014, the Department of Homeland Security (DHS) and the National Counterterrorism Center (NCTC) had a problem. For months, both agencies had spent countless hours setting up a large community engagement program in North Carolina. There were repeated calls and meetings with Muslim American religious leaders to explain why the two counterterrorism organizations thought it was imperative to run something called a Community Resilience Exercise in Raleigh. The CREX, as it was called within government, is a hypothetical scenario that unfolds in stages, appearing to show a person radicalizing to violence. Usually run with a crowd evenly split between law enforcement and community partners, it is meant to bring out a discussion on what role each side can play in terrorism prevention. Each side takes the role of the other, so community partners are law enforcement and vice versa. This role reversal helps set the stage for a better understanding of the limitations and misconceptions each possesses when trying to disengage an individual from extremist action.

On the government side, the local US Attorneys were supportive but hesitant to allow D.C.-based bureaucrats to sweep into their area and run a delicate conversation between law enforcement and the public about terrorism recruitment in the United States. After some hand holding, both agreed that March 20 would be the kickoff event. Representatives from DHS and NCTC had just begun the more than 280-mile trek from the nation's capital to Raleigh, North Carolina when their phones started ringing. The FBI had arrested Avin Marsalis Brown, the first American charged with attempting to travel to Syria to join ISIS.[1] Brown was handcuffed and charged while at Raleigh Durham International Airport, only a few minutes from the would-be community engagement venue. The case hinged on the use of an informant, a particularly sensitive touchpoint in community relations. Muslim American leaders wanted to cancel the event. Law enforcement was also reluctant to participate, citing concerns that they would have to answer questions about an ongoing investigation. After some careful negotiating and numerous conference calls, the CREX went off without a hitch.

The three-hour event helped both sides understand where the other was coming from on addressing homegrown terrorism. An action plan was developed, with specific roles and responsibilities for both community partners and government officials. The near failure of the Raleigh CREX was a microcosm of a larger issue with countering violent extremism programs. The public–private partnership hinged on trust and an understanding of what the efforts sought to accomplish. After years of only hard counterterrorism approaches to extremism in America, and administrations that struggled to define the scope of the initiative, that trust and understanding was in short supply.[2]

There is an ongoing, and perhaps never-ending, debate within policy circles on when and where countering violent extremism programs began in the United States. Some in the Bush Administration argue that the "ideas and actions" section of their national security strategy was the first marker.[3] Others say the story of the United States terrorism prevention program began in earnest in 2011 with the release of an Obama-era strategy entitled "Empowering Local Partners to Prevent Violent Extremism in the United States," that focused exclusively on the issue.[4]

There is, however, little debate on whether it has been implemented effectively. By every objective measure, it has not. The story of terrorism prevention in America is one of fits and starts. Countering violent extremism programs have had many bosses, quite a few iterations, and little coherency. To those true believers of prevention programs, it is the best of government, an attempt to save people from themselves. To those who saw the last two decades of counterterrorism approaches as government overreach, fraught with civil liberties abuses, countering violent extremism is another thinly veiled attempt to profile Muslim Americans and police their thoughts and religious beliefs. Like most extreme policy positions, both are wrong. The focus of countering violent extremism was shaped by a small but persistent band of bureaucrats in three different presidential administrations who were given a small mandate and little funding, but also believed that most people drawn to jihadist ideology, if given options and a way out, would choose to come back into the fold of normal society. To understand the evolution of countering violent extremism policy in the United States, it is important to start with a series of mundane government meetings in London.

A Transatlantic Idea

The concept of American counter-radicalization programs was born out of a series of conversations between British and American security officials in early 2004. A cross-pond collaboration structure called the Joint Contact Group included senior leadership from both countries' counterterrorism apparatus. The organization met every six months, rotating between Washington, D.C. and London.[5] In the summer of 2004, at a meeting in the Reagan Building in D.C., American officials pushed their British counterparts to be more forceful on counter-radicalization programs. Senior American counterterrorism leadership spoke of overarching efforts to conduct community engagement across the country. The conversation helped spark action, but only on one side of the table. The United Kingdom was about to put significant resources into countering violent extremism programs, while

American officials would talk about forthcoming efforts but take years until they caught up with their foreign colleagues.[6]

While the Americans were struggling to understand homegrown terrorism and create structures to address it, the United Kingdom was pushing ahead with an ambitious plan to implement counter-radicalization polices. These included efforts to deradicalize individuals who had already adopted extremist ideas and had taken part in or were contemplating violence, as well as those aimed at preventing radicalization in the first place. The flagship program of this effort was named *Prevent*, and it was included in the 2003 British counterterrorism strategy called CONTEST under the Labour Government headed by Prime Minister Tony Blair. Alongside standard hard-power counterterrorism measures such as pursuing and arresting terrorists was a new and ambitious plan to figure out how and why individuals were drawn to terrorism and address these factors further upstream, in the hope people could be guided away from violence before they committed, or even contemplated it.[7]

In its initial phases, *Prevent* was run by the UK Department for Communities and Local Government and acted as a funding and support system for community groups that were best placed to address the needs and concerns of local youth who may be vulnerable to radicalization. This came in the form of the Preventing Violent Extremism Pathfinder Fund, which was launched in late 2006.[8] Its stated aim was "to support priority local authorities in developing programs of activity to tackle violent extremism at a local level."[9] The idea was to increase what the government described as "the resilience of communities to violent extremism." The types of local programs that were funded ranged from religious organizations to debate and discussion forums and sports activities. Between 2007 and 2008 around six million pounds was disbursed to 261 separate local projects as part of the fund.[10]

Soon, however, the fund, and *Prevent* more widely, began to receive criticism from various angles. Among the first issues to arise was how precisely those implementing the program planned to evaluate the success and impact of the local projects that received funding. It soon became clear that there was no system in place to gauge this, despite the amount of taxpayer funds committed to it. Secondly, and perhaps most damagingly, civil liberties groups and Muslim activist organizations argued that *Prevent* was targeting and unfairly stigmatizing British Muslim communities. They were, it was argued, all being treated as potential terrorists by the state. It was also suggested, though with little evidence, that those organizations which received *Prevent* funding were being asked in return to spy on local Muslim communities and report back to the government.[11]

By 2011, these issues had turned *Prevent* into a toxic brand that was widely distrusted by British Muslims and in need of an urgent overhaul. Prime Minister David Cameron's new Conservative Government, elected in 2010, commissioned a review into the program which concluded, among other things, that *Prevent* should be significantly reduced in scope and moved from the Department for Communities and Local Government to the Office for Security and Counter-Terrorism. A broad-based engagement with communities was to be scrapped in favor of targeted interventions under what was called the Channel program.[12]

This approach to countering violent extremism stemmed from years of intervention strategies for other at-risk populations in different sectors of society, from child wellbeing to drug abusers and criminal offenders. Across the board, these strategies adhered to the principle of early intervention, and the approach to countering radicalization was to be no different. It is possible and necessary, the thinking went, to conduct early interventions before the individual is radicalized and considering undertaking a violent extremist act.[13] Because radicalization processes are incredibly diverse, comprehensive deradicalization and intervention programming needed to address a number of factors. How are individuals identified? How is risk and vulnerability to radicalization measured? How can accelerated radicalization processes (and faster mobilization to violence) be isolated from more gradual processes and assessed? How should intervention be staged? Once staged, how should intervention make the transition to deradicalization processes, and how are those processes monitored and evaluated?[14] It was these and other questions that practitioners grappled with in the UK's opening years of counter-radicalization programming.

To answer the first question regarding identification of at-risk individuals, they first turned to studies of convicted terrorists in the UK, using the individual factors from each of the cases in that population to build an assessment framework.[15] Once vulnerability factors from these past cases could be identified and pooled into the assessment framework, they were adopted by the Channel program. When Channel adopted the assessment framework in 2012, it organized those vulnerability factors into three broad dimensions: 1) engagement, 2) intent to cause harm, and 3) capacity to cause harm, the three together forming Channel's referral process.[16] Engagement factors, sometimes called "psychological hooks," detail the different push and pull factors that drive individual radicalization processes, including perceived grievances, threats to self, identity searching, adventure-seeking, family/friend/close social circle involvement in extremism, and mental health issues. Intent to cause harm, however, includes a number of factors that mark a separate stage in which individuals are ready to carry out violent acts. Intent factors range from dehumanization of perceived out-groups to attitudes that justify violence. Third, capacity to cause harm denotes the smallest pool of the three, specific to individuals who have the personal capability, resources, and/or networks to successfully carry out an attack. Operational skills and attack equipment are two obvious factors.[17]

Using the assessment framework, local area "Channel Panels"—made up of experts from local civil society sectors like education, social services, and mental health, along with religious figures—review individual case referrals to determine whether to provide a specialist intervention mentor, and who that mentor should be.[18] Part of Channel's *Prevent* duties include making sure that panel leadership either use the risk assessment framework or establish another one, develop capabilities to deal with risk, and maintain accountability both within the panel and publicly for communicating those duties.[19] One of the most critical dimensions of Channel Panels' duties ensures that panel leadership and law enforcement share information, built on relationships of trust that Channel programming would not "involve covert activity against people or communities."[20] Part of that trust stemmed from the fact that, once panel leadership agreed on intervention, referred individuals consent to taking part in the program voluntarily.[21]

The selection of who will conduct a specific intervention is largely dependent on panel assessments, where the honest question of "who needs what?" is answered. Interventions aimed at deradicalization can diverge significantly in structure from those aimed only at de-escalation and not deradicalization.[22] After starting, however, interventions can fold in any personnel evaluated to be appropriate and/ or necessary, and can last from several months up to two years.[23] The first stages are aimed at building trust and confidence between the interveners and the individual. One of the defining questions interveners face in these critical initial stages is what role religion should play, and whether religious components to countering violent extremism (CVE) intervention measures are effective, necessary, and/or ethical.[24] In response, Channel practitioners would say that programs do not aim to shape religious and political beliefs, but rather challenge individuals who justify violent behavior using underlying jurisprudence and theology to think through these beliefs. The ways in which mentors tackle these and other difficult challenges are closely monitored and evaluated both throughout the intervention and after deradicalization programming concludes.[25]

The United States was slow to implement its own thinking from the Reagan Building meeting and it represented a shift in the way the US Government had previously discussed addressing homegrown terrorism. By March 2007, the first Congressional hearings were starting to review the US Government's approach to the threat. Michael Chertoff, the then DHS Secretary, told senators that radicalization was a problem for outside America, not within: "The United States is fortunate that radicalization seems to have less appeal here than in other parts of the world." He credited that lack of appeal to a number of issues:

> Though it is difficult at this stage to determine the exact cause of these differences, there appear to be a set of advantages the US enjoys. Among these are economic advantages associated with low barriers to employment markets and business creation, traditional cultural acceptance of religious expression and free speech, unfettered participation in the US political process, and a high degree of social integration.[26]

From every outsider's perspective, the Department of Homeland Security's Civil Rights and Civil Liberties Office (CRCL) would be a strange place to provide the impetus for terrorism prevention programs in the United States. Largely tasked with ensuring that the department's programs did not run afoul of constitutional protections, its staff also found themselves explaining DHS policy to marginalized populations in America. In the mid-2000s, very few offices within the US Government were conducting routine and continuous engagement with Muslim American communities. Headed by Daniel Sutherland, an eternal optimist who was skilled at the interagency process, CRCL punched above its weight and largely set the future direction of CVE programs. Sutherland hired six full-time staffers to engage with Muslim American communities through dedicated community roundtables in places like Dearborn, Michigan and Chicago, Illinois. The roundtables were not specifically focused on counter-radicalization. To the contrary, the agendas were primarily about watchlisting, border screening, and other initiatives that were controversial within Muslim American communities because they were disproportionally affected by DHS' policy implementations. As the roundtables progressed throughout the country, a debate raged within both communities and government on what to call this new initiative.

Terminology to describe counter-radicalization programs has vacillated between broad and specific in the last 15 years. Originally called "countering radical Islam" during the early days of the Bush Administration, by the end of its second term, thinking had shifted on how to describe the programs. A series of engagements were initiated by CRCL with prominent Muslim American scholars and leaders about what name to give to countering violent extremism. In January 2008, it released a memo which summarized that community feedback [27] The opening lines hint at the difficulty US Government officials had at wrapping their heads around the issue.

> Words matter. The terminology that senior government officials use must accurately identify the nature of the challenges that face our generation. It is critical that all Americans properly understand the gravity of the threats we face, and prepare themselves to take the steps necessary to build a secure future. We are facing an enemy that holds a totalitarian ideology, and seeks to impose that ideology through force across the globe. We must resist complacency. The language that senior government officials use can help to rally Americans to vigilance.
>
> At the same time, the terminology should also be strategic—it should avoid helping the terrorists by inflating the religious bases and glamorous appeal of their ideology. One of the most common concerns expressed by Muslims in America, and indeed the West, is that senior government officials and commentators in the mass media regularly indict all Muslims for the acts of a few. They argue that terminology can create either a negative climate, in which acts of harassment or discrimination occur, or, by contrast, a positive climate, such as President Bush's remarks while visiting a mosque in the days after 9/11.
>
> If senior government officials carefully select strategic terminology, the government's public statements will encourage vigilance without unintentionally undermining security objectives. That is, the terminology we use must be accurate with respect to the very real threat we face. At the same time, our terminology must be properly calibrated to diminish the recruitment efforts of extremists who argue that the West is at war with Islam.[28]

Nearly one year to the day later, President Barack Obama was inaugurated into office. His new national security team was increasingly uncomfortable with the use of the word "Islamist" to describe the threat.[29] They were concerned that the general public would not understand the nuances between Islam, describing a religion, and Islamist, a fully-fledged political ideology based on the religion. There was no official memo about the shift, but as the new political appointees made their feelings known at National Security Council meetings, the rest of the bureaucracy fell in line.[30] As such, the term "countering violent extremism," which at the time was seen as controversial, was born.

As the Obama Administration was struggling with how to describe the budding homegrown threat, the summer and fall of 2009 represented an uptick in activity. A New York man, Najibullah Zazi, traveled with two friends to Afghanistan. While there, he received weapons and explosives training.[31] Zazi's return to the United States kicked off a nationwide manhunt that started in Colorado, where he was building a bomb, and ultimately ended with an arrest in New York City.[32] Zazi was just one of many homegrown terrorism arrests spanning Illinois, Minnesota, and North Carolina in late 2009.[33]

The homegrown threat continued unabated and culminated in, at that time, one of the deadliest terrorist attacks in the United States since September 11, 2011. On November 2009, Major Nidal Hasan, an army doctor, walked into the Fort Hood processing center in Texas and opened fire, killing 13 and injuring more than 30 others. An after-action review commissioned by the FBI and led by its former director, William Webster, found "shortcomings in FBI policy guidance, technology, information review protocols, and training."[34] A Congressional review by the US Senate Homeland Security and Governmental Affairs Committee also found systemic failures on the part of the Department of Defense and the FBI. The Senate report called for "a comprehensive approach to countering the threat of homegrown terrorism … [and to] develop a national approach to this challenge utilizing all relevant federal agencies including those not traditionally part of counterterrorism." The report requested that the Department of Homeland Security, Department of Justice, and the Office of the Director of National Intelligence lead the effort.[35]

In a speech to the largest mosque on the East Coast, Deputy National Security Advisor to the President Denis McDonough laid out the forthcoming White House approach to homegrown terrorism and countering violent extremism. In a dramatic shift from DHS Secretary Chertoff's rosy assertions to Congress on the homegrown threat two years prior, McDonough stated, "For a long time, many in the US thought that our unique melting pot meant we were immune from this threat—this despite the history of violent extremists of all kinds in the United States. That was false hope, and false comfort. This threat is real, and it is serious."[36]

For the first time, McDonough gave the contours of the Obama Administration's future terrorism prevention efforts.

So we're devoting extensive resources and expertise to this, including entire analytic units at the Department of Homeland Security and the National Counterterrorism Center. We have a new senior intelligence official focused full-time on radicalization that leads to violence. And we're constantly working with Congress, academic and research institutions, as well as foreign governments, to gain a more precise understanding of this challenge and how to address it.

Second, equipped with this information, we've expanded our engagement with local communities that are being targeted by terrorist recruiters. The departments of Homeland Security and Justice have created new advisory groups, instituted regular outreach sessions, and held dozens of roundtables across the country. It's all been with the goal of listening to your communities, sharing information on how al-Qaeda attempts to recruit and radicalize, and answering the question so many communities have asked us—what can we do to protect our young people?

But we've also recognized that this engagement can't simply be about terrorism. We refuse to "securitize" the relationship between the government and millions of law-abiding, patriotic Muslim Americans and other citizens. We refuse to limit our engagement to what we're against, because we need to forge partnerships that advance what we're for—which is opportunity and equal treatment for all.

. . .

Third, based on this engagement, we're increasing the support we offer to communities as they build their own local initiatives. Every community is unique, and our enemy—al-Qaeda—is savvy. It targets different communities differently. So we're working to empower local communities with the information and tools they need to build their own capacity to disrupt, challenge and counter propaganda, in both the real world and the virtual world.

. . .

Fourth, because the federal government cannot and should not be everywhere, we're expanding our coordination with state and local governments, including law enforcement, which work directly with communities every day. We are in close collaboration with local governments, like Minneapolis and Columbus, Ohio, and we're drawing on their best practices.[37]

McDonough was largely advocating for a national approach that had been piloted in Minnesota for a number of years. Before the ISIS mobilization in that city which is described in Chapter 3, between 2008 and early 2011, nearly two dozen individuals from the city traveled to Somalia to join the al-Qaeda-aligned terrorist organization, al-Shabaab.[38] The US Attorney's Office and the local FBI field office were, by their own admissions, caught flat-footed in addressing this issue. They had little, if any, systematic engagement with the Somali-American community in the area. Law enforcement was searching for ways to increase their connections with the Somali diaspora and looking for any existing programs. They found one through the CRCL roundtable, which had recently been established in Minneapolis.

The Brian Coyle Recreational Center, in the heart of the Somali-American community of Minneapolis, became ground zero for countering violent extremism efforts.[39] Representatives from the FBI, DHS, US Attorney's Office, Department of Justice, and the National Counterterrorism Center descended on the building on a regular basis. Each brought their own style and approach to countering violent extremism efforts. However, there was a downside to this new flood of government focus. Somali-American leaders expressed "engagement fatigue" with the US Government and resented that issues such as unemployment, gangs, and crimes were placed on the backburner while the US Government appeared only interested in stemming the tide of terrorist recruitment.[40]

In August 2011, the Obama Administration announced the release of a new strategy, *Empowering Local Partners to Prevent Violent Extremism in the United States.*[41] At only eight pages long, it was unlike most national strategies in that it read more like a policy speech than a guiding document with objectives, sub-objectives, and measures of effectiveness. The strategy did, however, have three main components: (1) Enhancing Federal Engagement with and Support to Local Communities that May be Targeted by Violent Extremists; (2) Building Government and Law Enforcement Expertise for Preventing Violent Extremism; and (3) Countering Violent Extremist Propaganda While Promoting Our Ideals. In its rollout, Administration officials stated that the National Security Council staff would take the lead on implementation.[42]

Congressional overseers, led by Senators Joseph Lieberman (I-CT) and Susan Collins (R-ME) expressed a continued interest in countering violent extremism efforts. In a September 2011 letter to the Administration, the Senators hammered the lack of a true strategy, stating, "the framework lacks the essential elements of a strategy ... there is no mission statement. Roles and responsibilities are not assigned to any agencies or individuals. And there are no stated strategic goals, performance goals or timelines, nor evaluation methods to measure performance. The framework also lacks resources and budget estimates."[43] They also lamented the lack of a defined lead for countering violent extremism, continuing:

> If your letter [to the Committee] meant that the National Security Staff (NSS) is assuming leadership, then we question the basis for the NSS' authority and are concerned that accountability for this critical mission is placed with a body led by officials who are not serving in statutorily-created roles, confirmed by the Senate, and subject to Congressional oversight — which is crucial to ensure these programs are operating effectively.[44]

Responding to Congressional pressure, the Obama Administration released a Strategic Implementation Plan (SIP) in December 2011.[45] The SIP was designed to act as a detailed blueprint for how the Administration planned to build community resilience against violent extremism, detailing the specifics of the 2011 strategy. While the SIP defines violent extremists as "individuals who support or commit ideologically-motivated violence to further political goals"[46] and notes that it applies all forms of extremism, it also specifies that it will "prioritize preventing violent extremism and terrorism that is inspired by al-Qaeda and its affiliates and adherents, which the 2010 National Security Strategy, the 2011 National Strategy for Counterterrorism, and the National Strategy for Empowering Local Partners identify as the preeminent security threats to our country."[47]

The plan fleshed out the objectives of the Empowering Local Partners strategy in a number of ways. Firstly, it aimed to enhance federal engagement with and support to local communities that may be targeted by violent extremists. It also sought to build up government and law enforcement expertise on methods for preventing violent extremism.[48] To achieve these objectives, the plan called for four fundamental activities that cut across different objectives: whole-of-government coordination, leveraging existing public safety, violence prevention, and community resilience programming, coordinating domestic and international CVE efforts within legal limits, and addressing technology and virtual space.[49] Federal responsibilities for pursuing the Strategic Implementation Plan's objectives by undertaking those activities were delegated through the 94 US Attorneys' Offices nationwide to four agencies: DHS, NCTC, FBI, and DOJ.[50] The SIP also notes that both the DHS and NCTC had begun "raising awareness about violent extremism among private sector actors and foundations and connected them with community civic activists interested in developing programs to counter violent extremism."[51]

The Community Awareness Briefing, known internally as the CAB, was the opening salvo in trying to enhance community engagement on terrorism prevention. To an outside observer, it is simply a PowerPoint presentation with the latest terrorism arrest numbers, examples of terrorism propaganda, and case studies of Americans who ultimately joined jihadist groups. But in the right hands, it is a powerful tool to convince a reluctant audience that terrorist recruitment in the United States is real. The CABs were delivered by a handful of trained community engagement officers at the DHS and NCTC to mosques, colleges, and community centers around the country. Through a small but committed cadre staff at the office of Civil Rights and Civil Liberties, the DHS began experimenting with the CABs at the Department of Justice's BRIDGES meetings, which was their established engagement meeting. The CAB went through many iterations but ultimately settled on an approach that highlighted the human aspect of terrorist recruitment. Instead of a data-heavy presentation, the CAB focused on stories of individuals who joined terrorist organizations with the hope that the audience would be able to recognize those who were drawn to groups like ISIS as individuals who would have been convinced otherwise if given the right community mentorship.

One particularly noteworthy CAB, attended by one of the authors in their official capacity as NCTC staff, occurred in November 2014 at the Abu Bakr mosque outside of Denver, Colorado.[52] A month prior, three young teenage girls from the area had been stopped in Germany with the intent to continue on to Turkey and then Syria to join the Islamic State. The case had shaken the relatively small but rapidly growing Muslim American community in Colorado. At the request of the imam of the mosque, officials from the NCTC and DHS presented the CAB to a room of more than 200 parents. The three-hour meeting kicked off the start of continued engagement with community partners. The US Attorney's Office made the unusual decision not to prosecute the young women for terrorism charges. This decision, which at the time was controversial within the Department of Justice, helped set the stage for achieving trust with community partners that the US Government was not solely interested in arresting their way out of the problem of terrorist recruitment.

The CABs were the most outward sign at the time of the US Government's efforts at countering violent extremism. However, there were problems. Chief among them were that there were too few staff to implement them and there was little follow-up after the initial engagement. At the time, the US Government had only six full-time CVE staffers. Most were assigned to the NCTC, which had little reach into communities outside of Washington, D.C. While events like the Denver CAB briefed well at National Security Council meetings, at the staff level there was growing frustration that not enough was being done to address the growing issue of radicalization of American ISIS supporters. Community engagement officers at the DHS, NCTC, FBI, and DOJ huddled together with an ambitious plan. Dubbed internally as the Group of Four, these staffers from the four main agencies working on CVE decided to refocus efforts on three pilot cities: Minneapolis–St. Paul, Boston, and Los Angeles.[53]

The plan was simple enough. Each of the cities had strong local partners who believed in the countering violent extremism mission. The Group of Four would spend the majority of their time helping build up programming in those three areas with the hope that lessons learned could be later expanded to more municipalities in the future. The "Three-City Pilot" had three distinct approaches: Boston's focused on one-on-one interventions of radicalized individuals, Los Angeles' on broad-based community engagement, and Minneapolis–St. Paul's on what they saw as societal-level root causes of terrorism.

However, while the Group of Four was coordinating in Washington D.C., a more organized effort was building in advocacy and community groups around the country against countering violent extremism. The organizations who opposed the initiatives of the Pilot City programs did not view countering violent extremism as a good-faith effort by the federal government to find alternatives to "counterterrorism as usual," but as an extension of it. The federal government effort to unroll the pilot programs was only in its nascent stages when a sustained pressure campaign against their implementation threatened to unravel the entire strategy.

Counter-Countering Violent Extremism

As the CVE strategy was being rolled out nationwide, concerns among civil rights activists and Muslim American organizations grew regarding the strategy's implementation in local communities and over the direction of the strategy more broadly. Responses ranged from calls for greater institutional checks from civil society on government programs to ending CVE as a strategy altogether. One of the criticisms most commonly raised among counter-CVE activists was, and continues to be, that only Muslim communities are highlighted and stigmatized as suspect communities.[54]

Those concerns and criticisms continued to rise after the initial 2011 SIP release. By 2014, just as the Three-City Pilot Program in Boston, Minneapolis, and Los Angeles was beginning to take shape, protests quickly followed. Organizing under the hashtag #StopCVE, local activists and organizations in each of the three cities staged protests and raised awareness online. In addition to framing their protests as a struggle for human and civil rights, community organizers and legal advocates also tried to situate the post-2011 CVE wave within the context of the War on Terror. By connecting the counter-CVE struggle to the longer history of America's domestic counterterrorism efforts, activists tapped into the fears and lived experiences of Muslim Americans across the US over a decade in the making. When the 2015 interagency CVE Task Force was announced, the FBI's "Shared Responsibilities Committees," modeled on UK *Prevent*'s Channel Panels for referrals and tailored intervention, received some of the greatest condemnation from activists.

In Boston, the Muslim Justice League—formed in 2014 "in response to a pressing need for local Muslim-led defense of our communities' human and civil rights against the 'War on Terror'"—drew support from a number of members, individual donors, and foundations like the Hyams Foundation, Episcopal City Mission, Barr Foundation, and others.[55] The Muslim Justice League went on to receive a seed grant from the Harvard Law School Public Service Venture Fund in 2015. In addition to organizing protests, the group also provided Know Your Rights workshops and pro-bono legal representation to community members who had been approached by the FBI.[56]

A Muslim advocacy group called Council on American–Islamic Relations (CAIR) soon took the lead in organizing resistance to CVE measures in Minneapolis, forming a coalition of over 40 organizations based in the Minneapolis area or in Minnesota more broadly. These organizations co-signed a letter penned by CAIR to CVE-affiliated organizations addressing concerns over what they deemed the "stigmatizing, divisive, and ineffective CVE Pilot Program" being implemented in Minneapolis' Somali-American community.[57]

Perhaps the most sophisticated resistance to CVE, however, came from Los Angeles. While #StopCVE had been organizing opposition protests since April 2016,[58] it was in June 2018 that a petition was signed criticizing the Los Angeles Mayor's Office of Public Safety, Human Relations Commission, and Police Department for failing to release documents regarding the federal CVE grant to the City.[59] This resulted in a lawsuit, filed on June 28, 2018, claiming that the City of Los Angeles had uncritically adopted CVE measures without community transparency, and aimed to publicize that funding stream to analyze and assess the impact on Los Angeles communities.[60] By August of that year, responding to the pressure, the City of Los Angeles announced it would not accept CVE funding.

Though not part of the Three-City Pilot Program, Chicago also witnessed significant counter-CVE resistance to the Illinois Criminal Justice Information Authority's (ICJIA) Targeted Violence Prevention Program (TVPP), a DHS-funded initiative that essentially renamed and rebranded CVE efforts in the city. The TVPP program built on ICJIA's experience with gang prevention models in Chicago's south and southwest neighborhoods, which alone drew significant backlash on the basis that the two issues are both fundamentally different and vary in scope. The unsuccessful track records of gang prevention models certainly did not alleviate these concerns.[61] In this environment, StopCVE–Chicago's coalition was able to draw on a number of organizations, including CAIR, to organize and resist CVE locally.

In a 2017 article for *Just Security*, Faiza Patel, co-director of the Brennan Center's Liberty and National Security Program, summed up many of the sentiments expressed by advocacy and community leaders nationwide.[62] Patel, a leader in the countering-CVE movement, identified three fundamental reasons why she believed countering violent extremism is bad policy. First, she stated that CVE programs are built on a behavioral science that, despite years of research, failed to deliver a concrete profile of an American terrorist or model of terrorist behavior, and which now uses overly-broad indicators to identify individuals who are vulnerable to radicalization. Second, virtually all of the CVE programs with government funding are directed towards Muslim American communities. Third, the high proportion of funding dedicated to policing or adjacent services laid bare the central role of law enforcement to the CVE mission, deepening fears of surveillance in target communities.

A number of the concerns raised by activists and other organizations and individuals involved in counter-CVE are valid. Among them was the criticism that CVE was an Islamist-focused initiative that turned a blind eye to other violent extremist threats facing the nation. Indeed, language in the National CVE Strategy and then the SIP made little to no mention of countering the surge in violence stemming from right-wing extremism, which had been rising steadily for years and continues to do so.[63] The one CVE program purportedly aimed at right-wing extremism interventions, Life After Hate, had its funding rescinded in the 2016 DHS CVE grant application round.[64] For counter-CVE activists and the public more broadly, the recall of the one right-wing-extremism-focused grant seemed to confirm their suspicions that the government was interested only in surveilling Muslim communities.[65]

There was very little organic grassroots support for CVE. Only a handful of government officials and family members of radicalized individuals seem truly committed to the cause of finding an alternative approach to homegrown terrorism besides arresting someone or doing nothing. Civil rights activists and community groups see the program as inherently flawed and thus not worthy of being saved. As one counter-CVE activist said in an interview, "It's not my job to fix CVE."[66] From the other side of the aisle, right-wing opponents of CVE lambast the program as "trying to hug terrorists," preferring traditional counterterrorism methods and decrying what it perceived as the Obama Administration's efforts to separate jihadist extremism from its religious foundations.[67]

The opponents of CVE have legitimate criticisms of the development of programming in the United States, but they are mistaken in believing that ending CVE altogether will fix their woes with the counterterrorism apparatus in the United States. Absent a robust CVE initiative, the US security apparatus will be forced to rely solely on its counterterrorism and law enforcement approach as it did prior to the rollout of CVE. Pure, traditional counterterrorism without alternatives to prosecution may be more likely to engender civil rights concerns and destroy relationships between law enforcement and local communities that are necessary to protect the US from homegrown extremists. Whether one advocates for or opposes CVE, it has now become a necessary component of the counterterrorism infrastructure in the United States and is likely to remain within US Government policy in some form or another for the considerable future.

Online CVE

The 2011 Strategic Implementation Plan also noted that there would be a forthcoming separate strategy on online radicalization. The plan noted that the Obama Administration would "develop a separate, more comprehensive strategy for countering and preventing violent extremist online radicalization and leveraging technology to empower community resilience."[68] However, these efforts were hamstrung by National Security Council (NSC) infighting. Because the internet was not simply domestic but global, it crossed over multiple policy directorates within the National Security Council. Its senior directors wrestled for control of who would own the internet radicalization policy portfolio. The result was an inter-agency process that could best be described as confused, and, at worst, fatally flawed. Staff at the NCTC, working with their State Department colleagues, drafted a more-than-25-page strategy with clear lines of responsibilities for departments and agencies and measures of effectiveness. The draft strategy was cleared at a staff level by the Group of Four. When it was presented to the NSC, they were told that it was dead on arrival and instead of a strategy, a policy statement would be issued from the Obama Administration.[69]

The statement, released in 2013, announced the creation of "a new Interagency Working Group to Counter Online Radicalization to Violence, chaired by the National Security Staff at the White House and involving specialists in countering violent extremism, internet safety experts, and civil liberties and privacy practitioners from across the United States Government." Its stated mission was to "be responsible for developing plans to implement an internet safety approach to address online violent extremism, coordinating the federal government's activities and assessing our progress against these plans, and identifying additional activities to pursue for countering online radicalization to violence."[70] In practical terms, the announcement was the end of a coordinated approach on the issue. The working group met less and less as the year progressed and finally ceased operating in 2014.[71] Both the Obama and now the Trump Administrations ceded the responsibility of online radicalization and recruitment to private technology companies.

This shift of responsibility is exemplified in a February 2016 meeting in Washington D.C. between high-ranking Obama Administration officials and "executives of major technology companies" who met to "discuss combating the activities of violent extremists online."[72] Internally, the meeting was referred to as "MadisonValleyWood" to reflect having participants from advertising (Madison Avenue), technology companies (Silicon Valley), and entertainment executives

(Hollywood). According to contemporaneous reporting and documents obtained by the Electronic Privacy Information Center, opening remarks by Assistant Attorney General John Carlin identified the purpose of the meeting as bringing together "relevant experts from the advertising, social media, and technology industries, along with civil society representatives to collaborate in generating and amplifying compelling content to undermine ISIL's online messaging and recruitment efforts."[73] The daylong meeting was a mix between presentations from intelligence officials on how terrorist use the online platforms and breakout sessions on how to address it.[74] While filled with enthusiasm, the meeting suffered what has always been the Achilles heel of countering violent extremism, in that there was little follow-up and no single lead to ensure implementation. The National Security Council staff tasked a number of agencies such as the NCTC and DHS to continue the conversation but those efforts largely died by attrition as press and White House focus waned.

The February 2016 meeting, coming months after the ISIS terror attacks in San Bernardino and Paris, was billed as an important step in the attempt to coordinate efforts between the government and the private sector on issues of national security and terrorist content online, at a time when calls were emanating loudly from Washington, D.C. for technology companies to act more aggressively to counter the growing use of their platforms by malign actors. Reflecting pressure from Congressional leaders who increasingly discussed publicly the idea of regulation against technology companies for allowing terrorist content on their platforms, the major online platforms set to roll out a solution which they hoped would placate detractors and address their concerns head on.

Established in 2017, The Global Internet Forum to Counter Terrorism, often referred to by its acronym GIFCT, was founded by four of the leading tech companies: Facebook, Microsoft, Twitter and YouTube. Utilizing existing networks, such as the European Union Internet Forum, the GIFCT began as a knowledge-sharing exercise, and has expanded to an independent organization, now partnered with other big tech companies including Dropbox, Amazon, LinkedIn, and WhatsApp. The main outcome of the GIFCT has been the Hash Sharing Consortium, a database of "hashes", or unique identifiers, of terrorist recruitment, propaganda, and violent imagery. With around 200,000 hashes in the database, the consortium database allows for different platforms to share and take down terrorist material in an increasingly efficient manner. Partners in the Hash Sharing Consortium include Ask.fm, Cloudinary, Facebook, Google, Instagram, Justpaste.it, LinkedIn, Microsoft, Verizon Media, Reddit, Snap, Twitter, and Yellow.

The GIFCT works with several partners, including governments, non-governmental organizations, and academics. One of its longest relationships has been with Tech Against Terrorism. Created in 2016 in cooperation with the United Nations Counter-Terrorism Executive Directorate (UN CTED), Tech Against Terrorism brings together UN Member States, academics, and tech companies as part of a public–private partnership to tackle terrorism online. The organization markets itself as "supporting the tech industry [to] tackle terrorist exploitation of the internet, whilst respecting human rights."[75] Since the creation of the GIFCT, one of Tech Against Terrorism's main focuses has been on helping smaller tech companies counter online extremism, as terrorists migrate from the larger platforms to lesser-known websites. These smaller platforms do not necessarily have the manpower or knowhow for countering these users, and Tech Against Terrorism helps provide support in this endeavor.

An emerging concern in the fight against extremist content online is the human cost associated with the moderation and removal of the vast quantities of hate speech and terrorist propaganda on social media platforms.[76] In 2017, YouTube CEO Susan Wojcicki, under significant pressure to take action against extremist use of its platform, announced an expansion of its "global workforce" of moderators to 10,000.[77] However, questions have been raised about the efficacy and ethics of relying on teams of human content moderators.[78] At Google, these content moderation teams are often staffed with recent immigrants who do not have the necessary language skills, and work for roughly minimum wage as contract workers with "almost no paid medical leave."[79]

The sheer scope of extremist content on these platforms is staggering. In a December 2017 official statement explaining their work against abuse on YouTube, Wojcicki claimed that the platform had manually reviewed nearly two million videos for violent extremist content over a six-month period. In October 2019, Google reported that it had removed 160,000 pieces of violent extremist content just from Blogger, Google Photos, and Google Drive.[80]

However, despite the well-documented concerns associated with human moderation of this content, there is equal skepticism within the broader community surrounding the effectiveness of artificial intelligence (AI) as a tool to curtail online hate.[81] Brian Fishman, who manages Facebook's global terrorism policy, describes the current conversation concerning AI and human content moderation as such:

> Computers do not get tired or make "mistakes" in the traditional sense. Algorithms, perhaps counterintuitively, also have some advantages for small companies because, once trained, they do not require the large human teams necessary for human review. But automated systems are only as good as the training data and labeling exercises used to program and maintain them. A poorly trained algorithm may have a systemic bias around certain types of content or certain organizations and, as a result, can produce false positives and false negatives, just as humans do. This carries real risk: Counter-speech campaigns sometimes purposefully emulate the visual style and language of terrorist propaganda, which might confuse some automated detection techniques, but not a human being. In other words, enabling an algorithm to remove content does not obviate the need to make difficult policy decisions. It just changes how those policy choices manifest.[82]

There appears to be little appetite within the current Administration to create and implement online counter-radicalization and counter-propaganda programs aimed at violent extremists in America. This is a reflection of both a lack of existing structure and the potential for serious constitutional freedom-of-speech concerns if the US Government waded into changing people's views online. For the time being, online countering violent extremism programs, whether that be content moderation or counter messaging, will be implemented by US technology companies.

ISIS Prisoners and Recidivism

As the United States was addressing an unprecedented number of ISIS-related arrests, a concern was quietly growing within the Administration on the aftereffects of those arrests. Law enforcement officials have not developed a comprehensive system to monitor convicted terrorists after they are released. Each is given drastically different terms of probation. Some are subjected to a lifetime review of their online activities, while a few have been ordered to participate in therapy.

Unlike most European countries, who have developed prison deradicalization programs, there is presently no such approach in US prisons, along with no systematic approach to terrorist re-entry and no support system to re-integrate them.[83] In September 2017, then-acting DHS Secretary Elaine Duke testified that "DHS is looking at what more can be done to counter terrorist recidivism ... We currently have a number of inmates with terrorism affiliations scheduled for release from US prisons in the next few years, and we need to work with interagency partners to make sure they do not return to violence once released."[84] This sentiment was reinforced three months later in Congressional testimony by the National Counterterrorism Center's Deputy Director, Russell Travers: "Even if [ISIS sympathizers] are arrested and put in jail, the chances are that the sentences will be relatively light in some cases, and they will be out on the streets in a few years. So this is going to be [a] recurring threat."[85] The 2018 *National Strategy for Counterterrorism* also raised both the concern and the profile of the policy gap, and admitted that limiting "prison radicalization by training prison staff and supporting rehabilitation" was a pressing yet unaddressed issue.[86]

Burgeoning research on the issue notes that the rate of criminal recidivism is lower for terrorist convicts than for the larger criminal population. However, the dataset of released terror convicts is relatively small. As the next significant wave of individuals are released, it may well test that early finding. What is clear for now is that American ISIS prisoners receive no support during their incarceration and many of them are likely to be released without having their views challenged, let alone moderated.

America's First Intervention Program?

In September 2019, the DHS announced the implementation of a new Strategic Framework for Countering Terrorism and Targeted Violence. Then-acting Homeland Security Secretary Kevin McAleenan introduced it at a joint Brookings

Institution and The Heritage Foundation event, stating that "There is evidence of this growing number of threat actors who seek to attack the seams of our diverse and violent social fabric and incite our nation's most vulnerable populations ... to violence against their fellow citizens."[87]

The ideas set forth in the Strategic Framework complement and expand upon those elucidated in both the Trump White House's 2018 National Strategy for Counterterrorism (NSCT) and the 2019 announcement of the establishment of the DHS Office for Targeted Violence and Terrorism Prevention (TVTP).[88] The White House strategy calls for the institutionalization of a nationwide prevention architecture which would "support local solutions and stakeholders" and details the importance of working to "strengthen and connect with our partners in civil society,"[89] while the TVTP launch statement described the importance of "moving beyond 'whole of government' efforts to 'whole of society' and [giving] prominence to the needs and leadership of states and local communities."[90] The TVTP will also function as the central hub responsible for coordinating the existing DHS prevention strategies, coordinating with state, local, and federal partners.[91]

Given the inconsistency associated with previous CVE and terrorism prevention initiatives, the campaign rhetoric by President Trump, and dramatic policy changes,[92] it is understandable that terrorism prevention efforts by the current Administration are met with skepticism from both sides of the conversation.[93]

According to Bennie Thompson, Chairman of the House Committee on Homeland Security, "This strategy could be a much-welcomed step in the right direction, and I applaud the Department for laying out a serious plan."[94] However, Thompson noted, "If we are going to have any success countering the threat of domestic terrorism ... the Administration needs to back up [the new Strategic Framework] with solid action."[95] Despite rhetoric to the contrary, the US Government's domestic CVE efforts will likely continue largely as they have for the past decade: underfunded, understaffed, and focused on individuals influenced by the Islamic State and other jihadi groups more than right-wing extremists.[96]

As the US Government retracts in the size of both its terrorism prevention staff and Congressional funding, a quiet shift has begun at the local level. The future of countering violent extremism programs will be determined by state-level and city initiatives. In New York, since 2014 the US Attorney's office has been inundated with new ISIS cases. According to one senior official, "There was a weekly meeting between local and federal law enforcement. We'd go around the room through all the ongoing cases. Each week, the meeting got longer and longer."[97] However, most cases did not rise to the level of an arrest for terrorism charges. Law enforcement could not keep up with the caseload and they also did not feel comfortable closing investigations on individuals they were still concerned about but who had not crossed the legal threshold for arrest.

As a result, the Eastern District of New York created a program called the "Disruption and Early Engagement Project" (DEEP). The goal was twofold: "provide counter terrorist across disciplines tools for early disruption and neutralization of individuals and groups" and "deny terrorist organizations personnel and other support and thereby degrade their capability to inspire or direct attacks."[98] DEEP is different from the national terrorism prevention efforts of the past in that it bypasses the traditional community engagement model of broad-based communication and focuses entirely on individuals who show signs of radicalizing to violence.

One of its first case studies involved "Mo," whom we had interviewed some years earlier after his return from Syria. As we detail in Chapter 3, Mo had become disillusioned with his time in the terrorist organization and, through a series of human smugglers, turned himself in to a US consulate in Turkey. Mo was ultimately charged with material support to terrorism, but as part of his cooperation, he assisted DEEP with some of its first interventions.[99] In one such case, he met with a 15-year-old New Yorker who had become interested in ISIS. Relying on his own experience, Mo deconstructed the group's ideology and explained the bleak reality of joining the group which he had experienced.

The DEEP program relies on threat assessment tools to "identify and assess individuals who appear to be on the path towards violent extremism." Using that assessment, trained law enforcement officials determine whether the individual is a good candidate for the program. DEEP does not, however, replace hard counterterrorism techniques. To the contrary, according to internal documents, "where federal prosecution is appropriate, DEEP prepares the federal court system to receive a defendant by providing detailed information to the court, Pretrial Services, the Probation Department, Defense Counsel, and the defendant's family. Such information may be relevant to bail determinations, agreed resolutions, specialized terms of supervised release and mental health evaluations and treatment plans." On other occasions, where the US Attorney's office deems that prosecution is not warranted, it coordinates with "family members, mental health professionals, mentors, and state and local officials to mitigate potential threats."[100]

The successes of the DEEP project, which currently only operates in New York, stem from the state and local-level interventions that have leveraged unique individual radicalization factors. These interventions, and a variety of other tools used in terrorism prevention, were identified by Attorney General William Barr as tactics that should be adopted at a federal level in order to prevent mass shootings, and he directed the FBI to better "identify and thwart such threats."[101]

In a memo released in October 2019, Barr notes that "Some of our most creative and effective disruption and early engagement tactics were born of the posture we adopted with respect to terrorist threats," and encourages authorities to adopt these disruption tactics when facing threats that "appear abruptly and with sometimes only ambiguous indications of intent."[102] However, given the criticism of and lack of institutional support for previous federally-led prevention and disengagement efforts, it remains to be seen whether this proposed adoption of terrorism prevention tools will garner sufficient buy-in. If the history of countering violent extremism is any guide, its implementation and success will rest entirely on whether a committed group of individuals within the US Government quietly shepherd it.

The Future of CVE in America

From its origins in the Bush Administration to its current course under President Trump, very little is certain about how countering violent extremism programming and strategy in the United States will develop. The program, unlike any other effort in the US counterterrorism arsenal, is subject to the political whims of senior managers in the US Government and factors in local communities. During the past eight years, this led to the uneven, patchwork development of US CVE policy. The implementation of the Strategic Framework led to vitriolic political disputes involving local communities, civil rights groups, and pundits on both sides of the aisle that left a small cadre of mid-level US Government bureaucrats caught in the crossfire as they attempted to carry programs to fruition. Certain concepts caught on in local environments; others, such as the DHS grant program, are now essentially dead in the water due to the hostile political environment surrounding the policy. In addition, CVE strayed further from its core mission of one-on-one interventions as developed by US and UK decision-makers during the mid-2000s. Over the past decade, CVE expanded into several new domains (online CVE, prison deradicalization and disengagement, community engagement), branched from three main sites of implementation into other areas throughout the country, and recently shifted to address new forms of ideological violence such as right-wing extremism or targeted violence.

The successes of CVE during the past few years are mainly in areas that fit its initial *raison d'être*: locally based, one-on-one interventions conducted quietly by local FBI field offices and US Attorneys' offices. These programs avoided the political spotlight and have a relatively strong record of often unsung success. The optimistic outlook on CVE, even in the face of confusion, is that new strategies like the DHS Strategic Framework for Countering Terrorism and Targeted Violence and the DEEP program are scaling up efforts that have proven successful in local environments and attempting to create the conditions for their success at the federal, strategic level. If the CVE of the future is to be an effective, politically sustainable alternative to traditional counterterrorism procedures in certain cases, the "bottom-up" approach exemplified in these recent documents may prove to be a more stable foundation than the top-down strategy of the past ten years.

CONCLUSION

For those familiar with jihadist recruitment in the West, the story of ISIS in America is simultaneously unique and typical of the broader dynamic. Due to the rise of ISIS and its establishment of the caliphate in 2014, several Western countries faced an unprecedented upsurge in supporters of jihadist groups attempting to fight overseas, commit attacks at home, or spread the message both online and off. ISIS augmented long-standing jihadist recruitment networks in Western Europe by coopting jihadist sentiment and through propaganda of the deed, recruiting thousands of Europeans to its cause. Yet in the United States, unlike its jihadist predecessors and unlike in other geographic contexts, ISIS had a unique ability to foment bottom-up, self-starting recruitment networks through virtual guidance. As this book explains, its activities in the country defy what many assume are essential factors for radicalization and mobilization. Through its American supporters, ISIS was able to establish a meaningful presence in a country where it had almost no on-the-ground presence or deep-rooted recruitment networks.

The lack of these important components certainly explains a relatively small American contingent of ISIS travelers, attackers, and other supporters in comparison to many Western European nations. However, contrary to popular belief, the lack of physical networks did not stop ISIS from finding ways to attract and mobilize a significant swathe of supporters in the United States. While many assume ISIS radicalization and mobilization processes in America largely targeted so-called "lone wolves," in reality it focused on small groups of twos and threes within American communities that, despite having no interaction with large extremist milieus, were able to conduct activities on behalf of the group. Because networks were smaller, and ISIS' physical presence diminished, these groups extensively used online communications to reach out to other supporters. Regardless of whether American ISIS members radicalized online, almost all used the online space to facilitate their activities.

ISIS was generally successful at radicalizing and recruiting American jihadists to their cause, but unlike in Europe, was far less effective at guiding successful and deadly attacks. Despite being firmly in the crosshairs of the ISIS terrorist strategy, America has proven to be the most difficult Western country for the group to gain a foothold in and plot large-scale attacks. As we have shown, the relatively low success rate for ISIS in America can be put down to three interrelated factors. Firstly, the geographic distance between the US and ISIS-controlled territory increases the length and difficulty of interactions between ISIS' central leadership and its American followers. Attackers could not physically contact ISIS handlers, and interested travelers needed to clear several logistical hurdles and plan relatively expensive journeys. In comparison, ISIS demonstrated the ability to send its fighters back into Europe to conduct physical recruitment of attackers. For a time, Western European ISIS fighters interested in returning home could plan a course back from Syria through Turkey for less than $500 and without a significant risk of interdiction.

Secondly, the US legal system has unique tools at its disposal to prosecute jihadist travelers and potential terrorist plotters. At the beginning of the ISIS mobilization, many European countries did not have laws criminalizing terrorist travel, meaning they could do little to stop citizens traveling to Syria despite having reason to suspect their intentions. In America, the material support statute and other legal tools made illegal most of the activity that American ISIS supporters conducted, and the law was in place well before the ISIS mobilization.[1] Currently, ISIS-related material support prosecutions in the US have just shy of a 100 percent conviction rate.[2] Moreover, those convicted of material support in the US can face prison sentences of up to 20 years. In Europe, there have been far fewer prosecutions of travelers, and even in cases where a prosecution is successful, convicted jihadists face smaller sentences.[3]

Finally, wide-reaching jihadist recruitment networks were far more established in the European context prior to the conflicts in Syria and Iraq. Militant Salafist groups, including al-Muhajiroun in the UK, Sharia4 in several European countries, Profetens Ummah (PU) in Norway, and Millatu Ibrahim in Germany, were all active in several European cities before 2011. When the Syrian conflict began, these groups began to mobilize their supporters to engage in networked travel to the Middle Eastern theater to participate in jihadist movements.[4] In assessing the stories of European jihadist travelers from these countries, many were active members of these groups prior to leaving. Similar initiatives existed in the United States (for example, Revolution Muslim), but they were not organized on the same scale as in Europe.[5]

Nevertheless, several aspects of ISIS recruitment mirrored dynamics in Europe and beyond. First, even though they occurred only in limited numbers in the United States, it remains clear that long-standing social networks are crucial to any sort of large-scale or community-wide mobilization. It is no coincidence, for example, that in Minnesota, the location of one of the only physical recruitment networks in America, we saw the single largest number of Americans travel and attempt to travel to ISIS. Like similar European recruitment networks, all participants in the Minnesota traveler network were connected through friendship, kinship, or community networks. Not only did the network pre-date ISIS, similar to many of those in Europe, but it also had direct and real connections to both al-Qaeda and ISIS members who facilitated communications between the network in America and operators in Syria and Iraq.

While the number of Americans involved with ISIS are proportionally a fraction of those from other Western nations, the findings of this book also show us that past assumptions about America being uniquely immune to homegrown jihadists were both premature and overly optimistic. This thinking was partly the result of a misunderstanding about the highly adaptable and dexterous nature of the global jihad movement. America may well be exceptional in its integration of different faiths and cultures, but the idea that it was protected from jihadism by the American Dream was a fantasy. While Muslim Americans are socioeconomically better off than those in most European countries, a statistic upon which this assumption was also based, this did not protect them from the new ideas and outreach strategies of one of the world's most rapidly growing extremist subcultures. If there is only one lesson to take from our findings, it is that extremists operating in liberal democracies almost always find a way to reach their target audiences and tailor their messages accordingly.

Jihadist activists and recruiters have shown yet again their acute sense of how to appeal to specific audiences using a range of tools and resources at their disposal. Issues such as race relations, the perceived maltreatment of Muslims and disrespect for their faith within the American government and society, and military involvement in conflicts in Muslim-majority countries were exploited yet again to great effect. Using messaging that resonated with their experiences, ISIS was able to strike a tone with disaffected Americans, some of whom did not even begin their engagement with the group's propaganda as Muslims but converted as a result.

We have seen how some Americans, driven by a mix of personal grievances, peer pressure, and commitment to an ideology often presented to them through the strategic messaging of influential ideologues decided to rebel against their country of birth in the most violent way possible. They plotted attacks on fellow Americans whom, while being civilians, they regarded as complicit in the crimes committed by their nation against Muslims and blamed for their own personal struggles and grievances. Thus, attacks like the Pulse nightclub and San Bernardino were indiscriminate; the attackers were given license by ISIS to kill anyone who resided in America including Muslims who, simply by choosing to remain living peacefully in the country, were considered apostates.

In other cases, attacks and plots were more targeted. Of particular interest to American ISIS supporters was the "Draw the Prophet Muhammad" event and those behind organizing and promoting it. At least seven different Americans mentioned this in discussions about possible attacks, and four directly plotted to attack either the event or those associated with it. They viewed this as the epitome of secular liberal American corruption in which the sacred value of free speech was little more than a weapon wielded by the enemies of Islam to attack and defame Islam and Muslims; proof, in their eyes, of a wide-ranging conspiracy to destroy the faith. Free speech was, in "Mo" the traveler's view, "used to desecrate Islam," a conclusion he came to after watching the film *Submission* in his Columbia University class.

For the majority of America's ISIS supporters, however, it was a new dimension of the global jihad project which attracted them more than homegrown terrorism:

the establishment of the caliphate. This purported utopian super-state promised a better, more meaningful life to American Muslims who had come to reject the values, beliefs, and governance of their home country. It was, to them, about more than just fighting and killing. Joining the caliphate offered them the chance to live the "real Islam" which they concluded was no longer possible in America, while also giving them a new way of understanding themselves. They found comfort in the collective identity and shared mission of the state-building project in which all races and classes were treated equally, and everyone had their role and place in society. The Islamic courts, which policed everything from personal beliefs and morality to violent crime, made up part of a totalitarian promise to fix all that was wrong with both the individual and the community. In a world many perceive as descending into chaos, where the line between truth and falsehood is becoming increasingly blurred and where objective truth about right and wrong often feels unattainable, movements like ISIS offer great comfort in their divinely guided certainty about these questions. Take, for example, the words of a female resident of the al-Hol camp in Syria where thousands of former residents of the caliphate now reside in Kurdish custody, many of whom continue to pine for their lost utopia. Asked why she still supports ISIS, she replied: "They told us what was right and what was wrong. It was better."[6]

While Americans traveled in search of this dream, many were disappointed by the reality. Some, like "Mo" and Mohamad Khweis, decided to defect after witnessing the dysfunction, corruption, and wanton violence of ISIS, or simply because they were not offered the perfect and heroic lives they were promised in the propaganda. Others, like the Minnesota travelers profiled in the third chapter of this book, died on the battlefield as committed jihadists who embraced martyrdom as the ultimate prize. At present, our data shows that the returnee threat to the US is negligible compared to that faced by most other Western nations. Unlike their European counterparts, which in some cases have been able to take advantage of open borders in the European Union and exploit refugee flows into the continent to move more freely, American travelers have so far found it more difficult to return home undetected. There is currently no publicly available evidence to suggest that American travelers have slipped into the country without the knowledge of authorities. Any who attempt to do so also face among the most daunting obstacles of any contingent of Western travelers wishing to return home.

New digital communications tools became a vehicle for much of the ISIS outreach in America, and offered Americans a myriad of ways to do their part for the advancement of ISIS in the country. For those who are not cut out for the rough and dangerous life of a traveler or could not quite bring themselves to commit mass murder at home, there are now many other options available. In most cases, they took on the role of propaganda creators and disseminators, helping to spread the ISIS message as far as they could via social media. Others, however, employed more innovative approaches. From hackers like Kim Anh Vo, to Ali Amin's cryptocurrency funding schemes, to Thomas Osadzinski's coding of new applications to help streamline the creation and spread of propaganda, American ISIS supporters found means to support the group despite increasing pressure in both the online and real world. This type of online activism also offered an easy and low-risk entryway into jihadist activism. For some, this was the first step towards more high-risk ventures.

In response to this threat, the United States has been largely successful in its application of pre-existing laws and traditional counterterrorism operations. As demonstrated in the case of Mohamed Bailor Jalloh, the stakes are high and the margin for error is minuscule. One small misjudgment or mistake could lead to another massacre. Law enforcement agencies, policymakers and the public all view the FBI's counterterrorism mission as an area where failure is unacceptable. The statistics show that the FBI, generally speaking, was able to interdict threats from ISIS supporters through arrests and prosecution, but whether the country will develop preventative alternatives remains to be seen. Unlike all of its major European partners who face a range of terrorist threats, from jihadists to the extreme right, the United States still has no clear program or roadmap in place to implement any form of counter- or deradicalization program. Of particular surprise and concern is the current lack of any rehabilitation program for extremists of any stripe in US prisons. Unlike the extensive drug or sexual offender programs on offer, those with extreme views that have led them to commit criminal acts that place them in prison have no clear path away from their old lives.

There are cases where American jihadists have reformed, but most of this is due to what one influential former American jihadist referred to as "self-deradicalization," rather than to any assistance or intervention from the state.[7] In some ways, American foot-dragging on countering violent extremism is a reflection of an uneasiness within American legal and policy arenas about undermining values such as freedom of speech, association, and religion that are enshrined in law. While this cultural difference may partly account for why Europe is further ahead on CVE programming, it is worth noting that European countries generally face a larger number of supporters of extremist groups, fewer and weaker prosecutorial tools, and a longer history of employing pre-crime prevention programs.

Meanwhile, American government employees on the front lines of CVE sometimes take matters into their own hands. Throughout the pages of this book, we examine cases where FBI agents have organized voluntary interviews with ISIS suspects who have yet to break the law. These meetings can act as informal interventions, in which the individual is given the opportunity to disengage from their behavior before they make a decision that will ruin their lives and, in many cases, those of their close family. While we have documented cases where these warnings went unheeded, it is likely that many such meetings have taken place and been successful and, as a result, remain unreported by the courts and media. The innovative DEEP program is also the product of bottom-up implementation by committed federal employees as opposed to a top-down directive from senior federal authorities. Those who devised it wanted to give authorities more options to deal with potential ISIS suspects that went beyond arrests and long-term, often expensive, investigations. Now, some are able to give young Americans who are on the edge of making bad and dangerous decisions a chance to change their ways.

The current lack of any fully functioning official effort to conduct prevention and deradicalization programs is, to some extent, being counterbalanced by an increase in the role that American technology companies are taking. Through collaborative initiatives, Facebook, Google, Twitter, and other platforms that ISIS has long exploited are now taking proactive roles and developing innovative ways to counter a savvy and rapidly adaptable foe. They have hired terrorism and radicalization experts to head up teams committed to combating extremism and given them a fair amount of freedom to pursue their objectives. Still very much in their infancy, the technology companies' initiatives have the potential to make a significant impact, in particular when it comes to coordinating cross-platform efforts to remove extremist propaganda as it emerges. It remains to be seen whether programs like these will be able to move beyond content removal into the far more complex and poorly understood world of online counter-extremism, through conducting online interventions or deradicalization initiatives.

All of these efforts aside, the main factor which will impact the threat posed by ISIS in America is the future direction of the group in Syria and Iraq. Under a new leadership and no longer in control of a significant amount of territory, it is as yet unclear what sort of terrorism strategy the group intends to pursue. With the territorial caliphate gone for now, the flow of travel from America to ISIS has all but dried up. However, as our statistical analysis demonstrated in Chapter 2, the ISIS territorial loss correlated with a rise in attacks and plots as Americans were told to stay in the belly of the beast and harm it from the inside. Even before the fall of the caliphate, American ISIS supporters were redirected by ISIS handlers, who encouraged their assets to refocus their efforts on attack planning as their chances of successful *hijra* dwindled.

In 2018 and 2019, ISIS lost its last vestige of its held territory in Syria and Iraq, its self-declared caliph, and the spokesperson who was first responsible for directing its followers to kill the disbelievers in the United States and beyond. But in the face of these losses, the FBI is still conducting over 1,000 open investigations of homegrown violent extremists in the United States. Today, the threat from ISIS supporters in America is more amorphous, but ever-present, and tacked on to a resurgence of activity from domestic right-wing terrorist groups and ISIS' foreign terrorist competitors alike. Given that al-Qaeda was able to mobilize Americans without anything resembling a territorial, state presence, ISIS should be expected to be able to find ways to remain capable and relevant as a terrorist presence in the United States for years to come. Even if another terrorist group arises from ISIS' ashes to overtake it as the major homegrown terrorist threat facing the country, it is likely to draw on the tactics, techniques, and procedures that ISIS used during the height of its reign to mobilize several hundred Americans to join the ranks of the caliphate.

NOTES

Introduction

1 Al-Adnani, Abu Muhammad. 2014. "Indeed, Your Lord is Ever Watchful." Al-Furqan Media Foundation, September 22, 2014.
2 Berger, J.M. 2011. *Jihad Joe: Americans Who Go to War in the Name of Islam.* 1st ed. Washington, D.C: Potomac Books; Bergen, Peter. 2016. *United States of Jihad: Investigating America's homegrown terrorists.* 1st ed. New York, NY: Crown Publishers; Bjelopera, Jerome P. 2013. "American Jihadist Terrorism: Combating a Complex Threat." Congressional Research Service, January 23, 2013; Vidino, Lorenzo. 2019. "Homegrown Jihadist Terrorism in the United States: A New and Occasional Phenomenon?" *Studies in Conflict & Terrorism* 32(1): 1–17.
3 See, for example: Jenkins, Brian. 2010. "Would-Be Warriors: Incidents of Jihadist Terrorist Radicalization in the United States Since September 11, 2001." RAND Corporation; Kurzman, Charles. 2018. "Muslim-American Involvement with Violent Extremism, 2017." Triangle Center on Terrorism and Homeland Security, 9th Annual Report.
4 For more on this see findings in Gilkes, Sarah. 2016. "Not Just The Caliphate: Non-Islamic State-Related Jihadist Terrorism in America." Washington, D.C: George Washington University Program on Extremism, December 2016.
5 "Open Source Jihad," *Inspire* 1, June 2010.
6 Ibid.
7 Based on their study of all ISIS-related attacks and plots in Europe between 2014 and 2016, Petter Nesser, Anne Stenersen, and Emilie Oftedal found that "what we can say with certainty is that although many think of the ISIS-threat to Europe in terms of inspired, so-called 'lone wolf' attacks, a minority of the cases, six plots, seemed based on inspiration only—and no contact with ISIS's networks." Nesser, Petter, Anne Stenersen, and Emilie Oftedal. 2016. "Jihadi Terrorism in Europe: The ISIS-Effect." *Perspectives on Terrorism* 10 (6): 8.

1. *The Islamic State in America*

1 "Criminal Complaint." 2014. *USA v. Avin Marsalis Brown and Akba Jihad Jordan.* United States District Court for the Eastern District of North Carolina. Case: 5:14-MJ-1181-WW. https://extremism.gwu.edu/sites/g/files/zaxdzs2191/f/Brown%20 Criminal%20Complaint.pdf.
2 Wray, Christopher. 2019. "Global Terrorism: Threats to the Homeland." Testimony of Federal Bureau of Investigation Director Christopher Wray before the House Homeland Security Committee, October 30, 2019. https://www.fbi.gov/news/ testimony/global-terrorism-threats-to-the-homeland-103019.
3 "ISIS in America." Program on Extremism. https://extremism.gwu.edu/isis-america.

4   Bergen, Peter, et al. "Terrorism in America After 9/11." *New America.* https://www. newamerica.org/in-depth/terrorism-in-america/.

5   Ibid.

6   Vidino, Lorenzo, and Seamus Hughes. 2015. "ISIS in America: From Retweets to Raqqa." Washington, D.C: George Washington University Program on Extremism, December 2015.

7   Berger, J.M. 2011. *Jihad Joe: Americans Who Go to War in the Name of Islam.* 1st ed. Washington, D.C: Potomac Books; Bergen, Peter. 2017. *United States of Jihad: Who Are America's Homegrown Terrorists, and How Do We Stop Them?* New York: Crown Publishers.

8   Berger. 2011. *Jihad Joe*; Bergen. 2017. *United States of Jihad*; Jenkins, Brian. 2014. "When Jihadis Come Marching Home: The Terrorist Threat Posed by Westerners Returning from Syria and Iraq." RAND Corporation. https://www.rand.org/content/dam/rand/pubs/perspectives/PE100/PE130-1/RAND_PE130-1.pdf.

9   Jenkins. 2014. "When Jihadis Come Marching Home."

10 Ibid.

11 Yuen, Laura, and Sasha Aslanian. 2013. "Minnesota Pipeline to Al-Shabab." *Minnesota Public Radio News*, September 25, 2013. http://minnesota.publicradio.org/projects/ongoing/somali_timeline/.

12 Meleagrou-Hitchens, Alexander, Shiraz Maher, and James Sheehan. 2012. "Lights, Camera, Jihad: Al-Shabaab's Western Media Strategy." London, UK: International Centre for the Study of Radicalisation. http://icsr.info/wp-content/uploads/2012/11/ICSR-Lights-Camera-Jihad-Report_Nov2012_ForWeb-2.pdf.

13 Jenkins. 2014. "When Jihadis Come Marching Home"

14 Lister, Charles. 2015. *The Syrian Jihad: Al-Qaeda, the Islamic State and the Evolution of an Insurgency.* Oxford, UK: Oxford University Press.

15 Fishman, Brian H. 2016. *The Master Plan: ISIS, al-Qaeda, and the Jihadi Strategy for Final Victory.* New Haven: Yale University Press.

16 Fishman. 2016. *The Master Plan.*

17 Lister, Charles. 2015. *The Syrian Jihad.*

18 Hegghammer, Thomas, and Aaron Y. Zelin. 2014. "How Syria's Civil War Became a Holy Crusade." *Foreign Affairs*, October 15, 2014. https://www.foreignaffairs.com/articles/middle-east/2013-07-03/how-syrias-civil-war-became-holy-crusade.

19 Ibid.

20 Carter, Joseph A., Shiraz Maher, and Peter Neumann. 2014. "#Greenbirds: Measuring Importance and Influence in Syrian Foreign Fighter Networks." London, UK: International Centre for the Study of Radicalisation. http://icsr.info/wp-content/uploads/2014/04/ICSR-Report-Greenbirds-Measuring-Importance-and-Infleunce-in-Syrian-Foreign-Fighter-Networks.pdf.

21 Vidino and Hughes. 2015. "ISIS in America: From Retweets to Raqqa."

22 "Inside the Mufid Elfgeeh Investigation." 2016. Federal Bureau of Investigation. May 16, 2016. https://www.fbi.gov/news/stories/inside-the-mufid-elfgeeh-investigation.

23 "Application for a Search Warrant and Affidavit." 2014. *USA v. Mufid Elfgeeh*, United States District Court for the Western District of New York. Case: 14-MJ-635. https://extremism.gwu.edu/sites/g/files/zaxdzs2191/f/Elfgeeh%20Affidavit.PDF.

24 Ibid.

25 Ibid.

26 Ibid.

27 "Inside the Mufid Elfgeeh Investigation." 2016. *Federal Bureau of Investigation.*

28 "Terrorist Designations of Groups Operating in Syria." 2014. *U.S. Department of State.* May 14, 2014. //2009-2017.state.gov/r/pa/prs/ps/2014/05/226067.htm.

29 BBC News. 2014. "Isis Rebels Declare 'Islamic State.'" June 30, 2014, sec. Middle East. https://www.bbc.com/news/world-middle-east-28082962.

30 Kelsay, John. 2009. *Arguing the Just War in Islam.* Cambridge, MA: Harvard University Press.

31 Ibid.

32 Wood, Graeme. 2015. "What ISIS Really Wants." *The Atlantic*, March 2015. https://www.theatlantic.com/magazine/archive/2015/03/what-isis-really-wants/384980/.

33 Winter, Charlie. 2015. "The Virtual 'Caliphate': Understanding Islamic State's Propaganda Strategy." London, UK: Quilliam; Winter, Charlie. 2018. "Apocalypse, Later: A Longitudinal Study of the Islamic State Brand." *Critical Studies in Media Communication* 35 (1): 103–21. https://doi.org/10.1080/15295036.2017.1393094.

34 Archetti, Cristina. 2015. "Terrorism, Communication and New Media: Explaining Radicalization in the Digital Age." *Perspectives on Terrorism* 9 (1): 49–59. http://www.terrorismanalysts.com/pt/index.php/pot/article/view/401/html.

35 Winter, Charlie. 2016. "ISIS Is Using the Media Against Itself." *The Atlantic*, March 23, 2016. https://www.theatlantic.com/international/archive/2016/03/isis-propaganda-brussels/475002/; Winter, Charlie, and Haroro J. Ingram. 2017. "Why ISIS Is So Good at Branding Its Failures as Success." *The Atlantic*, September 19, 2017. https://www.theatlantic.com/international/archive/2017/09/isis-propaganda/540240/.

36 Wray, Christopher. 2019. "Global Terrorism: Threats to the Homeland." Testimony of Federal Bureau of Investigation Director Christopher Wray before the House Homeland Security Committee, October 30, 2019. https://www.fbi.gov/news/testimony/global-terrorism-threats-to-the-homeland-103019.

37 Interview with senior FBI counterterrorism official, March 2018.

38 "Operation Inherent Resolve: Lead Inspector General Report to the United States Congress." 2019. https://www.stateoig.gov/system/files/q3fy2019_leadig_oir_report.pdf.

39 Goldman, Adam, and Eric Schmitt. 2016. "One by One, ISIS Social Media Experts Are Killed as Result of F.B.I. Program." *The New York Times*, November 24, 2016, sec. World. https://www.nytimes.com/2016/11/24/world/middleeast/isis-recruiters-social-media.html.

40 BBC News. 2017. "How the Battle for Mosul Unfolded." July 10, 2017, sec. Middle East. https://www.bbc.com/news/world-middle-east-37702442.

41 Clarke, Hilary, Nick Paton Walsh, Eliza Mackintosh, and Ghazi Balkiz. 2017. "ISIS Defeated in Raqqa Stronghold." *CNN*, October 18, 2017. https://edition.cnn.com/2017/10/17/middleeast/raqqa-isis-syria/index.html.

42 BBC News. 2019. "Fall of Islamic State 'caliphate' Announced." March 23, 2019, sec. Middle East. https://www.bbc.com/news/world-middle-east-47678157.

43 Callimachi, Rukmini, and Eric Schmitt. 2019. "ISIS Names New Leader and Confirms Al-Baghdadi's Death." *The New York Times*, October 31, 2019, sec. World. https://www.nytimes.com/2019/10/31/world/middleeast/isis-al-baghdadi-dead.html.

44 Mahood, Samantha, and Halim Rane. 2016. "Islamist Narratives in ISIS Recruitment Propaganda." *The Journal of International Communication* 18 (1): 97–111. https://www.tandfonline.com/doi/abs/10.1080/13216597.2016.1263231.

45 Byman, Daniel. 2017. "Frustrated Foreign Fighters." *Lawfare*, July 12, 2017. https://www.lawfareblog.com/frustrated-foreign-fighters; Byman, Daniel. 2019. *Road Warriors: Foreign Fighters in the Armies of Jihad.* Oxford, New York: Oxford University

Press.; Nesser, Petter. 2019. "Military Interventions, Jihadi Networks, and Terrorist Entrepreneurs: How the Islamic State Terror Wave Rose So High in Europe." *CTC Sentinel* 12 (3): 15–21. https://ctc.usma.edu/military-interventions-jihadi-networks-terrorist-entrepreneurs-islamic-state-terror-wave-rose-high-europe/.

46 Wilson, Lydia. 2017. "Understanding the Appeal of ISIS." *New England Journal of Public Policy* 29 (1). https://scholarworks.umb.edu/nejpp/vol29/iss1/5.

47 "Affidavit in Support of Criminal Complaint." 2019. *USA v. Abdul-Majeed Marouf Ahmed Alani*, United States District Court for the Southern District of Florida. Case: 1:19-mj-03419-JJO. https://extremism.gwu.edu/sites/g/files/zaxdzs2191/f/Alani%20 complaint.pdf.

48 Ibid.

49 "Three Florida Men Sentenced for Conspiring to Provide Material Support to ISIS." 2018. Department of Justice Press Release. May 16, 2018. https://www.justice.gov/opa/ pr/three-florida-men-sentenced-conspiring-provide-material-support-isis.

50 "Indictment." 2016. *USA v. Marie Antoinette Castelli*, United States District Court for the Eastern District of Kentucky. Case: 2:16-cr-00033-ART-CJS. https://extremism. gwu.edu/sites/g/files/zaxdzs2191/f/Castelli%20Indictment.pdf.

51 "Indictment." 2017. *State of New York v. Trevor William Forrest*. Supreme Court of the State of New York, County of New York. https://extremism.gwu.edu/sites/g/files/ zaxdzs2191/f/ForrestIndictment.pdf.

52 "Plea Agreement." 2016. *USA v. Santos Colon*, United States District Court for the District of New Jersey. Case: 1:17-cr-00119-NLH. https://extremism.gwu.edu/sites/g/ files/zaxdzs2191/f/Colon%20Plea%20Agreement.pdf.

53 "Criminal Complaint." 2017. *USA v. Zakariya Abdin*, United States District Court for the District of South Carolina. Case: 2:17-mj-00081-MCRI. https://extremism.gwu. edu/sites/g/files/zaxdzs2191/f/Abdin%20Criminal%20Complaint.pdf.

54 "South Carolina Man Sentenced for Attempting to Provide Material Support to ISIS." 2019. Department of Justice Press Release. June 11, 2019. https://www.justice.gov/opa/ pr/south-carolina-man-sentenced-attempting-provide-material-support-isis.

55 Kim, Elliot. 2018. "Summary: Supreme Court Decision in *Sessions v. Dimaya*." *Lawfare*, April 27, 2018. https://www.lawfareblog.com/summary-supreme-court-decision-sessions-v-dimaya; Zable, Stephanie. 2018. "How Dimaya v. Sessions Has Affected Sentencing for Terrorism Convictions." *Lawfare*, October 25, 2018. https://www. lawfareblog.com/how-dimaya-v-sessions-has-affected-sentencing-terrorism-convictions.

56 Hughes, Seamus, and Devorah Margolin. 2019. "The Fractured Terrorism Threat to America." *Lawfare*, November 10, 2019. https://www.lawfareblog.com/fractured-terrorism-threat-america.

57 Ibid.

58 Alexander, Audrey. 2019. "Key Considerations: Forward Thinking About Women, Gender, and Violent Extremism." In *Perspectives on the Future of Women, Gender, & Violent Extremism*. Washington, D.C: George Washington Program on Extremism. https://extremism.gwu.edu/sites/g/files/zaxdzs2191/f/Perspectives%20on%20the%20 Future%20of%20Women%2C%20Gender%20and%20Violent%20Extremism.pdf.

59 Lahoud, Nelly. 2014. "The Neglected Sex: The Jihadis' Exclusion of Women From Jihad." *Terrorism and Political Violence* 26 (5): 780–802. https://doi.org/10.1080/095465 53.2013.772511; Peresin, Anita, and Alberto Cervone. 2015. "The Western Muhajirat of ISIS." *Studies in Conflict & Terrorism* 38 (7): 495–509. https://doi.org/10.1080/10576 10X.2015.1025611.

60 Alexander, Audrey, and Rebecca Turkington. 2018. "Treatment of Terrorists: How Does Gender Affect Justice?" *CTC Sentinel* 11 (8): 24–9. https://ctc.usma.edu/ treatment-terrorists-gender-affect-justice/.

61 Peresin and Cervone. 2015. "The Western Muhajirat of ISIS".

62 "Complaint and Affidavit in Support of Arrest Warrants." 2015. *USA v. Noelle Velentzas and Asia Siddiqui.* United States District Court for the Eastern District of New York. Case: 1:15-mj-00303-WP. https://extremism.gwu.edu/sites/g/files/zaxdzs2191/f/ Velentzas%20and%20Siddiqui%20Criminal%20Complaint%2C%20Affidavit.pdf.

63 Ibid.

64 Ibid.

65 "Two Queens Women Plead Guilty in Connection with Plan to Build Explosive Devices Similar to Those Used in Prior Terrorist Attacks in the United States." 2019. Department of Justice Press Release. August 23, 2019. https://www.justice.gov/opa/pr/ two-queens-women-plead-guilty-connection-plan-build-explosive-devices-similar-those-used.

66 Margolin, Devorah, and Charlie Winter. 2017. "The Mujahidat Dilemma: Female Combatants and the Islamic State." *CTC Sentinel* 10 (7): 23–8. https://ctc.usma.edu/ the-mujahidat-dilemma-female-combatants-and-the-islamic-state/; al-Tamimi, Aymenn Jawad. 2019. "ISIS' Female Suicide Bombers Are No Myth." *Foreign Affairs*, August 14, 2019. https://www.foreignaffairs.com/articles/syria/2017-09-22/isis-female-suicide-bombers-are-no-myth.

67 Ibid.

68 Fishman, Brian H. 2016. *The Master Plan: ISIS, al-Qaeda, and the Jihadi Strategy for Final Victory.* New Haven: Yale University Press.

69 Alexander, Audrey. 2016. "Cruel Intentions: Female Jihadists in America." Washington, D.C: George Washington Program on Extremism. https://cchs.gwu.edu/sites/cchs.gwu. edu/files/downloads/Female%20Jihadists%20in%20America.pdf.

70 "Homegrown Violent Extremist Mobilization Indicators." 2019. National Counterterrorism Center. https://www.dni.gov/files/NCTC/documents/news_ documents/NCTC-FBI-DHS-HVE-Mobilization-Indicators-Booklet-2019.pdf.

71 McGarrity, Michael. 2019. "Confronting the Rise of Domestic Terrorism in the Homeland." Testimony of Federal Bureau of Investigation Counterterrorism Division Assistant Director Michael McGarrity before the House Homeland Security Committee. May 8, 2019. https://homeland.house.gov/imo/media/doc/Testimony-McGarrity.pdf.

72 Wray, Christopher. 2018. "Countering the Terrorist Threat Through Partnerships, Intelligence, and Innovation." Presented at the Utah National Security and Anti-Terrorism Conference, Salt Lake City, Utah, August 29. https://www.fbi.gov/news/ speeches/countering-the-terrorist-threat-through-partnerships-intelligence-and-innovation.

73 Vidino, Lorenzo, Francesco Marone, and Eva Entenmann. 2017. "Fear Thy Neighbor: Radicalization and Jihadist Attacks in the West." Milan, Italy: Joint George Washington Program on Extremism, ICCT-The Hague, ISPI Report. https://extremism.gwu.edu/ sites/extremism.gwu.edu/files/FearThyNeighbor%20 RadicalizationandJihadistAttacksintheWest.pdf.

74 Ibid.

75 Vidino and Hughes. 2015. "ISIS in America: From Retweets to Raqqa."

76 Ruffini, Christina. 2016. "Molenbeek: Terror Recruiting Ground." *CBS News*, March 18, 2016. https://www.cbsnews.com/news/molenbeek-brussels-belgium-isis-terror-

recruiting-ground/; "Lunel: The Tiny French Town That Became the Symbol of Jihad."
2018. *AFP*, April 5, 2018. https://www.thelocal.fr/20180405/lunel-the-tiny-french-
town-that-became-the-symbol-of-jihad.

77 Al-Adnani, Abu Muhammad. 2016. "And Those Who Lived [In Faith] Would Live
Upon Evidence." *al-Furqan Media*, May 20, 2016.

78 Hegghammer, Thomas. 2013. "Should I Stay or Should I Go? Explaining Variation in
Western Jihadists' Choice between Domestic and Foreign Fighting." *American Political
Science Review* 107 (1): 1–15. https://doi.org/10.1017/S0003055412000615.

79 "Criminal Complaint." 2015. *USA v. Emanuel Lutchman*, United States District Court
for the Western District of New York. Case: 6:15-mj-04212-MWP. https://extremism.
gwu.edu/sites/g/files/zaxdzs2191/f/Lutchman%20Complaint.pdf

80 Ibid.

81 Ibid.

82 "Criminal Complaint." 2017. *USA v. Kaan Sercan Damlarkaya*, United States District
Court for the Southern District of Texas. Case: 4:17-mj-01871. https://extremism.gwu.
edu/sites/g/files/zaxdzs2191/f/Damlarkaya%20Criminal%20Complaint.pdf.

83 Ibid.

84 Ibid.

85 Byman, Daniel. 2017. "Frustrated Foreign Fighters." *Lawfare*, July 12, 2017. https://
www.lawfareblog.com/frustrated-foreign-fighters; Byman, Daniel. 2019. *Road
Warriors: Foreign Fighters in the Armies of Jihad*. Oxford, New York: Oxford University
Press.

86 Wray, Christopher. 2018. "Countering the Terrorist Threat Through Partnerships,
Intelligence, and Innovation." Presented at the Utah National Security and Anti-
Terrorism Conference, Salt Lake City, Utah, August 29. https://www.fbi.gov/news/
speeches/countering-the-terrorist-threat-through-partnerships-intelligence-and-
innovation.

87 Ibid.

88 De Block, Simon. 2016. "Using Human Sources in Counterterrorism Operations:
Understanding the Motivations and Political Impact." FBI: Law Enforcement
Bulletin. April 8, 2016. https://leb.fbi.gov/articles/featured-articles/using-human-
sources-in-counterterrorism-operations-understanding-the-motivations-and-
political-impact.

89 Aaronson, Trevor. 2011. "The Informants." *Mother Jones*, October 2011. https://www.
motherjones.com/politics/2011/07/fbi-terrorist-informants/.

90 VanLandingham, Rachel. 2017. "Jailing the Twitter Bird: Social Media, Material
Support to Terrorism, and Muzzling the Modern Press." *Cardozo Law Review*,
February. https://papers.ssrn.com/abstract=2953309.

91 Doyle, Charles. 2016. "Terrorist Material Support: An Overview of 18 U.S.C. §2339A
and §2339B." CRS Report. Congressional Research Service. https://fas.org/sgp/crs/
natsec/R41333.pdf.

92 Ibid.

93 Ibid.

94 "Terrorist Designations of Groups Operating in Syria." 2014. U.S. Department of State.
May 14, 2014. //2009-2017.state.gov/r/pa/prs/ps/2014/05/226067.htm.

95 Doyle. 2016. "Terrorist Material Support: An Overview of 18 U.S.C. §2339A and
§2339B."

96 Daniels, Lisa. 2016. "Prosecuting Terrorism in State Court." *Lawfare*, October 26, 2016.
https://www.lawfareblog.com/prosecuting-terrorism-state-court.

97 Pishko, Jessica. 2016. "The FBI Accused Him of Terrorism. He Couldn't Tie His Shoes." *Esquire*, September 8, 2016. https://www.esquire.com/news-politics/a47390/alabama-isis-peyton-pruitt/.

98 Clifford, Bennett. 2018. "Radicalization in Custody: Towards Data-Driven Terrorism Prevention in the United States Federal Correctional System." Policy Paper. Washington, D.C: George Washington Program on Extremism. https://extremism.gwu.edu/sites/g/files/zaxdzs2191/f/Prisons%20Policy%20Paper.pdf.

99 Ibid.

100 Ibid.

101 The Economist. 2015. "The Terrorists' Prison." May 21, 2015. https://www.economist.com/united-states/2015/05/21/the-terrorists-prison.

102 Authors' interview with senior Bureau of Prisons counterterrorism official, July 2018.

103 Vidino, Lorenzo, and Bennett Clifford. 2019. "A Review of Transatlantic Best Practices for Countering Radicalisation in Prisons and Terrorist Recidivism." EUROPOL, July 12. https://www.europol.europa.eu/publications-documents/review-of-transatlantic-best-practices-for-countering-radicalisation-in-prisons-and-terrorist-recidivism.

104 Ibid.

105 Ibid.

106 Clifford. 2018. "Radicalization in Custody: Towards Data-Driven Terrorism Prevention in the United States Federal Correctional System."

107 Author's interview with Probation Administrator for Violent Extremists, US Probation and Pretrial Services Office, July 2018.

108 Hodwitz, Omi. 2019. "The Terrorism Recidivism Study (TRS): Examining Recidivism Rates for Post-9/11 Offenders." *Perspectives on Terrorism* 13 (2): 54–64; Wright, Christopher J. 2019. "An Examination of Jihadi Recidivism Rates in the United States." *CTC Sentinel* 12 (10). https://ctc.usma.edu/examination-jihadi-recidivism-rates-united-states/.

2. The Terrorists

1 Vidino, Lorenzo, Francesco Marone, and Eva Entenmann. 2017. "Fear Thy Neighbor: Radicalization and Jihadist Attacks in the West." Milan, Italy: Joint George Washington Program on Extremism, ICCT-The Hague, ISPI Report. https://extremism.gwu.edu/sites/extremism.gwu.edu/files/FearThyNeighbor%20RadicalizationandJihadistAttacksintheWest.pdf.

2 Ibid.

3 Al-Adnani, Abu Muhammad. 2014. "Indeed, Your Lord is Ever Watchful." *al-Furqan Media Foundation*. September 9, 2014.

4 Nesser, Petter, Anne Stenersen, and Emilie Oftedal. 2016. "Jihadi Terrorism in Europe: The ISIS-Effect." *Perspectives on Terrorism* 10 (6): 8.; Nesser, Petter. 2019. "Military Interventions, Jihadi Networks, and Terrorist Entrepreneurs: How the Islamic State Terror Wave Rose So High in Europe."

5 Ibid.

6 Ibid.

7 Ibid.

8 Database compiled by the Program on Extremism at George Washington University. The methodology for determination of a "successful jihadist attack" is explained in

Vidino, Marone, and Entenmann. 2017. "Fear Thy Neighbor: Radicalization and Jihadist Attacks in the West."

9 ISIS also claimed a shooting in Las Vegas, Nevada on October 1, 2017 that left 58 dead, in the worst mass shooting in United States history. However, in an investigation conducted after the attack, the FBI found no evidence that the shooter had any inspiration or connection to ISIS. We assess that ISIS falsely claimed this attack, and do not include it in our statistics on jihadist attacks in the United States. Wood, Graeme. 2017. "Why Did the Islamic State Claim the Las Vegas Shooting?" *The Atlantic*, October 2, 2017. https://www.theatlantic.com/international/archive/2017/10/isis-amaq-las-vegas/541746/.

10 Yan, Holly. 2015. "ISIS Claims Responsibility for Garland, Texas, Shooting." *CNN*, May 5, 2015. https://www.cnn.com/2015/05/05/us/garland-texas-prophet-mohammed-contest-shooting/index.html.

11 Karimi, Faith, Jason Hanna and Yousuf Basil. 2015. "ISIS: San Bernardino Shooters Were 'Supporters.'" *CNN*, December 5, 2015. https://www.cnn.com/2015/12/05/us/san-bernardino-shooting/index.html.

12 Reuters. 2016. "Islamic State Claims Responsibility for Orlando Nightclub Shooting." June 12, 2016. https://www.reuters.com/article/us-florida-shooting-claim-idUSKCN0YY0VU.

13 Narayan, Chandrika, and Steve Visser. 2016. "ISIS Wing Claims Responsibility for Minnesota Mall Attack." *CNN*, September 18, 2016. https://www.cnn.com/2016/09/18/us/minnesota-mall-stabbing/index.html.

14 Smith, Mitch, Rukmini Callimachi and Richard Pérez-Peña. 2016. "ISIS Calls Ohio State University Attacker a 'Soldier.'" *The New York Times*, November 29, 2016, sec. U.S. https://www.nytimes.com/2016/11/29/us/ohio-state-university-abdul-artan-islamic-state.html.

15 Callimachi, Rukmini, Benjamin Mueller, Michael Schwirtz, and Adam Goldman. 2017. "Islamic State Claims Responsibility for Lower Manhattan Terrorist Attack." *The New York Times*, November 2, 2017, sec. New York. https://www.nytimes.com/2017/11/02/nyregion/manhattan-terror-attack-wedding.html.

16 An-Naba. 2017. "Events of the Week." December 15, 2017.

17 Almasy, Steve, and Chuck Johnston. 2018. "Police: Florida Teen Who Stabbed Friend to Death Was Known to FBI." *CNN*, March 15, 2018. https://www.cnn.com/2018/03/14/us/florida-teen-fatal-stabbing-muslim/index.html.

18 "Airport Terrorist Sentenced." 2019. Story. Federal Bureau of Investigation. July 8, 2019. https://www.fbi.gov/news/stories/canadian-man-sentenced-for-stabbing-airport-police-officer-070819.

19 Nesser, Petter. 2012. "Research Note: Single Actor Terrorism: Scope, Characteristics and Explanations." *Perspectives on Terrorism* 6 (6). http://www.terrorismanalysts.com/pt/index.php/pot/article/view/231.

20 Nesser, Stenersen, and Oftedal. 2016. "Jihadi Terrorism in Europe: The ISIS-Effect."

21 Burke, Jason. 2017. "The Myth of the 'Lone Wolf' Terrorist." *The Guardian*, March 30, 2017, sec. News. https://www.theguardian.com/news/2017/mar/30/myth-lone-wolf-terrorist.

22 Meleagrou-Hitchens, Alexander, and Seamus Hughes. 2017. "The Threat to the United States from the Islamic State's Virtual Entrepreneurs." *CTC Sentinel* 10 (3): 1–8. https://www.ctc.usma.edu/posts/the-threat-to-the-united-states-from-the-islamic-states-virtual-entrepreneurs; Moreng, Bridget. 2016. "ISIS' Virtual Puppeteers." *Foreign Affairs*, September 21, 2016. https://www.foreignaffairs.com/articles/2016-09-21/

isis-virtual-puppeteers; Gartenstein-Ross, Daveed, and Madeleine Blackman. 2017. "ISIL's Virtual Planners: A Critical Terrorist Innovation." *War on the Rocks*, January 4, 2017. https://warontherocks.com/2017/01/isils-virtual-planners-a-critical-terrorist-innovation/.

23 Meleagrou-Hitchens and Hughes. 2017. "The Threat to the United States from the Islamic State's Virtual Entrepreneurs."

24 Ibid.

25 Carlin, John P. 2018. *Dawn of the Code War: America's Battle Against Russia, China, and the Rising Global Cyber Threat*. New York: PublicAffairs.

26 Ibid.

27 Ibid.

28 Meleagrou-Hitchens and Hughes. 2017. "The Threat to the United States from the Islamic State's Virtual Entrepreneurs."

29 *The Guardian*. 2016. "Sister of Parramatta Shooter Was 'Top Isis Recruiter', Says Pentagon," May 8, 2016, sec. World news. https://www.theguardian.com/world/2016/may/08/sister-of-parramatta-shooter-was-top-isis-recruiter-says-pentagon.

30 "Factual Basis." 2016. *USA v. Justin Nojan Sullivan*, United States District Court for the Western District of North Carolina. Case 1:16-cr-00005-MR-DLH. https://extremism.gwu.edu/sites/g/files/zaxdzs2191/f/Sullivan%20Factual%20Basis.pdf

31 Ibid.

32 Ibid.

33 Ibid.

34 Mueller, John. 2017. "The Cybercoaching of Terrorists: Cause for Alarm?" *CTC Sentinel* 10 (9): 29–35. https://ctc.usma.edu/the-cybercoaching-of-terrorists-cause-for-alarm/.

35 Ellis, Ralph, Ashley Fantz, Faith Karimi, and Elliott McLaughlin. 2016. "49 Killed in Florida Nightclub Terror Attack." *CNN*, June 13, 2016. https://www.cnn.com/2016/06/12/us/orlando-nightclub-shooting/index.html.

36 Hong, Nicole, and Dan Frosch. 2016. "Transcripts Show ISIS Influence on Orlando Gunman." *Wall Street Journal*, September 28, 2016, sec. US. https://www.wsj.com/articles/transcripts-show-isis-influence-on-orlando-gunman-1475023090.

37 Ellis, Fantz, Karimi, and McLaughlin. 2016. "49 Killed in Florida Nightclub Terror Attack."

38 *The New York Times*. "Pulse Nightclub Shooting." Accessed December 16, 2019. https://www.nytimes.com/news-event/2016-orlando-shooting.

39 Reuters. 2016. "Islamic State Claims Responsibility for Orlando Nightclub Shooting." June 12, 2016. https://www.reuters.com/article/us-florida-shooting-claim-idUSKCN0YY0VU.

40 Nagourney, Adam, Ian Lovett, and Richard Pérez-Peña. 2015. "San Bernardino Shooting Kills at Least 14; Two Suspects Are Dead." *The New York Times*, December 2, 2015, sec. U.S. https://www.nytimes.com/2015/12/03/us/san-bernardino-shooting.html.

41 Mueller, Benjamin, and Michael Schwirtz. 2017. "Driver in Manhattan Attack Had Been Planning for Weeks, Police Say." *The New York Times*, November 1, 2017, sec. N.Y. / Region. https://www.nytimes.com/2017/11/01/nyregion/driver-had-been-planning-attack-in-manhattan-for-weeks-police-say.html.

42 Ibid.

43 Callimachi, Rukmini, Benjamin Mueller, Michael Schwirtz, and Adam Goldman. 2017. "Islamic State Claims Responsibility for Lower Manhattan Terrorist Attack." *The New York Times*, November 2, 2017, sec. New York. https://www.nytimes.com/2017/11/02/nyregion/manhattan-terror-attack-wedding.html.

44 BBC News. 2016. "California Attacker 'Inspired by ISIS.'" March 18, 2016, sec. US & Canada. https://www.bbc.com/news/world-us-canada-35838588.

45 Ibid.

46 Detman, Gary. 2016. "Orlando Gunman Omar Mateen Investigated Twice by FBI." *WPEC*, June 12, 2016. https://cbs12.com/news/local/fbi-omar-mateen-investigated-for-ties-to-fort-pierce-suicide-bomber.

47 Apuzzo, Matt, Michael S. Schmidt, and Julia Preston. 2015. "U.S. Visa Process Missed San Bernardino Wife's Online Zealotry." *The New York Times*, December 12, 2015, sec. U.S. https://www.nytimes.com/2015/12/13/us/san-bernardino-attacks-us-visa-process-tashfeen-maliks-remarks-on-social-media-about-jihad-were-missed.html.

48 Ibid.

49 Interview with FBI Joint Terrorism Task Force agents, March 2018.

50 "Affidavit in Support of a Criminal Complaint." 2016. *USA v. Mohamed Bailor Jalloh*, United States District Court for the Eastern District of Virginia. Case 1:16-mj-00296-TCB. https://extremism.gwu.edu/sites/g/files/zaxdzs2191/f/Jalloh%20Affidavit%20in%20Support%20of%20Criminal%20Complaint.pdf.

51 Ibid.

52 Hong, Nicole, and Dan Frosch. 2016. "Transcripts Show ISIS Influence on Orlando Gunman." *Wall Street Journal*, September 28, 2016, sec. US. https://www.wsj.com/articles/transcripts-show-isis-influence-on-orlando-gunman-1475023090.

53 Interview with FBI Joint Terrorism Task Force agents, March 2018.

54 Ibid.

55 "Department of Defense Press Briefing by Pentagon Press Secretary Peter Cook." 2016. United States Department of Defense. May 5, 2016. https://www.defense.gov/Newsroom/Transcripts/Transcript/Article/752789/department-of-defense-press-briefing-by-pentagon-press-secretary-peter-cook-in/.

56 Meleagrou-Hitchens and Hughes. 2017. "The Threat to the United States from the Islamic State's Virtual Entrepreneurs."

57 Interview with FBI Joint Terrorism Task Force agents, March 2018.

58 Ibid.

59 Ibid.

60 Ibid.

61 "Affidavit in Support of a Criminal Complaint." 2016. *USA v. Mohamed Bailor Jalloh*.

62 Ibid.

63 Interview with FBI Joint Terrorism Task Force agents, March 2018.

64 Ibid.

65 Ibid.

66 Ibid.

67 Ibid.

68 Ibid.

69 Ibid.

70 Ibid.

71 Ibid.

72 Ibid.

73 Ibid.

74 Ibid.

75 Ibid.

76 Ibid.

77 Ibid.

78 Ibid.

79 Ibid.

80 "Affidavit in Support of a Criminal Complaint." 2016. *USA v. Mohamed Bailor Jalloh.*

81 Ibid.

82 Ibid.

83 Interview with FBI Joint Terrorism Task Force agents, March 2018.

84 Ibid.

85 Ibid.

86 Ibid.

87 Ibid.

88 Ibid.

89 Ibid.

90 Ibid.

91 Ibid.

92 Ibid.

93 Ibid.

94 Ibid.

95 Ibid.

96 Ibid.

97 Callimachi, Rukmini. 2015. "Clues on Twitter Show Ties Between Texas Gunman and ISIS Network." *The New York Times*, May 11, 2015, sec. U.S. https://www.nytimes.com/2015/05/12/us/twitter-clues-show-ties-between-isis-and-garland-texas-gunman.html.

98 Ibid.

99 Ibid.

100 Ibid.

101 "Suspects Dead In Garland Art Show Shooting." 2015. CBS DFW. May 4, 2015. https://dfw.cbslocal.com/2015/05/04/garland-shooting-investigation/.

102 Ibid.

103 Ibid.

104 "Arizona Man Sentenced to 30 Years for Conspiracy to Support ISIL and Other Federal Offenses." 2017. Department of Justice Press Release. February 8, 2017. https://www.justice.gov/opa/pr/arizona-man-sentenced-30-years-conspiracy-support-isil-and-other-federal-offenses.

105 "Defendant Found Guilty for Making False Statements in Garland Shooting Investigation." 2019. Department of Justice Press Release. June 7, 2019. https://www.justice.gov/usao-az/pr/defendant-found-guilty-making-false-statements-garland-shooting-investigation.

106 Amarasingam, Amarnath. 2015. "Elton 'Ibrahim' Simpson's Path to Jihad in Garland, Texas." *War on the Rocks*, May 14, 2015. https://warontherocks.com/2015/05/elton-ibrahim-simpsons-path-to-jihad-in-garland-texas/.

107 Ibid.

108 Ibid.

109 Murphy, Esme. 2015. "Former Minnesota Man Played Key Role In Inciting Texas Terror Attack." CBS Minnesota. May 4, 2015. https://minnesota.cbslocal.com/2015/05/04/former-minnesota-man-played-key-role-in-inciting-texas-terror-attack/.

110 Yuen, Laura, and Sasha Aslanian. 2013. "Minnesota Pipeline to Al-Shabab." *Minnesota Public Radio News*, September 25, 2013. http://minnesota.publicradio.org/projects/ongoing/somali_timeline/.

111 *Washington Post.* 2015. "Minn. Man Whose Tweets Urged Jihad Is Held in Africa." December 8, 2015, sec. National Security. https://www.washingtonpost.com/world/national-security/minn-man-whose-tweets-urged-jihad-is-held-in-africa/2015/12/08/8fb7a1b4-9d4c-11e5-8728-1af6af208198_story.html.

112 Callimachi. 2015. "Clues on Twitter Show Ties Between Texas Gunman and ISIS Network."

113 Ibid.

114 Ibid.

115 Ibid.

116 Ibid.

117 Sanger, David E., and Nicole Perlroth. 2015. "F.B.I. Chief Says Texas Gunman Used Encryption to Text Overseas Terrorist." *The New York Times*, December 9, 2015, sec. U.S. https://www.nytimes.com/2015/12/10/us/politics/fbi-chief-says-texas-gunman-used-encryption-to-text-overseas-terrorist.html.

118 Koerner, Claudia. 2015. "The Garland, Texas, Shooters' Quiet Path To Violent Jihad." *BuzzFeed News*, May 14, 2015. https://www.buzzfeednews.com/article/claudiakoerner/the-garland-texas-shooters-quiet-path-to-violent-jihad.

119 Ibid.

120 Ibid.

121 Ibid.

122 Ibid.

123 "Arizona Man Sentenced to 30 Years for Conspiracy to Support ISIL and Other Federal Offenses." 2017. Department of Justice Press Release. February 8, 2017. https://www.justice.gov/opa/pr/arizona-man-sentenced-30-years-conspiracy-support-isil-and-other-federal-offenses.

124 "Second Superseding Indictment." 2015. *USA v. Abdul Malik Abdul Kareem*, United States District Court for the District of Arizona. Case 2:15-cr-00707-SRB. https://extremism.gwu.edu/sites/g/files/zaxdzs2191/f/Kareem%20Second%20Superseding%20Indictment.pdf

125 Ibid.

126 "AP: FBI Agent Drove Past Shooters in 2015 Garland Attack, Records Say." 2017. *WFAA*, February 10, 2017. https://www.wfaa.com/article/news/local/ap-fbi-agent-drove-past-shooters-in-2015-garland-attack-records-say/287-406741839.

127 Ibid.

128 Martin, Naomi. 2017. "Security Guard Injured in Garland Terror Attack Tormented by Belief That FBI Knew of ISIS Plot." *Dallas News*, May 26, 2017. https://www.dallasnews.com/news/crime/2017/05/26/security-guard-injured-in-garland-terror-attack-tormented-by-belief-that-fbi-knew-of-isis-plot/.

129 Grassley, Charles. 2017. "Letter to FBI Director James Comey, Jr." April 27, 2017. https://www.grassley.senate.gov/sites/default/files/constituents/2017-04-27%20CEG%20to%20FBI%20%28Garland%20Texas%20Incident%29.pdf.

130 "60 Minutes Investigates First ISIS-Claimed Attack in U.S. and What the FBI Knew." 2017. *CBS News*, August 20, 2017. https://www.cbsnews.com/news/terrorism-in-garland-texas-what-the-fbi-knew-before-the-2015-attack-2/.

131 Shane, Scott. 2015. "F.B.I. Says It Sent Warning on One Gunman in Attack at Texas Gathering." *The New York Times*, May 7, 2015, sec. U.S. https://www.nytimes.com/2015/05/08/us/fbi-says-it-warned-of-gunman-in-garland-texas-attack.html.

132 "Affidavit in Support of an Application for Criminal Complaint and Arrest Warrant." 2015. *USA v. Robert McCollum*, United States District Court for the Northern District of Ohio. https://extremism.gwu.edu/sites/g/files/zaxdzs2191/f/McCollum%20Affidavit.pdf.

133 Ibid.
134 Affidavit in Support of an Application for Criminal Complaint and Arrest Warrant."
    2016. *USA v. Erick Jamal Hendricks*, United States District Court for the Northern
    District of Ohio. Case: 1:16-mj-02128. https://extremism.gwu.edu/sites/g/files/
    zaxdzs2191/f/Hendricks%20Affidavit%20in%20Support%20of%20a%20Criminal%20
    Complaint.pdf.
135 Ibid.
136 Ibid.
137 Ibid.
138 Ibid.
139 Ibid.
140 Ibid.
141 Ibid.
142 Ibid.
143 Ibid.
144 Ibid.
145 Ibid.
146 Ibid.
147 Ibid.
148 Ibid.
149 Ibid.
150 "North Carolina Man Sentenced to 15 Years in Prison for Attempting and Conspiring
    to Provide Material Support to ISIS." 2019. Department of Justice Press Release.
    February 4, 2019. https://www.justice.gov/opa/pr/north-carolina-man-sentenced-15-
    years-prison-attempting-and-conspiring-provide-material.
151 "Two Men Charged with Conspiracy to Provide Material Support to Islamic State."
    2015. Department of Justice Press Release. June 12, 2015. https://www.justice.gov/
    opa/pr/two-men-charged-conspiracy-provide-material-support-islamic-state.
152 "Government's Sentencing Memorandum." 2017. *USA v. David Wright*, United States
    District Court for the District of Massachusetts. Case 1:15-cr-10153-WGY. https://
    extremism.gwu.edu/sites/g/files/zaxdzs2191/f/David%20Wright%20Government%20
    Sentencing%20Memo.pdf.
153 Ibid.
154 Hughes, Seamus, Alexander Meleagrou-Hitchens, and Bennett Clifford. 2018. "A New
    American Leader Rises in ISIS." *The Atlantic*, January 13, 2018. https://www.
    theatlantic.com/international/archive/2018/01/isis-america-hoxha/550508/.
155 "Government's Sentencing Memorandum." 2017. *USA v. David Wright*, United States
    District Court for the District of Massachusetts. Case 1:15-cr-10153-WGY. https://
    extremism.gwu.edu/sites/g/files/zaxdzs2191/f/David%20Wright%20Government%20
    Sentencing%20Memo.pdf.
156 Ibid.
157 "Trial Transcript." 2017. *USA v. David Wright*, United States District Court for the
    District of Massachusetts. Case 1:15-cr-10153-WGY. October 12, 2017.
158 Ibid.
159 Ibid.
160 Ibid.
161 "Government's Sentencing Memorandum." 2017. *USA v. David Wright*, United States
    District Court for the District of Massachusetts. Case 1:15-cr-10153-WGY. https://
    extremism.gwu.edu/sites/g/files/zaxdzs2191/f/David%20Wright%20Government%20
    Sentencing%20Memo.pdf.

162 Ibid.

163 Ibid.

164 Ibid.

165 Ibid.

166 Ibid.

167 Ibid.

168 Ibid.

169 "Massachusetts Man Sentenced to 28 Years in Prison for Supporting ISIS and Conspiring to Murder U.S. Citizens." 2017. Department of Justice Press Release. December 19, 2017. https://www.justice.gov/opa/pr/massachusetts-man-sentenced-28-years-prison-supporting-isis-and-conspiring-murder-us-citizens; "Rhode Island Man Sentenced for Conspiring to Commit Acts of Terrorism to Support ISIS." 2017. Department of Justice Press Release. December 20, 2017. https://www.justice.gov/usao-ma/pr/rhode-island-man-sentenced-conspiring-commit-acts-terrorism-support-isis.

170 Sanger, David E., and Nicole Perlroth. 2015. "F.B.I. Chief Says Texas Gunman Used Encryption to Text Overseas Terrorist." *The New York Times*, December 9, 2015, sec. U.S. https://www.nytimes.com/2015/12/10/us/politics/fbi-chief-says-texas-gunman-used-encryption-to-text-overseas-terrorist.html.

171 Affidavit in Support of an Application for Criminal Complaint and Arrest Warrant." 2016. *USA v. Erick Jamal Hendricks*, United States District Court for the Northern District of Ohio. Case: 1:16-mj-02128. https://extremism.gwu.edu/sites/g/files/zaxdzs2191/f/Hendricks%20Affidavit%20in%20Support%20of%20a%20Criminal%20Complaint.pdf.

172 Carlin. 2018. *Dawn of the Code War.*

173 Ibid.

174 Ibid.

175 Hamid, Nafees. 2018. "The British Hacker Who Became the Islamic State's Chief Terror Cybercoach: A Profile of Junaid Hussain." *CTC Sentinel* 11 (4): 30–37. https://ctc.usma.edu/british-hacker-became-islamic-states-chief-terror-cybercoach-profile-junaid-hussain/.

176 Hughes, Meleagrou-Hitchens, and Clifford. 2018. "A New American Leader Rises in ISIS."

177 Ibid.

178 Ibid.

179 Ibid.

180 Interview with U.S. Government official, December 2017.

181 Davies, Wyre. 2018. "The Terror Cell Started in Pontypridd." *BBC News*, July 16, 2018, sec. Wales. https://www.bbc.com/news/uk-wales-44826806.

182 Ibid.

183 Ibid.

184 Rassler, Don. 2018. "The Islamic State and Drones: Supply, Scale and Future Threats." West Point: Combating Terrorism Center. https://ctc.usma.edu/app/uploads/2018/07/Islamic-State-and-Drones-Release-Version.pdf.

185 Ibid.

186 Ibid.

187 Ibid.

188 "Discovery." 2018. *USA v. Mohamed Elshinawy*, United States District Court for the District of Maryland. Case: ELH-16-009.

189 Interview with FBI Joint Terrorism Task Force agents, June 2018.

190 Ibid.
191 Ibid.
192 Ibid.
193 Ibid.
194 Ibid.
195 Ibid.
196 Ibid.
197 Ibid.
198 Ibid.
199 Ibid.
200 Ibid.
201 Ibid.
202 Ibid.
203 Ibid.
204 Ibid.
205 Ibid.
206 Ibid.
207 Ibid.
208 Ibid.
209 "Diligencias Previas Proc. Abreviado 000020/2016." 2016. Juzgado Central de Instruccion N. 003 Madrid.
210 Davies. 2018. "The Terror Cell Started in Pontypridd."
211 "Diligencias Previas Proc. Abreviado 000020/2016." 2016. Juzgado Central de Instruccion N. 003 Madrid.
212 Ibid.
213 Ibid.
214 "Coalition Killed 10 Senior ISIL Leaders in December." 2015. United States Department of Defense. December 29, 2015. https://www.defense.gov/Explore/News/Article/Article/639489/coalition-killed-10-senior-isil-leaders-in-december/.
215 Ibid.
216 "Maryland Man Charged With Attempting to Provide Material Support to ISIL." 2015. Department of Justice Press Release. December 14, 2015. https://www.justice.gov/opa/pr/maryland-man-charged-attempting-provide-material-support-isil.
217 "Terrorist Sentenced." 2018. Story. Federal Bureau of Investigation. June 17, 2018. https://www.fbi.gov/news/stories/maryland-man-sentenced-in-terrorism-planning-and-financing-conspiracy-071718.
218 Rassler. 2018. "The Islamic State and Drones."
219 Mueller. 2017. "The Cybercoaching of Terrorists: Cause for Alarm?"
220 Cruickshank, Paul. 2018. "A View from the CT Foxhole: Nicholas Rasmussen, Former Director, National Counterterrorism Center." *CTC Sentinel* 11 (1): 12–17. https://ctc.usma.edu/view-ct-foxhole-nicholas-rasmussen-former-director-national-counterterrorism-center/.
221 Ibid.
222 Ingram, Haroro J., Craig Whiteside, and Charlie Winter. 2019. "The Guerrilla 'Caliph': Speeches That Bookend the Islamic State's 'Caliphate' Era." *CTC Sentinel* 12 (2): 41–5. https://ctc.usma.edu/guerrilla-caliph-speeches-bookend-islamic-states-caliphate-era/.
223 Brantly, Aaron. 2017. "Banning Encryption to Stop Terrorists: A Worse than Futile Exercise." *CTC Sentinel* 10 (7): 29–33. https://ctc.usma.edu/posts/banning-encryption-to-stop-terrorists-a-worse-than-futile-exercise.

224 Wray, Christopher. 2019. "Global Terrorism: Threats to the Homeland." Testimony of Federal Bureau of Investigation Director Christopher Wray before the House Homeland Security Committee, October 30, 2019. https://www.fbi.gov/news/testimony/global-terrorism-threats-to-the-homeland-103019.

225 Ibid.

226 Ebner, Julia. 2017. *The Rage: The Vicious Circle of Islamist and Far-Right Extremism.* London: I.B. Tauris.

227 "Criminal Complaint." 2019. *USA v. Mark Domingo*, United States District Court for the Central District of California. Case: 2:19-MJ-01751-DUTY. https://extremism.gwu.edu/sites/g/files/zaxdzs2191/f/Mark%20Domingo%20Criminal%20Complaint.pdf p.2

228 Ibid., 23.

229 Ibid., 5.

230 Ibid.

3. The Travelers

1 Clapper, James. 2016. Testimony before Senate Select Committee on Intelligence, February 9, 2016. https://www.dni.gov/files/documents/2016-02-09SSCI_open_threat_hearing_transcript.pdf; The Soufan Group. "Foreign Fighters: An Updated Assessment of the Flow of Foreign Fighters into Syria and Iraq." 2015. New York: The Soufan Group. http://soufangroup.com/wpcontent/uploads/2015/12/TSG_ForeignFightersUpdate3.pdf.

2 Ibid.

3 Cruickshank, Paul. 2017. "The Inside Story of the Paris and Brussels Attacks." *CNN*, October 30, 2017. https://www.cnn.com/2016/03/30/0urope/inside-paris-brussels-terror-attacks/index.html.

4 Ibid.

5 Ibid.

6 Comey, James. 2014. "Worldwide Threats to the Homeland." Statement by Director James B. Comey before the House Homeland Security Committee. Federal Bureau of Investigation. September 17, 2014. https://www.fbi.gov/news/testimony/worldwide-threats-to-the-homeland.

7 Witte, Griff, Sudarsan Raghavan, and James McAuley. 2016. "Flow of Foreign Fighters Plummets as Islamic State Loses Its Edge." *Washington Post*, September 9, 2016, sec. Europe. https://www.washingtonpost.com/world/1urope/flow-offoreign-fighters-plummets-as-isis-loses-its-edge/2016/09/09/ed3e0dda-751b-11e6-9781-49e591781754_story.html.

8 Cook, Joana and Gina Vale. 2018. "From Daesh to Diaspora: Tracing the Women and Minors of the Islamic State." London, UK: International Centre for the Study of Radicalisation. https://icsr.info/wp-content/uploads/2018/07/ICSR-Report-From-Daesh-to-%E2%80%98Diaspora%E2%80%99-Tracing-the-Women-and-Minors-of-Islamic-State.pdf.

9 Authors' interview with Federal Bureau of Investigation officials on October 24, 2017. This number includes travelers, attempted travelers, and participants of jihadist and non-jihadist groups.

10 Mendick, Robert, and Robert Verkaik. 2016. "Only One in Eight Jihadists Returning to UK Is Caught and Convicted." *The Telegraph*, May 21, 2016. http://www.telegraph.co.

uk/news/2016/05/21/only-one-in-eight-jihadists-returning-to-uk-is-caught-and-convic.

11 Ibid.

12 Berger, J.M. 2011. *Jihad Joe: Americans Who Go to War in the Name of Islam*. 1st ed. Washington, D.C: Potomac Books. xi.

13 Malet, David. 2013. *Foreign Fighters: Transnational Identity in Civic Conflicts*. New York, NY: Oxford University Press.

14 Bennett, Gina. 1993. "The Wandering Mujahidin: Armed and Dangerous." *U.S. Department of State Bureau of Intelligence and Research Weekend Edition*, August 22, 1993.

15 Jenkins, "When Jihadis Come Marching Home."

16 "Complaint and Affidavit In Support of Arrest Warrant." 2016. *USA v. Mohamed Rafik Naji*, United States District Court for the Eastern District of New York. Case: 1:16-mj-01049. https://extremism.gwu.edu/sites/extremism.gwu.edu/files/Naji%20 Complaint%2C%20Affidavit%20in%20Support%20of%20Arrest%20Warrant.pdf.

17 "Affidavit in Support of a Criminal Complaint." 2016. *USA v. Mohamed Bailor Jalloh*.

18 Wright, Robin. 2018. "America's ISIS Jihadists Were Largely Duds." *The New Yorker*, February 6, 2019. https://www.newyorker.com/news/news-desk/americas-isis-fighters-were-largely-duds.

19 Wood, Graeme. 2017. "The American Climbing the Ranks of ISIS." *The Atlantic*, March 2017. https://www.theatlantic.com/magazine/archive/2017/03/the-american-leader-in-the-islamic-state/510872.

20 Hughes, Seamus, and Bennett Clifford. 2017. "First He Became an American—Then He Joined ISIS." *The Atlantic*, May 25, 2017. https://www.theatlantic.com/international/archive/2017/05/first-he-became-an-americanthen-he-joined-isis/527622.

21 Anderson, Karen. 2014. "FBI on Mass. Terror Suspect: 'Don't Know Where He Is, What He's Doing.'" *WCVB*, October 15, 2014. http://www.wcvb.com/article/fbi-on-mass-terror-suspect-don-t-know-where-he-is-what-he-s-doing/8209979.

22 Ibid.

23 Ibid.

24 "Superseding Indictment." 2009. *USA v. Tarek Mehanna and Ahmad Abousamra*. United States District Court for the District of Massachusetts. Case: 09-CR-I0017.

25 Singman, Brooke. 2015. "Moderate Imam Reveals How Radicals Won Battle for Soul of Boston Mosques." *Fox News*, July 26, 2015. http://www.foxnews.com/us/2015/07/22/moderate-imam-reveals-how-radicals-won-battle-for-soul-boston-mosques.html.

26 Ibid.

27 "Superseding Indictment." 2009. *USA v. Tarek Mehanna and Ahmad Abousamra*.

28 Ibid.

29 Ibid.

30 Lavoie, Denise. 2011. "Witness Says Mass. Men Discussed Mall Shooting." *Boston.com*, November 28, 2011. http://archive.boston.com/news/local/massachusetts/articles/2011/11/28/witness_in_mass_terror_case__sought_terror_camp.

31 "Superseding Indictment." 2009. *USA v. Tarek Mehanna and Ahmad Abousamra*.

32 Valencia, Milton. 2011. "Mehanna Friend Said to Seek Camps for Training." *The Boston Globe*, November 16, 2011. https://www.bostonglobe.com/metro/2011/11/16/man-who-trained-terrorist-testifies-gave-mehanna-associate-contacts-yemen/Xtg5EQTfJNj8RqUHC0nrRL/story.html.

33 Ibid.

34 "Superseding Indictment." 2009. *USA v. Tarek Mehanna and Ahmad Abousamra*.

35 Ibid.

36 Ibid.

37 Ibid.

38 Ibid.

39 Ibid.

40 Ibid.

41 Ibid.

42 Ibid.

43 "Tarek Mehanna Sentenced in Boston to 17 Years in Prison on Terrorism-Related Charges." 2012. FBI. April 12, 2012. https://www.fbi.gov/boston/press-releases/2012/tarek-mehanna-sentenced-in-boston-to-17-years-in-prison-on-terrorism-related-charges.

44 "FBI Engages Social Media in Terrorist Manhunt." 2012. *Public Radio International*, October 4, 2012. https://www.pri.org/stories/2012-10-04/fbi-engages-social-media-terrorist-manhunt.

45 Ibid.

46 "Wanted Fugitive Ahmad Abousamra Added to the FBI's Most Wanted Terrorists List." 2013. FBI. December 18, 2013. https://www.fbi.gov/boston/press-releases/2013/wanted-fugitive-ahmad-abousamra-added-to-the-fbis-most-wanted-terrorists-list.

47 Ibid.

48 McPhee, Michele, and Brian Ross. 2014. "Official: American May Be Key in ISIS Social Media Blitz." *ABC News*, September 3, 2014. http://abcnews.go.com/blogs/headlines/2014/09/official-american-may-be-key-in-isis-social-media-blitz; Cruickshank, Paul. 2017. "ISIS Lifts Veil on American at Heart of Its Propaganda Machine." *CNN*, April 7, 2017. http://www.cnn.com/2017/04/06/middleeast/isis-american-propaganda-editor/index.html.

49 *Rumiyah*. 2017. "Among the Believers Are Men." April 2017.

50 Ibid.

51 Ibid.

52 Ibid.

53 Ibid.

54 Ibid.

55 Ibid.

56 Abousamra, Ahmad. 2016. "Jews of Jihad: Zawahiri's Al Qaeda." https://www.longwarjournal.org/wp content/uploads/2017/04/Arabic-version-of-Jews-of-Jihad.pdf.

57 *Rumiyah*. 2017. "Among the Believers Are Men."

58 *Rumiyah*. Issue 1, September 2016.

59 Warrick, Joby. 2016. "ISIS's Second-in-Command Hid in Syria for Months. The Day He Stepped Out, the U.S. Was Waiting." *Washington Post*, November 28, 2016, sec. National Security. https://www.washingtonpost.com/world/national-security/isiss-second-in-command-hid-in-syria-for-months-the-day-he-stepped-out-the-us-was-waiting/2016/11/28/64a32efe-b253-11e6-840f-e3ebab6bcdd3_story.html; BBC News. 2016. "US Strike 'Kills ISIS Propaganda Chief,'" September 16, 2016, sec. Middle East. http://www.bbc.com/news/world-middle-east-37390408.

60 *Rumiyah*. 2017. "Among the Believers Are Men."

61 Joscelyn, Thomas. 2017. "How a US Citizen Became a Key Player in the Islamic State's Rivalry with Al Qaeda." *FDD's Long War Journal*, April 7, 2017. https://www.longwarjournal.org/archives/2017/04/how-a-us-citizen-became-a-key-player-in-the-islamic-states-rivalry-with-al-qaeda.php.

62 Ibid.

63 *Rumiyah*. 2017. "Among the Believers Are Men."

64 Ibid.

65 Yusuf, Hamza. 2016. "When Evil Fails." *Sandala* (blog), July 31, 2016. https://sandala. org/when-evil-fails.

66 "Criminal Complaint." 2015. *USA v. Asher Abid Khan*, United States District Court for the Southern District of Texas. Case: H15-712 M. https://extremism.gwu.edu/sites/ extremism.gwu.edu/files/Khan%2C%20A.%20Criminal%20Complaint.pdf.

67 "Factual Basis." 2017. *USA v. Mohommad Hasnain Ali*, United States District Court for the Eastern District of Texas. Case: 4:17-cr-00087-MAC-CAN. https://extremism.gwu. edu/sites/extremism.gwu.edu/files/MAliFactualBasis.pdf.

68 Vidino, Marone, and Entenmann. 2017. "Fear Thy Neighbor: Radicalization and Jihadist Attacks in the West."

69 Yuen, Laura, and Sasha Aslanian. 2013. "Minnesota Pipeline to Al-Shabab." *Minnesota Public Radio News*, September 25, 2013. http://minnesota.publicradio.org/projects/ ongoing/somali_timeline.

70 "U.S. Attorney: We Have a Terror-Recruiting Problem in Minnesota." 2015. *NBC News*, April 20, 2015. https://www.nbcnews.com/dateline/ video/u-s-attorney-we-have-a-terror-recruiting-problem-in-minnesota-430813251584.

71 "Indictment." 2017. *USA v. Abdullahi Ahmed Abdullahi*, United States District Court for the Southern District of California. Case: 3:17-cr-00622. https://extremism.gwu. edu/sites/g/files/zaxdzs2191/f/Abdullahi%20Indictment.pdf.

72 Ibid.

73 Ibid.

74 Ibid.

75 Ibid.

76 Ibid.

77 Omar, Ammar Cheikh, and Saphora Smith. 2014. "ISIS' Douglas McCain, Best Friend Troy Kastigar Both Waged Jihad." *NBC News*, August 27, 2014. https://www.nbcnews. com/news/world/isis-douglas-mccain-best-friend-troy-kastigar-both-waged- jihad-n190001; "Details Emerge About Douglas McCain, American Jihadist Killed in Syria." 2014. *VOA*, August 27, 2014. https://www.voanews.com/a/us-man-suspected- of-fighting-alongside-militants-killed-in-syria/2429355.html.

78 Ibid.

79 Ibid.

80 "Details Emerge About Douglas McCain, American Jihadist Killed in Syria." 2014. "Superseding Indictment." 2017. *USA v. Marchello Dsaun Mccain*, United States District Court for the Southern District of California. Case: 3:15-cr-00174. https://extremism. gwu.edu/sites/g/files/zaxdzs2191/f/McCain%20Superseding%20Indictment.pdf.

81 "Affidavit in Support of Application for a Search Warrant." 2015. United States District Court for the District of Minnesota. Case: 014-mj-00973, pp. 8–9.

82 Ibid.

83 Ibid.

84 "Indictment." 2017. *USA v. Abdullahi Ahmed Abdullahi*, United States District Court for the Southern District of California. Case: 3:17-cr-00622.

85 "Details Emerge About Douglas McCain, American Jihadist Killed in Syria."

86 Ibrahim, Mukhtar M. 2017. "As Life's Pressures Mounted, He Left Minnesota for ISIS." *Minnesota Public Radio News*, December 6, 2017. https://www.mprnews.org/ story/2017/12/06/minnesota-isis-fighter-abdifatah-ahmed-court-documents.

87 Huncar, Andrea. 2015. "3 Canadians Believed Killed Fighting for ISIS." *CBC News*, January 14, 2015. http://www.cbc.ca/news/canada/edmonton/3-isis-recruits-from- edmonton-believed-killed-1.2901146.

88 Temple-Raston, Dina. 2017. "An American Teen Tried to Join ISIS. Then Came His Second Chance." *New York Magazine*, November 26, 2017. http://nymag.com/daily/intelligencer/2017/11/abdullahi-yusuf-isis-syria.html.

89 Ibid.

90 "Criminal Complaint." 2015. *USA v. Mohamed Abdihamid Farah et. al.* United States District Court for the District of Minnesota. Case: 0:15-cr-00049. https://extremism.gwu.edu/sites/extremism.gwu.edu/files/Omar%20Criminal%20Complaint.pdf.

91 Ibid.

92 Ibid.

93 "Criminal Complaint." 2014. *USA v. Abdullahi Yusuf and Abdi Nur.* United States District Court for the District of Minnesota. Case: 14-mj-1024. https://extremism.gwu.edu/sites/extremism.gwu.edu/files/Yusuf%20Criminal%20Complaint.pdf.

94 Ibid.

95 Ibid.

96 Ibid.

97 Ibid.

98 Ibid.

99 Ibid.

100 "Criminal Complaint." 2015. *USA v. Mohamed Abdihamid Farah et. al.*

101 Ibid.

102 Ibid.

103 "Criminal Complaint." 2016. *USA v. Mohamed Ali Amiin Roble.* United States District Court for the District of Minnesota. Case: 16-mj-584. https://extremism.gwu.edu/sites/extremism.gwu.edu/files/Roble%20Criminal%20Complaint%2C%20Signed%20Affidavit.pdf.

104 Ibid.

105 Ibid.

106 Ibid.

107 Yuen, Laura, Mukhtar Ibrahim, and Sasha Aslanian. 2015. "From MN Suburbs, They Set out to Join ISIS." *Minnesota Public Radio News*, March 25, 2015. https://www.mprnews.org/story/2015/03/25/minnesota-teens-isis.

108 Ibid.

109 Ibid.; "Brother of San Diego Man Killed Fighting for ISIS Sentenced to 10 Years for Terrorism Related Charges and Illegal Firearms Possession." Department of Justice Press Release, January 12, 2018. https://www.justice.gov/opa/pr/brother-san-diego-man-killed-fighting-isis-sentenced-10-years-terrorism-related-charges-and.

110 "Canadian National Extradited to San Diego to Face Terrorism Charges." Department of Justice Press Release, October 25, 2019. https://www.justice.gov/usao-sdca/pr/canadian-national-extradited-san-diego-face-terrorism-charges.

111 Montemayor, Stephen. 2017. "After Prison, Will Minnesota's ISIS Defendants Come out Better or Worse?" *Star Tribune*, July 1. http://www.startribune.com/after-years-in-prison-will-minnesota-s-isis-defendants-come-out-better-or-worse/432015773.

112 Temple-Raston. 2017. "An American Teen Tried to Join ISIS. Then Came His Second Chance."

113 Montemayor. 2017. "After Prison, Will Minnesota's ISIS Defendants Come out Better or Worse?"

114 Stahl, Brandon. 2019. "Two of three convicted in ISIS trial ask U.S. Supreme Court to hear appeal." *Star Tribune*, February 5. http://www.startribune.com/two-of-three-convicted-in-isis-trial-ask-u-s-supreme-court-to-hear-appeal/505377472/.

115 "SCOTUS denies hearing on case of Minnesotan who tried to join ISIS." *KSTP Eyewitness News*, March 13. https://kstp.com/news/scotus-denies-hearing-case-of-minnesotan-mohamed-farah-tried-to-join-isis/5277672/.

116 Yuen, Laura, Mukhtar Ibrahim, and Sasha Aslanian. 2015. "Called to Fight: Minnesota's ISIS Recruits." *Minnesota Public Radio News*, March 25. https://www.mprnews.org/story/2015/03/25/minnesota-isis.

117 "Sentencing Position of the United States of America." *USA v. Abdullahi Mohamed Yusuf.* United States District Court for the District of Minnesota. Case: 0:15-cr-00046. p. 8.

118 "Criminal Complaint." *USA v. Yusra Ismail.* United States District Court for the District of Minnesota. Case: 0:14-mj-01047. https://extremism.gwu.edu/sites/extremism.gwu.edu/files/Ismail%20Criminal%20Complaint.pdf.

119 Montemayor, Stephen. 2017. "Feds Have at Least Six Open Cases Looking at ISIS Support in Minnesota." *Star Tribune*, September 9. http://www.startribune.com/on-vacation-in-morocco-normandale-student-made-break-for-isis/443462893.

120 Basra, Rajan, Peter Neumann, and Claudia Brunner. 2016. "Criminal Pasts, Terrorist Futures: European Jihadists and the New Crime-Terror Nexus." London, UK: International Centre for the Study of Radicalisation. http://icsr.info/wp-content/uploads/2016/10/Criminal-Pasts-Terrorist-Futures.pdf.

121 Authors' interview with "Mo", May 9, 2017.

122 Ibid.

123 Ibid.

124 Ibid.

125 Ibid.

126 Ibid.

127 Ibid.

128 Ibid.

129 Ibid.

130 Ibid.

131 Ibid.

132 Ibid.

133 Ibid.

134 Ibid.

135 Ibid.

136 Ibid.

137 Ibid.

138 Burke, Jason. 2014. "Indian Police Arrest Owner of pro-Islamic State Twitter Account." *The Guardian*, December 13. http://www.theguardian.com/world/2014/dec/13/india-isis-twitter-mehdi-masroor-biswas-shamiwitness.

139 Authors' interview with "Mo."

140 Ibid.

141 Ibid.

142 Ibid.

143 Ibid.

144 Ibid.

145 Ibid.

146 Ibid.

147 Ibid.

148 Gordon, Scott. 2016. "Two North Texas College Students Listed as ISIS Fighters." *NBCDFW*, May 16, 2016. https://www.nbcdfw.com/news/local/Two-North-Texas-College-Students-Listed-As-ISIS-Fighters-379675901.html.

149 Authors' interview with "Mo."
150 Ibid.
151 Ibid.
152 Ibid.
153 Ibid.
154 Ibid.
155 Ibid.
156 Ibid.
157 Ibid.
158 Ibid.
159 Ibid.
160 Ibid.
161 Ibid.
162 Ibid.
163 Ibid.
164 Ibid.
165 Ibid.
166 Ibid.
167 Ibid.
168 Ibid.
169 Ibid.
170 Ibid.
171 Ibid.
172 "Criminal Complaint," 2014. *USA v. John Doe*, United States District Court for the Eastern District of New York. Case: 1:14-cr-00612.
173 Authors' interview with "Mo."
174 Ibid.
175 Authors' interview with senior law enforcement official familiar with the investigation, May 2017.
176 Authors' interview with "Mo."
177 Ibid.
178 "Information," 2014. *USA v. John Doe*, United States District Court for the Eastern District of New York. Case: 1:14-cr-00612.
179 Authors' interview with senior law enforcement official familiar with the investigation, May 2017.
180 Authors' interview with "Mo," alongside discussions with federal agents involved in his case.
181 Nordland, Rob. 2017. "Captured ISIS Fighters' Refrain: 'I Was Only a Cook'". *The New York Times*, October 1, 2017. https://www.nytimes.com/2017/10/01/world/middleeast/iraq-islamic-state-kurdistan.html.
182 Authors' interview with "Mo."
183 Ibid.
184 "Trial Transcript." 2017. *USA v. Mohamad Jamal Khweis*, United States District Court for the Eastern District of Virginia. Case 1:16-cr-00143., 909.
185 Numbers based on a database collected and maintained by the Program on Extremism at George Washington University.
186 Alexander and Turkington. 2018. "Treatment of Terrorists: How Does Gender Affect Justice?"
187 Peresin, Anita, and Alberto Cervone. 2015. "The Western Muhajirat of ISIS." *Studies in Conflict & Terrorism* 38 (7): 495–509. https://doi.org/10.1080/1057610X.2015.1025611.

188 Loken, Meredith, and Anna Zelenz. 2018. "Explaining Extremism: Western Women in Daesh." *European Journal of International Security* 3 (1): 45–68. https://doi. org/10.1017/eis.2017.13.

189 Authors' interview with Tania Joya, January 2019.

190 Ibid.

191 Ibid.

192 Ibid.

193 Hall, Ellie. 2015. "How One Young Woman Went From Fundamentalist Christian To ISIS Bride." *BuzzFeed News*, July 20, 2015. https://www.buzzfeednews.com/article/ ellievhall/woman-journey-from-chattanooga-to-isis.

194 Ibid.

195 Ibid.

196 Alexander, Audrey. 2016. "Cruel Intentions: Female Jihadists in America." Washington, D.C.: George Washington Program on Extremism. https://cchs.gwu. edu/sites/cchs.gwu.edu/files/downloads/Female%20Jihadists%20in%20America.pdf.

197 Saltman, Erin Marie, and Melanie Smith. 2015. "'Till Martyrdom Do Us Part': Gender and the ISIS Phenomenon." London: Institute for Strategic Dialogue. https:// www.isdglobal.org/wpcontent/uploads/2016/02/Till_Martyrdom_Do_Us_Part_ Gender_and_the_ISIS_Phenomenon.pdf.

198 Engel, Richard, Ben Plesser, Tracy Connor, and Jon Schuppe. 2016. "The Americans: 15 Who Left the U.S. to Join ISIS." *NBC News*, May 16, 2016. https://www.nbcnews.com/ storyline/isis-uncovered/americans-15-who-left-united-states-join-isis-n573611.

199 Ibid.

200 Ibid.

201 Lahoud, Nelly. 2014. "The Neglected Sex: The Jihadis' Exclusion of Women From Jihad." *Terrorism and Political Violence* 26 (5): 780–802. https://doi.org/10.1080/09546 553.2013.772511.

202 Ibid.

203 Alexander and Turkington. 2018. "Treatment of Terrorists: How Does Gender Affect Justice?"

204 Ibid.

205 Cook, Joanna, and Gina Vale. 2019. "From Daesh to 'Diaspora' II: The Challenges Posed by Women and Minors After the Fall of the Caliphate." *CTC Sentinel* 12 (6): 30–45. https://ctc.usma.edu/daesh-diaspora-challenges-posed-women-minors-fall- caliphate/.

206 Berger, Miriam. 2019. "Here's What We Know about the ISIS Prisons Controlled by the Syrian Kurds." *Washington Post*, October 12, 2019. https://www.washingtonpost. com/world/2019/10/12/inside-isis-prisons-controlled-by-syrian-kurds/.

207 "North East Syria: Al-Hol Camp," United Nations Office for the Coordination of Humanitarian Affairs, January 13, 2020.

208 Albeck-Ripka, Livia. 2019. "Desperate Pleas to Free Women and Children From ISIS Camps in Syria." *The New York Times*, October 21, 2019, sec. World. https://www. nytimes.com/2019/10/21/world/australia/isis-camp-syria.html.

209 Sommerville, Quentin. 2019. "The Women and Children No-One Wants." *BBC News*, April 12, 2019, sec. Middle East. https://www.bbc.com/news/world-middle- east-47867673.

210 Ibid.

211 "Press Briefing with Ambassador James F. Jeffrey, Special Representative for Syria Engagement and Special Envoy, Global Coalition to Defeat ISIS, and Deputy Assistant Secretary of State Joel Rayburn." 2019. United States Department of State

(blog). June 11, 2019. https://www.state.gov/ambassador-james-f-jeffrey-special-representative-for-syria-engagement-special-envoy-global-coalition-to-defeat-isis-deputy-assistant-secretary-of-state-joel-rayburn/.

212 Among prominent examples are the United Kingdom, Germany, and Denmark. Rawlinson, Kevin, and Vikram Dodd. 2019. "Shamima Begum: Isis Briton Faces Move to Revoke Citizenship." *The Guardian*, February 19, 2019, sec. UK news. https://www.theguardian.com/world/2019/feb/19/isis-briton-shamima-begum-to-have-uk-citizenship-revoked; Chazan, Guy. 2019. "Germany to Strip Dual-Nationals Who Fight for Isis of Citizenship." *Financial Times*, March 4, 2019. https://www.ft.com/content/1c929f90-3e6b-11e9-9bee-efab61506f44; "Denmark to Strip Suspected ISIS Fighters of Consular Assistance." 2019. *Euronews*, November 17, 2019. https://www.euronews.com/2019/11/17/denmark-to-strip-suspected-isis-fighters-of-consular-assistance.

213 An Ohioan named Abdirahman Sheik Mohamud was planning a jihadist attack in the United States after he returned from Syria, but Mohamud fought with al-Qaeda affiliate Jabhat al-Nusra, not ISIS. Hughes, Seamus, Alexander Meleagrou-Hitchens, and Bennett Clifford. 2018. "The Travelers: American Jihadists in Syria and Iraq." Washington, D.C.: George Washington Program on Extremism. https://extremism.gwu.edu/sites/g/files/zaxdzs2191/f/TravelersAmericanJihadistsinSyriaandIraq.pdf.

214 Authors' interview with FBI Joint Terrorism Task Force agents, March 2018.

215 Ibid.

216 Ibid.

217 Ibid.

218 Hughes, Seamus, and Jon Lewis. 2019. "It's Not Only Iraq and Syria." *Lawfare*, August 23, 2019. https://www.lawfareblog.com/its-not-only-iraq-and-syria.

219 Hall, Ellie. 2019. "An Alabama 'ISIS Bride' Wants To Come Home. Can We Forgive Her Horrifying Social Media Posts?" *BuzzFeed News*, May 4, 2019. https://www.buzzfeednews.com/article/elliehall/hoda-muthana-isis-instagram-twitter-tumblr-alabama.

220 Ibid.

221 Hall, Ellie. 2019. "A Judge Has Ruled That A Woman Who Left The US For ISIS Is Not An American Citizen." *BuzzFeed News*, November 14, 2019. https://www.buzzfeednews.com/article/elliehall/hoda-muthana-isis-not-american-citizen.

222 Savage, Charlie, Rukmini Callimachi, and Eric Schmitt. 2018. "American ISIS Suspect Is Freed After Being Held More Than a Year." *The New York Times*, October 29, 2018, sec. U.S. https://www.nytimes.com/2018/10/29/us/politics/isis-john-doe-released-abdulrahman-alsheikh.html.

223 Ibid.

224 Pokalova, Elena. 2019. *Returning Islamist Foreign Fighters: Threats and Challenges to the West*. New York: Palgrave Macmillan.

225 Ibid.

226 "Women and Children First: Repatriating the Westerners Affiliated with ISIS." 2019. 208. Brussels, Belgium: International Crisis Group. https://www.crisisgroup.org/middle-east-north-africa/eastern-mediterranean/syria/208-women-and-children-first-repatriating-westerners-affiliated-isis.

227 Hughes, Seamus, Emily Blackburn, and Andrew Mines. 2019. "The Other Travelers: American Jihadists Beyond Syria and Iraq." Washington, D.C.: GW Program on Extremism. https://extremism.gwu.edu/sites/g/files/zaxdzs2191/f/The%20Other%20Travelers%20Final.pdf.

228 Winter, Charlie, and Haroro J. Ingram. 2017. "Why ISIS Is So Good at Branding Its Failures as Success." *The Atlantic*, September 19, 2017. https://www.theatlantic.com/international/archive/2017/09/isis-propaganda/540240/.

229 Hughes, Blackburn, and Mines. 2019. "The Other Travelers: American Jihadists Beyond Syria and Iraq."

230 "Michigan Residents Arrested for Conspiracy to Provide Material Support to ISIS." 2019. Department of Justice Press Release. January 22, 2019. https://www.justice.gov/opa/pr/michigan-residents-arrested-conspiracy-provide-material-support-isis.

231 "Two Men Arrested for Conspiring to Provide Material Support to ISIS." 2019. Department of Justice Press Release. July 29, 2019. https://www.justice.gov/opa/pr/two-men-arrested-conspiring-provide-material-support-isis.

232 "Texas Man Charged by Criminal Complaint with Conspiring to Provide Material Support to a Foreign Terrorist Organization." 2019. Department of Justice Press Release. February 8, 2019. https://www.justice.gov/opa/pr/texas-man-charged-criminal-complaint-conspiring-provide-material-support-foreign-terrorist; "New York Man Arrested for Attempting and Conspiring to Provide Material Support to Terrorist Organization." 2019. Department of Justice Press Release. February 8, 2019. https://www.justice.gov/opa/pr/new-york-man-arrested-attempting-and-conspiring-provide-material-support-terrorist.

4. The E-Activists

1 Koerner, Brendan. 2016. "Why ISIS Is Winning the Social Media War—And How to Fight Back." *Wired*, April 2016. https://www.wired.com/2016/03/isis-winning-social-media-war-heres-beat/.

2 Winter, Charlie. 2017. "Media Jihad: The Islamic State's Doctrine for Information Warfare." London, UK: International Centre for the Study of Radicalisation. https://icsr.info/wp-content/uploads/2017/02/Media-jihad_web.pdf.

3 For more information, see: "ISIS Online Project." Washington D.C.: George Washington Program on Extremism. https://extremism.gwu.edu/isis-online.

4 "ISIS Online Project." Program on Extremism, George Washington University. https://extremism.gwu.edu/isis-online.

5 Weinberg, Leonard and Jeffrey Kaplan. 1998. *The Emergence of a Euro-American Radical Right*. New Brunswick, NJ: Rutgers University Press, 160.

6 Schafer, Joseph. 2002. "Spinning the Web of Hate: Web-based Hate Propagation by Extremist Organisations." *Journal of Criminal Justice and Popular Culture* 9(2), 69; Kaplan, Jeffrey and Leonard Weinberg. 1998. *The Emergence of a Euro-American Radical Right*. New Brunswick, NJ: Rutgers University Press, 160.

7 Zelin, Aaron. 2013. *The State of Global Jihad Online*. Washington, D.C: New America Foundation. https://www.washingtoninstitute.org/uploads/Documents/opeds/Zelin20130201-NewAmericaFoundation.pdf; Neumann, Peter. 2012. *Countering Online Radicalization in America*. Washington, D.C.: Bipartisan Policy Centre, 16.

8 Della Porta, Donatella and Lorenzo Mosca. 2009. "Searching the Net: Web Sites' Qualities in the Global Justice Movement." *Information, Communication and Society* 12(6): 777.

9 Bari Atwan, Abdel. 2006. *The Secret History of al-Qaeda*. London: Saqi Books, 127; Di Justo, Patrick. 2002. "How Al-Qaida Site Was Hijacked." *Wired*, August 10, 2002. http://www.wired.com/culture/lifestyle/news/2002/08/54 455.

10 Rogan, Hanna. 2006. "Jihadism Online – A Study of How al-Qaida and Radical Islamist Groups Use the Internet for Terrorist Purposes." Kjeller, Norway: Norwegian Defence Research Establishment. https://admin.ffi.no/no/Rapporter/06-00915.pdf.

11 Hussain, Ghaffar, Erin Saltman, and Quilliam Foundation. 2014. *Jihad Trending: A Comprehensive Analysis of Online Extremism and How to Counter It*, 32; Zelin. 2013. *The State of Global Jihad Online*, 5.

12 Ramsay, Gilbert. 2008. "Conceptualising Online Terrorism." *Perspectives on Terrorism* 2(7): 3–10; Zelin. 2013. *The State of Global Jihad Online*, 5.

13 Ducol, Benjamin. 2012. "Uncovering the French-speaking Jihadisphere: An Exploratory Analysis." *Media, War & Conflict* 5 (1): 52. https://doi.org/10.1177/1750635211434366.; Awan, Akil. 2007. "Radicalization on the Internet? The Virtual Propagation of Jihadist Media and its Effects." *RUSI Journal* 152 (3): 76–81.

14 Ibid.

15 Zelin. 2013. *The State of Global Jihad Online*, 5.

16 McFarlane. Bruce. 2010. *Online Violent Radicalisation (OVeR): Challenges Facing Law Enforcement Agencies and Policy Stakeholders*. Monash University, 5.; Sageman, Marc. 2004. *Understanding Terror Networks*. Philadelphia, Pennsylvania: University of Pennsylvania Press.

17 Bunt, Gary. 2003. *Islam in the Digital Age: E-jihad, Online Fatwas and Cyber Islamic Environments*. London, UK: Pluto Press; Weimann, Gabriel. 2010. 'Terror on Facebook, Twitter and YouTube', *Brown Journal of World Affairs* (16) 2: 45–54; National Coordinator for Counterterrorism. 2010. *Jihadists and the Internet: 2009 Update*. Netherlands: The Hague; Singh, Bilveer. 2013. "Youth Self-radicalisation: Lessons from the Singapore Narrative." *The Southeast Asia Regional Centre for Counter-Terrorism (SEARCCT) Journal* (August): 87–103.

18 Suler, John. 2005. "The Online Disinhibition Effect." *International Journal of Applied Psychoanalytic Studies* 2: 2, June 2005, 184–8. It is also worth noting that, in his work with former German far-right extremists who were active online, Daniel Koehler identified anonymity as the second most common attribute among the interviewees as it provoked individuals to speak out more than they normally would offline. Koehler, Daniel. 2014. "The Radical Online: Individual Radicalization Processes and the Role of the Internet." *Journal for Deradicalization* 1 (Winter): 118.

19 Klausen, Jytte. 2015. "Tweeting the Jihad: Social Media Networks of Western Foreign Fighters in Syria and Iraq." *Studies in Conflict and Terrorism* (38) 1: 6. https://doi.org/10.1080/1057610X.2014.974948.

20 Whiteside, Craig. 2016. "Lighting the Path: The Evolution of the Islamic State Media Enterprise (2003–2016)." International Centre for Counter-Terrorism, The Hague; Zelin. 2013. *The State of Global Jihad Online*.; Prucha, Nico. 2016. "ISIS and the Jihadist Information Highway – Projecting Influence and Religious Identity via Telegram." *Perspectives on Terrorism* 10 (6): 48–58. http://www.terrorismanalysts.com/pt/index.php/pot/article/view/556

21 Milton, Daniel. 2016. "Communication Breakdown: Unraveling the Islamic State's Media Efforts." Combating Terrorism Center at West Point.

22 Prucha. 2016. "ISIS and the Jihadist Information Highway." 54.

23 Joscelyn, Thomas. 2015. "Graphic Promotes the Islamic State's Prolific Media Machine." *FDD's Long War Journal*. http://www.longwarjournal.org/archives/2015/11/graphic-promotes-islamic-states-prolific-mediamachine.php.

24 Koerner. 2016. "Why ISIS Is Winning the Social Media War."

25 Milton. 2016. "Communication Breakdown."

26 Ibid., 23–9.

27 Ingram, Haroro J. 2016. "An Analysis of Islamic State's *Dabiq* Magazine." *Australian Journal of Political Science* 51(3): 458–77. https://doi.org/10.1080/10361146.2016.1174188.

28 Koerner. 2016. "Why ISIS Is Winning the Social Media War."

29 Alexander, Audrey, and Helen Powell. 2018. "Gray Media Under the Black and White Banner." *Lawfare* (blog), May 6, 2018. https://www.lawfareblog.com/gray-media-under-black-and-white-banner.

30 Carter, Joseph A., Shiraz Maher, and Peter Neumann. 2014. "#Greenbirds: Measuring Importance and Influence in Syrian Foreign Fighter Networks." London, UK: International Centre for the Study of Radicalisation. http://icsr.info/wp-content/uploads/2014/04/ICSR-Report-Greenbirds-Measuring-Importance-and-Infleunce-in-Syrian-Foreign-Fighter-Networks.pdf.

31 Fisher, Ali and Nico Prucha. 2013. 'Tweeting for the Caliphate: Twitter as the new frontier for jihadi propaganda', *CTC Sentinel* 6 (62).

32 Alkhouri, Laith and Alex Kassirer. 2016. "Tech for Jihad: Dissecting Jihadists' Digital Toolbox." Flashpoint report, July 2016.

33 Clifford, Bennett, and Helen Powell. 2019. "Encrypted Extremism: Inside the English-Speaking Islamic State Ecosystem on Telegram." Washington, D.C.: George Washington Program on Extremism. https://extremism.gwu.edu/sites/g/files/zaxdzs2191/f/EncryptedExtremism.pdf.

34 Nesser, Petter, Anne Stenersen, and Emilie Oftedal. 2016. "Jihadi Terrorism in Europe: The ISIS-Effect." *Perspectives on Terrorism* 10 (6): 3–24.

35 According to Milton, "[ISIS battlefield] setbacks suggest that the efficacy of the media is not a foregone conclusion, but a subjective reality contingent on a wide array of other factors such as counterterrorism pressure, battlefield conditions, and personnel availability". For more see: Milton. 2016. "Communication Breakdown," 50.

36 Prucha, Nico. 2016. "ISIS and the Jihadist Information Highway – Projecting Influence and Religious Identity via Telegram." *Perspectives on Terrorism*, 10 (6); Berger, J.M. and Heather Perez. 2016. "The Islamic State's Diminishing Returns on Twitter: How Suspensions are Limiting the Social Networks of English-speaking ISIS Supporters." Program on Extremism Occasional Paper, February 2016. https://cchs.gwu.edu/sites/g/files/zaxdzs2371/f/downloads/Berger_Occasional%20Paper.pdf

37 "Telegram F.A.Q." Telegram. https://telegram.org/faq.

38 Ibid.

39 Clifford and Powell. 2019. "Encrypted Extremism"

40 Ibid.

41 "About the Internet Archive." The Internet Archive. https://archive.org/about/

42 In the official 'Twitter Rules,' the company identifies "Violent threats (direct or indirect)" as grounds for temporarily locking and/or permanently suspending accounts, explaining, "You may not make threats of violence or promote violence, including threatening or promoting terrorism." "The Twitter Rules." 2017. Twitter Help Center. https://help.twitter.com/articles/18311?lang=en. See also, "Upload Media," Twitter Developer.

43 Analysis and discussion for this case is based on a mix of court documents, news reports, and notes from Mohamad Khweis' trial in 2017, which was attended by the authors.

44 Ibid.

45 Kheel, Rebecca. 2016. "Report: American ISIS Fighter Captured." *The Hill*. March 14, 2016. http://thehill.com/policy/defense/272884-reports-american-isis-fighter-captured-while-defecting.

46 Zapotosky, Matt, and Rachel Weiner. 2016. "American ISIS Fighter Who 'Found It Hard' Returns to Face Criminal Charges." *Washington Post*, June 9. https://www.washingtonpost.com/world/national-security/american-isis-fighter-who-found-it-hard-returns-to-face-criminal-charges/2016/06/08/b6990ea2-efa5-11e5-a61f-e9c95c06edca_story.html.

47 Much of the subsequent analysis of this case is based on the authors' observations of the *Khweis* court proceedings, in which details that are not found in the court documents were revealed by federal prosecutors.

48 "Trial Transcript." 2017. *USA v. Mohamad Jamal Khweis*, United States District Court for the Eastern District of Virginia. Case 1:16-cr-00143,741.

49 Ibid., 678.

50 Ibid., 798.

51 Ibid., 908.

52 Ibid., 622.

53 Ibid., 579.

54 Ibid., 909.

55 Ibid., 752–4.

56 Ibid., 754.

57 The Google Mail account, mkhweis123, was created on December 12th. Ibid., 952.

58 Ibid., 537.

59 Ibid.

60 Ibid.

61 Ibid., 692.

62 Ibid., 1012–13.

63 Among the physical evidence recovered by the FBI from Khweis were three mobile phones (a Samsung Galaxy, iPhone, and a BLU phone) and two SIM cards. The phones all had the cameras covered by tape, presumably a measure taken to prevent authorities from possibly accessing these and surveilling his activities. The activity on Khweis' phone that investigators were able to uncover helped them to both map out his route from Virginia to Syria and what his intentions were once arriving there. Among his location searches were a map of Gatwick Airport in London, along with maps of Istanbul and Gaziantep in Turkey. He used Google Maps to view the Gaziantep area and query which border crossings were controlled by ISIS. These searches matched to locations where Khweis' phone had connected to wireless routers, with investigators identifying connections at Gatwick Airport in the UK on December 17, 2015, in Istanbul on the 20th, in Gaziantep on the 24th, and in the border town of Elbaily on the 23rd, 24th and 25th. He also made a number of revealing inquiries on Google, searching names such as "Al amriki", "Abu zak al Canada", "Al Canada", "Al Canada in Arabic", and "Al Kanadi." Other search terms included translations into Turkish of "how do I get to Gaziantep", "can you take a bus", "can you take a train", "good morning," and "thank you." "Government's Amended Trial Exhibit List, Exhibits 4–26, 36–42, 57–71." *USA v. Mohamad Jamal Khweis.*

64 The Apple ID 001Freedom007, registered to Khweis, was used to create the account. "Trial Transcript." *USA v. Mohamad Jamal Khweis*, 1024.

65 Ibid., 702.

66 Virtual private networks, or VPNs, allow users of public internet networks to access private networks that otherwise might be geographically restricted. Tor is a downloadable browser which allows its users to browse the internet anonymously, masking their location and activity through relaying connections via several nodes, rather than making a single, traceable connection.

67 "Government's Amended Trial Exhibit List, Exhibits 64 and 67." *USA v. Mohamad Jamal Khweis.*

68 Ibid.

69 "Trial Transcript." *USA v. Mohamad Jamal Khweis*, 703–4.

70 Ibid., 704.

71 The account he contacted was @islamispeacexxx. Ibid., 975–81.

72 Ibid., 657.

73 The National Investigation Agency of India, in a 2016 case, found that this account's owner was connected to the recruitment of an Indian national to join ISIS in Syria. "Charge Sheet." 2016. *State (NIA) v/s Mohamed Naser and Others*, Honourable Special Court, NIA Patiala House Courts, New Delhi, India. http://www.nia.gov.in/writereaddata/Portal/CasesPdfDoc/CS_RC-14_2015_NIA_DLI-1.pdf.

74 Before his death in a coalition airstrike in September 2015, Parson was a member of "the Legion," a group of English-speaking recruiters and attack planners who guided supporters in Anglophone countries to travel to join ISIS and commit attacks. He is connected to at least one attempted travel case in the US. Robles, Frances. 2017. "Trying to Stanch Trinidad's Flow of Young Recruits to ISIS." *The New York Times*, February 21. https://www.nytimes.com/2017/02/21/world/americas/trying-to-stanch-trinidads-flow-of-young-recruits-to-isis.html.

75 "Trial Transcript." *USA v. Mohamad Jamal Khweis.*, 658–9.

76 Ibid., 545.

77 Ibid., 990–99.

78 Ibid., 990.

79 Ibid., 997.

80 Ibid., 992–4.

81 Alexander, Audrey, and Bennett Clifford. 2019. "Doxing and Defacements: Examining the Islamic State's Hacking Capabilities." *CTC Sentinel* 12 (4): 22–8. https://ctc.usma.edu/doxing-defacements-examining-islamic-states-hacking-capabilities/.

82 Ibid.

83 Archived versions of the site in authors' possession.

84 "ISIL-Linked Kosovo Hacker Sentenced to 20 Years in Prison." 2016. DOJ Press Release. September 23, 2016. https://www.justice.gov/opa/pr/isil-linked-kosovo-hacker-sentenced-20-years-prison.

85 As articulated in the government's sentencing memo, please note, a record of this site from May 23, 2015 is accessible via archive.org: "PenVid Homepage" 2015. PenVid. May 23, 2015. https://web.archive.org/web/20150523022321/http://penvid.com/.

86 "Position of the United States with Respect to Sentencing." 2016. *USA v. Ardit Ferizi*, U.S. District Court in the Eastern District of Virginia.

87 Ibid., 3.

88 "Statement of Facts." 2016. *USA v. Ardit Ferizi*, U.S. District Court in the Eastern District of Virginia.

89 Ibid.

90 Ibid., 4.

91 For more on Hussain's legacy as a hacker, see Hamid, Nafees. 2018. "The British Hacker Who Became the Islamic State's Chief Terror Cybercoach: A Profile of Junaid Hussain." Combating Terrorism Center at West Point 11(4). https://ctc.usma.edu/ british-hacker-became-islamic-states-chief-terror-cybercoach-profile-junaid-hussain/.

92 "Statement of Facts." 2016. *USA v. Ardit Ferizi.* 4.

93 Ibid.

94 "Position of the United States with Respect to Sentencing." 2016. *USA v. Ardit Ferizi,* U.S. District Court in the Eastern District of Virginia.

95 "ISIL-Linked Hacker Arrested in Malaysia on U.S. Charges." 2015. Department of Justice Press Release October 15, 2015. https://www.justice.gov/opa/pr/isil-linked-hacker-arrested-malaysia-us-charges.

96 "ISIL-Linked Kosovo Hacker Sentenced to 20 Years in Prison." 2016.

97 Ibid.

98 Alexander and Clifford. 2019. "Doxing and Defacements"; Bernard, Rose. 2017. "These Are Not the Terrorist Groups You're Looking For: An Assessment of the Cyber Capabilities of Islamic State." *Journal of Cyber Policy* 2 (2): 255–65. https://doi.org/10.1080/23738871.2017.1334805.

99 Starks, Tim. 2017. "How the Islamic State Is Doing in Cyberspace." *POLITICO,* December 7, 2017. http://politi.co/2BdWNYP.

100 Bernard. 2017. "These Are Not the Terrorist Groups You're Looking For."

101 "Complaint." 2019. *USA v. Kim Anh Vo,* United States District Court for the Southern District of New York. Case: 19-mj-2334. https://www.justice.gov/opa/press-release/file/1143071/download.

102 Ibid.

103 Ibid.

104 Ibid.

105 Ibid.

106 Ibid.

107 Ibid.

108 Ibid.

109 Ibid.

110 Ibid

111 "Affidavit." 2018. *USA v. Waheba Issa Dais,* U.S. District Court in the Eastern District of Wisconsin.

112 Ibid.

113 "Wisconsin Woman Charged With Attempting to Provide Material Support to ISIS." 2018. Department of Justice Press Release. June 13, 2018. https://www.justice.gov/opa/pr/wisconsin-woman-charged-attempting-provide-material-support-isis.

114 "Affidavit." 2018. *USA v. Waheba Issa Dais,* U.S. District Court in the Eastern District of Wisconsin. 4.

115 Ibid.

116 Ibid.

117 Ibid.

118 Ibid., 12.

119 Ibid.

120 Ibid.

121 "Wisconsin Woman Charged With Attempting to Provide Material Support to ISIS." 2018.

122 "Affidavit." 2016. *USA v. Safya Roe Yassin*, U.S. District Court for the Western District of Missouri. Case: 16-3024-01-CR-S-MDH.

123 Ibid.

124 "Criminal Complaint," 2016. *USA v. Safya Roe Yassin*, U.S. District Court for the Western District of Missouri. Case: 16-3024-01-CR-S-MDH, 4.

125 Ibid.

126 Pearson, Elizabeth, and Emily Winterbotham. 2017. "Women, Gender and Daesh Radicalisation." *The RUSI Journal* 162 (3): 60–72. https://doi.org/10.1080/03071847.2017.1353251; Cook, Joana. 2019. "Women and Terror After 9/11: The Case of Islamic State." *Handbook of Terrorism and Counter Terrorism Post 9/11*, December. https://www.elgaronline.com/view/edcoll/9781786438010/9781786438010.00018.xml.

127 "Criminal Complaint," *USA v. Safya Roe Yassin*, 12.

128 Sidner, Sara and Ed Payne. 2015. "Mohammed Cartoon Contest: Protest Held Outside Phoenix mosque." *CNN*, May 30, 2015, https://edition.cnn.com/2015/05/29/us/mohammed-cartoon-contest/index.html.

129 "Criminal Complaint," *USA v. Safya Roe Yassin*, 6.

130 Ibid.

131 "Affidavit," *USA v. Safya Roe Yassin*.

132 "Criminal Complaint," *USA v. Safya Roe Yassin*, 9.

133 Ibid., 8.

134 Peralta, Edyer. 2015. "Shootings in Chattanooga: What We Know About The Alleged Gunman." *NPR*, July 17, 2015. https://www.npr.org/sections/thetwo-way/2015/07/17/423746603/shootings-in-chattanooga-what-we-know-about-the-alleged-gunman.

135 "Criminal Complaint," *USA v. Safya Roe Yassin*, 10.

136 Ibid., 12.

137 Ibid., 12–13.

138 Tweets and ISIS Hacking Division website archived by authors.

139 "Criminal Complaint," *USA v. Safya Roe Yassin*, 15.

140 "Statement of Facts," 2016. *USA v. Haris Qamar*, U.S. District Court for the Eastern District of Virginia.

141 Weiner, Rachel, and Justin Jouvenal. 2016. "Northern Virginia Man Accused of Supporting the Islamic State." *Washington Post*, July 8, 2016. https://www.washingtonpost.com/local/public-safety/northern-virginia-man-accused-of-supporting-the-islamic-state/2016/07/08/37e47f00-4523-11e6-88d0-6adee48be8bc_story.html.

142 "Criminal Complaint," 2016, *USA v. Haris Qamar*, U.S. District Court for the Eastern District of Virginia.

143 Ibid.

144 "Statement of Facts," 2016, *USA v. Haris Qamar*.

145 Ibid., 9.

146 "Criminal Complaint," 2016, *USA v. Haris Qamar*.

147 Ibid.

148 "Virginia Man Charged with Attempting to Provide Material Support to ISIL." 2016. Department of Justice Press Release. Friday, July 8, 2016. https://www.justice.gov/usao-edva/pr/virginia-man-charged-attempting-provide-material-support-isil.

149 "Criminal Complaint." 2019. *USA v. Thomas Osadzinski*, U.S. District Court for the Northern District of Illinois. Case 1:19-cr-00869, 14.

150 "Flames of War: The Fighting Has Just Begun." 2014. *al-Hayat Media Centre*, September 17, 2014.

151 "Criminal Complaint," *Osadzinski*, 16.

152 Ibid., 16.

153 Ibid., 20.

154 Ibid., 21–4.

155 Ibid., 22.

156 Ibid., 35.

157 BBC News. 2019. "Europol Disrupts ISIS Propaganda Machine." November 25, 2019, sec. Middle East. https://www.bbc.com/news/world-middle-east-50545816.

158 "Criminal Complaint," *Osadzinski*, 27.

159 Ibid., 35.

160 Ibid., 29.

161 Ibid., 24.

162 Ibid., 34

163 Ibid., 33

164 "Chicago Man Charged with Attempting to Provide Material Support to ISIS." 2019. Department of Justice Press Release. November 19, 2019. https://www.justice.gov/usao-ndil/pr/chicago-man-charged-attempting-provide-material-support-isis.

165 "Statement of Facts." 2015. *USA v. Ali Shukri Amin*. U.S. District Court for the Eastern District of Virginia. Case l:15-cr-001642.

166 al-Munthir, Taqi'ul Deen (Ali Amin). 2014. "Bitcoin wa Sadaqat al-jihad." *Al-Khilafa Aridat.*

167 "Letter to Judge Tomlinson." 2017. *USA v. Zoobia Shahnaz*, U.S. District Court in the Eastern District of New York.

168 Ibid., 3.

169 Ibid., 2.

170 Ibid.

171 Ibid., 4.

172 Ibid., 5.

173 Ibid., 6.

174 Sageman. 2004. *Understanding Terror Networks.*

175 Macdonald, Stuart, and Joe Whitaker. 2019. "Online Radicalization." In *Online Terrorist Propaganda, Recruitment, and Radicalization*, edited by John R. Vacca. Boca Raton: CRC Press.

176 Bjelopera, Jerome P., and Mark Randol. 2010. *American Jihadist Terrorism: Combating a Complex Threat.* United States Congressional Research Service, 19.

177 Costello, Matthew, James Hawdon, and Thomas N. Ratliff. 2017. "Confronting Online Extremism: The Effect of Self-Help, Collective Efficacy, and Guardianship on Being a Target for Hate Speech." *Social Science Computer Review* 35 (5): 587–605. https://doi.org/10.1177/0894439316666272; Manrique, Pedro D., Minzhang Zheng, Zhenfeng Cao, Elvira Maria Restrepo, and Neil F. Johnson. 2018. "Generalized Gelation Theory Describes Onset of Online Extremist Support." *Physical Review Letters* 121 (4): 048301. https://doi.org/10.1103/PhysRevLett.121.048301. Koehler, Daniel. 2014. "The Radical Online: Individual Radicalization Processes and the Role of the Internet." *Journal for Deradicalization* 0 (1): 116–34.

178 Edwards, Charlie, and Luke Gribbon. 2013. "Pathways to Violent Extremism in the Digital Era." *The RUSI Journal* 158 (5): 40–47. https://doi.org/10.1080/03071847.2013.847714.

179 O'Hara, Kieron, and David Stevens. 2015. "Echo Chambers and Online Radicalism: Assessing the Internet's Complicity in Violent Extremism." *Policy & Internet* 7 (4): 401–22. https://doi.org/10.1002/poi3.88.

180 Ibid.
181 Neumann, Peter R. 2013. "Options and Strategies for Countering Online Radicalization in the United States." *Studies in Conflict & Terrorism* 36 (6): 431–59. https://doi.org/10.1080/1057610X.2013.784568.
182 Tufekci, Zeynep. 2018. "YouTube, the Great Radicalizer." *The New York Times*, March 10, 2018, sec. Opinion. https://www.nytimes.com/2018/03/10/opinion/sunday/youtube-politics-radical.html. Baugut, Philip, and Katharina Neumann. 2019. "Online Propaganda Use During Islamist Radicalization." *Information, Communication & Society* (forthcoming), 1–23. https://doi.org/10.1080/1369118X.2019.1594333.
183 Alexander, Audrey, and William Braniff. 2018. "Marginalizing Violent Extremism Online." *Lawfare*, January 21, 2018. https://www.lawfareblog.com/marginalizing-violent-extremism-online.
184 Ibid.
185 Conway, Maura, Moign Khawaja, Suraj Lakhani, Jeremy Reffin, Andrew Robertson, and David Weir. 2017. "Disrupting Daesh: Measuring Takedown of Online Terrorist Material and Its Impacts." *VoxPol*. http://www.voxpol.eu/download/vox-pol_publication/DCUJ5528-Disrupting-DAESH-1706-WEB-v2.pdf. See also Alexander and Braniff. 2018. "Marginalizing Violent Extremism Online."

5. The Ideologues

1 Wiktorowicz, Quintan. 2005. *Radical Islam Rising*. London: Rowman and Littlefield, 135–6.
2 Precht, Tomas. 2007. "Home Grown Terrorism and Islamist Radicalization in Europe: From Conversion to Terrorism." Copenhagen: Danish Ministry of Justice, 50.
3 Ibid., 53.
4 Ingram, Haroro J. 2013. *The Charismatic Leadership Phenomenon in Radical and Militant Islamism*. Religion and International Security. Farnham, England; Burlington, Vermont: Ashgate, 49.
5 Casciani, Dominic. 2018. "Who Is Radical Cleric Anjem Choudary?" *BBC News*, October 19, 2018, sec. UK. https://www.bbc.com/news/uk-45903314.
6 Ibid.
7 Koppelman, Andrew. 2017. "Entertaining Satan: Why We Tolerate Terrorist Incitement." *Fordham Law Review* 86: 535.
8 See, for instance, Simpson, Glenn R. 2002. "U.S. Indicts Head of Charity For Helping Fund al Qaeda." *Wall Street Journal*, October 10, 2002, sec. News. https://www.wsj.com/articles/SB1034185882821997916; "Feds Launch 'Operation Green Quest.'" 2001. *CBS News*, October 25, 2001. https://www.cbsnews.com/news/feds-launch-operation-green-quest/; Singman, Brooke. 2015. "Moderate Imam Reveals How Radicals Won Battle for Soul of Boston Mosques." *Fox News*, July 25, 2015. https://www.foxnews.com/us/moderate-imam-reveals-how-radicals-won-battle-for-soul-of-boston-mosques.
9 Ibid.
10 Gendron, Angela. 2017. "The Call to Jihad: Charismatic Preachers and the Internet." *Studies in Conflict and Terrorism* 40 (1): 157–91. https://doi.org/10.1080/1057610X.2016.1157406.
11 Brachman, Jarret M., and Alix N. Levine. 2011. "You Too Can Be Awlaki!" *Fletcher Forum on International Affairs* 35 (1). https://static1.squarespace.com/

static/579fc2ad725e253a86230610/t/57ec9034f7e0abf8c055c74b/1475121204759/
Brachman-Levine_35-1.pdf.

12 Ibid.

13 This debate is exemplified by the argument between the French political scientists
    Olivier Roy and Gilles Kepel, with Roy arguing that most recruits to jihadist groups are
    motivated primarily by socioeconomic and political factors rather than religious ones
    and Kepel arguing that religious ideology is at the center of their decision-making. See
    Nossiter, Adam. 2016. "'That Ignoramus': 2 French Scholars of Radical Islam Turn
    Bitter Rivals." *The New York Times*, July 12, 2016, sec. World. https://www.nytimes.
    com/2016/07/13/world/europe/france-radical-islam.html. Other scholars arguing in
    favor of the role of religion in radicalization include: Reinares, Fernando. 2017.
    "Jihadist Mobilisation, Undemocratic Salafism and Terrorist Threat in the EU." Elcano
    Royal Institute, March 10 2017; Armstrong, Karen. 2017. "Wahhabism to ISIS: How
    Saudi Arabia Exported the Main Source of Global Terrorism." *The New Statesman*,
    November 24, 2017. https://www.newstatesman.com/world-affairs/2014/11/
    wahhabism-isis-how-saudi-arabia-exported-main-source-global-terrorism; Wood,
    Graeme. 2015. "What ISIS Really Wants." *The Atlantic*, March 2015, https://www.
    theatlantic.com/magazine/archive/2015/03/what-isis-really-wants/384980/. Others
    arguing against the role of religious ideology include: Parvez, Z. Fareen. 2016. "Prayer
    and Pedagogy: Redefining Education among Salafist Muslim women In France."
    Journal of Religious and Political Practice 2 (1); Esposito, John L. 2015. "Islam and
    Political Violence." *Religions* 6 (3): 1067–81. https://doi.org/10.3390/rel6031067;
    Coolsaet, Rik. 2016. "Facing The Fourth Foreign Fighters Wave: What Drives
    Europeans To Syria, And To Islamic State? Insights From The Belgian Case." Brussels,
    Belgium: Egmont Institute, March 2016, 3.

14 Wagemakers, Joas. 2016. "Salafism." Oxford Research Encyclopedia of Religion, August
    2016. https://doi.org/10.1093/acrefore/9780199340378.013.255.

15 Ibid.

16 Ibid.

17 Lauziere, Henry. 2016. *The Making of Salafism: Islamic Reform in the Twentieth
    Century*. New York: Columbia University Press, 6–7.

18 Commins, David, "From Wahhabi to Salafi," in Bernard Haykel, Thomas Hegghammer
    and Stephane Lacroix. 2015. *Saudi Arabia in Transition: Insight on Social, Political,
    Economic and Religious Change*. Cambridge: Cambridge University Press., 152–3.

19 Wiktorowicz, Quintan. 2006. "Anatomy of the Salafi Movement." *Studies in Conflict &
    Terrorism* 29 (3): 207–39. https://doi.org/10.1080/10576100500497004.

20 Wiktorowicz, Quintan. 2001. "The New Global Threat: Transnational Salafis and
    Jihad," *Middle East Policy* 8 (4): 21. https://doi.org/10.1111/j.1475-4967.2001.tb00006.x.

21 Wiktorowicz, Quintan. 2006. "Anatomy of the Salafi Movement."

22 Ibid.

23 Wagemakers, Joas. 2012. *A Quietist Jihadi: The Ideology and Influence of Abu
    Muhammad Al-Maqdisi*. Cambridge, UK: Cambridge University Press.

24 For more on the *sahwa* see Lacroix, Stephane. 2011. *Awakening Islam*. Cambridge, MA:
    Harvard University Press.

25 Wagemakers. 2012. *A Quietist Jihadi*.

26 Wiktorowicz. 2006. "Anatomy of the Salafi Movement."

27 Meleagrou-Hitchens, Alexander. 2018. "Salafism in America: History, Evolution,
    Radicalization." Washington, D.C.: George Washington Program on Extremism.
    https://extremism.gwu.edu/sites/g/files/zaxdzs2191/f/Salafism%20in%20America.pdf.

28 Ibid.
29 Maher, Shiraz. 2016. *Salafi-Jihadism: The History of an Idea*. Oxford, UK: Oxford University Press.
30 Ibid.
31 Ibid.
32 Wagemakers, Joas. 2009. "The Transformation of a Radical Concept: *al-wala' wa-l-bara'* in the Ideology of Abu Muhammad al-Maqdisi." in Roel Meijer (ed.). 2009. *Global Salafism: Islam's New Religious Movement*. London, UK: Hurst, 81–2.
33 Maher. 2016. *Salafi-Jihadism: The History of an Idea*.
34 Ibid.
35 Hegghammer, Thomas. 2013. "'Abdallah 'Azzam and Palestine." 0043-2539. https://doi.org/10.1163/15685152-5334P0003; Nesser, Petter. 2011. "Ideologies of Jihad in Europe." *Terrorism and Political Violence* 23 (2): 173–200. https://doi.org/10.1080/0954 6553.2010.537587; Hegghammer, Thomas. 2020. *The Caravan: Abdallah Azzam and the Rise of Global Jihad*. Cambridge, UK: Cambridge University Press.
36 Nesser. 2011. "Ideologies of Jihad in Europe."
37 Hegghammer. 2013. "'Abdallah 'Azzam and Palestine."; Hegghammer. 2020. *The Caravan*.
38 Al-Qaeda's global jihad model is most commonly associated with the group's senior strategist, Abu Musab al-Suri. Lia, Brynjar. 2009. *Architect of Global Jihad: The Life of Al-Qaeda Strategist Abu Mus'ab Al-Suri*. 1st edition. New York: Oxford University Press.
39 Atran, Scott. 2006. "The Moral Logic and Growth of Suicide Terrorism." *The Washington Quarterly* 29 (2): 127–47. https://doi.org/10.1162/wash.2006.29.2.127.
40 Hoffman, Bruce. 2004. "The Changing Face of Al Qaeda and the Global War on Terrorism." *Studies in Conflict & Terrorism* 27 (6): 549–60. https://doi.org/10.1080/10576100490519813.
41 While the term has not been used in print, it was applied to ISIS by Joas Wagemakers at a conference attended by one of the authors.
42 Wood, Graeme. 2016. *The Way of the Strangers: Encounters with the Islamic State*. New York: Random House Publishing Group.
43 Ibid.
44 Lea-Henry, Jed. 2018. "The Life and Death of Abdullah Azzam." *Middle East Policy* 25 (1): 64–79. https://doi.org/10.1111/mepo.12325.
45 Berger, J.M. 2011. *Jihad Joe: Americans Who Go to War in the Name of Islam*. 1st ed. Washington, D.C: Potomac Books.
46 Meleagrou-Hitchens. 2018. "Salafism in America: History, Evolution, Radicalization."
47 Ibid.
48 Bergen, Peter. 2017. *United States of Jihad: Who Are America's Homegrown Terrorists, and How Do We Stop Them?* New York: Crown Publishers, 251–3.
49 Mazzetti, Mark, Eric Schmitt, and Robert F. Worth. 2011. "American-Born Qaeda Leader Is Killed by U.S. Missile in Yemen." *The New York Times*, September 30, 2011, sec. Middle East. https://www.nytimes.com/2011/10/01/world/middleeast/anwar-al-awlaki-is-killed-in-yemen.html.
50 Ibid.
51 Reuters. 2012. "Prosecutors Say al Qaeda Leader Awlaki Directed Underwear Bomber." February 10, 2012. https://www.reuters.com/article/us-usa-security-abdulmutallab-idUSTRE8191VL20120210.
52 "Zachary Chesser: A Case Study in Online Islamist Radicalization and Its Meaning for the Threat of Homegrown Terrorism." 2012. *U.S. Senate Committee on Homeland*

Security and Governmental Affairs. https://www.hsgac.senate.gov/imo/media/doc/CHESSER%20FINAL%20REPORT(1)2.pdf.

53 Poppe, Katharine. 2018. "Nidal Hasan: A Case Study in Lone-Actor Terrorism." Washington, D.C.: George Washington Program on Extremism. https://extremism.gwu.edu/sites/g/files/zaxdzs2191/f/Nidal%20Hasan.pdf.

54 This data is provided by the New America Foundation, and takes into account the period between January 2007 and January 2015. "Terrorism in America After 9/11." 2017. New America.

55 "Case by Case: ISIS Prosecutions in the United States." 2016. New York, NY: Center for National Security at Fordham Law. https://static1.squarespace.com/static/55dc76f7e4b013c872183fea/t/577c5b43197aea832bd486c0/1467767622315/ISIS+Report+-+Case+by+Case+-+July2016.pdf.

56 Program on Extremism Twitter database.

57 Al-Awlaki, Anwar. 2000. "Stories from the Hadith." CIIE. https://www.halaltube.com/stories-from-hadith.

58 Meleagrou-Hitchens, Alexander. 2020. *Incitement: Anwar al-Awlaki's Western Jihad.* Cambridge, MA: Harvard University Press; Meleagrou-Hitchens, Alexander. 2011. "As American as Apple Pie: How Anwar al-Awlaki Became the Face of Western Jihad." London, UK: International Centre for the Study of Radicalisation. http://icsr.info/wp-content/uploads/2012/10/1315827595ICSRPaperAsAmericanAsApplePieHowAnwaralAwlakiBecametheFaceofWesternJihad.pdf.

59 Ibid.

60 Meleagrou-Hitchens. 2020. *Incitement: Anwar al-Awlaki's Western Jihad.*

61 Shane, Scott. 2015. "The Lessons of Anwar Al-Awlaki." *The New York Times,* August 27, 2015, sec. Magazine. https://www.nytimes.com/2015/08/30/magazine/the-lessons-of-anwar-al-awlaki.html.

62 Ibid.

63 Ibid.

64 Shane, Scott. 2015. "From Minneapolis to ISIS: An American's Path to Jihad." *The New York Times,* March 21, 2015, sec. World. https://www.nytimes.com/2015/03/22/world/middleeast/from-minneapolis-to-isis-an-americans-path-to-jihad.html.

65 Fernandez, Manny, Richard Pérez-Peña, and Fernanda Santos. 2015. "Gunman in Texas Shooting Was F.B.I. Suspect in Jihad Inquiry." *The New York Times,* May 4, 2015, sec. U.S. https://www.nytimes.com/2015/05/05/us/garland-texas-shooting-muhammad-cartoons.html.

66 Shane, Scott. 2016. "The Enduring Influence of Anwar Al-Awlaki in the Age of the Islamic State." *CTC Sentinel* 9(7): 15–19. https://ctc.usma.edu/the-enduring-influence-of-anwar-al-awlaki-in-the-age-of-the-islamic-state/.

67 "From the Words of Scholars about the Project of the Islamic State." *al-Hayat Media Center,* December 10, 2013.

68 The first reference to this is in issue 1 of *Inspire,* released in January 2010. *Inspire.* 2010. "Open Source Jihad." https://azelin.files.wordpress.com/2010/06/aqap-inspire-magazine-volume-1.pdf.

69 Meleagrou-Hitchens. 2020. *Incitement: Anwar al-Awlaki's Western Jihad.*

70 Ibid.

71 Meleagrou-Hitchens. 2011. "As American as Apple Pie."

72 Reed, Alastair, and Haroro J. Ingram. 2017. "Exploring the Role of Instructional Material in AQAP's *Inspire* and ISIS' *Rumiyah.*" European Counter Terrorism Centre (ECTC). https://icct.nl/wp-content/uploads/2017/06/reeda_ingramh_

instructionalmaterial.pdf; Clifford, Bennett. 2018. "'Trucks, Knives, Bombs, Whatever:' Exploring Pro-Islamic State Instructional Material on Telegram." *CTC Sentinel* 11(5). https://ctc.usma.edu/trucks-knives-bombs-whatever-exploring-pro-islamic-state-instructional-material-telegram/.

73 Sarat-St. Peter, Hilary. 2017. "'Make a Bomb in the Kitchen of Your Mom': Jihadist Tactical Technical Communication and the Everyday Practice of Cooking." *Technical Communication Quarterly* 26 (1): 76–91. https://doi.org/10.1080/10572252.2016.1275862.

74 Ibid.

75 Miller, Greg. 2015. "Al-Qaeda Figure Seen as Key Inspiration for San Bernardino Attacker." *Washington Post*, December 18, 2015, sec. National Security. https://www.washingtonpost.com/world/national-security/al-qaeda-figure-seen-as-key-inspiration-for-san-bernardino-attacker/2015/12/18/f0e00d80-a5a0-11e5-9c4e-be37f66848bb_story.html.

76 Ibid.

77 Brachman, Jarret M., and Alix N. Levine. 2011. "You Too Can Be Awlaki!" *Fletcher Forum on International Affairs* 35 (1). https://static1.squarespace.com/static/579fc2ad725e253a86230610/t/57ec9034f7e0abf8c055c74b/1475121204759/Brachman-Levine_35-1.pdf.

78 Ibid.

79 Meleagrou-Hitchens. 2020. *Incitement: Anwar al-Awlaki's Western Jihad.*

80 Meleagrou-Hitchens. 2011. "As American as Apple Pie."

81 Meleagrou-Hitchens. 2020. *Incitement: Anwar al-Awlaki's Western Jihad.*

82 Ibid.

83 Ibid.

84 Lemieux, Anthony F., Jarret M. Brachman, Jason Levitt, and Jay Wood. 2014. "Inspire Magazine: A Critical Analysis of Its Significance and Potential Impact Through the Lens of the Information, Motivation, and Behavioral Skills Model." *Terrorism and Political Violence* 26 (2): 354–71. https://doi.org/10.1080/09546553.2013.828604.

85 Ibid.

86 Reed, Alastair, and Haroro J. Ingram. 2017. "Exploring the Role of Instructional Material in AQAP's *Inspire* and ISIS' *Rumiyah*." In European Counter Terrorism Centre (ECTC). https://icct.nl/wp-content/uploads/2017/06/reeda_ingramh_instructionalmaterial.pdf.

87 "The Dust Will Never Set Down Campaign." *Inspire*, Issue 1 (2010).

88 Ibid.

89 Reed, Alastair, and Haroro J. Ingram. 2017. "Exploring the Role of Instructional Material in AQAP's *Inspire* and ISIS' *Rumiyah*." European Counter Terrorism Centre (ECTC). https://icct.nl/wp-content/uploads/2017/06/reeda_ingramh_instructionalmaterial.pdf.

90 "The Ruling on Dispossessing the Disbelievers' Wealth in Dar Al-Harb." *Inspire*, Issue 4 (2011).

91 "Indictment." 2016. *USA v. Abdullahi Ahmed Abdullahi*, U.S. District Court for the Southern District of California. Case 3:17-cr-00622. https://extremism.gwu.edu/sites/g/files/zaxdzs2191/f/Abdullahi%20Indictment.pdf

92 "The Ruling on Dispossessing the Disbelievers' Wealth in Dar Al-Harb." *Inspire*, Issue 4 (2011).

93 Ibid.

94 Basra, Rajan, Peter Neumann, and Claudia Brunner. 2017. "Criminal Pasts, Terrorist Futures: European Jihadists and the New Crime-Terror Nexus." ICSR Report. London, UK: International Centre for the Study of Radicalisation. http://icsr.info/wp-content/uploads/2017/05/Criminal-Pasts-Terrorist-Futures.pdf.

95 Ibid.

96 Ibid.

97 Ibid.

98 Biography found on his personal website, ahmadjibril.com. http://ahmadjibril.com/aboutus.html.

99 Ibid.

100 Ibid.

101 Jibril, Ahmad Musa. 2001. "Salman al-Odah: An Imam of our Time." alSalafyoon. com.: https://web.archive.org/web/20010215150201/http://alsalafyoon.com:80/EnglishPosts/salamanalodahanimam.htm; Jibril, Ahmad Musa. 2003. "SheikhRabi'a bin Hadi or Muhammad Amaan on the website al-Salafyoon?" alSalafyoon.com. 138 https://web.archive.org/web/20030629012512/http://www.alsalafyoon.com/ArabicPosts/RabeeAmanSafarSalman.htm

102 Ibid.

103 Jibril, Ahmad Musa. 2001. "The Call to Jihad in the Quran." alSalafyoon.com. https://web.archive.org/web/20011108093442/http://alsalafyoon.com:80/EnglishPosts/jihad2.html; Jibril, Ahmad Musa. 2001. "Al-Jihad." alSalafyoon.com. https://web.archive.org/web/20010831133234/http://www.alsalafyoon.com:80/EnglishPosts/poem2.html.

104 Levitt, Matthew. 2015. "Anatomy of a Bombing." *Foreign Affairs*, September 22, 2015. https://www.foreignaffairs.com/articles/lebanon/2015-09-01/anatomy-bombing.

105 "Trial Exhibit B." 2005. *USA vs. Ahmad Musa Jebril and Musa Abdullah Jebril*, United States District Court for the Eastern District of Michigan.

106 Sacirbey, Omar. 2006. "Extremism in Our Own Communities?" Beliefnet. http://www.beliefnet.com/Faiths/Islam/2006/06/Extremism-In-Our-Own-Communities.aspx.

107 Ibid.

108 Ibid.

109 The original alsalafyoon.com site has been taken down. The authors are in possession of a full archived copy of the posts on the site, and several URLs to the content are available through the Internet Archive.

110 Jibril, Ahmad Musa. 2001. "The Call to Jihad in the Quran." *Alsalafyoon.com*, August, 2001. https://web.archive.org/web/20011108093442/http://alsalafyoon.com:80/EnglishPosts/jihad2.html.

111 Jibril, Ahmad Musa. 2001. "Jihad in Allah's Cause." *Alsalafyoon.com*, September 2001. https://web.archive.org/web/20010904200013/http://www.alsalafyoon.com:80/EnglishPosts/jihad.html.

112 Jibril, Ahmad Musa. 2001. "Jihad and Expedition." *Alsalafyoon.com*, https://web.archive.org/web/20011108092143/http://alsalafyoon.com:80/EnglishPosts/jihad1.html.

113 Jibril, Ahmad Musa. 2001. "Al-Jihad." *Alsalafyoon.com*, https://web.archive.org/web/20010831133234/http://www.alsalafyoon.com:80/EnglishPosts/poem2.html.

114 Jibril, Ahmad Musa. 2001. "What Scholars Say About Shi'a Sect." *alSalafyoon.com*, https://web.archive.org/web/20010107210400/http://www.alsalafyoon.com:80/EnglishPosts/shclarsonshia.htm.

115 Jibril. 2001. "Al-Jihad."

116 "DawahSchedule." ahmadjibril.com. https://web.archive.org/web/20030326102150/http://ahmadjibril.com:80/.

117 "AhmadJibril-IslamClasses." Yahoo! Group. https://groups.yahoo.com/neo/groups/AhmadJibril/info.

118 Back in action," Yahoo! Group post, September 13, 2003. https://groups.yahoo.com/
neo/groups/AhmadJibril/conversations/messages/17; "Riyaad," Yahoo! Group post,
September 14, 2003. https://groups.yahoo.com/neo/groups/AhmadJibril/
conversations/messages/18.

119 Abdo, Geneive. 2006. *Mecca and Main Street: Muslim Life in America After 9/11.*
Oxford; New York: Oxford University Press.

120 "Anyone Want to get boating?" Yahoo! Group post, August 13, 2003. https://groups.
yahoo.com/neo/groups/AhmadJibril/conversations/messages/5.

121 "FERAZ & SUMEERA(GREAT NEWS)." Yahoo! Group post. https://groups.yahoo.
com/neo/groups/AhmadJibril/conversations/messages/6.

122 "No Classes this week." Yahoo! Group post, August 17, 2003. https://groups.yahoo.
com/neo/groups/AhmadJibril/conversations/messages/7.

123 "If You Didn't Kill Him, He Would Have Died." Yahoo! Group post, January 2, 2004.
https://groups.yahoo.com/neo/groups/AhmadJibril/conversations/messages/39.

124 Ibid.

125 "Ibn Taimieh in Prison." Yahoo! Group post, February 24, 2004. https://groups.yahoo.
com/neo/groups/AhmadJibril/conversations/messages/66.

126 "Today is the 1st of Dhul Hijjah." Yahoo Group post, January 12, 2005. https://groups.
yahoo.com/neo/groups/AhmadJibril/conversations/messages/257.

127 "Jury Verdict Form." 2004. *USA v. Ahmad Musa Jebril et. al.* United States District
Court for the Eastern District of Michigan. Case: 2:03-cr-80810.

128 "Supplemental Sentencing Memorandum." 2004. *USA v. Ahmad Musa Jebril et. al.*
United States District Court for the Eastern District of Michigan. Case: 2:03-cr-
80810.

129 Ibid.

130 Ibid.

131 Authors' interview with senior Bureau of Prisons counterterrorism official, July 2018.

132 "Communications Management Units." 2015. National Institute of Corrections.
February 2, 2015. https://nicic.gov/communications-management-units.

133 Ibid.

134 Johnson, Carrie, and Margot Williams. 2011. "'Guantanamo North': Inside Secretive
U.S. Prisons." *NPR*, March 3, 2011. https://www.npr.org/2011/03/03/134168714/
guantanamo-north-inside-u-s-secretive-prisons.

135 Authors' interview with senior Bureau of Prisons counterterrorism official, July 2018.

136 "A Letter from A Muslim CMU Inmate," ahmadjibril.com. http://ahmadjibril.com/
articles/cmuprison.html.

137 Ibid.

138 Horton, Alex, and Michael Brice-Saddler. 2019. "The 'American Taliban' Will Be Free
after 17 Years. Is the U.S. Ready to Welcome Him Back?" *Washington Post*, May 22,
2019. https://www.washingtonpost.com/national-security/2019/05/20/american-
taliban-will-be-free-after-years-is-us-ready-welcome-him-back/.

139 "A Letter from A Muslim CMU Inmate." http://ahmadjibril.com/page-96/page-150/.

140 Jibril, Ahmad Musa. "A Forgotten Prisoner! The Smiling Somali Pirate." ahmadjibril.
com. http://ahmadjibril.com/articles/ssomali.html.

141 Ibid.

142 With thanks to Audrey Alexander, who drew these figures from a database used to
author her study "Digital Decay: Tracing Change Over Time Among English-
Language Islamic State Sympathizers on Twitter." Program on Extremism, George
Washington University, 2017.

143 These figures are from a database from the Program on Extremism study "Encrypted Extremism: Inside the English-Language Pro-Islamic State Ecosystem on Telegram." Washington, D.C.: George Washington Program on Extremism, 2019.

144 Warikoo, Niraj. 2017. "London Terror Suspect Was Influenced by Dearborn Cleric, Says Friend." *Detroit Free Press*, June 5, 2017. http://www.freep.com/story/ news/2017/06/06/london-terror-suspect-influenced-dearborn-cleric-says-friend/370329001/.

145 Carter, Joseph A., Shiraz Maher, and Peter Neumann. 2014. "#Greenbirds: Measuring Importance and Influence in Syrian Foreign Fighter Networks." London, UK: International Centre for the Study of Radicalisation. http://icsr.info/wp-content/ uploads/2014/04/ICSR-Report-Greenbirds-Measuring-Importance-and-Infleunce-in-Syrian-Foreign-Fighter-Networks.pdf.

146 Ibid.

147 Jibril, Ahmad Musa. "The Only Path to Victory." https://archive.org/details/ VictoryJibril.

148 Ibid.

149 Another lecture where this message appears includes Jibril, Ahmad Musa. "Advice on Hijra: You be the Judge." undated. https://www.youtube.com/watch?v= JbDvbIqDhMk.

150 Undated and untitled Ahmad Musa Jibril sermon, digital archived version in author's possession.

151 Jibril. "The Only Path to Victory."

152 Jibril, Ahmad Musa. "Syria in Our Hearts." undated. https://www.youtube.com/watch? v=BUMUjQN773k&t=1122s.

153 Jibril. "Syria in Our Hearts."

154 Jibril. "Advice on Hijra: You be the Judge."

155 Warikoo, Niraj. 2017. "London Terror Suspect Was Influenced by Dearborn Cleric, Says Friend."

156 Affidavit in Support of Search Warrants (Under Seal). *USA vs. Mohamed Elshinawy*, United States District Court for the District of Maryland. Case: ELH-16-009.

157 Warikoo, Niraj. 2017. "Dearborn Heights Man Accused of Supporting ISIS Sentenced to 5 Years." *Detroit Free Press*, April 6, 2017. https://www.freep.com/story/news/local/ michigan/detroit/2017/04/06/khalil-abu-rayyan-isis/100090964/.

158 Snell, Robert. 2016. "FBI Probes Md. Terror Link in Detroit Case." *Detroit News*, September 21, 2016. https://www.detroitnews.com/story/news/local/detroit-city/2016/09/21/fbi-probes-md-terror-link-detroit-case/90815642/.

159 Moore, Jack. 2017. "YouTube Hasn't Blocked Radical U.S. Cleric Ahmad Musa Jibril in Hate Speech Crackdown." *Newsweek*, November 13, 2017. https://www.newsweek. com/youtube-taking-down-anwar-al-awlakis-sermons-not-us-cleric-who-inspired-isis-709114.

160 Warikoo, Niraj. 2017. "London Terror Suspect Was Influenced by Dearborn Cleric, Says Friend."

161 Shane, Scott, and Adam Goldman. 2016. "Extremist Imam Tests F.B.I. and the Limits of the Law." *The New York Times*, September 30, 2016, sec. U.S. https://www.nytimes. com/2016/10/01/us/maryland-imam-fbi-suleiman-anwar-bengharsa.html; Jouvenal, Justin. 2016. "Maryland Imam's Advocacy of ISIS Lands Him at Center of Terrorism Probe." *Washington Post*, October 7, 2016, sec. Public Safety. https://www.washingtonpost. com/local/public-safety/maryland-imams-advocacy-of-isis-lands-him-at-center-of-terrorism-probe/2016/10/06/421c6627-c715-4fe7-a246-70871169cf49_story.html.

162 Shane and Goldman. 2016. "Extremist Imam Tests F.B.I. and the Limits of the Law."

163 The authors are in possession of an archived copy of the now-defunct IJC website. According to official business filings, Suleiman set up two separate companies, The Islamic Jurisprudence Center (IJC), which was founded in October 2015 and is still active, and The Islamic Jurisprudence Center, Inc., which was dissolved in February 2017, just six months after it was created. However, the IJC's now defunct Facebook page states that it was founded in June 2015.

164 "Sheikh Suleiman Anwar." Accessed November 1, 2019. https://www.youtube.com/user/sbengharsa.

165 "Sheikh Suleiman Anwar Evening Lecture." Fiqh of interaction with non-Muslims 1 of 13.m4v." 2010. YouTube. https://www.youtube.com/watch?v=SkCTL6ETpw8

166 Ibid.

167 Bengharsa, Suleiman Anwar. 2016. "The Dilemma of Muslim Marriages," suleimananwar.com, June 24, 2016. https://suleimananwar.com/2016/06/muslim-marriage-islamic-marriage; Bengharsa, Suleiman Anwar. 2016. "Some Fundamentals Regarding Islamic Business Practices." suleimananwar.com, April 27, 2016. https://suleimananwar.com/2016/04/some-fundamentals-regarding-islamic-business-practices/.

168 Bengharsa, Suleiman Anwar. 2016. "Fatwa #1: Prohibition of Adherence to Partial Sharia/Islam (Based on Period of Revelation)." suleimananwar.com, March 20, 2016. https://suleimananwar.com/2016/03/fatwa-prohibition-adherence-partial-sharia-islam/.

169 Bengharsa, Suleiman Anwar. 2017. "Fatwa #11: Democracy — Part of the Creed of the Disbelievers." suleimananwar.com, June 17, 2017. https://suleimananwar.com/2017/06/democracy-religion-disbelievers/

170 Ibid.

171 IJC site archive.

172 Ibid.

173 Bengharsa. 2017. "Fatwa #11: Democracy."

174 Bengharsa, Suleiman Anwar. 2018. "Fatwa #15: Attending Mosques Propagating Western/Modern Islam." suleimananwar.com, June 1, 2018. https://suleimananwar.com/2018/06/injunction-fatwa-16-attending-mosques-propagating-western-modern-islam/

175 Ibid.

176 "Affidavit in Support of an Application for Search Warrant." *USA vs. Gregerson*, United States District Court for the Eastern District of Michigan, 5–6.

177 Ibid.

178 Ibid.

179 Ibid.

180 Ibid.

181 Ibid.

182 Shane and Goldman. 2016. "Extremist Imam Tests F.B.I. and the Limits of the Law."

183 Affidavit in Support of an Application for Search Warrant. *USA vs. Gregerson*.

184 Ibid.

185 Shane and Goldman. 2016. "Extremist Imam Tests F.B.I. and the Limits of the Law."

186 "Affidavit in Support of an Application for Search Warrant." *USA vs. Gregerson*, 14.

187 Ibid.

188 "Detroit Resident Pleads Guilty to Illegally Acquiring a Firearm." 2017. U.S. Department of Justice, May 2, 2017. https://www.justice.gov/usao-edmi/pr/detroit-resident-pleads-guilty-illegally-acquiring-firearm.

189 Ibid.

190 "Government Sentencing Memorandum." *USA vs. Gregerson*. 26.

191 "Affidavit in Support of an Application for Search Warrant." *USA vs. Gregerson*, 15

192 Ibid.

193 Shane and Goldman. 2016. "Extremist Imam Tests F.B.I. and the Limits of the Law."

194 Weiner, Rachel. 2017. "He Talked about Committing a Terrorist Attack. He'll Go to Prison for 10 Years." *Washington Post*, July 14, 2017, sec. Public Safety. https://www.washingtonpost.com/local/public-safety/he-talked-about-committing-a-terrorist-attack-hell-go-to-prison-for-10-years/2017/07/14/dc312e82-67dc-11e7-9928-22d00a47778f_story.html.

195 Ibid.

196 Shane and Goldman. 2016. "Extremist Imam Tests F.B.I. and the Limits of the Law."

197 "Affidavit in Support of Complaint and Arrest Warrant." 2018. *USA v. Damon Joseph*, United States District Court for the Northern District of Ohio. https://extremism.gwu.edu/sites/g/files/zaxdzs2191/f/Joseph%20Affidavit%20in%20Support%20of%20Complaint%20and%20Arrest%20Warrant%202018.pdf.

198 "Toledo Terror Suspect Showed Social Media Evolution." 2019. *Homeland Security Today*, January 5, 2019. https://www.hstoday.us/subject-matter-areas/terrorism-study/memri-toledo-terror-suspect-showed-social-media-evolution-from-pot-smoking-student-to-jihadi/.

199 Bengharsa, Suleiman Anwar. 2017. "Radicalization or Guidance?" October 1, 2017. https://suleimananwar.com/2017/10/radicalization-or-guidance/.

200 Bengharsa, Suleiman Anwar. 2017. "Online Study Program: Introduction to Usool-ud-Deen (The Foundations of the Islamic Religion)." November 2, 2018. https://suleimananwar.com/2018/11/new-study-program-introduction-yo-usool-ul-deen-the-fundamentals-of-the-islamic-religion/.

201 Anwar, Suleiman. SoundCloud Account. https://soundcloud.com/user-634448699.

202 Bengharsa, Suleiman Anwar. 2018. "Salafism in America." October 28, 2018. https://suleimananwar.com/2018/10/salafism-in-america/

203 Morton, Jesse, and Mitch Silber. 2018. "'Sheikh' Abdullah Faisal: Ideologue of Hate." New York, NY: Anti-Defamation League.

204 Ibid.

205 Ibid.

206 Ibid.

207 Ibid.

208 Ibid.

209 Ibid.

210 Faisal, Abdullah. 2014. "The Importance of Hijrah." July 9, 2014. https://archive.org/details/TheImportanceOfHijrah.

211 Ibid.

212 Ibid.

213 Ibid.

214 Faisal, Abdullah. 2016. "Can the Caliphate Survive?" November 5. https://archive.org/details/CanTheCaliphateSurvive.

215 Faisal. 2014. "The Importance of Hijrah."

216 Ibid.

217 Ibid. Faisal relies here on the work of Ibn Hazim, a scholar from the early tenth century who followed the Zahiri school of jurisprudence. While not strictly a Salafi source, his work is respected and used by many Salafis.

218 Ibid.
219 "Affidavit in Support of Criminal Complaint," 2018. *USA v. Masoud Khan,* United States District Court for the District of Columbia. Case: 1:19-cr-00007-TSC, 7,11.
220 "Transcript of Sentencing Hearing." *USA v. Masoud Khan,* United States District Court for the District of Columbia. Case: 1:19-cr-00007-TSC, 29.
221 "Affidavit in Support of Criminal Complaint." *USA v. Masoud Khan,* 7–8.
222 Ibid., 8.
223 Ibid., 15.
224 Ibid., 14.
225 Ibid., 17–20.
226 "Indictment," 2017. *State of New York v Trevor William Forrest* Supreme Court for the State of New York., 5.
227 Criminal Complaint, 2015. *USA v. Keonna Thomas,* United States District Court for the Eastern District of Pennsylvania. https://extremism.gwu.edu/sites/g/files/zaxdzs2191/f/Thomas%20Criminal%20Complaint.pdf.
228 "Notice of Unsealed Filings." *USA v. Keonna Thomas,* 14.
229 "Transcript of Sentencing Hearing." *USA v. Masoud Khan,* 21.
230 "Indictment." *State of New York v Trevor William Forrest.*
231 Morton, Jesse, and Mitch Silber. 2018. "'Sheikh' Abdullah Faisal: Ideologue of Hate." New York, NY: Anti-Defamation League.
232 Treasury Sanctions Jamaica-based ISIS Recruiter for Terror Support." 2017. U.S. Department of the Treasury Press Release, December 5, 2017. https://www.treasury.gov/press-center/press-releases/Pages/sm0231.aspx.
233 "Indictment." 2017. *State of New York v. Trevor William Forrest.*
234 "Counter-Terrorism Designation." 2017. U.S. Department of the Treasury, December 5, 2017. https://www.treasury.gov/resource-center/sanctions/OFAC-Enforcement/Pages/20171205.aspx.
235 "Treasury Sanctions Jamaica-based ISIS Recruiter for Terror Support." U.S. Department of the Treasury, Press Release, December 5, 2017. https://www.treasury.gov/press-center/press-releases/Pages/sm0231.aspx.
236 Goldman, Adam, and Scott Shane. 2017. "A Long-Pursued ISIS Preacher Is Finally Charged in New York." *The New York Times,* September 1, 2017, sec. U.S. https://www.nytimes.com/2017/09/01/us/abdullah-faisal-al-qaeda.html.
237 Kelly, Louise. 2017. "Preparing To Leave, National Counterterrorism Center Director Reviews Threats." *NPR,* December 7, 2017. https://www.npr.org/2017/12/07/569222289/preparing-to-leave-national-counterterrorism-center-director-reviews-threats.
238 "Dallas Man Found Guilty of Conspiring to Support ISIS." 2019. Department of Justice Press Release. May 6, 2019. https://www.justice.gov/usao-ndtx/pr/dallas-man-found-guilty-conspiring-support-isis.
239 "Criminal Complaint." 2017. *USA v. Said Azzam Mohamad Rahim.* United States District Court for the Northern District of Texas. Case: 3:17-mj-00171. https://extremism.gwu.edu/sites/g/files/zaxdzs2191/f/S.%20Rahim%20Complaint.pdf.
240 Ibid.
241 Ibid.
242 Shane, Scott. 2017. "In 'Watershed Moment,' YouTube Blocks Extremist Cleric's Message." *The New York Times,* November 12, 2017, sec. U.S. https://www.nytimes.com/2017/11/12/us/politics/youtube-terrorism-anwar-al-awlaki.html.

243 Alexander, Audrey, and William Braniff. 2018. "Marginalizing Violent Extremism Online." *Lawfare*, January 21, 2018. https://www.lawfareblog.com/marginalizing-violent-extremism-online."

6. Countering Violent Extremism in America

1 Office of Public Affairs. "Raleigh Man Pleads Guilty to Conspiring to Provide Material Support for Terrorism." Department of Justice, October, 2014. https://www.justice.gov/opa/pr/raleigh-man-pleads-guilty-conspiring-provide-material-support-terrorism.

2 This information is a first-hand account from Seamus Hughes, who was directly involved in organizing and running CREX.

3 Interview with Bush Administration National Security Council official, March 2019.

4 White House. 2011. *Empowering Local Partners to Prevent Violent Extremism in the United States*. Washington, DC: White House.

5 Interview with senior U.S. Government official tasked with implementing countering violent extremism programs, March 2018.

6 Ibid.

7 The four pillars of CONTEST are: 1) Pursue (to stop terrorist attacks); 2) Prevent (to stop people becoming terrorists or supporting terrorism; 3) Protect (to strengthen protection against terrorist attacks); and 4) Prepare (to mitigate the impact of terrorist attacks). *CONTEST: The United Kingdom's Strategy for Countering Terrorism*. UK Home Office, July 2011. https://assets.publishing.service.gov.uk/government/uploads/system/uploads/attachment_data/file/97994/contest-summary.pdf.

8 Department for Communities and Local Government. 2008. *Preventing Violent Extremism Pathfinder Fund Mapping of project activities 2007/2008*. London: Communities and Local Government Publications.

9 Ibid., 5.

10 Ibid., 8.

11 Dodd, Vikram. "Government anti-terrorism strategy 'spies' on innocent." *The Guardian*, October 16, 2009.

12 May, Theresa. 2011. "Prevent Strategy." HM Government, June 2011.

13 Ali, Rashad. "Roots of Violent Radicalization." Counter Extremism Consultancy, Training, Research and Interventions, February 2012.

14 Ali, Rashad. 2015. "De-radicalization and Integration: The United Kingdom's Channel Programme." Washington, D.C.: George Washington Program on Extremism, October 2015. https://extremism.gwu.edu/sites/g/files/zaxdzs2191/f/downloads/Rashad%20Ali.pdf.

15 Ibid.

16 See statutory guidance explaining the framework, HM Government. *Channel: Vulnerability Assessment Framework*. UK Home Office, October 2012. https://www.gov.uk/government/uploads/system/uploads/attachment_data/file/118187/vul-assessment.pdf.

17 HM Government. 2010. *Channel: Supporting Individuals Vulnerable to Recruitment by Violent Extremists*. HM Government: London. https://assets.publishing.service.gov.uk/government/uploads/system/uploads/attachment_data/file/118187/vul-assessment.pdf.

18 Ali, Rashad. 2015. "De-radicalization and Integration."

19 HM Government. 2015. *Prevent Duty Guidance: for England and Wales*. UK Home Office. https://www.lbhf.gov.uk/sites/default/files/Prevent_Duty_Guidance_for_England_and_Wales.pdf.

20 Ibid.

21 Ibid.

22 Ali, Rashad. 2015. "De-radicalization and Integration."

23 Ibid.

24 Rafiq, Haras and Rashad Ali. 2010. "When Will The Authorities Learn That Extremists Can't Be Used to Tackle Other Extremists?" *Conservative Home*, December 21, 2010.

25 Ali, Rashad. 2015. "De-radicalization and Integration."

26 Chertoff, Michael. 2007. "Written Testimony of Michael Chertoff Secretary of the Department of Homeland Security Before the Senate Committee on Homeland Security and Governmental Affairs on Radicalization." US Senate, March 2007. http://www.hsgac.senate.gov/download/031407chertoff.

27 Office for Civil Rights and Civil Liberties. 2008. "Terminology to Define the Terrorists: Recommendations from American Muslims." US Department of Homeland Security, January 2008. https://www.dhs.gov/xlibrary/assets/dhs_crcl_terminology_08-1-08_accessible.pdf.

28 Ibid.

29 Interview with former National Security Council staffer, May 2019.

30 Interview with U.S. Government countering violent extremism policy staffer, November 2019.

31 "Government's Proffer and Memorandum of Law in Support of Motion for Detention." *USA vs. Najibullah Zazi,* United States District Court of Colorado, September 2009. https://www.justice.gov/archive/usao/co/news/2009/September09/Zazi_Detention_Motion.pdf.

32 Office of Public Affairs. 2009. "Najibullah Zazi Indicted for Conspiracy." Department of Justice, September 2009. https://www.justice.gov/opa/pr/najibullah-zazi-indicted-conspiracy.

33 Office of Public Affairs. 2011. "Illinois Man Admits Plotting to Bomb Federal Courthouse and is Sentenced to 28 Years in Prison." *Department of Justice*, May 2011. https://www.justice.gov/opa/pr/illinois-man-admits-plotting-bomb-federal-courthouse-and-sentenced-28-years-prison; Office of Public Affairs. "Seven Charged with Terrorism Violations in North Carolina." Department of Justice, July 2009. https://www.justice.gov/opa/pr/seven-charged-terrorism-violations-north-carolina.

34 FBI National Press Office. 2012. "Judge Webster Delivers Webster Commission Report on Fort Hood." Federal Bureau of Investigation, July 2012. https://www.fbi.gov/news/pressrel/press-releases/judge-webster-delivers-webster-commission-report-on-fort-hood.

35 Lieberman, Joseph I. and Susan M. Collins. 2011. "A Ticking Time Bomb: Counterterrorism Lessons from the U.S. Government's Failure to Prevent the Fort Hood Attack." U.S. Senate Committee on Homeland Security and Governmental Affairs, February 2011. https://www.hsgac.senate.gov/imo/media/doc/Fort_Hood/FortHoodReport.pdf.

36 Office of the Press Secretary. 2011. "Remarks of Denis McDonough Deputy National Security Advisor to the President—As Prepared for Delivery." *Obama White House*, March 2011. https://obamawhitehouse.archives.gov/the-press-office/2011/03/06/remarks-denis-mcdonough-deputy-national-security-advisor-president-prepa.

37 Ibid.

38 Full Committee Hearing. 2009. "Violent Islamist Extremism: al-Shabaab Recruitment in America." *US Senate Homeland Security and Governmental Affairs Committee*, March 2009. http://www.hsgac.senate.gov/hearings/violent-islamist-extremism-al-shabaab-recruitment-in-america.

39 Mukhtar, Abdirahman. 2009. "Testimony by Abdirahman Mukhtar, Youth Program Manager, Brian Coyle Center of Pillsbury United Communities." *US Senate Homeland Security and Governmental Affairs Committee*, March 2009. http://www.hsgac.senate. gov/download/031109mukhtar.

40 Interview with Minnesota Somali American community members, October 2019.

41 The White House. 2011. *Empowering Local Partners to Prevent Violent Extremism in the United States.* Washington, D.C.: White House. https://obamawhitehouse.archives. gov/sites/default/files/empowering_local_partners.pdf.

42 Temple-Raston, Dina. 2019. "Officials Detail Plan To Fight Terrorism At Home." *NPR*. https://www.npr.org/2011/12/08/143319965/officials-detail-plans-to-fight-terrorism-at-home.

43 Lieberman, Joseph and Susan Collins, letter to John Brennan September 12, 2011. https://www.hsgac.senate.gov/media/senators-urge-administration-to-address-internet-radicalization.

44 Ibid.

45 The White House. 2011. *Strategic Implementation Plan for Empowering Local Partners to Prevent Violent Extremism in the United States.* Washington, D.C.: White House. https://obamawhitehouse.archives.gov/sites/default/files/sip-final.pdf

46 Ibid., 1.

47 Ibid., 2.

48 Ibid.

49 Ibid., 4–5.

50 Vidino, Lorenzo, and Seamus Hughes. 2015. "Countering Violent Extremism in America." Center for Cyber and Homeland Security, June 2015. https://extremism. gwu.edu/sites/g/files/zaxdzs2191/f/downloads/CVE%20in%20America.pdf.

51 The White House. 2011. "Strategic Implementation Plan for Empowering Local Partners to Prevent Violent Extremism in the United States," 11.

52 "After Girls' Jihadi Quest, a Focus on Outreach." *Associated Press*, November 14, 2014.

53 Speech by Attorney General Eric Holder. September 15, 2014. http://www.justice.gov/ opa/video/countering-violent-extremism.

54 Brennan Center for Justice, "Counter Violent Extremism (CVE): A Resource Page." New York, NY: Brennan Center for Justice, February 2015. https://www.brennancenter. org/our-work/research-reports/countering-violent-extremism-cve-resource-page.

55 Muslim Justice League. "Our Work." Boston, MA: Muslim Justice League. https://www. muslimjusticeleague.org/our-work/.

56 Ibid.

57 Undersigned Organizations. "Minnesota Muslims Concerned About New 'Stigmatizing, Divisive, and Ineffective' CVE Pilot Program." http://files.ctctcdn.com/ bd15115b001/d068ad69-9ad8-46a0-bdcd-b9d57454ed20.pdf.

58 STOPCVE. "Los Angeles." http://www.stopcve.com/la.html.

59 *Council on American-Islamic Relations-California; Vigilant Love Coalition; Asian Americans Advancing Justice-Los Angeles; and American Civil Liberties Union Foundation of Southern California, Petitioners vs. Los Angeles Mayor's Office of Public Safety; Los Angeles Human Relations Commission; and Los Angeles Police Department, Respondents,* Verified Petition for Alternative Writ of Mandate and Writ of Mandate Ordering Compliance with the California Public Records Act, June 2018. http://www. stopcve.com/uploads/1/1/2/4/112447985/conformed_cve_pra_writ_petition.pdf.

60 StopCVE. "LA CVE Resources." http://www.stopcve.com/resources.html.

61 Greene, Judith and Kevin Pranis. 2007. "Gang Wars: The Failure of Enforcement Tactics and the Need for Effective Public Safety Strategies." Washington D.C. :Justice Policy Institute, July 2007. http://www.justicepolicy.org/uploads/justicepolicy/documents/07-07_rep_gangwars_gc-ps-ac-jj.pdf.

62 Patel, Faiza. 2017. "The Trump Administration Provides One More Reason to Discontinue CVE." *Just Security*, July 12. https://www.justsecurity.org/42998/trump-administration-reason-discontinue-cve/.

63 Center on Extremism. 2019. "Murder and Extremism in the United States in 2018." Anti-Defamation League, January 2019. https://www.adl.org/media/12480/download.

64 Life After Hate. 2016. "Preventing Violent Radicalization and Supporting the De-Radicalization Process via Targeted Online and Offline Individualized Interventions." Chicago, IL: Life After Hate, 2016. http://www.stopcve.com/uploads/1/1/2/4/112447985/2016_life_after_hate_proposal_cve_grant_programmanaging_intervention_activities_nd_grants_submission.pdf.

65 In the media backlash that followed the news cycle covering the rescinding of Life After Hate's DHS grant, Chicago native and founder of Life After Hate, Christian Picciolini, was able to raise over $500,000 in donations to his organization. Davies, Dave. 2018. "A Former Neo-Nazi Explains Why Hate Drew Him in—and How He Got Out." *NPR*, January, 2018. https://www.npr.org/transcripts/578745514?storyId=578745514.

66 Interview with anti-CVE activist, December 2019.

67 Hudson, John. 2017. "The Gorka That Matters Isn't Leaving The Trump Administration." *BuzzFeed News*, August 29, 2017. https://www.buzzfeednews.com/article/johnhudson/the-gorka-that-matters-isnt-leaving-the-trump-administration.

68 The White House. 2011. "Strategic Implementation Plan for Empowering Local Partners to Prevent Violent Extremism in the United States," 20.

69 Interview with U.S. Government officials, August and November 2019.

70 Wiktorowicz, Quintan. 2013. "Working to Counter Online Radicalization to Violence in the United States." Obama White House, February, 2013. https://obamawhitehouse.archives.gov/blog/2013/02/05/working-counter-online-radicalization-violence-united-states.

71 Interview with former U.S. government countering violent extremism official, June 2019.

72 Kang, Cecilia, and Matt Apuzzo. 2016. "U.S. Asks Tech and Entertainment Industries Help in Fighting Terrorism." *The New York Times*, February, 2016. https://www.nytimes.com/2016/02/25/technology/tech-and-media-firms-called-to-white-house-for-terrorism-meeting.html.

73 Carlin, John. 2016. "Remarks by Assistant Attorney General John Carlin Opening of Madison Valleywood Project." Department of Justice, February, 2016. https://epic.org/foia/MadisonValleywood_2.pdf.

74 Interview with four participants of the MadisonValleyWood meeting, January 2019.

75 "Tech Against Terrorism." https://www.techagainstterrorism.org.

76 Newton, Casey. 2019. "Google and YouTube Moderators Speak out on the Work That Gave Them PTSD." *The Verge*, December 2019. https://www.theverge.com/2019/12/16/21021005/google-youtube-moderators-ptsd-accenture-violent-disturbing-content-interviews-video.

77 Levin, Sam. 2017. "Google to Hire Thousands of Moderators after Outcry over YouTube Abuse Videos." *The Guardian*, December 5, 2017. https://www.theguardian.com/technology/2017/dec/04/google-youtube-hire-moderators-child-abuse-videos.

78 Chotiner, Isaac. 2019. "The Underworld of Online Content Moderation." *The New Yorker*, July 2019. https://www.newyorker.com/news/q-and-a/the-underworld-of-online-content-moderation; Arsht, Andrew and Daniel Etcovitch, "The Human Cost of Online Content Moderation." *JOLT Digest*, March, 2018. https://jolt.law.harvard.edu/digest/the-human-cost-of-online-content-moderation; Vincent, James. 2019. "AI Won't Relieve the Misery of Facebook's Human Moderators." *The Verge*, February, 2019. https://www.theverge.com/2019/2/27/18242724/facebook-moderation-ai-artificial-intelligence-platforms.

79 Newton, Casey. 2019. "Google and YouTube Moderators Speak out on the Work That Gave Them PTSD."

80 Ibid.

81 Matthews, Kyle, and Nicolai Pogadl. 2018. "Big Tech Is Overselling AI as the Solution to Online Extremism." *The Conversation*, September 2018. http://theconversation.com/big-tech-is-overselling-ai-as-the-solution-to-online-extremism-102077.

82 Fishman, Brian. 2019. "Crossroads: Counter-Terrorism and the Internet." *Texas National Security Review*, February 2019. https://tnsr.org/2019/02/crossroads-counter-terrorism-and-the-internet/.

83 Vidino, Lorenzo and Seamus Hughes. 2018. "America's Terrorism Problem Doesn't End with Prison—It Might Just Begin there." *Lawfare* (blog), June 17, 2018. https://www.lawfareblog.com/americas-terrorism-problem-doesnt-end-prison-it-might-just-begin-there.

84 Duke, Elaine. 2017. "Written Testimony of DHS Acting Secretary Elaine Duke for a Senate Committee on Homeland Security and Governmental Affairs Hearing Titled 'Threats to the Homeland.'" Department of Homeland Security. September 27, 2017. https://www.dhs.gov/news/2017/09/27/written-testimony-dhs-acting-secretary-elaine-duke-senate-committee-homeland.

85 Kitfield, James. 2017. "Taking on 'Foreign Fighters': How the West Tracks—and Targets—Jihadis Fleeing the Collapse of ISIS." Yahoo News. December 1, 2017. https://www.yahoo.com/news/taking-foreign-fighters-west-tracks-targets-jihadis-fleeing-collapse-isis-100045440.html.

86 The White House. 2018. "National Strategy for Counterterrorism of the United States of America." Washington DC: White House.

87 McAleenan, Kevin. "A Strategic Framework for Countering Terrorism and Targeted Violence." Washington, D.C.: The Brookings Institution, September 2019. https://www.brookings.edu/wp-content/uploads/2019/09/fp_20190920_dhs_terrorism_transcript.pdf p. 8.

88 The White House. 2018. "National Strategy for Counterterrorism of the United States of America."; Office of Public Affairs. "Acting Secretary McAleenan Announces Establishment of DHS Office for Targeted Violence and Terrorism Prevention." Department of Homeland Security, April 2019. https://www.dhs.gov/news/2019/04/19/acting-secretary-mcaleenan-announces-establishment-dhs-office-targeted-violence-and.

89 The White House. 2018. "National Strategy for Counterterrorism of the United States of America."

90 Ibid.

91 Office of Public Affairs. "Targeted Violence and Terrorism Prevention." Department of Homeland Security, March 2016. https://www.dhs.gov/tvtp.

92 Undersigned Organizations. "Minnesota Muslims Concerned About New 'Stigmatizing, Divisive, and Ineffective' CVE Pilot Program." http://files.ctctcdn.com/bd15115b001/d068ad69-9ad8-46a0-bdcd-b9d57454ed20.pdf; American Civil Liberties Union. "The Problem with 'Countering Violent Extremism' Programs." https://www.aclu.org/other/problem-countering-violent-extremism-programs.

93　American Civil Liberties Union. "The Problem with 'Countering Violent Extremism' Programs"; Simcox, Robin, 2018. "Can America's Countering Violent Extremism Efforts Be Salvaged?" Washington, D.C.: The Heritage Foundation, December 2018. https://www.heritage.org/terrorism/commentary/can-americas-countering-violent-extremism-efforts-be-salvaged.

94　Thompson, Rep. Bennie G. (D-MS). 2019. "Thompson Statement on DHS Strategy for Combating Terrorism and Targeted Violence." House Committee on Homeland Security, September, 2019. http://homeland.house.gov/news/press-releases/thompson-statement-on-dhs-strategy-for-combating-terrorism-and-targeted-violence.

95　Ibid.

96　Hughes, Seamus, and Haroro Ingram. 2019. "Trump's Domestic Countering Violent Extremism Policies Look a Lot Like Obama's." *Lawfare* (blog), March 10, 2019. https://www.lawfareblog.com/trumps-domestic-countering-violent-extremism-policies-look-lot-obamas.

97　Interview with senior law enforcement official, February 2018.

98　Internal U.S. Government documents, DEEP.

99　Hong, Nicole. 2017. "Former ISIS Recruit Now a Weapon Against Terrorism." *Wall Street Journal*, March 2017. https://www.wsj.com/articles/former-isis-recruit-becomes-prosecutors-aide-1488898751.

100　Internal U.S. Government documents, DEEP.

101　Gurman, Sadie. 2019. "Barr Wants to Adopt Terrorism-Prevention Tactics to Stop Mass Shootings." *Wall Street Journal*, October 2019. https://www.wsj.com/articles/barr-wants-to-adopt-terrorism-prevention-tactics-to-stop-mass-shootings-11571864324; Reilly, Ryan J. 2019. "William Barr: Anti-Terror Tactics Can Help Thwart Mass Shooters." *HuffPost*, October 2019. https://www.huffpost.com/entry/william-barr-mass-shooting-domestic-terrorism_n_5db05fbee4b0a7dbe8e27e61.

102　Gurman. "Barr Wants to Adopt Terrorism-Prevention Tactics to Stop Mass Shootings."

Conclusion

1　Doyle, Charles. 2016. "Terrorist Material Support: An Overview of 18 U.S.C. §2339A and §2339B." CRS Report. Congressional Research Service. https://fas.org/sgp/crs/natsec/R41333.pdf.

2　Noor Salman, wife of Pulse nightclub shooter Omar Mateen, was the first ISIS-related case to be acquitted of terrorism charges.

3　Rotella, Sebastian. 2016. "How Europe Left Itself Open to Terrorism." *Frontline*, October 18. http://www.pbs.org/wgbh/frontline/article/how-europe-left-itself-open-to-terrorism/.

4　Raymond, Catherine Zara. 2010. "Al Muhajiroun and Islam4UK: The Group behind the Ban." London, UK: International Centre for the Study of Radicalisation. http://icsr.info/wpcontent/uploads/2012/10/1276697989CatherineZaraRaymondICSRPaper.pdf; Reynolds, Sean C., and Mohammed M. Hafez. 2017. "Social Network Analysis of German Foreign Fighters in Syria and Iraq." *Terrorism and Political Violence*, 31: 661–86. https://doi.org/10.1080/09546553.2016.1272456; Lia, Brynjar, and Petter Nesser. 2016. "Jihadism in Norway: A Typology of Militant Networks in a Peripheral European Country." *Perspectives on Terrorism* 10 (6): 121–134. http://www.terrorismanalysts.com/pt/index.php/pot/article/view/563.

5　Levin, Brian. 2015. "The Original Web of Hate: Revolution Muslim and American Homegrown Extremists." *American Behavioral Scientist* 59 (12):1609–30. https://doi.org/10.1177/0002764215588815.

6   Cunningham, Eric. 2019. "True ISIS Believers Regroup Inside Refugee Camp, Terrorize The 'Impious.'" *Washington Post*, April 19, 2019.

7   Speaking about his turn away from jihadism, former American al-Qaeda recruiter Jesse Morton described how during his time in prison he reflected on his actions and beliefs, further studied his faith and wider political ideas and, as a result, "self-deradicalised." Jesse Morton, "'I Believed al-Qaeda When They Said 9/11 Was Justified. . . 15 Years On, I Work for Homeland Security,'" *The Telegraph*, September 10, 2016.

INDEX

Abdin, Zakariya 20–21
Abdulazeez, Mohammad Youssef 38, 103
Abdullahi, Abdullahi Ahmed 63, 66
Abdulmutallab, Umar Farouk 119, 139
Abdurahman, Zacharia 65
Abedi, Salman 146
Abousamra, Ahmad 58–61, 75–76
Abousamra, Dr. Abdulbadi 58
Abual-Fayad, Wa'il 60
Abu-Rayyan, Khalil 133
Abu-Salha, Moner 36
ADMAX (administrative security facility) 28
Afghanistan 13, 117–18, 135
ahmadjibril.com see Jibril, Ahmad Musa
Ahmed, Abdifatah 63–64, 66
Ahmed, Hamza 66
'AJ' *see* Jibril, Ahmad Musa
akhlaq (disposition) 70
al-Adnani, Abu Muhammad 2, 25, 31–32, 60, 131
al-Amriki, Abu Isa *see* Sudani, Abu Sa'ad
Alani, Abdul-Majeed Marouf Ahmed 20
al-Assad, President Bashar,
    atrocities of 4, 13, 16
    and ISI affiliates 14
    and jihadist groups fighting against 132
al-Awda, Salman 125
Alawites 4, 14
al-Awlaki, Anwar,
    and Abdullah Faisal 142, 145–47
    and Ahmad Musa Jibril 131, 134–35
    an essential source for American ISIS supporters 119–35
    an outsized influence 114
    and Damon Joseph 138–39
    English-language jihadist preacher 93
    life of 38
    and Masoud Khan 142, 144
    and Nadir Soofi 43

    ruling by 63
    Western al-Qaeda strategist 4–5, 13
Al-Azhar University, Egypt 134
al-Bab, Syria 34
al-Baghdadi, Abu Bakr,
    and Ahmad Jibril 131
    death of 1, 9, 18, 54
    the new caliph 140
    and Omar Mateen 35
    re-establishment of the caliphate 15, 71
    self-proclaimed caliph 119
    territory both sides of Syria–Iraq border 14
    top US target 48
al-Britani, Abu Rahman 70
al-Britani, Abu Sa'eed *see* Hussain, Omar
'Al Capone tactics' 113
al-Dulaimi, Shaker Wahib al-Fahdawi 35
Alexander, Audrey 22
al-Fayad, Wa'il 60
al-Furqan, Abu Muhammad *see* al-Fayad, Wa'il
al-Ghazi, Amir Said Abdul Rahman *see* McCollum, Robert
al-Hawali, Safar 125
al-Hayat Media Center 60, 105, 121
al-Hindi, Abu Salman 71
al-Hol camp 79
Ali, Arman and Omar 62
Ali, Ayaan Hirsi 123
al-Julani, Abu Muhammad 14
al-Kasasbeh, Muath 16, 93
'Al-Khilafa Aridat' (blog) 106
al-Madioum, Abdelhamid 66
al-Maqdisi, Abu Muhammad 117
al-Muhajir, Abu Hassan 18
al-Muhajiroun network 94, 112, 170
al-neda.com 86
al-Nusra, Jabhat 56
al-Qaeda,
    ability to mobilize Americans 174

affiliate network of 13
aggressive pursuit of 1
and Ahmad Abousamra 58–59
and Anwar al-Awlaki 114, 120–23
in the Arabian Peninsula (AQAP) 4,
    13, 22, 59, 61, 122–23
and Global jihad 117–18
in Iraq (AQI) 22, 27, 61
and Jabhat al-Nusra 56
and Khobar Towers bombing 125–26
and Minnesota traveler network 170
official websites of 87
and open source Jihad 122
overlap with ISIS 3–4
recruitment and radicalization 156
and Salafi-jihadist ideologues 131
and social media 5
and suicide bombing 69
al-salaf al-salih (Salafism) 155
alSalafyoon.com see Jibril, Ahmad Musa
al-Shabaab 13, 42, 63–65, 67, 119, 135
al-Sham 5
al-Sheikh, Abdulrahman Ahmad 80
al Sudani, Abu Sa'ad 34, 37–38, 46
al-Thawrah, Syria 61
al-Uyayri, Yusuf 123
al-Wahhab, Muhammad ibn Abd 129
Al wala wal bara (loyalty/disavowal)
    116–17, 126–27, 132, 135, 141
al-Zarqawi, Abu Musab 22, 126
al-Zawahiri, Ayman 117
Amaq 2
'Amari' 72
American ISIS,
    introduction 92
    technology attacks, cyber operations,
        travel 96–100
    technology and financing 106–8
    technology and propaganda 100–106
    technology and travel 92–96
    terrorism and the Internet 108–10
Amin, Ali 106–8, 172
Anarchist's Cookbook, The 22
anti-Christ 5
anwaralawlaki.com 123
Apple 95
Application Programming Interface
    (Twitter) 6
archive.org 91

Arkan, Colonel 92
Artan, Abdul Razaq Ali 144
artificial intelligence (AI) 164
ash-Shami, Abu Maysarah *see* Al-Fayad,
    Wa'il
Australia 64
Authentic Tauheed Paltalk room 142
'Authentic Tauheed' (web platform)
    139–40
Azzam, Abdallah 117

Baghuz Fawqani, Syria 17–18
Bahrain 80
Bangladesh 50–51
Bara'a, Abu 94
Barr, William 167
Beam, Louis 86
Bengharsa, Suleiman Anwar 8, 114,
    134–39, 145, 147, 212n.163
bin Laden, Osama 15, 117, 119, 126–27,
    131
Bin Mikaayl, Abdurrahman *see* Gregerson,
    Sebastian
Birmingham 34
Biswas, Mehdi 70
Bitcoin 106–7
'Bitcoin wa Sadaqat al-jihad' (article) 106
Bjelopera, Jerome 109
Black, Donald 86
Blair, Tony 97, 151
Bosnia 118
Boston 46–47, 58, 61, 122, 159–60
Boston Marathon bombers (2013) 122
Brachman, Jarret 113
Bradley, Ariel 77
Brian Coyle Recreational Center,
    Minneapolis 156
BRIDGES meetings 158
Brown, Avin Marsalis 11, 149
Brussels attacks (2016) 55
Bush, George W. 150, 154, 168
Byman, Daniel 25

caliphate jihadism 118, 209n.41
caliphate, the *see* Islamic State
'Call to Jihad in the Quran, The' (Jibril)
    126–27
Cameron, David 151
Camp Abdallah Azzam (Camp AA) 72–73

Camp Farooq 71–72
Canada 135
capital punishment 16
'Capture and Slaughter of a Safavid
    Soldier' (Bengharsa) 137
Carlin, John 98, 163
Castelli, Marie 20
Channel Panels 152, 160
Channel program 151–53
Charlie Hebdo (newspaper) 45
Chattanooga attack (2015) 77, 103
Chechnya 118
Chertoff, Michael 153, 155
Chesser, Zachary Adam 119, 139
Choudary, Anjem 112
Christians 141
Civil Rights and Civil Liberties Office
    (CRCL) 153–54, 156
Clark Jr, John Bailey 34
Collins, Susan 157
Colon, Santos 20
Combating Terrorism Center 88–89
Combined Joint Task Force–Operation
    Inherent Resolve (CJTF–OIR)
    17–18, 51
Comey, James 43–44, 55
Communication Breakdown (Combating
    Terrorism Center) 88–89
Communications Management Unit
    (CMU), FCC Terre Haute 130
Community Awareness Briefing (CAB)
    158–59
Community Resilience Exercise (CREX)
    149, 218n.2
'Constants on the Path of Jihad' (al-
    Awlaki) 123
CONTEST (British counterterrorism
    strategy) 151
Costello, Matthew 109
Council on American–Islamic Relations
    (CAIR) 160–61
Countering Violent Extremism (CVE) 8,
    29, 153, 155, 158–61, 166, 173
counter-radicalization programs 150–54
counterterrorism,
    and American responses 145, 221n.65
    criticism of investigations 36
    and CVE 161–62, 173
    and domestic drivers of radicalization 23

FBI tactics in 53
    and government overreach 150
    and releases of convicted jihadists 29
    and using technology in investigations
        26
cryptocurrencies 1, 107–8, 172
Curtis Culwell Center attack, Texas (2015)
    32–33, 41–47, 65, 102, 121, 144
'cyberbalkanization' 109

Dabiq (online magazine) 5, 58, 60, 89, 97,
    124, 137
Dais, Waheba Issa 99–100
Damlarkaya, Kaan Sercan 25
Dar al-Farooq Youth and Family Center,
    Minneapolis 64–65
dar al-harb 140
dar al-kufr 140
dark web 89
Daud, Abdirahman 65–66
dawla 140–41
Dearborn 128–31, 133, 146, 154
Deir ez-Zor, Syria 72
Department of Homeland Security (DHS)
    23, 149, 158, 163, 165–66
DHS grant program 168
DHS Strategic Framework for Countering
    Terrorism and Targeted Violence
    168
Disruption and Early Engagement Project
    (DEEP) 166–68, 173
DOJ 28
Domingo, Mark Steven 54
'Draw the Prophet Muhammad' contest
    50, 123, 171
drones 49, 53
Dropbox 50
Duke, Elaine 165
Dulles International Airport 39
Durov, Pavel and Nikolai 90
'Dust Will Never Settle Down, The' (al-
    Awlaki) 123
'DustyFeet' *see* al-Awlaki, Anwar

e activists,
    American ISIS *see* American ISIS
    extremist communications 86–89
    introduction 85–86
    Twitter to Telegram 90–92

'echo chambers' 109
Egypt 82
Electronic Privacy Information Center
   163
Elfgeeh, Mufid 14–15
Elkhodary, Tamer 49–50
Elshinawy, Mohamed 48–52
Emni (ISIS intelligence wing) 55
'Empowering Local Partners' 150
Empowering Local Partners (strategy) 157
Emwazi, Mohammed 48
Episcopal City Mission Barr Foundation
   160
Ethiopia 13
Euphrates River 17
European Union Internet Forum 163

Facebook,
   and Abdurrahman Bin Mikaayl 137
   and Ahmad Jibril 131–32, 134
   and Anwar al-Awlaki 121
   and Damon Joseph 138
   and echo chambers 109–10
   and Faisal Shehzad 139
   global terrorism policy 164
   and ISIS 5, 174
   Islamic State propaganda on 137
   and Marie Castelli 20
   and Mohamad Khweis 95
   and Mohamed Abdullahi Hassan 65
   and Waheba Issa Dais 99
Faisal, Abdullah 8, 20, 93, 114, 139–45,
   147
Farah, Adnan 65
Farah, Mohamed 65–66
Farook, Syed Rizwan 1–2, 35, 122
fatwas (religious rulings) 60
FBI,
   and Ahmad Jibril 134
   arrest of 3 Michigan men for
      conspiracy 82
   arrest of North Carolina men 11
   arrests of Guled Omar and others 65
   and Avin Marsalis Brown 149
   and confidential human sources (CHS)
      26
   counterterrorism mission of 36, 173
   and Culwell Center attack 43–46
   and detained ISIS fighters 80

   and Elton Simpson 42
   and Hamza Yusuf 64
   and homegrown violent extremists
      174
   investigations of 7, 17–18
   and jihadist attacks 35–36, 53
   and Junaid Hussain 48
   and Kaan Sercan Damlarkaya 25
   and Kalachnikv E-Security Team 98
   and Kim Anh Vo 98–99
   and Major Nidal Hasan 155
   and Masoud Khan 143
   and 'Mo' 73–74
   and Mohamad Khweis 92–96
   and Mohamed Bailor Jalloh 37–41
   and Mohamed Elshinawy 49–50, 133
   and Safya Yassin 100–103
   and Sebastian Gregerson 136
   and 'Shared Responsibilities
      Committees' 160–61
   and terrorism cases 25, 53–54
   and Thomas Osadzinski 105
   and undercover agents (UCEs) 26–27
   and William Barr 167
Federal Bureau of Prisons (BOP) 28, 130
Federal Correctional Complex, Terre
   Haute 129–32
Ferizi, Ardit 97–98, 103
'filter bubble effect' 109
First Amendment 112, 145
First Annual Muhammad Art Exhibit and
   Contest 39, 42, 45–46
Fisher, Ali 89
Fishman, Brian 164
'Flames of War' (video) 104
Flint Airport shooting (2017) 33
foreign terrorist organizations (FTO) 27
Forrest, Trevor William *see* Faisal,
   Abdullah
Fort Hood shooting (2009) 38, 119
'44 Ways to Support Jihad' (al-Awlaki) 123
France 56
Francis, Pope 20
Freedom of Information Act (FOIA) 6, 57
free-speech 112
Free Syrian Army 15, 63–64
'frustrated foreign fighter' phenomenon
   19, 25
Ftouhi, Amor 33

Garcia, Sixto Ramiro 62
Gendron, Angela 113
Georgelas, John 58, 77
Germany 56, 170
Global Internet Forum to Counter
    Terrorism (GIFCT) 163–64
Global War on Terror 118
God 116–17, 132
'going dark' problem 53
Gonzalez, Ana Maria 51
Google 164, 174
Google Drive 91
Grassley, Chuck 44
Great Mosque of al-Nuri 15
'Greenbird' *see* Khweis, Mohamad Jamal
    Amin
Gregerson, Sebastian 133, 136–39
Group of Four 159, 162
Gulf War 125

hacktivists 98
hadith 120, 140
Hakimiyyah 117
Haque, Ataul 49, 51
Haque, Siful Sujan 51
Harb, Abu 44
Harvard Law School Public Service
    Venture Fund 160
Hasan, Nidal Malik 38, 119
Hash Sharing Consortium 163
Hassan, Mohamed Abdullahi *see* Miski,
    Mujahid
Hassan, Nidal Malik 119
Hassan, Tnuza 33
Hegghammer, Thomas 25
Hendricks, Erick Jamal 44–46
'Hereafter, The' (al-Awlaki) 122
Hersi, Mahad 63–64
hijra 25, 33, 82, 95, 133, 139, 141–42,
    174
hisba (religious police) 78
homegrown violent extremists (HVE) 23
Hossain, Delowar Mohammed 82
Hostey, Raphael 34
House Committee on Homeland Security
    53
Hoxha, Zulfi 46–48
Hubbard, Gregory 20
Hughes, Seamus 8

Hussain, Junaid 25, 34, 42–43, 46–51,
    96–99, 103
Hussain, Omar 34
Hussein, Abdi Yemani 82
Hyams Foundation 160

IBACS Group 49–51
Ibacstel Electronics Limited 49–50
ibn Abd al-Wahhab, Muhammad 115
Ibn Taymiyya 129
ibn Taymiyya, Taqi ad-Din Ahmad 115
ideologues,
    Abdullah Faisal 139–44
    Ahmad Musa Jibril 125–31
    American Salafi-Jihadists 118–20
    Anwar al-Awlaki 119–20
    future of American jihadists 144–47
    introduction 111–14
    Jibril and the Jihad in Syria 131–34
    open source jihad 121–25
    Salafi-Jihadism Americanization
        120–21
    Salafism and Salafi-Jihadism 114–18,
        208n.13
    Suleiman Anwar Bengharsa 134–39
idol worship (*shirk*) 117
Illinois Criminal Justice Information
    Authority (ICJIA) 160
Imam Muhammad ibn Saud University,
    Saudi Arabia 139
'Importance of Hijrah, The' (Faisal)
    140
improvised explosive devices (IED)
    122
inghimasi 72
Ingram, Haroro 111–12
inshallah (God willing) 95
Inspire 4–5, 22, 121–24
International Centre for Study of
    Radicalisation (ICSR) 131
Internet Archive *see* Archive.org
Iran 14
Iraq,
    and Abdi Nur 65
    and Abdullahi Ahmed Abdullahi 63
    and Ahmad Abousamra 59
    and the Elshinawy plot 51
    foreign fighter travel to 55–56, 62
    and ISIS 2, 7–9, 16, 52, 57, 174

and Islamic State 17–18, 52, 136
jihadists in 3, 13–14
and Junaid Hussain 48
and Kim Anh Vo 98
and lone actors 33
and the Minnesota traveler network
      66, 79–83, 170
mobilization to 67
and Salafi-jihadists in 131
travel to 25
and Twitter 5
women travelers to 76–79
irhabeen (terrorists) 71
Islamic Community Center, Phoenix,
      Arizona 102
Islamic Jurisprudence Center (IJC)
      135–36
Islamic State,
      and Abdi Nur 64
      Americans supporting 18–19, 145,
            174
      and the caliphate 5, 15, 24, 32, 53, 118,
            136, 172
      and the Elshinawy plot 51
      and Elton Simpson 42
      fall of 174
      Hacking Division 96, 98, 103
      importance of foreign women to 78
      jihadist groups in 122
      and 'khilafa' brothers 38
      last territorial holding of 79
      leadership succession within 54
      the only true Islamic utopia 69
      pledges of allegiance to 27
      significant setbacks to 17
      Western foreign fighters traveling to
            92, 131
Islamic State in Iraq (ISI) 14, 60, 121
Ismail, Yusra 66
Israel 127
ISYNCTEL Technologies 51

Jabhat al-Nusra 14, 36, 60
Jackson, Darren Arness 20
Jalloh, Mohamed Bailor 37–41, 46, 57, 173
Jamaica 144
Jama, Yusuf 65–66
Jeffrey, James 79
Jews 141

Jibril, Ahmad Musa 8, 93, 114, 119,
      125–36, 138, 145–47, 212n.109
Jibril, Musa 128
Jibril, Musa Abdallah 125
'Jihad in Allah's Cause' (post) 127
'Jihad and Expedition' (post) 127
'Jihadi John' *see* Emwazi, Mohammed
jihadism,
      and the American Dream 171
      brides 77–78
      husbands 77
      and ideologues 112–13
      online networks driven underground
            88
'jihadisphere' 87
Johnson, Corey 32
Johnson, Ron 44
Joiner, Bruce 44
Joint Contact Group 150
Joint Terrorism Task Force (JTTF) 22, 36,
      39–40, 53, 59, 69, 73
Jordan, Akba 'Jihad' 11
Joseph, Damon 138
Joya, Tania 77
juba1911 45
Justpaste.it 91
Just Security (Patel) 161
Jyllands-Posten (newspaper) 123

kafirs 48, 106
Kalachnikv E-Security Team 98
Kareem, Abdul Malik 42–43, 144
Karie, Hamsa 63–64, 66
Karie, Hersi 63–64, 66
Kastigar, Troy 63
Kenya 59
Khan, Asher Abid 62
Khan, Masoud 142–43
Khan, Reyaad 34
Khan, Samir 4, 13, 22, 122–23
Khilafa 39
Khobar Towers bombing (1995) 125–26
khutba (sermons) 118
Khweis, Mohamad Jamal Amin 92–96,
      107–8, 172, 202n.63, 203n.74
Kik 47–48, 70, 90
King's College London 89
Kobani, siege of (2014) 64
Koehler, Daniel 109

kuffar (non-believers) 63, 136, 141
kufr (disbelief) 132
Kurds 79, 92, 108

Lahoud, Nelly 78
Lashkar-e-Taiba (LeT) 58–59, 61, 83
Las Vegas shooting (2017) 32, 182n.9
Legion, The 34
Levant, the 13–14, 56–57, 68–69, 79–80, 82
Levine, Alix 113
Liberty and National Security Program (Brennan Center) 161
Libya 39
Lieberman, Joseph 157
Life After Hate (CVE program) 161
Lindh, John Walker 131
Loken, Meredith 77
London Bridge/Borough Market attacks (2017) 133
lone-actors 4, 8, 33–37, 67–76
Los Angeles 54, 159–60
Lower Manhattan truck-ramming attack (2017) 32
Luger, Andrew 62
Lunel, France 24
Lutchman, Emanuel 25

McAleenan, Kevin 165–66
McCain, Douglas 63–66
McCain, Marchello 63, 66
McCollum, Robert 44
McDonough, Denis 155–56
'MadisonValleyWood 162–63
Mad Mullah (@martenyiii) 95–96
Maersk Alabama (ship) 131
Maher, Shiraz 116
'Make a Bomb in the Kitchen of Your Mom' (article) 122
Malaysia 86
Maldonado, Daniel 58, 59
Malik, Tashfeen 1–2, 22, 35–36, 42
Manbij, Syria 73–74
Manrique, Pedro 109
Mateen, Omar 28, 35–36, 40, 42
material support statute 27–28
Maududi, Abu Ala 117
Mehanna, Tarek 58–59
Millat Ibrahim (l-Maqdisi) 117

Millatu Ibrahim 170
Minneapolis 63–67
Minneapolis Passport Agency 64
Minnesota 24, 62–67, 75, 170
Miski, Mujahid 42, 64–66
'Mo' 67–74, 81, 94, 96, 167, 171
Mohallim, Hanad Abdullahi 63–66
Mohamed, Ahmed Mahad 82
Mohammad, Faisal 36
Mohammad, Shadi Jabar Khalil 34
Mohammad, Younus Abdullah 139
Mojoe's pizzeria 15
Molenbeek, Belgium 24
MoneyGram 142
monotheism (*tawhid*) 115
mosque shooting (2019) Christchurch, New Zealand 54
Mosul, Iraq 15, 17
Mueller, John 51
muhajireen (foreigners) 55
Muhammad ibn Saud university 142
Muhammad (Prophet) 42, 45, 113–15, 119–20, 123, 140
mujahideen 117
Mujahid Miski *see* Hassan, Mohamed Abdullahi
'multiplatform zeitgeist' 88
Mu'mineen, Amirul 41
Muse, Abduwali 131
mushriqin (idol worshippers) 132
Muslim Brotherhood 49, 58, 116, 125
Muslim Justice League 160
Muslim Student Associations (MSAs) 136
Musse, Hanad 65
Muthana, Hoda 80

Naji, Mohamed Rafik 57
Nasrin, Zakia 78
National Counterterrorism Center (NCTC) 8, 23, 149, 158, 162–65
National CVE Strategy 161
National Security Council (NSC) 162
National Security Staff (NSS) 157
National Strategy for Counterterrorism (2018) 165–66
Nesser, Petter 7, 90, 175n.7
networked travelers 62–67
Neumann, Peter 109
New America Foundation 12

newerajihadi *see* Qamar, Haris
New York 22
New York City subway incident (2009)
    56
Nidal Hasan, Major 155
Nigeria 38–39, 57
Niknejad, Reza 106
9/11,
    and Ahmad Musa Jibril 126
    and American Salafi-jihadism 118
    and Anwar al-Awlaki 120
    and arrest of jihadist imams 113
    and centrally controlled top-down
        websites 87
    jihadist mobilization since 3
    and Salafists 116, 127
    US interventions after 13
    and US jihadist travelers 56
Northwest Airlines suicide attack (2009)
    119
Norway 170
Nur, Abdi 64–67, 121
NYPD 144

Obama, Barack 9, 48, 80, 150, 154–57,
    161–62
Office of Foreign Assets Control (OFAC)
    144
Oftedal, Emilie 7, 175n.7
Ohio State University stabbings (2016) 32
Omar, Ahmed Ali 64
Omar, Guled 64–66
Omar, Mullah 127
online,
    communications 90, 201n.35
    counter-extremism 174
    disinhibition 87
    ISIS sympathizers 89
    Jihadist groups 88
    propaganda 88
    radicalization 16
open source Jihad 4, 122
'Operation: Heralds of the Internet' 105
Osadzinski, Thomas 104–6, 172

Pakistan,
    al-Qaeda networks in 58–59
    historical credibility for jihadists 13
    LeT training camps in 59

Paltalk (forum site) 46, 123, 139–40, 142,
    144
Paris attacks (2015) 55
Parson, Shawn 95–96, 203n.74
Patel, Faiza 161
PayPal 50
Pazara, Abdullah Ramo 58
Penvid.com 97
Peshmerga forces 93
pioneers 57–62
Pippin, Jason 59
Port Authority bombing, New York (2017)
    32
Precht, Tomas 111
Preventing Violent Extremism Pathfinder
    Fund 151
Prevent program 151–52, 160
Probations and Pretrial Services 29
Profetens Ummah (PU) 170
Program on Extremism 11–12, 79, 86,
    119, 131, 138
ProtonMail (encrypted email service) 90
Prucha, Nico 88–89
Public Access Line (PAL) 100
Public Access to Court Electronic Records
    (PACER) 12
Pulse night club shooting, Florida (2016)
    27, 35, 51, 171

qadhis (Islamic judges) 106
Qamar, Haris 104
Quran, the 5, 115, 140
Qutb, Sayyid 117

radicalization,
    by al-Qaeda 156
    diverse processes of 152
    online 16, 109
    and Syed Farook 122
    the tipping point 68
    women travelers 77
    of young Muslims 138
Rahim, Said Azzam Mohamad 146
Rahim, Usaamah 46–48
Rahman, Talmeezur 71
Raihan, Raisel 78
Raleigh, North Carolina 149
Ramadan 39
Randol, Mark 109

Raqqa, Syria 17, 34, 48, 51, 72–74
Rasulullah (Prophet of Allah) 42
returning travelers 79–83
Revolution Muslim (website) 119, 170
ribat (front lines) 61
Robbinsdale Cooper High School 63
Roble, Mohamed Amiin Ali 65–66
Rovinski, Nicholas 46–48
Rumiyah (online magazine) 58, 60–61, 89, 124
Rushdie, Salman 123

Saeed, Hafiz Muhammad 58
sahwa (movement) 125, 129
St. Cloud Mall stabbing, Minnesota (2016) 32
Saipov, Sayfullo 35
Salafi jihadism 116, 132, 135–36, 138–39, 144–47
Salafi-Jihadism: The History of an Idea (Maher) 116
Salafi-jihadist movement 116, 125, 132, 135, 139
Salafi politicos (activists) 116
Salafi purists (quietists) 116
Salafism 125, 127, 132, 135, 138, 170
Salman, Noor Zahi 28
Saltman, Erin 78
Samad, Abdul 50–51
Sana'a University, Yemen 134
San Bernardino shooting, California (2015) 1–2, 32–33, 35, 122, 163, 171
San Diego, California 65
Satanic Verses, The (Rushdie) 123
Saudi Arabia 68, 115–16, 125, 130, 136
Self-deradicalization 173
Sessions v. Dimaya 20–21
shadow banning 146
Shahnaz, Zoobia 107
Sham 5
Sharia4 170
sharia law 69–71, 128, 132, 135, 141
Sharon Mosque 58
Shaytan (the Devil) 72
Shi'a Muslims 118, 127, 132, 133
Shiao, Lora 98
shirk 132
Siddiqui, Asia 22
Sierra Leone 38–39

Simpson, Elton 42–46, 121, 144
sirah (prophetic biographies) 120
Skype 7, 46
Smith, Melanie 78
Snaptube 95
social media 26, 88–89
Somalia,
    and al-Shabaab 59, 64–65, 119, 135, 156
    and Americans supporting jihadist groups 13
    and Douglas McCain 63
    jihadist groups in 67
    and Mujahid Miski 42
Somali Civil War (2006) 13
Sommerville, Quentin 79
Soofi, Nadir 42–43, 45–46, 144
SoundCloud 138
South Park (cartoon show) 119
Soviet Union 117–18
Stag Arms AR-15 gun 40
START 21
Steam (video-gaming platform) 46
Stenersen, Anne 7, 175n.7
#StopCVE 160–61
Strategic Implementation Plan (SIP) 157, 159
Submission (film) 68, 171
Sudani, Abu Sa'ad 34, 37, 48, 59
suicide bombing 69, 71
Sujan, Siful Haque 48–51
suleimananwar.com see Bengharsa, Suleiman Anwar
Suler, John 87
Sullivan, Justin Nojan 34
Sunni Muslims,
    and Ahmad Musa Jibril 132–33
    and ISIS 4, 118
    in rebellion against Alawites 14
Surespot (application) 48, 50, 90
Sutherland, Daniel 153–54
Syria,
    and Abdullahi Ahmed Abdullahi 63
    and Ahmad Abousamra 59–60, 75
    and Ahmad Musa Jibril 132–33
    al-Hol camp in 172
    and Avin Marsalis Brown 149
    conflict in 4, 170
    and the Elshinawy plot 51

foreign fighters travelling to 55–56, 62
Hasakah governorate of 79
and ISIS 2, 7–9, 12, 16, 22, 46, 52, 57, 170, 174
and Islamic State 17–18, 42, 52, 136
jihadists in 3, 14
and Junaid Hussain 48
and Keonna Thomas 143
and lone actors 33
and Masoud Khan 142–43
and the Minnesota traveler network 66, 170
and 'Mo' 68–74, 167
mobilization to 67
and Mohamad Khweis 92, 95, 96
and Mohamed Abdullahi Hassan 65
and Mohamed Elshinawy 50
and Salafi-jihadists to 131
and Sham 5
travel to 25, 79–83
and Twitter 5
underground routes to Turkey 73
women travelers to 76–79
and Zoobia Shahnaz 107
Syrian Democratic Forces (SDF) 17, 79–80
'Syria in our Hearts' (Jibril) 133

taghut (tyrant) 133, 136, 141
takfir 118, 132, 135–36, 141
Taliban,
    in Afghanistan 135
    and Delowar Mohammed Hossain 82–83
    and John Walker Lindh 131
Targeted Violence Prevention Program (TV PP) 160
Targeted Violence and Terrorism Prevention (TVTP) 166
Tariq, Hamayun 97
tawaghit (tyrants/idols) 117, 128
Tawhid 116–17
tawhid alhakimiyya 132
tazkiyah 70
TeaMp0isonN (hacking group) 97
Tech Against Terrorism 163–64
Telegram (instant messaging) 6, 50, 86, 90–91, 96, 104–6, 142
'The Only Path to Victory' (Jibril) 132
Thomas, Keonna 143–44

Thompson, Bennie 166
'Three-City Pilot' 159–60
Times Square incident (2010) 56, 139
Title 18 of the US Code, Section 2339B *see* material support statute
Top4top.net 91
Tor (internet browser) 90, 105
Travers, Russell 165
Tree of Life synagogue shooting (2018) 138
TriCk *see* Hussain, Junaid
Trump, Donald 162, 166, 168
Tufekci, Zeynep 109
Turkey,
    divine punishment of major earthquake 127
    and foreign fighters 14, 70
    and Hamza Yusuf 64
    and ISIS 80
    and Islamic State 3
    and Mohamad Khweis 95
    and underground routes to Syria 73
Twitter,
    and Ahmad Jibril 131–32, 134
    and Ardit Ferizi 97
    and echo chambers 109–10
    and Faisal Shehzad 139
    and ISIS 5–6, 41–42, 46, 89–90, 174
    and Junaid Hussain 98
    and 'MO' 69–70
    and Mohamad Khweis 95–96
    and Safya Yassin 100–103

ummah (global Muslim community) 116, 118
underwear bomber (2008) 139
United Arab Emirates 59
United Cyber Caliphate (UCC) 98–99
United Kingdom 56, 112, 139, 150–51
United Nations Counter-Terrorism Executive Directorate (UN CTED) 163
United States Penitentiary, Florence 28
United States Secret Service 143

Velentzas, Noelle 22
violent extremism,
    counter-countering 159–62
    and CVE 162–65, 168

first intervention program 165–67
introduction 149–50
ISIS Prisoners and Recidivism 165
transatlantic idea 150–59
virtual entrepreneurs 33–34, 51–53
Vo, Kim Anh 98–99, 172
VPN Browser 95, 203n.66

Wagemakers, Joas 116
Wahhabism 72, 115
Wahid, Abdul Khabir 35, 42
Wahmi Technologies 50–51
'wandering mujahideen' problem 56
Warren, Colonel Steve 51
Warsame, Abidirizak 66
Washington Field Office 40
waswas 72
Webster, William 155
Wehelie, Yusuf 138
Western Union 142
WhatsApp 90, 139
Wiktorowicz, Quintan 111, 116
wilayat (provinces) 82
Wojcicki, Susan 164
women,
    in jihadist groups 21–22
    rape, torture, murder of Syrian
        132–33
    travelers 76–79
World Trade Center bombing (1993) 56
Wray, Christopher 23, 53

Wright, David 'Daoud' 46–48
wudu (ritual ablution) 70

Yahoo! 128
Yahud al-Jihad: Qaidat al-Zawahiri 60
Yassin, Safya 100–104
Yemen,
    and al-Qaeda 4, 43
    and American jihadist propagandists 13
    and Jason Pippin 59
    and Mohamed Rafik Naji 57
YouTube 91, 95
    abuse on 164
    and Ahmad Jibril 131–32, 134
    and Anwar al-Awlaki 146
    and Faisal Shehzad 139
    and ISIS 91
    and Kim Anh Vo 99
    and Mohamad Jamal Khweis 95
    and Suleiman Anwar Bengharsa 135
Yusuf, Abdullahi 66
Yusuf, Hamza 61, 64

'Zach K' *see* Khweis, Mohamad Jamal
        Amin
Zaytuna College 61
Zazi, Najibullah 155
Zelenz, Anna 77
Zelin, Aaron 87
Zello (walkie-talkie app) 146
zero-fail missions 36